LATIN
AMERICA,
1983–1987

LATIN AMERICA, 1983-1987

A Social Science Bibliography

Compiled by
ROBERT L. DELORME

Bibliographies and Indexes in Sociology, Number 14

G P

Greenwood Press
New York • Westport, Connecticut • London

Library of Congress Cataloging-in-Publication Data

Delorme, Robert, 1931-
    Latin America, 1983-1987 : a social science bibliography /
compiled by Robert L. Delorme.
        p.   cm. — (Bibliographies and indexes in sociology, ISSN
0742-6895 ; no. 14)
    Includes index.
    ISBN 0-313-26406-6 (lib. bdg. : alk. paper)
    1. Latin America—Economic conditions—1945- —Bibliography.
2. Latin America—Social conditions—1945- —Bibliography.   3. Latin
America—Politics and government—1948- —Bibliography.   I. Title.
II. Series.
Z7165.L3D4395 1988
[HC125]
016.98—dc19   88-25081

British Library Cataloguing in Publication Data is available.

Library of Congress Catalog Card Number: 88-25081
ISBN: 0-313-26406-6
ISSN: 0742-6895

First published in 1988

Greenwood Press, Inc.
88 Post Road West, Westport, Connecticut 06881

Printed in the United States of America

The paper used in this book complies with the
Permanent Paper Standard issued by the National
Information Standards Organization (Z39.48-1984).

10 9 8 7 6 5 4 3 2 1

CONTENTS

PREFACE

This reference source has been produced as a sequel to two previously published works: *Latin America, 1967-1979: Social Science Information Sources* and *Latin America, 1979-83: A Social Science Bibliography*. The volume contains titles to books, monographs, articles and chapters in edited books that have been published since the completion of the second bibliography (September 1983) through December 1987. A majority of works are in English, but about one-fifth are in a foreign language. It should be noted that not all issues of journals published in 1987 were available in the library when the collection of materials was ended. This is especially true of journals published in foreign countries. It is also inevitable that some book titles published in 1987 were not available.

The purpose of *Latin America, 1983-1987* is to provide an up-to-date and in-depth listing of scholarly books and journal articles of interest to social scientists concerned with the study and research of Latin America. The country-by-country listing complements the *Handbook of Latin American Studies* and the *Hispanic American Periodical Index,* which are both arranged by subject. The arrangement in this volume is advantageous for those interested only in specific regions or individual countries; yet the subject index facilitates cross-country comparisons. This compilation is intended especially for university and college instructors as well as for librarians who provide guidance to students researching Latin America. As a reference tool, the volume may also be useful to scholars in the social sciences and other disciplines interested in the multifaceted dimensions of the region and countries of Latin America.

The articles have been selected from a systematic survey of 110 journals that are listed at the beginning of the book. All major articles dealing with Latin America have been included. Over eighty-five of these journals do not specialize in Latin America, and have been selected to include a broad spectrum of the social sciences, divergent points of view, different levels of scholarship, and a wide range of topics. The vast majority of the journals surveyed are the same ones used to compile the first two bibliographies. However, a small number of journals were dropped and replaced with others in an effort to achieve greater geographic and subject matter balance.

Chapters in edited volumes have been selected from seventy-five edited works which are also listed in the beginning of the book. Chapters dealing with specific countries, or with subjects not indicated from the title of the book, have been selected from those anthologies dealing exclusively with Latin America. All chapters pertaining to Latin America have been included from the more general edited works.

Book and monograph titles have been obtained from announcements of leading publishers and from notices and reviews contained in the major Latin American Journals including the *Latin American Research Review, Hispanic American Historical Review, Journal of Inter-American Studies and World Affairs, Latin American Perspectives, Journal of Latin American Studies,* and *The Americas.* Once this initial phase of collecting the book titles was completed, an additional search was conducted using a variety of sources to supplement geographic areas or subject areas which were insufficiently represented in the results of the first search. For example, the initial search yielded only one book on Uruguay, reflecting a neglect among United States scholars of that rather unique country. The subsequent search produced an additional eighteen titles, the majority in Spanish.

In collecting the book titles, emphasis with respect to publication was placed on trade and university publications, publications of Latin American research institutes and centers and some private research entities. Therefore, few government publications are included, although selected publications from such organizations as the World Bank, the United Nations, the Organization of American States, and the Economic Commission for Latin America are included. The Melvyle Online Catalog, which provides access to the book holdings at eight University of California campuses including Los Angeles and Berkeley, was used to verify the bibliographic information. Books that were not available at any of the University of California libraries were generally not included because most of them would appear not to be readily available to most prospective users of this volume.

Some noteworthy trends about the literature published in the past few years emerge from an analysis of items indexed in this volume. The crisis in Central America and the Caribbean region has led to an outpouring of books and articles on this region. Several countries that were previously somewhat neglected in the scholarship are now represented more fully. The role of the United States in Latin America, both in its historical context as well as its present aspects, is receiving increased attention and examination. There is also more scholarly interest in the foreign policies of Latin American countries. These developments have been accompanied by a decrease in the number of works devoted to the Organization of American States which is also evidence of its lack of relevance in the current struggle in Central America.

The decline in popularity of dependency theory as an explanation of Latin American under-development is also indicated by the literature published over the past few years. However, interest in the problem of modernization is still evident and of concern to many writers on the region. This is reflected in the many studies focusing on the economic, social, political, industrial, and rural aspects of development. The matter of the international debt and the economic crisis of the past several years are also major issues of interest and analysis.

Additional trends in the literature include a renewed interest in the subject of democracy and redemocratization, no doubt reflecting the return to civilian rule in many of the countries in recent years. Interest in indigenous peoples and women also continues to command attention in the literature. For example, with respect to the former, there are over forty-five specific indigenous groups identified in the index in addition to a good number of more general studies on indigenous groups. Areas such as the agrarian sector and agriculture, population migration, the Catholic Church, labor, and peasants continue to receive considerable study. Overall, the topics associated with the disciplines of political science, history, sociology and economics are by far the most numerous.

The organization of this work follows the pattern established in the earlier editions. The first section, Bibliographies and Reference Sources, is followed by sections devoted to each of the three geographic regions — The Caribbean, Central America, and Latin America. These four general sections are followed by country-by-country listings arranged alphabetically. One category in the list, Lesser Antilles, contains specific studies of various islands in the Caribbean that are not listed separately. Citations dealing with two or three countries are repeated in the listing of each country. Where more than three countries are covered, the title is placed in the appropriate regional category. Each bibliographical reference is entered by author. Within each section books and monographs are listed separately from chapter titles and articles.

Citations are numbered consecutively from 1 to 3942. These numbers are used in both the author and subject index to locate the appropriate bibliographical entry. The subject index is intended as a guide for the researcher, and is arranged into both broad topics suitable for a general approach and into more specific topics suitable for narrow research. The citations under each index subject or topic are further classified by geographical region or country. In an attempt to provide a more detailed access than in the two previous volumes, the number of subjects in this index has been greatly expanded. Entries dealing with two or more subjects, which is the case in the overwhelming number of entries, are cited under each of the appropriate subject terms, and there are many cross-references to guide the researcher further. Citations in foreign languages are identified by an asterisk in the subject index. The author index includes the names of all authors, coauthors, editors, and coeditors, and includes citation numbers.

The publication of this bibliography was made possible by a sabbatical leave granted by California State University, Long Beach. I owe special thanks to Raudel Márquez Dorado and Eliane de Abreu Sawyer who generously volunteered their time to assist in proofreading the Spanish and Portuguese sources. I also wish to acknowledge Jill Serrao who typeset the bibliography utilizing a Compaq Deskpro 286, Hewlett-Packard LaserJet printer, and WordPerfect word processing software. Her promptness and accuracy greatly assisted in the final production of this work.

Robert L. Delorme
California State University, Long Beach
May 1988

LIST OF BOOKS SURVEYED

Note: *The following edited volumes have been surveyed for chapters which are included as separate entries. Chapters dealing with specific countries or with subjects not evident from the title of the book have been selected from those works devoted exclusively to Latin America. The main entries for these volumes are also included in the bibliography under the book listing of the appropriate geographical area or country. All chapters dealing with Latin America have been included from the more general edited works. These volumes are not included as main entries in the bibliography.*

Abel, Christopher, and Colin M. Lewis, eds. *Latin America, Economic Imperialism and the State: The Political Economy of the External Connection from Independence to the Present.* London; Dover, NH: Athlone, 1985. 540p.

Adams, Dale W., Douglas H. Graham, and J.D. Von Pischke, eds. *Undermining Rural Development with Cheap Credit.* Boulder, CO: Westview, 1984. 307p.

Albert, Bill, and Adrian Graves, eds. *Crisis and Change in the International Sugar Economy, 1860-1914.* Edinburgh, Scotland: ISC Press, 1984. 381p.

Baloyra, Enrique A., ed. *Comparing New Democracies: Transition and Consolidation in Mediterranean Europe and the Southern Cone.* Boulder, CO: Westview, 1987. 318p.

Becker, David G., Jeff Frieden, Sayre P. Schatz, and Richard L. Sklar, eds. *Postimperialism, International Capitalism and Development in the Late Twentieth Century.* Boulder, CO: Lynne Rienner, 1987. 250p.

Blachman, Morris J., William M. LeoGrande, and Kenneth Sharpe, eds. *Confronting Revolution: Security through Diplomacy in Central America.*

Falcoff, Mark, and Robert Royal, eds. *Crisis and Opportunity: U.S. Policy in Central America and the Caribbean.* Washington, DC: Ethics and Public Policy Center, 1984. 491p.

Feinberg, Richard E., and Valeriana Kallab, eds. *Adjustment Crisis in the Third World.* Rutgers, NJ: Transaction, 1984. 186p.

Ghadar, Fariborz. *The Petroleum Industry in Oil-Importing Developing Countries.* Lexington, MA: Lexington, 1983. 240p.

Grabendorff, Wolf, and Riordan Roett, eds. *Latin America, Western Europe, and the United States: Reevaluating the Atlantic Triangle.* New York: Praeger, 1985. 295p.

Grabendorff, Wolf, Heinrich-W. Krumwiede and Jörg Todt, eds. *Political Change in Central America: Internal and External Dimensions.* Boulder, CO: Westview Press, 1984. 312p.

Greaves, Thomas, and William Culver, eds. *Miners and Mining in the Americas.* Manchester, England; Dover, NH: Manchester University Press, 1985. 358p.

Hardoy, Jorge, and David Satterthwaite, eds. *Small and Intermediate Urban Centers.* Boulder, CO: Westview, 1986. 416p.

Hartland-Thunberg, Penelope, and Charles K. Ebinger, eds. *Banks, Petrodollars, and Sovereign Debtors.* Boulder, CO: Westview, 1986. 193p.

Hartlyn, Jonathan, and Samuel A. Morley, eds. *Latin American Political Economy: Financial Crisis and Political Change.* Boulder, CO: Westview, 1986. 386p.

Hilhorst, Jos G.M., and Matty Klatter, eds. *Social Development in the Third World: Level of Living Indicators and Social Planning.* London: Croom Helm, 1985. 233p.

Irvin, George, and Xabier Gorostiaga, eds. *Towards an Alternative for Central American and the Caribbean.* London; Boston: Allen & Unwin, 1985. 273p.

Kaplan, Morton A., ed. *Global Policy: Challenge of the 80s.* Washington, DC: Washington Institute for Values in Public Policy, 1984. 281p.

Katz, James Everett, ed. *Arms Production in Developing Countries: An Analysis of Decision Making.* Lexington, MA: Lexington, 1984. 370p.

Katz, James Everett, ed. *Implications of Third World Military Industrialization: Showing the Serpents Teeth.* Lexington, MA: Lexington, 1986. 327p.

Keogh, Dermot, ed. *Central America: Human Rights and U.S. Foreign Policy.* Cork, Ireland: Cork University Press, 1985. 168p.

Kim, Kwan S., and David F. Ruccio, eds. *Debt and Development in Latin America.* Notre Dame, IN: University of Notre Dame Press, 1985. 226p.

Levine, Barry B., ed. *The Caribbean Exodus.* New York: Praeger, 1987. 293p.

Kirkpatrick, Colin H., and Frederick I. Nixson, eds. *The Industrialisation of Less*

Developed Countries. Manchester, England; Dover, NH: Manchester University Press, 1983. 231p.

Leacock, Eleanor Burke, and Helen I. Safa, eds. *Women's Work: Development and the Division of Labor by Gender.* South Hadley, MA: Bergin & Garvey, 1986. 300p.

Levine, Daniel H., ed. *Religion and Political Conflict in Latin America.* Chapel Hill: University of North Carolina Press, 1986. 266p.

Lincoln, Jennie K., and Elizabeth G. Ferris, eds. *The Dynamics of Latin American Foreign Policies: Challenge for the 1980s.* Boulder, CO: Westview, 1984. 325p.

Little, Peter D., and Michael M. Horowitz, eds. *Lands at Risk in the Third World: Local-Level Perspectives.* Boulder, CO: Westview, 1987. 416p.

Lowenthal, Abraham F., and Samuel Fitch, eds. *Armies and Politics in Latin America.* Rev. ed. New York: Holmes & Meier, 1986. 489p.

Maguire, Andrew, and Janet Welsh Brown, eds. *Bordering On Trouble: Resources and Politics in Latin America.* Bethesda, MD: Adler and Adler, 1986. 448p.

Malloy, James M., and Mitchell A. Seligson, eds. *Authoritarians and Democrats: Regime Transition in Latin America.* Pittsburgh, PA: University of Pittsburgh Press, 1987. 268p.

Muñoz, Heraldo, and Joseph S. Tulchin, eds. *Latin American Nations in World Politics.* Boulder, CO: Westview, 1984. 278p.

Nash, June, and Helen Safa, eds. *Women and Change in Latin America.* South Hadley, MA: Bergin & Garvey, 1986. 372p.

Newfarmer, Richard, ed. *From Gunboats to Diplomacy: New U.S. Policies for Latin America.* Baltimore, MD: Johns Hopkins University Press, 1984. 254p.

O'Brien, Philip J., and Paul Cammack, eds. *Generals in Retreat: The Crisis of Military Rule in Latin America.* Dover, NH: Manchester University Press, 1985. 208p.

O'Donnell, Guillermo, Philippe C. Schmitter, and Laurence Whitehead, eds. *Transition from Authoritarian Rule.* Baltimore, MD: Johns Hopkins University Press, 1986. 244p.

Pastor, Robert A., ed. *Migration and Development in the Caribbean: The Unexplored Connection.* Boulder, CO: Westview, 1985. 454p.

Payne, Anthony, and Paul Sutton, eds. *Dependency under Challenge: The Political Economy of the Commonwealth Caribbean.* Dover, NH: Manchester University Press, 1984. 295p.

Petras, James F. *Capitalist and Socialist Crises in the Late Twentieth Century.* Totowa, NJ: Rowman & Allanheld, 1984. 350p.

Ritter, Archibald R.M., and David H. Pollock, eds. *Latin American Prospects for the 1980s: Equity, Democratization and Development.* New York: Praeger,

1983. 330p.

Ropp, Steve C., and James A. Morris, eds. *Central America: Crisis and Adaptation.* Albuquerque: University of New Mexico Press, 1984. 311p.

Sanderson, Steven E., ed. *The Americas in the New International Division of Labor.* New York: Holmes & Meier, 1985. 296p.

Saulniers, Alfred H., ed. *The Public Sector in Latin America.* Austin: Institute of Latin American Studies, University of Texas, 1984. 235p.

Schulz, Donald E., and Douglas H. Graham, eds. *Revolution and Counterrevolution in Central America and the Caribbean.* Boulder, CO: Westview, 1984. 555p.

Segal, Aaron, with Brijen Gupta, Wallace C. Koehler, Jr., Ward Morehouse, Richard P. Suttmeier, and Wenlee Ting. *Learning by Doing: Science and Technology in the Developing World.* Boulder, CO: Westview, 1987. 239p.

Seligson, Mitchell A., ed. *The Gap between Rich and Poor: Contending Perspectives on the Political Economy of Development.* Boulder, CO: Westview, 1984. 418p.

Slatta, Richard W., ed. *Bandidos: The Varieties of Latin American Banditry.* Westport, CT: Greenwood, 1987. 218p.

Stewart, Frances, ed. *Macro Policies for Appropriate Technology in Developing Countries.* Boulder, CO: Westview, 1987. 315p.

Super, John C., and Thomas C. Wright, eds. *Food, Politics, and Society in Latin America.* Lincoln: University of Nebraska Press, 1985. 261p.

Tardanico, Richard, ed. *Crises in the Caribbean Basin.* Beverly Hills, CA: Sage, 1987. 263p.

Tullis, F. LaMond, and W. Ladd Hollist, eds. *Food, the State and International Political Economy.* Lincoln: University of Nebraska Press, 1986. 351p.

Tussie, Diana, ed. *Latin America in the World Economy: New Perspectives.* New York: St. Martin's, 1983. 238p.

Varas, Augusto, ed. *Soviet-Latin American Relations in the 1980s.* Boulder, CO: Westview, 1987. 290p.

Wesson, Robert G., ed. *Politics, Policies, and Economic Development in Latin America,* Stanford, CA: Hoover Institution Press, 1984. 262p.

Wiarda, Howard J., ed. *The Iberian-Latin American Connection: Implications for U.S. Foreign Policy.* Boulder, CO: Westview, 1986. 482p.

Wiarda, Howard J., ed. *Rift and Revolution: The Central American Imbroglio.* Washington, DC: American Enterprise Institute, 1984. 392p.

Williamson, John, ed. *Inflation and Indexation: Argentina, Brazil, and Israel.* Washington, DC: Institute for International Economics (dist. by M.I.T. Press), 1985. 181p.

Wionczek, Miguel S., ed., in collaboration with Luciano Tomassini. *Politics and Economics of External Debt Crisis: The Latin American Experience.* Boulder, CO: Westview, 1985. 482p.

Young, Alma H., and Dion E. Phillips, eds. *Militarization in the Non-Hispanic Caribbean.* Boulder, CO: Lynne Rienner, 1986. 178p.

LIST OF JOURNALS SURVEYED

Note: *The following journals have been consistently surveyed for relevant articles published since the completion of the second volume in the summer of 1983. Most, although not all, issues of journals published in 1987 were available when work on collecting the materials was ended in January, 1988. Societies that sponsor the journals are identified within parenthesis after the publisher's name.*

América Indígena. Mexico City: Instituto Indigenista Interamericano.

Anerican Anthropologist. Washington, DC: American Anthropological Association.

American Economic Review. Nashville, TN: American Economic Association.

American Ethnologist. Washington, DC: American Ethnological Society.

American Journal of Agricultural Economics. Ames, IA: American Agricultural Economics Association.

American Journal of Economics and Sociology. New York: American Journal of Economics and Sociology. (Robert Schalkerbach Foundation and Francis Neilson Fund.)

American Journal of International Law. Washington, DC: American Society of International Law.

American Journal of Sociology. Chicago: University of Chicago Press.

The Americas. West Bethesda, MD: Academy of American Franciscan History.
Boletín de Antropología Americana. Mexico City: Instituto Panamericano de Geografía e Historia.

Boletín de Estudios Latinoamericanos y del Caribe. Amsterdam: Centro de Estudios y Documentación Latinoamericanos.

British Journal of Sociology. London: Routledge & Kegan Paul, Ltd. (London School of Economics and Political Science.)

Bulletin of Latin American Research. Oxford, England: Pergamon Press, Inc. (Society for Latin American Studies.)

Canadian Journal of Political Science. Waterloo, Ontario, Canada: Wilfred Laurier University Press. (Canadian Political Science Association.)

Caribbean Quarterly. Mona, Kingston, Jamaica: University of the West Indies, Department of Extral Mural Studies.

CEPAL Review. New York: United Nations.

Commentary. New York: American Jewish Committee.

Comparative Political Studies. Beverly Hills, CA: Sage Publications.

Comparative Politics. New York: Political Science Program, City University of New York.

Comparative Studies of Society and History. Cambridge, England; New York: Cambridge University Press.

Cuban Studies. Pittsburgh, PA: University of Pittsburgh Press. (Center for Latin American Studies, University of Pittsburgh.)

Current History. Philadelphia: Current History, Inc.

Daedalus. Cambridge, MA: American Academy of Arts and Sciences.

Desarrollo Económico. Buenos Aires, Argentina: Instituto de Desarrollo Económico y Social.

Developing Economies. Tokyo: Institute of Developing Economies.

Dissent. New York: Foundation for the Study of Independent Social Ideas.

Economic Development and Cultural Change. Chicago: University of Chicago Press. (University of Chicago, Research Center in Economic Development and Cultural Change.)

Economic History Review. Norwich, England: University of East Anglia, School of Economic and Social Studies.

Economy and Society. London: Routledge & Kegan Paul, Ltd.

Estudios Rurales Latinoamericanos. Bogotá, Colombia: Consejo Latinoamericano de Ciencias Sociales.

Estudios Sociales Centroamericanos. San José, Costa Rica: Confederación Universitaria Centroamericana, Programa Centroamericano de Ciencias Sociales.

Ethnohistory. Durham, NC: Duke University Press. (American Society for

Ethnohistory.)

Ethnology. Pittsburgh, PA: University of Pittsburgh, Department of Anthropology.

Foreign Affairs. New York: Council on Foreign Relations, Inc.

Foreign Policy. Washington, DC: Carnegie Endowment for International Peace.

Foro Internacional. Mexico City: El Colegio de México.

Geographical Review. New York: American Geographical Society.

Government and Opposition. London: Government and Opposition, Ltd. (London School of Economics and Political Science.)

Hispanic American Historical Review. Durham, NC: Duke University Press. (American Historical Association, Conference on Latin American Studies.)

Human Organization. Oklahoma City, OK: Society for Applied Anthropology.

Inter-American Economic Affairs. Washington, DC: Inter-American Affairs Press.

Inter-American Review of Bibliography. Washington, DC: Organization of American Studies.

International Affairs. Guildford, England: Butterworth Scientific Ltd. (Royal Institute of International Affairs.)

International Journal of Comparative Sociology. Leiden, Netherlands: E.J. Brill. (York University, Department of Sociology.)

International Journal of Political Economy. Armonk, New York: M.E. Sharpe, Inc.

International Journal of Sociology. Armonk, NY: M.E. Sharpe, Inc.

International Labour Review. Geneva, Switzerland: International Labour Office-Bureau of International Travail, Publications Sales Service.

International Organization. Cambridge, MA: M.I.T. Press. (World Peace Foundation.)

International Review of Administrative Sciences. Brussels, Belgium: International Institute of Administrative Sciences.

International Social Science Journal. Paris: UNESCO.

Journal of Anthropological Research. Albuquerque: University of New Mexico, Department of Anthropology.

Journal of Caribbean History. Bridgetown, Barbados: University of the West Indies, Department of History.

Journal of Church and State. Waco, TX: Baylor University, Institute of Church and State.

Journal of Contemporary History. Beverly Hills, CA: Sage Publications, Inc.

Journal of Developing Areas. Macomb, IL: Western Illinois University.

Journal of Development Economics. Amsterdam: North-Holland Publishing Co.

Journal of Development Studies. London: Frank Cass & Co., Ltd.

Journal of Economic History. Wilmington, DE: Economic History Association.

Journal of Economic Issues. Lincoln, NE: Association for Evolutionary Economics.

Journal of Family History. Greenwich, CT: JAI Press, Inc. (National Council on Family Relations.)

Journal of Inter-American Studies and World Affairs. Miami, FL: University of Miami, North-South Center. (Institute of Interamerican Studies.)

Journal of Interdisciplinary History. Cambridge, MA: M.I.T. Press.

Journal of International Affairs. New York: Columbia University, School of International Affairs.

Journal of Latin American Studies. Cambridge, England: Cambridge University Press. (Centers of Latin American Studies at Universities of Cambridge, Glasgow, Liverpool, London and Oxford.)

Journal of Peace Research. Oslo: Universitetsforlaget. (International Peace Research Institute.)

Journal of Peasant Studies. London: Frank Cass & Co., Ltd.

Journal of Political and Military Sociology. DeKalb: Northern Illinois University, Department of Sociology.

Journal of Political Economy. Chicago: University of Chicago Press.

Journal of Politics. Gainesville, FL: Southern Political Science Association.

Journal of Public Health Policy. South Burlington, VT: Journal of Public Health Policy, Inc.

Journal of Social, Political and Economic Studies. Washington, DC: Council for Social and Economic Studies.

Journal of Social Psychology. Washington, DC: Heldref Publications. (Helen Dwight Reid Educational Foundation.)

Journal of Third World Studies. Americus, GA: Association of Third World Studies.

Land Economics. Madison: University of Wisconsin Press. (University of Wisconsin-Madison, Land Tenure Center.)

Latin American Perspectives. Beverly Hills, CA: Sage Publications, Inc.

Latin American Research Review. Albuquerque, NM: Latin American Studies

Association.

Luso-Brazilian Review. Madison: University of Wisconsin Press.

Mexican Studies/Estudios Mexicanos. Berkeley: University of California Press.

Monthly Review. New York: Monthly Review, Inc. (Monthly Review Foundation.)

New Left Review. London: New Left Review, Ltd.

Orbis. Philadelphia: Foreign Policy Research Institute.

Political Science Quarterly. New York: Academy of Political Science.

Politics and Society. Los Altos, CA: Geron-X, Inc., Publishers.

Polity. Amherst, MA: Northeastern Political Science Association.

Population Bulletin. Washington, DC: Population Reference Bureau.

Problems of Communism. Washington, DC: U.S. Information Agency.

Review. Beverly Hills, CA: Sage Publications, Inc. (Fernand Braudel Center.)

Review of Radical Political Economics. New York: Union for Radical Political Economics.

Revista Brasileira de Economia. Rio de Janeiro: Fundação Getúlio Vargas. (Instituto Brasileiro de Economia.)

Revista Brasileira de Estudos Políticos. Belo Horizonte, Brazil: Universidade Federal de Minas Gerais.

Revista de Ciencias Sociales. Rio Piedras: Universidad de Puerto Rico, Centro de Investigaciones Sociales.

Revista de Estudios Políticos. Madrid: Librería Europa. (Instituto de Estudios Políticos.)

Revista Mexicana de Sociología. Mexico City: Universidad Nacional Autónoma de México, Instituto de Investigaciones Sociales.

Revista Paraguaya de Sociología. Asunción, Paraguay: Centro Paraguayo de Estudios Sociológicos.

Rural Sociology. Bozeman, MT: Rural Sociological Society.

Science and Society. New York: Science and Society Quarterly, Inc.

Social and Economic Studies. Mona, Jamaica: University of the West Indies, Institute of Social and Economic Research.

Social Forces. Chapel Hill: University of North Carolina Press.

Social Science Journal. Greenwich, CT: JAI Press, Inc. (Western Social Science Association.)

Socialist Review. Berkeley, CA: Center for Social Research and Education.

Studies in Comparative Communism. Guildford, England: Butterworth Scientific, Ltd.

Studies in Comparative International Development. New Brunswick, NJ: Transaction Periodicals Consortium.

Third World Quarterly. London: Third World Foundation for Social and Economic Studies.

El Trimestre Económico. Mexico City: Fondo de Cultura Económica.

World Affairs. Washington, DC: Heldref Publications. (American Peace Society.)

World Development. Elmsford, NY: Pergamon Press, Inc.

World Politics. Princeton, NJ: Princeton University Press. (Princeton University, Center of International Studies.)

World Policy Journal. New York: World Policy Institute.

World Today. London: Oxford University Press. (Royal Institute of International Affairs.)

Yale Review. New Haven, CT: Yale University Press.

LIST OF ABBREVIATIONS/ ACRONYMS

ADLAI	Latin American Integration Association
AIFLD	American Institute for Free Labor Development
ANUC	Asociación Nacional de Usuarios Campesinos
APP	Area de Propriedad del Pueblo
APRA	Alianza Popular Revolucionaria Americana
BWI	British West Indies
CAD	Diseno asistido por computadoras
CAM	Manufactura assistida por computadoras
CARICOM	Caribbean Community and Common Market
CEDE	Centro de Estudios de Desarrollo y Economía
CEDES	Centro de Estudios de Estado y Sociedad
CEDLA	Centro de Estudios y Documentación Latinoamericanos, Amsterdam
CELAM	Conferencia Espiscopal Latinoamericana
CEPAL	Comisión Económica para América Latina
CFP	Concentración de Fuerzas Populares
ECLA	Economic Commission for Latin America
CIEPLAN	Corporación de Investigaciones Económicas para Latinoamérica
CLALI	Consejo Latinoamericano de Apoyo a las Luchas Indígenas
CONAR	O Conselho Nacional de Autoregulamentaçao Publicitária
DESCO	Centro de Estudios y Promoción de Desarrollo
Dist.	Distributed
DRI	Desarrollo Rural Integrado
ECLA	Economic Commission for Latin America
ECLAC	Economic Commission for Latin America and the Caribbean
EDUCA	Editorial Universitaria Centroamérica
EEC	European Economic Community
EUA	Estados Unidos da America
FAO	Food and Agriculture Organization
FDR	Frente Democrático Revolucionario
FEDECAMARAS	Federación Venezolana de Camaras y Associaciones de Comercio y Producción
FMI	Fondo Monetario Internacional
FMLN	Frente Farabundo Martí de Liberación Nacional

FSLN	Frente Sandinista de Liberación Nacional
GATT	General Agreement on Tariffs and Trade
ICS	Institute for Contemporary Studies
IDES	Instituto de Desarrollo Económico y Social
IEP	Instituto de Estudios Peruanos
IIE	Instituto de Investigaciones Económicas
IJC	International Court of Justice
ILDIS	Instituto Latinoamericano de Investigaciones Sociales
ILV	Instituto Lingüístico de Verano
IMF	International Monetary Fund
INDI	Instituto de Desenvolvimento Industrial
IRDP II	Second Integrated Rural Development Project
ISHI	Institute for the Study of Human Issues
LDCs	Less Developed Countries
MAS	Movimiento al Socialismo
M.I.T.	Massachusetts Institute of Technology
PMEX	Petróleos Mexicanos
OECS	Organization of Eastern Caribbean States
ONG	Organizaciones no gubernamentales
PMDB	Partido Movimento Democrático Brasileiro
PRB	Population Reference Bureau
PT	Partido dos Trabalhadores
SAM	Sistema Alimentario Mexicano
UCA	Universidad Centroamericana
UCLA	University of California, Los Angeles
UNAM	Universidad Nacional Autónoma de México
UNESCO	United Nations Educational, Scientific and Cultural Organization
UNIDO	United Nations Industrial Development Organization
WICP	Women in the Caribbean Project

LATIN AMERICA, 1983–1987

BIBLIOGRAPHIES AND REFERENCE SOURCES

Books and Monographs

1. Alvarez, Jesús, and María Teresa Uribe de H. *Indice de prensa colombiana, 1840-1890; periódicos existentes en la Biblioteca Central*. Medellín, Colombia: Universidad de Antioquia, 1984. 240p.

2. Anzaldúa Montoya, Ricardo, and Wayne A. Cornelius, eds. *International Inventory of Current Mexico-Related Research*. Vol. 4. San Diego: Center for U.S.-Mexican Studies, University of California, 1984. 324p.

3. Arrigunaga Coello, Maritza. *Catálogo de las fotocopias de los documentos y periódicos yucatecos en la Biblioteca de la Universidad de Texas en Arlington*. Arlington: University of Texas at Arlington Press, 1983. 211p.

4. Barry, Tom, and Deb Preusch. *The Central American Fact Book*. New York: Grove, 1986. 357p.

5. Barry, Tom, Beth Wood, and Deb Preusch. *Dollars and Dictators: A Guide to Central America*. New York: Grove, 1983. 282p.

6. Becco, Horacio Jorge. *Simón Bolívar, El Libertador, 1783-1830: Bibliografía selectiva*. Washington, DC: Organization of American States, 1983. 61p.

7. Beloch, Israel, and Alzira Alves de Abreu, coords. *Dicionário histórico-biográfico brasileiro, 1930-1983*. Rio de Janeiro: Forense-Universitária, 1984. 4 vols.

8. Besa García, José. *Bibliografía sobre la dueda externa, 1970-1983*. Santiago, Chile: ECLA, 1984. 85p.

9. *Bibliographic Guide to Latin American Studies: 1985*. Boston. G.K. Hall, 1986. 3 vols.

10. Bierhorst, John. *A Nahuatl-English Dictionary and Concordance to the "Cantares Mexicanos."* Stanford, CA: Stanford University Press, 1985. 751p.

11. Boehm, Eric H., Marie S. Ensign, and Barbara H. Pope. *Historical Periodicals Directory.* Vol. 4: *Latin America and West Indies.* Santa Barbara, CA: ABC-Clio, 1984. 157p.

12. Brana-Shute, Rosemary, comp. and ed. *A Bibliography of Caribbean Migration and the Caribbean Immigrant Communities.* Gainesville: Reference and Bibliographic Department, University of Florida Libraries in cooperation with Center for Latin American Studies, University of Florida, 1983. 339p.

13. Bryant, Solena V. *Brazil.* World Bibliographical Series, No. 57. Santa Barbara, CA: ABC-Clio, 1985. 245p.

14. Burkholder, Mark. A. *Biographical Dictionary of Councilors of the Indies, 1717-1808.* Westport, CT: Greenwood, 1986. 194p.

15. Burton Julianne. *The New Latin American Cinema: An Annotated Bibliography of Sources in English, Spanish, and Portuguese, 1960-1980.* New York: Smyra, 1983. 80p.

16. Busey, James L. *Latin American Political Guide: A Quarter Century of Latin American Politics.* 18th ed. New York: Robert Schalkenback Foundation, 1985. 192p.

17. Byrne, Pamela R., and Suzanne Robitaille Ontiveros. *Women in the Third World: A Historical Bibliography.* Santa Barbara, CA: ABC-Clio, 1986. 152p.

18. Castro de Salmerón, Alicia, Elen Saucedo Lugo, and Graciela Alvarez de Pérez, comps. *Bibliografía sobre educación superior en América Latina.* Mexico City: UNAM, 1983. 197p.

19. Cevallos, Elena. *Puerto Rico.* World Bibliographical Series, No. 52. Santa Barbara, CA: ABC-Clio, 1985. 193p.

20. Chilcote, Ronald H., with Sheryl Lutjens, eds. and comps. *Cuba, 1953-1978: A Bibliographical Guide to the Literature.* White Plains, NY: Kraus International, 1986. 2 vols.

21. Collier, Simon, Harold Blakemore, and Thomas E. Skidmore, eds. *The Cambridge Encyclopedia of Latin and the Caribbean.* Cambridge, England; New York: Cambridge University Press, 1985. 456p.

22. Danby, Colin, and Richard Swedberg. *Honduras Bibliography and Research Guide.* Cambridge, MA: Camino, 1984. 330p.

23. Delorme, Robert L. *Latin America: 1979-1983, A Social Science Bibliography.* Santa Barbara, CA: ABC-Clio, 1984. 225p.

24. England, Nora C. *A Grammar of Mam, a Mayan Language.* Austin: University of Texas Press, 1983. 353p.

25. Fenton, Thomas P., and Mary J. Heffron, comps. and eds. *Latin America*

and Caribbean: A Director of Resources. Maryknoll, NY: Orbis, 1986. 142p.

26.   Garst, Rachel. *Bibliografía anotada de obras de referencia sobre Centroamérica y Panamá en el campo de las ciencias sociales.* San José: Instituto de Investigaciones Sociales, Universidad de Costa Rica, 1983. 2 vols.

27.   Goodman, Edward J., comp. *The Exploration of South America: An Annotated Bibliography.* New York: Garland, 1983. 174p.

28.   Goyer, Doreen S., and Eliane Domschke. *The Handbook of National Population Censuses: Latin America and the Caribbean, North America and Oceania.* Westport, CT: Greenwood, 1983. 711p.

29.   Graham, Norman A., and Keith L. Edwards. *The Caribbean Basin to the Year 2000: Demographic, Economic, and Resource Use Trends in Seventeen Countries: A Compendium of Statistics and Projections.* Boulder, CO: Westview, 1984. 166p.

30.   Grieb, Kenneth J., ed. *Research Guide to Central America and the Caribbean.* Madison: University of Wisconsin Press, 1985. 431p.

31.   Hartness-Kane, Ann. *Revolution and Counterrevolution in Guatemala, 1944-1963: An Annotated Bibliography of Materials in the Benson Latin American Collection.* Austin: University of Texas Press, 1984. 174p.

32.   Hinds, Harold E., Jr., and Charles M. Tatum, eds. *Handbook of Latin American Popular Culture.* Westport, CT: Greenwood, 1985. 259p.

33.   Hispanic Division, Library of Congress, comp. and ed. *Human Rights in Latin America 1964-1980: A Selected Annotated Bibliography.* Washington, DC, 1983. 257p.

34.   Hopkins, Jack W., ed. *Latin America and Caribbean Contemporary Record.* New York: Holmes & Meier, 1983-86. 1 vol. per year.

35.   Howard, Pamela, and Ann E. Smith. *Author Index to the Publications of the Middle American Research Institute, Tulane University, 1926-1985.* New Orleans, LA: Middle American Research Institute, 1985. 33p.

36.   Ingram, K.E. *Jamaica.* World Bibliographical Series, No. 45. Santa Barbara, CA: ABC-Clio, 1984. 369p.

37.   Ingram, K.E., comp. and ed. *Sources for West Indian Studies: A Supplementary Listing, with Particular Reference to Manuscript Sources.* Zug, Switzerland: Inter Documentation, 1983. 412p.

38.   *International Guide to Research on Mexico.* Tijuana, Mexico: El Colegio de la Frontera Norte; La Jolla: Center for U.S.-Mexican Studies, University of California, San Diego, 1986. 502p.

39.   Jara, Alvaro, and Sonia Pinto. *Fuentes para la historia del trabajo en el reino de Chile: legislación, 1546-1810.* Santiago, Chile: Andres Bello, 1982-83. 2 vols.

40. Jeffrey, Phillip, and Maureen Newton, comps. *Selected Annotated Bibliography of Studies on the Caribbean Community.* Georgetown, Guyana: Information and Documentation Section, Caribbean Community Secretariat, 1983. 17p.

41. Jordan, Alma, and Barbara Comissiong, eds. *The English-Speaking Caribbean: A Bibliography of Bibliographies.* Boston, MA: G.K. Hall, 1984. 411p.

42. Karttunen, Frances. *An Analytical Dictionary of Nahuatl.* Austin: University of Texas Press, 1983. 349p.

43. Latin American Bibliographic Foundation, and Ministerio de Cultura de Nicaragua. *Nicaraguan National Bibliography, 1800-1978.* Redlands, CA: Managua, Nicaragua, 1986. 3 vols.

44. Lockhart, James, Frances Berdan, and Arthur J.O. Anderson. *The Tlax-calan Actas: A Compendium of Records of the Cabildo of Tlaxcala, 1545-1627.* Salt Lake City: University of Utah Press, 1986. 156.p.

45. Lombardi, Cathryn L., John V. Lombardi, with K. Lynn Stoner. *Latin American History: A Teaching Atlas.* Madison: Published for the Conference on Latin American History by the University of Wisconsin Press, 1983. 144p.

46. Loroña, Lionel V., comp. *Bibliography of Latin American Bibliographies.* Madison, WI: Seminar on the Acquisition of Latin American Library Materials, Memorial Library, University of Wisconsin, 1984-. Annual.

47. Ludwig, Armin K. *Brazil: A Handbook of Historical Statistics.* Boston, MA: G.K. Hall, 1985. 487p.

48. Mamalakis, Markos J., comp. *Historical Statistics of Chile.*   Westport, CT: Greenwood.
     Vol. 4: *Money, Prices, and Credit Services,* 1983, 598p.
     Vol. 5: *Money, Banking and Financial Services,* 1985. 532p.

49. Martin, Dolores Moyano, ed. *Handbook of Latin American Studies: No. 45, Social Sciences.* Austin: University of Texas Press, 1983. 811p.

50. Martin, Dolores Moyano, ed. *Handbook of Latin American Studies: No. 47, Social Sciences.* Austin: University of Texas Press, 1985. 810p.

51. Medeiros, Ana Ligia Silva, and Maria Celina Soares D'Araujo, comps. and eds. *Vargas e os anos cinquenta: bibliografia.* Rio De Janeiro: Editora de Fundaçao Getúlio Vargas, 1983. 155p.

52. Miller, E. Willard, and Ruby M. Miller. *Doing Business in and with Latin America: An Information Sourcebook.* Phoenix, AZ: Oryx, 1987. 117p.

53. Mitchell, B.R. *International Historical Statistics: The Americas and Australia.* Detroit, MI: Gale Research, 1984. 949p.

54. Moral, Paul, et al., *Atlas d'Haiti.* Talence, France: Centre d'Etudes de Géographie Tropicale et Universite de Bordeaux 3, 1985. 146p.

55. Mundo Lo, Sara de. *The Falkland/Malvinas Islands: A Bibliography of*

Books, 1619-1982. Urbana, IL: Albatross, 1983. 65p.

56. Mundo Lo, Sara de, ed. *Index to Spanish American Collective Bibliography.* Boston: D.K. Hall, 4 vols.
    Vol. 3: *The Central American and the Caribbean Countries,* 1984. 360p.
    Vol. 4: *The River Platt Countries,* 1985. 388p.

57. Nauman, Ann K. *A Handbook of Latin American and Caribbean National Archives.* Detroit, MI: Blaine Ethridge, 1983. 127p.

58. Oberg, Larry R., comp. *Human Services in Postrevolutionary Cuba: An Annotated International Bibliography.* Westport, CT: Greenwood, 1984. 433p.

59. Organization of American States. *Directory of Inter-American and Other Associations in the Americas.* Washington, DC, 1986. 81p.

60. Organization of American States. *Handbook of Existing Rules Pertaining to Human Rights in the Inter-American System.* Washington, DC, 1985. 201p.

61. Organization of American Studies. *Inter-American Treaties and Conventions, Signatures, Ratifications and Deposits with Explanatory Notes.* Rev. ed. Washington, DC, 1986. 524p.

62. Perl, Raphael. *The Falkland Islands Dispute in International Law and Politics: A Documentary Source Book.* New York: Oceana, 1983. 722p.

63. Reich, Peter L., ed. *Statistical Abstract of the United States-Mexico Borderlands.* Los Angeles: Latin American Center, University of California, 1984, 120p.

64. Robbins, Naomi C., and Sheila R. Herstein. *Mexico.* World Bibliographical Series, No. 48. Santa Barbara, CA: ABC-Clio, 1984. 165p.

65. Schlachter, Gail A., ed. *Latin American Politics: A Historical Bibliography.* Santa Barbara, CA: ABC-Clio, 1984. 290p.

66. Snyder, Frederick E., comp. *Latin American Society and Legal Culture: A Bibliography.* Westport, CT: Greenwood, 1985. 188p.

67. Sonntag, Gabriela. *Eva Perón: Books, Articles, and Other Sources of Study: An Annotated Bibliography.* Madison, WI: Seminar on the Acquisition of Latin American Library Materials, Memorial Library, University of Wisconsin, 1983. 54p.

68. Spores, Ronald, with the assistance of Patricia A. Andrews, ed. *Supplement to the Handbook of Middle American Indians.* Vol. 4: *Ethnohistory.* Austin: University of Texas Press, 1986. 232p.

69. Sullivan, William M., and Brian S. McBeth. *Petroleum in Venezuela: A Bibliography.* Boston, MA: G.K. Hall, 1985. 538p.

70. Thomas, Jack Ray, ed. *Biographical Dictionary of Latin American Historians and Historiography.* Westport, CT: Greenwood, 1984. 420p.

71.   Waggoner, Barbara Ashton, and George R. Waggoner, comps. *Universities of the Caribbean Region — Struggles to Democratize: An Annotated Bibliography*. Boston, MA: G.K. Hall, 1986. 310p.

72.   Weeks, John M. *Maya Ethnohistory: A Guide to Spanish Colonial Documents at Tozzer Library, Harvard University*. Nashville, TN: Vanderbilt University, 1987. 121p.

73.   Wilkie, Richard W., ed. *Latin American Population and Urbanization Analysis: Maps and Statistics, 1950-1982*. Los Angeles: Latin American Center, University of California, 1984. 433p.

74.   Wilson, Lofton, ed. *Guide to Latin American Pamphlets from the Yale University Library: Selections from 1600-1900*. New York: Clearwater, 1985. 7 vols.

Articles and Chapters

75.   Bloch, Thomas. "Regional Sources of Economic and Social Information on Central America," *Latin America Research Review* 20:2 (1985), 142-147.

76.   Cherpak, Evelyn M. "Latin American Sources in the U.S. Naval War College's Naval Historical Collection," *Inter-American Review of Bibliography* 35:4 (1985), 422-430.

77.   Elkin, Judith Laikin. "Latin America's Jews: A Review of Sources," *Latin American Research Review* 20:2 (1985), 124-141.

78.   Etchepareborda, Roberto. "La bibliografía reciente sobre la cuestión Malvinas," *Inter-American Review of Bibliography* 34:1 (1984), 1-52.

79.   Etchepareborda, Roberto. "La bibliografía reciente sobre la cuestión Malvinas (Segunda Parte)," *Inter-American Review of Bibliography* 34:2 (1984), 227-288.

80.   Girbal de Blacha, Noemí M. "Aportes bibliográficos para el estudio de un área marginal: el Gran Chaco Argentino y la explotación forestal, 1880-1914," *Inter-American Review of Bibliography* 33:3 (1983), 331-354.

81.   Girbal de Blacha, Noemí M. "Política agrícola de los gobiernos radicales en Argentina, 1916-1930: Fuentes para la investigación," *Inter-American Review of Bibliography* 37:2 (1987), 160-189.

82.   LaFrance, David. "The Madero Collection in Mexico's Archivo General de la Nación," *Inter-American Review of Bibliography* 33:2 (1983), 191-197.

83.   McQuade, Frank. "Exile and Dictatorship in Latin America since 1945: An Annotated Bibliography," *Third World Quarterly* 9:1 (January 1987), 254-270.

84.   Pérez, Louis A., Jr. "Armed Struggle and Guerrilla Warfare in Latin America: A bibliography of Cuban Sources, 1959-1979," *Inter-American Review of Bibliography* 33:4 (1983), 507-544.

85.   Potash, Robert A. "A Computer-Based Guide to Notarial Records," *Inter-American Review of Bibliography* 33:2 (1983), 238-247.

86.   Sandos, James A. "Latin American Holdings of the U.S. Military History Institute," *Inter-American Review of Bibliography* 33:1 (1983), 21-27.

87.   Snarr, D. Neil. "Nicaragua: An Annotated Bibliography, 1979-1984," *Inter-American Review of Bibliography* 37:1 (1987), 18-49.

88.   Ward, Christopher, and Richard J. Junkins. "Panamanian Historical Sources," *Latin American Research Review* 21:3 (1986), 129-136.

CARIBBEAN

Books and Monographs

89. Abrahams, Roger D. *The Man-of-Words in the West Indies: Performance and the Emergence of Creole Culture.* Baltimore, M.D.: Johns Hopkins University Press, 1983. 203p.

90. Abrahams, Roger D., and John F. Szwed, eds., assisted by Leslie Baker and Adrian Stackhouse. *After Africa: Extracts from British Travel Accounts and Journals of the Seventeenth, Eighteenth and Nineteenth Centuries Concerning the Slaves, Their Manners and Customs in the British West Indies.* New Haven, CT: Yale University Press, 1983. 444p.

91. Anderson, Thomas D. *Geopolitics of the Caribbean: Ministates in a Wider World.* New York: Praeger, 1984. 175p.

92. Ashby, Timothy. *The Bear in the Back Yard: Moscow's Caribbean Strategy.* Lexington, MA: Lexington, 1987. 240p.

93. Axline, W. Andrew. *Agricultural Policy and Collective Self-Reliance in the Caribbean.* Boulder, CO: Westview, 1986. 134p.

94. Bark, Dennis L., ed. *The Red Orchestra Instruments of Soviet Policy in Latin America and the Caribbean.* Stanford, CA: Hoover Institution Press, 1986. 140p.

95. Barry, Tom, Beth Wood, and Deb Preusch. *The Other Side of Paradise: Foreign Control in the Caribbean.* New York: Grove, 1984. 405p.

96. Cortada, James N., and James W. Cortada. *U.S. Foreign Policy in the Caribbean, Cuba and Central America.* New York: Praeger, 1985. 251p.

97. Economic Commission for Latin America and the Caribbean. *Economic Survey of Latin America and the Caribbean 1984.* Vol. 2: *The Caribbean Economies.* Santiago, Chile; New York, 1986. 216p.

98.   Erisman, H. Michael, ed. *The Caribbean Challenge: U.S. Policy in a Volatile Region.* Boulder, CO: Westview, 1984. 208p.

99.   Falcoff, Mark, and Robert Royal, eds. *The Continuing Crisis: U.S. Policy in Central America and the Caribbean.* Lanham, MD: Ethics and Public Policy Center (dist. by University Press of America), 1987. 503p.

100.   Falcoff, Mark, and Robert Royal, eds. *Crisis and Opportunity: U.S. Policy in Central America and the Caribbean.* Washington, DC: Ethics and Public Policy Center, 1984. 491p.

101.   Fortune, Stephen Alexander. *Merchants and Jews: The Struggle for British West Indian Commerce, 1650-1750.* Gainesville: University of Florida Press, 1984. 244p.

102.   Gomes, P.I., ed. *Rural Development in the Caribbean.* London: C. Hurst; New York: St. Martin's, 1985. 246p.

103.   Greene, James R., and Brent Scowcroft, eds. *Western Interests and U.S. Policy Options in the Caribbean Basin: Report of the Atlantic Council's Working Group on the Caribbean Basin.* Boston, MA: Oelgeschlager, Gunn & Hain, 1984. 331p.

104.   Higman, B.W. *Slave Populations of the British Caribbean, 1807-1834.* Baltimore, MD: Johns Hopkins University Press, 1984. 781p.

105.   Hope, Kempe Ronald. *Economic Development in the Caribbean.* New York: Praeger, 1986. 215p.

106.   Hope, Kempe Ronald. *Urbanization in the Commonwealth Caribbean.* Boulder, CO: Westview, 1986. 129p.

107.   Ince, Basil, Anthony Bryan, Herb Addo, and Ramesh Ramsaran, eds. *Issues in Caribbean International Relations.* Washington, DC: University Press of America, 1983. 360p.

108.   Irvin, George, and Xabier Gorostiaga, eds. *Towards an Alternative for Central America and the Caribbean.* London; Boston: Allen & Unwin, 1985. 273p.

109.   Jhabvala, Farrokh, ed. *Maritime Issues in the Caribbean.* Gainesville: University Presses of Florida, 1983. 130p.

110.   Kiple, Kenneth F. *The Caribbean Slave: A Biological History.* New York: Cambridge University Press, 1984. 274p.

111.   Klein, Herbert S. *African Slavery in Latin America and the Caribbean.* New York: Oxford University Press, 1986. 311p.

112.   Krehm, William. *Democracies and Tyrannies of the Caribbean.* Westport, CT: L. Hill, 1984. 244p.

113.   La Belle, Thomas J. *Nonformal Education in Latin America and the Caribbean: Stability, Reform, or Revolution?* New York: Praeger, 1986. 367p.

114.   Langley, Lester D. *The United States and the Caribbean in the Twen-tieth Century.* Rev. ed.   Athens: University of Georgia Press, 1985. 342p.

115.   Lemoine, Maurice. *Bitter Sugar: Slaves Today in the Caribbean.* Trans-lated by Andrea Johnston. Chicago: Banner, 1985. 308p.

116.   Levine, Barry B., ed. *The Caribbean Exodus.* New York: Praeger, 1987. 293p.

117.   Marable, Manning. *African and Caribbean Politics: From Kwame Nkrukmah to the Grenada Revolution.* New York: Verso, 1987. 314p.

118.   Mintz, Sidney W., and Sally Price, eds. *Caribbean Contours.* Baltimore, MD: Johns Hopkins University Press, 1985. 254p.

119.   Montaner, Carlos Alberto. *Cuba, Castro and the Caribbean: The Cuban Revolution and the Crisis in Western Conscience.* Translated by Nelson Duran. New Brunswick, NJ: Transaction, 1985. 116p.

120.   Moorer, Thomas H., and Georges A. Fauriol. *Caribbean Basin Security.* New York: Praeger; Washington DC: Center for Strategic and Inter-national Studies, Georgetown University, 1983. 108p.

121.   Moreno Fraginals, Manuel, Frank Moya Pons, and Stanley L. Engerman, eds. *Between Slavery and Free Labor: The Spanish-Speaking Carib-bean in the Nineteenth Century.* Baltimore, MD: Johns Hopkins University Press, 1985. 294p.

122.   Organization of American States. *The Economy of Latin America and the Caribbean: Analysis and Interpretations Prompted by the Finan-cial Crisis.* Washington, DC: 1984. 100p.

123.   Palmer, Ransford W. *Problems of Development in Beautiful Countries: Perspectives on the Caribbean.* Lanham, MD: North-South, 1984. 91p.

124.   Payne, Anthony. *The International Crisis in the Caribbean.* Baltimore, MD: Johns Hopkins University Press, 1984. 177p.

125.   Payne, Anthony, and Paul Sutton, eds. *Dependency under Challenge: The Political Economy of the Commonwealth Caribbean.* Dover, NH: Manchester University Press, 1984. 295p.

126.   Ramsaran, Ramesh F. *U.S. Investment in Latin America and the Caribbean.* New York: St. Martin's, 1985. 196p.

127.   Richardson, Ronald. *Moral Imperium: Afro-Caribbeans and the Trans-formation of British Rule, 1776-1838.* Westport, CT: Greenwood, 1987. 211p.

128.   Ronfeldt, David. *Geopolitics, Security, and U.S. Strategy in the Caribbean Basin.* Santa Monica, CA: Rand Corporation, 1983. 93p.

129.   Schulz, Donald E., and Douglas H. Graham, eds. *Revolution and Coun-terrevolution in Central America and the Caribbean.* Boulder, CO: Westview, 1984. 555p.

130.   Sheridan, Richard B. *Doctors and Slaves: A Medical and Demographic History of Slavery in the British West Indies, 1680-1834.* New York: Cambridge University Press, 185. 420p.

131.   Stone, Carl. *Power in the Caribbean Basin: A Comparative Study of Political Economy.* Philadelphia, PA: ISHI, 1986. 159p.

132.   Sunshine, Catherine A. *The Caribbean: Survival and Sovereignty.* Washington, DC: Ecumenical Program for Interamerican Communication and Action (Boston, MA: Dist. by South End Press), 1985. 232p.

133.   Tardanico, Richard, ed. *Crises in the Caribbean Basin.* Beverly Hills, CA: Sage, 1987. 263p.

134.   United Nations. *Economic Survey of Latin America and the Caribbean 1982.* Santiago, Chile, 1984. 2 vols.

135.   Wasserstrom, Robert, ed. *Grassroots Development in Latin America and the Caribbean: Oral Histories of Social Change.* New York: Praeger, 1985. 197p.

136.   Young, Alma H., and Dion E. Phillips, eds. *Militarization in the Non-Hispanic Caribbean.* Boulder, CO: Lynne Rienner, 1986. 178p.

Articles and Chapters

137.   Abel, Christopher. "Review of the House of Commons Foreign Affairs Select Committee Report on Central America and the Caribbean," *Journal of Latin American Studies* 15:2 (November 1983), 471-480.

138.   Albuquerque, Klaus de. "A Comparative Analysis of Violent Crime in the Caribbean," *Social and Economic Studies* 33:3 (September 1984), 93-142.

139.   Auty, R.M. "Multinational Resource Corporations, Nationalization and Diminished Viability: Caribbean Plantations, Mines and Oilfields in the 1970s." In *Multinational Companies and the Third World,* edited by C.J. Dixon, David Drakakis-Smith and H.D. Watts. London: Croom Helm, 1986. pp. 160-188.

140.   Axline, W. Andrew. "Agricultural Co-operation in CARICOM." In *Dependency under Challenge: The Political Economy of the Commonwealth Caribbean,* edited by Anthony Payne and Paul Sutton. Dover, NH: Manchester University Press, 1984. pp. 152-173.

141.   Barraclough, Solon, and Peter Marchetti. "Agrarian Transformation and Food Security in the Caribbean Basin." In *Towards an Alternative for Central America and the Caribbean,* edited by George Irvin and Xabier Gorostiaga. London; Boston: Allen & Unwin, 1985. pp. 154-193.

142.   Basdeo, Sahadeo. "Walter Citrine and the British Caribbean Workers Movement during the Moyne Commission Hearing 1938-39," *Journal of Caribbean History* 18:2 (November 1983), 43-59.

143.   Beckford, George L. "Caribbean Peasantry in the Confines of the Plantation Mode of Production," *International Social Science Journal* 37:3 (1985), 401-414.

144.   Beckles, Hilary, and Andrew Downes. "An Economic Formalization of the Origins of Black Slavery in the BWI 1624-1645," *Social and Economic Studies* 34:2 (June 1985), 1-25.

145.   Benn, Denis. "The Commonwealth Caribbean and the New International Economic Order." In *Dependency under Challenge: The Political Economy of the Commonwealth Caribbean,* edited by Anthony Payne and Paul Sutton. Dover, NH: Manchester University Press, 1984. pp. 259-280.

146.   Bennett, Karl. "The Caribbean Basin Initiative and Its Implications for CARICOM Exports," *Social and Economic Studies* 36:2 (June 1987), 21-40.

147.   Bennett, Karl. "A Note on Exchange Rate Policy and Caribbean Integration," *Social and Economic Studies* 34:3 (December 1985), 35-43.

148.   Bernal, Richard, Mark Figueroa, and Michael Witter. "Caribbean Economic Thought: The Critical Tradition," *Social and Economic Studies* 33:2 (June 1984), 5-95.

149.   Bourne, Compton. "The Propensities to Consume Labour and Property Incomes in the Commonwealth Caribbean," *Journal of Development Studies* 22:3 (April 1986), 583-597.

150.   Carrington, Selwyn H.H. "The American Revolution and the British West Indies Economy," *Journal of Interdisciplinary History* 17:4 (Spring 1987), 823-850.

151.   Carrington, Selwyn H.H. "'Econocide' — Myth or Reality? — The Question of West Indian Decline, 1783-1806," *Boletín de Estudios Latinoamericanos y de Caribe* 36 (June 1984), 13-48.

152.   Casimir, Jean. "Culture, Discourse (Self-Expression) and Social Development in the Caribbean," *CEPAL Review* 25 (April 1985), 149-162.

153.   Clarke, Roberta, "Women's Organisations, Women's Interests," *Social and Economic Studies* 35:3 (September 1986), 107-155.

154.   Cumiford, William L. "The Political Role of Organized Labor in the Caribbean," *Journal of Third World Studies* 4:1 (Spring 1987), 119-127.

155.   Delson, Roberta M. "Sugar Production for the Nineteenth Century British Market: Rethinking the Roles of Brazil and the British West Indies." In *Crisis and Change in the International Sugar Economy, 1860-1914,* edited by Bill Albert and Adrian Graves. Edinburgh, Scotland: ISC Press, 1984. pp. 59-82.

156.   Dickson, Helen McEachrane. "Negotiation and Cooperation as a Strategy for Development in the Caribbean Basin." In *Conflict in Central America: Approaches to Peace and Security,* edited by Jack Child.

London: C. Hurst, 1985. 132-141.

157. Dietz, James L. "Destabilization and Intervention in Latin America and the Caribbean," *Latin American Perspectives* 11:3 (Summer 1984), 3-14.

158. Executive Secretariat, ECLAC. "Crisis and Development in Latin America and the Caribbean," *CEPAL Review* 26 (August 1985), 9-56.

159. Feinberg, Richard E., and Richard Newfarmer. "The Caribbean Basin Initiative: Bold Plan or Empty Promise?" In *From Gunboats to Diplomacy: New U.S. Policies for Latin America*, edited by Richard E. Feinberg and Richard Newfarmer. Baltimore, MD: Johns Hopkins University Press, 1984. pp. 210-227.

160. Feinberg, Richard E., Richard Newfarmer, and Bernadette Orr. "Caribbean Basin Initiative: Pros and Cons." In *Crisis and Opportunity: U.S. Policy in Central America and the Caribbean*, edited by Mark Falcoff and Robert Royal. Washington, DC: Ethics and Public Policy Center, 1984. pp. 101-118.

161. Galenson, David W. "Population Turnover in the English West Indies in the Late Sixteenth Century," *Journal of Economic History* 45:2 (June 1985), 227-235.

162. Gonzalez, Edward. "The Cuban and Soviet Challenge in the Caribbean Basin," *Orbis* 29:1 (Spring 1985), 73-94.

163. Grabendorff, Wolf. "El papel de Europa occidental en la cuenca del Caribe," *Foro Internacional* 23:4 (April-June 1983), 400-422.

164. Grant, Rudolph W., and Una M. Paul. "Perceptions of Caribbean Regional Integration: A Comparative Study of Caribbean Teacher Trainees," *Social and Economic Studies* 34:1 (March 1985), 1-26

165. Greene, J. Edward. "Challenges and Responses in Social Science Research in the English Speaking Caribbean," *Social and Economic Studies* 33:1 (March 1984), 9-46.

166. Griffith, David C. "Social Organizational Obstacles to Capital Accumulation among Returning Migrants: The British West Indies Temporary Alien Labor Program," *Human Organization* 45:1 (Spring 1986), 34-42.

167. Guimaráea, Robert P. "Co-operativism and Popular Participation: New Considerations Regarding an Old Subject," *CEPAL Review* 28 (April 1986), 187-201.

168. Halliday, Fred. "Cold War in the Caribbean," *New Left Review* 141 (September-October 1983), 5-22.

169. Hendrickson, Embert J. "Twilight of the Old Guard: Parties and Leadership in the Commonwealth Caribbean," *World Today* 43:2 (February 1987), 33-35.

170. Hertogs, Erik Jan. "Western European Responses to Revolutionary Developments in the Caribbean Basin Region." In *Towards an Alternative for Central America and the Caribbean*, edited by George

Irvin and Xabier Gorostiaga. London; Boston: Allen & Unwin, 1985. pp. 69-83.

171.   Higman, B.W. "Theory, Method and Techniques in Caribbean Social History," *Journal of Caribbean History* 20:1 (1985-86), 1-29.

172.   Hope, Kempe Ronald. "Urban Population Growth and Urbanization in the Caribbean," *Inter-American Economic Affairs* 39:1 (Summer 1985), 31-49.

173.   James-Bryan, Meryl. "Youth in the English-Speaking Caribbean: The High Cost of Dependent Development," *CEPAL Review* 29 (August 1986), 133-152.

174.   Johnson, Howard. "The United States and the Establishment of the Anglo-American Caribbean Commission," *Journal of Caribbean History* 19:1 (May 1984), 26-47.

175.   Jones, Edwin. "Politics, Bureaucratic Corruption, and Maladministration in the Third World: Some Commonwealth Caribbean Considerations," *International Review of Administrative Sciences* 51:1 (1985), 19-23.

176.   Jones-Hendrickson, S. "Rational Expectations, Causality and Integrative Fiscal-Monetary Policy in the Caribbean," *Social and Economic Studies* 34:4 (December 1985), 111-138.

177.   Jorge, Antonio, and Raúl Moncarz. "Aspectos teóricos de la inflación en la América Latina y el Caribe, *El Trimestre Económico* 51:204 (October-December 1984), 871-883.

178.   Koehler, Wallace C., Jr., and Aaron Segal. "The Caribbean: Can Liliput Make It?" In *Learning by Doing: Science and Technology in the Developing World,* by Aaron Segal, et al. Boulder, CO: Westview, 1987. pp. 55-81.

179.   Leiken, Robert S. "Soviet and Cuban Policy in the Caribbean Basin." In *Revolution and Counter-revolution in Central America and the Caribbean,* edited by Donald E. Schulz and Douglas H. Graham. Boulder, CO: Westview, 1984. pp. 447-477.

180.   Lewis, Vaughan A. "The Caribbean Experience of the 1970s: Some Lessons in Regional and International Relations," *Social and Economic Studies* 32:4 (December 1983), 107-127.

181.   McCoy, Terry L., and Timothy J. Power. "La Cuenca del Caribe como subsistema regional," *Estudios Sociales Centroamericanos* 43 (January-April 1987), 13-26).

182.   MacDonald, Scott B. "The Future of Foreign Aid in the Caribbean after Grenada: Finlandization and Confrontation in the Eastern Tier," *Inter-American Economic Affairs* 38:4 (Spring 1985), 59-74.

183.   MacDonald, Scott B., and F. Joseph Demetrius. "The Caribbean Sugar Crisis: Consequences and Challenges," *Journal of Inter-American Studies and World Affairs* 28:1 (Spring 1986), 35-58.

184.   McIntyre, Arnold. "Finance, Growth and the Balance of Trade in OECS Countries," *Social and Economic Studies* 35:4 (Dec. 1986), 177-212.

185.   McKee, David L. "Some Specifics on the Loss of Professional Personnel from the Commonwealth Caribbean," *Inter-American Economic Affairs* 37:3 (Winter 1983), 57-76.

186.   McKenzie, Hermoine. "The Educational Experiences of Caribbean Women," *Social and Economic Studies* 35:3 (September 1986), 65-105.

187.   Mandle, Jay R. "Caribbean Dependency and Its Alternatives," *Latin American Perspectives* 11:3 (Summer 1984), 111-124.

188.   Mars, Perry. "Destabilization and Socialist Orientation in the English-Speaking Caribbean," *Latin American Perspectives* 11:3 (Summer 1984), 83-110.

189.   Massiah, Joycelin. "Establishing a Programme of Women and Development Studies in the University of the West Indies," *Social and Economic Studies* 35:1 (March 1986), 151-197.

190.   Massiah, Joycelin. "Postscript: The Utility of WICP Research in Social Policy Formation," *Social and Economic Studies* 35:3 (September 1986), 157-181.

191.   Massiah, Joycelin. "Work in the Lives of Caribbean Women," *Social and Economic Studies* 35:2 (June 1986), 177-239.

192.   Mason, Keith, "Demography, Disease and Medical Care in Caribbean Slave Societies," *Bulletin of Latin American Research* 5:1 (1986), 109-119.

193.   Mintz, Sidney W. "Labor and Ethnicity: The Caribbean Conjuncture." In *Crises in the Caribbean,* edited by Richard Tardanico. Beverly Hills, CA: Sage, 1987. pp. 47-57.

194.   Morrissey, Marietta. "Women's Work, Family Formation, and Reproduction among Caribbean Slaves," *Review* 9:3 (Winter 1986), 339-367.

195.   Mosher, Lawrence. "At Sea in the Caribbean?" In *Bordering On Trouble: Resources and Politics in Latin America,* edited by Andrew Maguire and Janet Welsh Brown. Bethesda, MD: Adler & Adler, 1986. pp. 235-269.

196.   Munroe, Trevor. "Caribbean Politics and the Faculty of Social Sciences," *Social and Economic Studies* 33:1 (March 1984), 59-81.

197.   Newfarmer, Richard S. "Economic Policy toward the Caribbean Basin: The Balance Sheet," *Journal of Inter-American Studies and World Affairs* 27:1 (February 1985), 63-89.

198.   Norton, Graham. "The Caribbean: Towards Democratic Differentiation?" *World Today* 43:8-9 (August-September 1987), 152-154.

199.   Norton, Graham. "Defending the Eastern Caribbean," *World Today* 40:6 (June 1984), 254-260.

200.   Palmer, Annette. "The United States in the British Caribbean 1940-1945: Rum and Coca Cola," *The Americas* 43:4 (April 1987), 441-451.

201.   Pantin, Dennis. "Long Waves and Caribbean Development," *Social and Economic Studies* 36:2 (June 1987), 1-20.

202.   Pastor, Robert, and Sergio Díaz-Briquets. "The Caribbean: More People and Fewer Resources." In *Bordering On Trouble: Resources and Politics in Latin America,* edited by Andrew Maguire and Janet Welsh Brown. Bethseda, MD: Adler & Adler, 1986. pp. 308-336.

203.   Payne, Anthony. "Regional Industrial Programming in CARICOM." In *Dependency under Challenge: The Political Economy of the Commonwealth Caribbean,* edited by Anthony Payne and Paul Sutton. Dover, NH: Manchester University Press, 1984. pp. 131-151.

204.   Pérez Salgado, Ignacio, and Bernardo Kliksberg. "Políticas de gestión pública: el rol del Estado en la presente situación de América Latina y el Caribe," *International Review of Administrative Sciences* 51:3 (1985), 221-238.

205.   Powell, Dorian. "Caribbean Women and Their Response to Familial Experiences," *Social and Economic Studies* 35:2 (June 1986), 83-130.

206.   Powell, Dorian. "The Role of Women in the Caribbean," *Social and Economic Studies* 33:2 (June 1984), 97-122.

207.   Ramsaran, Ramesh F. "Issues in Commonwealth Caribbean-United States Relations." In *Dependency under Challenge: The Political Economy of the Commonwealth Caribbean,* edited by Anthony Payne and Paul Sutton. Dover, NH: Manchester University Press, 1984. pp. 179-203.

208.   Reddock, Rhoda E. "Women and Slavery in the Caribbean: A Feminist Perspective," *Latin American Perspectives* 12:1 (Winter 1985), 63-80.

209.   Rosenberg, Mark B. "Pequeños países y potencias hegemónicas: Centroamérica y el Caribe en el contexto global," *Estudios Sociales Centroamericanos* 43 (January-April 1987), 27-40.

210.   Ross, David F. "The Caribbean Basin Initiative: Threat or Promise? In *The Central American Crisis: Sources of Conflict and the Failure of U.S. Policy,* edited by Kenneth M. Coleman and George C. Herring. Wilmington, DE: Scholarly Resources, 1985. pp. 137-155.

211.   Rubenstein, Hymie. "Remittances and Rural Underdevelopment in the English-Speaking Caribbean," *Human Organization* 42:4 (Winter 1983), 295-306.

212.   Safa, Helen I. "Economic Autonomy and Sexual Equality in Caribbean Society," *Social and Economic Studies* 35:3 (September 1986), 1-21.

213.   Schnakenbourg, Christian. "From the Sugar Estate to Central Factory: The Industrial Revolution in the Caribbean, 1840-1905." In *Crisis and Change in the Internatinal Sugar Economy, 1860-1914,* edited by Bill Albert and Adrian Graves. Edinburgh, Scotland: ISC Press, 1984. 381p.

214.   Segal, Aaron. "Caribbean Realities," *Current History* 84:500 (March 1985), 127-130.

215.   Slater, Jerome. "Estados Unidos y las revoluciones en el Caribe: el mito de los intereses vitales," *Foro Internacional* 26:2 (October-December 1985), 267-283.

216.   Smith, M.G. "Some Future Directions of Social Research in the Commonwealth Caribbean," *Social and Economic Studies* 33:2 (June 1984), 123-155.

217.   Soares, João Clemente Baena. "A Different Perspective for the Financial Crisis in Latin America and the Caribbean," *Journal of Inter-American Studies and World Affairs* 27:4 (Winter 1985-86), 9-20.

218.   Sutton, Paul. "From Neo-colonialism to Neo-colonialism: Britain and the EEC in the Commonwealth." In *Dependency under Challenge: The Political Economy of the Commonwealth Caribbean,* edited by Anthony Payne and Paul Sutton. Dover, NH: Manchester University Press, 1984. 204-237.

219.   Thrower, Mary M. "Background to Revolution: U.S. Intervention in Central America and the Caribbean," *Journal of Third World Studies* 3:2 (Fall 1986), 97-101.

220.   Tomich, Dale W. "White Days, Black Days: The Working Day and the Crisis of Slavery in the French Caribbean." In *Crises in the Caribbean Basin,* edited by Richard Tardanico. Beverly Hills, CA: Sage, 1987, pp. 31-45.

221.   Valenta, Jiri, and Virginia Valenta. "Soviet Strategy and Policies in the Caribbean Basin." In *Rift and Revolution: The Central American Imbroglio,* edited by Howard J. Wiarda. Washington, DC: American Enterprise Institute, 1984. pp. 197-252.

222.   Watson, Hillbourne. "Transnational Banks and Financial Crisis in the Caribbean." In *Towards an Alternative for Central America and the Caribbean,* edited by George Irvin and Xabier Gorostiaga. London; Boston: Allen & Unwin, 1985. pp. 126-153.

223.   White, Averille. "Profiles: Women in the Caribbean Project," *Social and Economic Studies* 35:2 (June 1986), 59-81.

224.   Williams, Marion. "An Analysis of Regional Trade and Payment Arrangements in CARICOM; 1971-82," *Social and Economic Studies* 34:4 (December 1985), 3-33.

225.   Wong, David C. "A Review of Caribbean Political Economy," *Latin American Perspectives* 11:3 (Summer 1984), 125-140.

CENTRAL AMERICA

Books and Monographs

226.   Alonso, Marcelo, ed. *Central America in Crisis.* Rev. ed. New York: Paragon House, 1984. 227p.

227.   Andrews, Anthony P. *Maya Salt Production and Trade.* Tucson: University of Arizona Press, 1983. 173p.

228.   Bagley, Bruce Michael, ed. *Contadora and the Diplomacy of Peace in Central America.* Boulder, CO: Westview, 1987. 2 vols.
                    Vol. 1:   *The United States, Central America and Contadora,* 320p.
                    Vol. 2:   *The Contadora Process,* 288p.

229.   Bagley, Bruce Michael, Roberto Alvarez, and Katherine J. Hagedorn, eds. *Contadora and the Central Peace Process: Selected Documents.* Boulder, CO: Westview, 1985. 297p.

230.   Berryman, Phillip. *Inside Central America.* New York: Pantheon, 1985. 166p.

231.   Berryman, Phillip. *The Religious Roots of Revolution: Christians in Central American Revolutions.* Maryknoll, NY: Orbis, 1984. 452p.

232.   Best, Edward. *U.S. Policy and Regional Security in Central America.* New York: St. Martin's, 1987. 182p.

233.   Blachman, Morris J., William M. LeoGrande, and Kenneth E. Sharpe, eds. *Confronting Revolution: Security through Diplomacy in Central America.* New York: Pantheon, 1986. 438p.

234.   Bonpane, Blase. *Guerrillas of Peace: Liberation Theology and the Central American Revolution.* Boston, MA: South End, 1985. 119p.

235.   Buckley, Tom. *Violent Neighbors: El Salvador, Central America, and the USA*. New York: Times Book, 1984. 358p.

236.   Burbach, Roger, and Patricia Flynn, eds. *The Politics of Intervention: The United States in Central America*. New York: Monthly Review Press, 1984. 255p.

237.   Chace, James. *Endless War: How We Got Involved in Central America and What Can Be Done*. New York: Vintage, 1984. 144p.

238.   Child, Jack, ed. *Conflict in Central America: Approaches to Peace and Security*. London: Published for the International Peace Academy by Hurst, 1986. 208p.

239.   Chomsky, Noam. *Turning the Tide: U.S. Intervention in Central America and the Struggle for Peace*. Boston, MA: South End, 1985. 298p.

240.   Cirincione, Joseph, ed. *Central America and the Western Alliance*. New York: Holmes & Meier, 1985. 238p.

241.   Colburn, Forrest D., ed. *Centroamérica: estratégias de desarrollo*. San José, Costa Rica: EDUCA, 1987. 206p.

242.   Coleman, Kenneth M., and George C. Herring, eds. *The Central American Crisis: Sources of Conflict and the Failure of U.S. Policy*. Wilmington, DE: Scholarly Resources, 1985. 240p.

243.   Cortada, James N., and James W. Cortada. *U.S. Foreign Policy in the Caribbean, Cuba and Central America*. New York: Praeger, 1985. 251p.

244.   Diskin, Martin, ed. *Trouble in Our Backyard: Central America and the United States in the Eighties*. New York: Pantheon, 1983. 264p.

245.   Dixon, Marlene, and Susanne Jonas, eds. *Revolution and Intervention in Central America*. Rev. ed. San Francisco: Synthesis, 1983. 344p.

246.   Domínguez, Jorge I., and Marc Lindenberg. *Central America: Current Crisis and Future Prospects*. New York: Foreign Policy Association, 1985. 80p.

247.   Economic Commission for Latin America. *Industrialización en Centroamérica, 1960-1980*. Santiago, Chile; New York: United Nations, 1983. 168p.

248.   Etheredge, Lloyd S. *Can Governments Learn?: American Foreign Policy and Central American Revolutions*. NY: Pergamon, 1985. 227p.

249.   Fagen, Richard. *Forging Peace: The Challenge of Central America*. Hagerston, MD: Basil Blackwell, 1987, 160p.

250.   Fagen, Richard R., and Olga Pellicer, eds. *The Future of Central America: Policy Choices for the U.S. and Mexico*. Stanford, CA: Stanford University Press, 1983. 228p.

251.   Falcoff, Mark, and Robert Royal, eds. *The Continuing Crisis: U.S. Policy in Central America and the Caribbean*. Lanham, MD: Ethics and

Public Policy Center (dist. by University Press of America), 1987. 503p.

252. Falcoff, Mark, and Robert Royal, eds. *Crisis and Opportunity: U.S. Policy in Central America and the Caribbean.* Washington, DC: Ethics and Public Policy Center, 1984. 491p.

253. Feinberg, Richard E., and Bruce M. Bagley. *Development Postponed: The Political Economy of Central America in the 1980s.* Boulder, CO: Westview, 1986. 65p.

254. Findling, John E. *Close Neighbors, Distant Friends: United States-Central American Relations.* Westport, CT: Greenwood, 1987. 240p.

255. González Casanova, Pablo. *La hegemonía del pueblo y la lucha Centro-américa.* Managua: Nueva Nicaragua, 1986. 171p.

256. González Casanova, Pablo. *El poder al pueblo.* Mexico City: Oceano, 1985. 145p.

257. González Casanova, Pablo, coord. *Historia del movimiento obrero en América Latina.* Vol. 2: *Guatemala, Honduras, El Salvador, Nicaragua, Costa Rica, Panamá.* Mexico City: Siglo Veintiuno, 1985. 319p.

258. Grabendorff, Wolf, Heinrich-W. Krumwiede, and Jörg Todt. *Political Change in Central America: Internal and External Dimensions.* Boulder, CO: Westview, 1984. 312p.

259. Gutiérrez, Margo, and Milton H. Jamail. *It's No Secret: Israel's Military Involvement in Central America.* Belmont, MA: Association of Arab-American University Graduates, 1986. 117p.

260. Hahn, Walter F. ed. *Central America and the Reagan Doctrine.* Lanham, MD: University Press of America, 1987. 318p.

261. Irvin, George, and Xabier Gorostiaga, eds. *Towards an Alternative for Central America and the Caribbean.* London; Boston: Allen & Unwin, 1985. 273p.

262. Kendall, Carl, John Hawkins, and Laurell Bossen, eds. *Heritage of Conquest: Thirty Years Later.* Albuquerque: University of New Mexico Press, 1983. 368p.

263. Keogh, Dermot, ed. *Central America: Human Rights and U.S. Foreign Policy.* Cork, Ireland: Cork University Press, 1985. 168p.

264. Kerns, Virginia. *Women and the Ancestors: Black Carib Kinship and Ritual.* Urbana: University of Illinois Press, 1983. 229p.

265. LaFeber, Walter. *Inevitable Revolutions: The United States in Central America.* New York: Norton, 1983. 357p.

266. Lange, Frederick W., and Doris Stone, eds. *Archaeology of Lower Central America.* Albuquerque: University of New Mexico Press, 1983. 476p.

267.   Langley, Lester D. *Central America, the Real Stakes: Understanding Central America before It's Too Late.* New York: Crown, 1985. 280p.

268.   Leiken, Robert S., ed. *Central America: Anatomy of a Conflict.* New York: Pergamon, 1984. 351p.

269.   Leiken, Robert S., and Barry Rubin, eds. *The Central American Crisis Reader.* New York: Summit, 1987. 717p.

270.   Leonard, Thomas M. *Central America and United States Policies, 1820s-1980s: A Guide to Issues and References.* Claremont, CA: Regina, 1985. 133p.

271.   Leonard, Thomas M. *The United States and Central America, 1944-1949: Perceptions of Political Dymanics.* University: University of Alabama Press, 1984. 215p.

272.   Lernoux, Penny. *Fear and Hope: Toward Political Democracy in Central America.* New York: Field Foundation, 1984. 47p.

273.   McCuen, Gary E., ed. *Political Murder in Central America: Death Squads and U.S. Policies.* Hudson, WI: Gary E. McCuen, 1985. 136p.

274.   Marnham, Patrick. *So Far From God: A Journey to Central America.* New York: Viking, 1985. 253p.

275.   Miller, Arthur G., ed. *Highland-Lowland Interaction in Mesoamerica: Interdisciplinary Approaches.* Washington, DC: Dumbarton Oaks Research Library and Collection, 1983. 263p.

276.   Munro, Dana G. *A Student in Central America, 1914-1916.* New Orleans, LA: Middle American Research Institute, Tulane University, 1983. 75p.

277.   National Bipartisan Commission on Central America. *The Report of the President's National Bi-partisan Commission on Central America.* New York: Macmillan, 1984. 158p.

278.   Nuccio, Richard A., with research by Kelly A. McBride. *What's Wrong, Who's Right in Central America? A Citizens Guide.* Washington, DC: Roosevelt Center for American Policy Studies, 1986. 136p.

279.   Pearce, Kenneth. *The View from the Top of the Temple: Ancient Maya Civilization and Modern Maya Culture.* Albuquerque: University of New Mexico Press, 1984. 273p.

280.   Pérez Brignoli, Héctor. *Breve historia de Centroamérica.* Madrid, Spain: Alianza, 1985. 169p.

281.   Pierre, Andrew J., ed. *Third World Instability: Central America as a European-American Issue.* New York: New York University Press, 1985. 156p.

282.   Policy Alternatives for Central America and the Caribbean. *Changing Course: Blueprint for Peace in Central America.* Washington, DC: Institute for Policy Studies, 1984. 112p.

283.   Ropp, Steve C., and James A. Morris, eds. *Central America: Crisis and Adaptation.* Albuquerque: University of New Mexico Press, 1984, 311p.

284.   Schulz, Donald E., and Douglas H. Graham, eds. *Revolution and Counterrevolution in Central America and the Caribbean.* Boulder, CO: Westview, 1984. 555p.

285.   Soto, Max Alberto, Carlos Alberto Sevilla, and Charles R. Frank, Jr. *Integración economíca y empleo en la industria centroamericana.* San José, Costa Rica EDUCA, 1983. 188p.

286.   Weeks, John. *The Economies of Central America.* New York: Holmes & Meier, 1985. 209p.

287.   White, Richard Alan. *The Morass: United States Intervention in Central America.* New York: Harper & Row, 1984. 319p.

288.   Wiarda, Howard J., ed. *Rift and Revolution: The Central American Imbroglio.* Washington, DC: American Enterprise Institute, 1984. 392p.

289.   Willey, Gordon Randolf. *Essays in Maya Archaeology.* Albuquerque: University of New Mexico Press, 1987. 245p.

290.   Williams, Robert C. *Export Agriculture and the Crisis in Central America.* Chapel Hill: University of North Carolina Press, 1986. 257p.

Articles and Chapters

291.   Woodward, Ralph Lee, Jr. *Central America: A Nation Divided.* 2d ed. New York: Oxford University Press, 1985. 390p.

292.   Abel, Christopher. "Review of the House of Commons Foreign Affairs Select Committee Report on Central America and the Caribbean," *Journal of Latin American Studies* 15:2 (November 1983), 471-480.

293.   Adam, Dale W. "Foreign Assistance, Economic Policies, and Agriculture in Central America," *Inter-American Economic Affairs* 38:2 (Autumn 1984), 45-60.

294.   Aguila, Juan M. del. "Central American Vulnerability to Soviet/Cuban Penetration," *Journal of Inter-American Studies and World Affairs* 27:2 (Summer 1985), 77-97.

295.   Arias Sánchez, Oscar. "A Time for Peace," *Government and Opposition* 22:4 (Autumn 1987), 452-456.

296.   Bagley, Bruce Michael. "Contadora: The Failure of Diplomacy," *Journal of Inter-American Studies and World Affairs* 28:3 (Fall 1986), 1-32.

297.   Baloyra, Enrique A. "Central America on the Reagan Watch," *Journal of Inter-American Studies and World Affairs* 27:1 (February 1985), 35-62.

298.   Baloyra-Herp. Enrique A. "Reactionary Despotism in Central America," *Journal of Latin American Studies* 15:2 (November 1983), pp. 295-319.

299.   Barry, Peter. "The EEC, Human Rights and Central America." In *Central America: Human Rights and U.S. Foreign Policy,* edited by Dermot Keogh. Cork, Ireland: Cork University Press, 1985. pp. 71-79.

300.   Benítez Manaut, Raúl. "Youth: A Solution to the Crisis in Central America," *International Social Science Journal* 37:4 (1985), 519-529.

301.   Benítez Manaut, Raúl, and Ricardo Córdova. "Il Informe Kissinger y las maniobras militares de Estados Unidos en Centroamérica: preludio de la intervención directa," *Revista Mexicana de Sociología* 46:3 (July-September 1984), 65-90.

302.   Bermúdez T., Lilia. "Centroamérica: la militarización en cifras," *Revista Mexicana de Sociología* 46:3 (July-September 1984), 27-48.

303.   Bischof, Henrik. "The Socialist Countries and Central America: In *Political Change in Central America: Internal and External Dimensions,* edited by Wolf Grabendorff, Heinrich-W. Krumwiede and Jörg Todt. Boulder, CO: Westview, 1984. pp. 228-244.

304.   Blasier, Cole. "The Soviet Union." In *Confronting Revolution: Security through Diplomacy in Central America,* edited by Morris J. Blachman, William M. LeoGrande and Kenneth E. Sharpe. New York: Pantheon, 1986. pp. 226-270.

305.   Blee, Kathleen M. "The Catholic Church and Central American Politics." In *The Central American Crisis: Sources of Conflict and the Failure of U.S. Policy,* edited by Kenneth M. Coleman and George C. Herring. Wilmington, DE: Scholarly Resources, 1985. pp. 55-71.

306.   Bolin, William H. "Central America: Real Economic Help is Workable Now," *Foreign Affairs* 62:5 (Summer 1984), 1096-1106.

307.   Bonachea, Rolando E. "The United States and Central America: Policy Options in the 80s." In *Global Policy: Challenge of the 80s,* edited by Morton A. Kaplan. Washington, DC: Washington Institute for Values in Public Policy, 1984. pp. 209-250.

308.   Booth, John A. "'Trickle-up' Income Redistribution and Development in Central America during the 1960s and 1970s." In *The Gap between Rich and Poor,* edited by Mitchell A. Seligson. Boulder, CO: Westview, 1984. pp. 351-365.

309.   Bossert, Thomas John. "Health-Policy Innovation and International Assistance in Central America," *Political Science Quarterly* 99:3 (Fall 1984), 441-455.

310.   Bulmer-Thomas, Victor. "Central American Integration, Trade Diversification and the World Market." In *Towards an Alternative for Central America and the Caribbean.* London; Boston: Allen & Unwin, 1985. pp. 194-212.

311.   Bulmer-Thomas, Victor. "Crisis in Central America: Economic Roots and Historical Dimensions," *World Today* 39:9 (September 1983), 328-335.

312.   Bulmer-Thomas, Victor. "Economic Development over the Long Run: Central America since 1920," *Journal of Latin American Studies* 15:2

(November 1983), 269-294.

313. Burbach, Roger. "Revolution and Reaction: U.S. Policy in Central America," *Monthly Review* 36:2 (June 1984), 1-20.

314. Cerezo, Vinicio. "Replacing Ideology with a Spirit of Compromise: Consolidating Democracy in Central America," *Journal of Third World Studies* 4:1 (Spring 1987), 113-118.

315. Chomsky, Noam. "Intervention in Vietnam and Central America: Parallels and Differences," *Monthly Review* 37:4 (September 1985), 1-29.

316. Coleman, Kenneth M. "The Consequence of Excluding Reformists from Power." In *The Central American Crisis: Sources of Conflict and the Failure of U.S. Policy,* edited by Kenneth M. Coleman and George C. Herring. Wilmington, DE: Scholarly Resources, 1985. pp. 73-93.

317. Coll, Alberto R. "Soviet Arms and Central American Turmoil," *World Affairs* 148:1 (Summer 1985), 7-17.

318. Connell-Smith, Gordon. "The Crisis in Central America: President Reagan's Options," *World Today* 39:10 (October 1983), 385-392.

319. Coraggio, José Luis. "Estado, política económica y transición en Centroamérica: notas para su investigación," *Estudios Sociales Centroamericanos* 13:37 (January-April 1984), 73-87.

320. Crahan, Margaret E. "The Central American Church and Regime Transformation: Attitudes and Options." In *Political Change in Central America: Internal and External Dimensions,* edited by Wolf Grabendorff, Heinrich-W. Krumwiede and Jörg Todt. Boulder, CO: Westview, 1984. pp. 139-152.

321. Creamer, Winifred. "Mesoamerica as a Concept: An Archaeological View from Central America," *Latin American Research Review* 22:1 (1987), 35-62.

322. Dawson, Frank Griffith. "William Pitt's Settlement at Black River on the Mosquito Shore: A Challenge to Spain in Central America, 1732-87," *Hispanic American Historical Review* 63:4 (November 1983), 677-707.

323. DeWalt, Billie R. "The Agrarian Bases of Conflict in Central America." In *The Central American Crisis: Sources of Conflict and the Failure of U.S. Policy,* edited by Kenneth M. Coleman and George C. Herring. Wilmington, DE: Scholarly Resources, 1985. pp. 43-54.

324. Díaz-Polanco, Héctor. "*Neoindígenismo* and the Ethnic Question in Central America," *Latin American Perspectives* 14:1 (Winter 1987), 87-100.

325. Dickey, Christopher. "Central America: From Quagmire to Cauldron?" *Foreign Affairs* 62:3 (1983), 659-694.

326. Dunkerley, James. "Central America: Collapse of the Military System." In *The Political Dilemmas of Military Regimes,* edited by Christopher Clapham, Ian Campbell, and George Philip. Totowa, NJ: Rowman &

Allanheld, 1985. pp. 171-200.

327.   Durán, Esperanza. "The Contadora Approach to Peace in Central America," *World Today* 40:8-9 (August-September 1984), 347-354.

328.   ECLA Mexican Office. "The Crisis in Central America: Its Origins, Scope and Consequences," *CEPAL Review* 22 (April 1984), 53-80.

329.   ECLAC Mexico Subregional Headquarters. "Central America: Bases for a Reactivation and Development Policy," *CEPAL Review* 28 (April 1986), 11-48.

330.   Falcoff, Mark. "Central America: A View from Washington," *Orbis* 28:4 (Winter 1985), 665-673.

331.   Falcoff, Mark. "How to Understand Central America," *Commentary* 78:3 (September 1984), 30-38.

332.   Farer, Tom J. "Contadora: The Hidden Agenda," *Foreign Policy* 59 (Summer 1985), 59-72.

333.   Farer, Tom J. "Desarrollo político en América Central: democracia y diplomacia inhumanitaria," *Revista Mexicana de Sociología* 46:3 (July-September 1984), 49-64.

334.   Farer, Tom J. "Manage the Revolution?" *Foreign Policy* 52 (Fall 1983), 96-117.

335.   Feinberg, Richard E. "The Kissinger Commission Report: A Critique," *World Development* 12:8 (August 1984), 867-876.

336.   Ferris, Elizabeth G. "Central America: The Political Impact of Refugees," *World Today* 41:5 (May 1985), 100-101.

337.   Figueres, José, Daniel Oduber, Rodrigo Carazo, Javier Solís. "Reflections on U.S. Policy," *World Policy Journal* 3:2 (Spring 1986), 317-345.

338.   Fischer, Robert. "The U.S. Response to Central American Problems," *Journal of Third World Studies* 2:2 (Fall 1985), 42-45.

339.   Fuerst Weigand, Edgar. "Industrialización y exportaciones no tradicionales: opciones estratégicas para una nueva política industrial del estado frente a la crisis económica en Centroamérica," *Estudios Sociales Centroamericanos* 13:37 (January-April 1984), 107-135.

340.   Gleijeses, Piero. "The Reagan Doctrine and Central America," *Current History* 85:515 (December 1986), 401-404.

341.   González, Vinicio. "The History of Ethnic Classification in Central America, 1700-1950," *International Social Science Journal* 39:1 (February 1987), 61-84.

342.   González del Valle, Jorge. "The Role of External Debt Problems in Central America." In *Politics and Economics of External Debt Crisis: The Latin American Experience,* edited by Miguel S. Wionczek in collaboration with Luciano Tomassini. Boulder, CO: Westview, 1985.

pp. 427-436.

343. Grabendorff, Wolf. "The Role of Regional Powers in Central America: Mexico, Venezuela, Cuba, and Colombia." In *Latin American Nations in World Politics*, edited by Heraldo Muñoz and Joseph S. Tulchin. Boulder, CO: Westview, 1984. pp. 83-100.

344. Grabendorff, Wolf. "West European Perceptions of the Crisis in Central America." In *Political Change in Central America: Internal and External Dimensions*, edited by Wolf Grabendorff, Heinrich-W. Krumwiede and Jörg Todt. Boulder, CO: Westview, 1984. pp. 285-297.

345. Gugliotta, Guy. "The Central American Exodus: Grist for the Migrant Mill." In *The Caribbean Exodus*, edited by Barry B. Levine. New York: Praeger, 1987. pp. 171-192.

346. Herring, George C., and Kenneth M. Coleman. "Beyond Hegemony: Toward a New Central American Policy." In *The Central American Crisis: Sources of Conflict and the Failure of U.S. Policy*, edited by Kenneth M. Coleman and George C. Herring. Wilmington, DE: Scholarly Resources, 1985. pp. 219-228.

347. Hintermeister, Alberto. "Subempleo y pobreza rural en Centroamérica," *Estudios Rurales Latinoamericanos* 9:2 (May-August 1986), 33-47.

348. Hufford, Larry. "The U.S. in Central America: The Obfuscation of History," *Journal of Peace Research* 22:2 (1985), 93-100.

349. Hunter, John M., and Renate De Kleine. "Geophagy in Central America," *Geographical Review* 74:2 (April 1984), 157-169.

350. Jiménez, Edgar. "Comentarios en torno de las recomendaciones económicas del Informe Kissinger," *Revista Mexicana de Sociología* 46:3 (July-September 1984), 91-108.

351. Kenworthy, Eldon. "Central America: Beyond the Credibility Trap." In *The Central American Crisis: Sources of Conflict and the Failure of U.S. Policy*, edited by Kenneth M. Coleman and George C. Herring. Wilmington, DE: Scholarly Resources, 1985. pp. 111-135.

352. Kenworthy, Eldon. "United States Policy in Central America: A Choice Denied," *Current History* 84:500 (March 1985), 97-100.

353. Kenworthy, Eldon. "United States Policy toward Central America," *Current History* 86:524 (December 1987), 401-404.

354. Kornbluh, Peter. "Test Case for the Reagan Doctrine: The Covert Contra War," *Third World Quarterly* 9:4 (October 1987), 1118-1128.

355. Krauss, Clifford. "Revolution in Central America," *Foreign Affairs* 65:3 (1986), 564-581.

356. LaFeber, Walter. "The Reagan Administration and Revolution in Central America," *Political Science Quarterly* 99:1 (Spring 1984), 1-25.

357. LaFeber, Walter. "The Reagan Policy in Historical Perspective." In *The*

Central American Crisis: Sources of Conflict and the Failure of U.S. Policy, edited by Kenneth M. Coleman and George C. Herring. Wilmington, DE: Scholarly Resources, 1985. pp. 1-16.

358.   LaFeber, Walter. "The United States and Central America: The Perspective of History." In *Central America: Human Rights and U.S. Foreign Policy,* edited by Dermot Keogh. Cork, Ireland: Cork University Press, 1985. 5-20.

359.   Lemco, Jonathan. "Canadian Foreign Policy Interests in Central America: Some Current Issues," *Journal of Inter-American Studies and World Affairs* 28:2 (Summer 1986), 119-146.

360.   LeoGrande, William M. "Through the Looking Glass: The Report on the National Bipartisan Commission on Central America," *World Policy Journal* 1:2 (Winter 1984), 251-284.

361.   Lernoux, Penny. "Revolution and Counterrevolution in the Central American Church." In *Revolution and Counterrevolution in Central America and the Caribbean,* edited by Donald E. Schultz and Douglas H. Graham. Boulder, CO: Westview, 1984. pp. 117-155.

362.   Libby, Ronald T. "Listen to the Bishops," *Foreign Policy* 52 (Fall 1983), 78-95.

363.   Lincoln, Jennie K. "Central America: Regional Security Issues." In *The Dymanics of Latin American Foreign Policies,* edited by Jennie K. Lincoln and Elizabeth G. Ferris. Boulder, CO: Westview, 1984. 195-212.

364.   Loehr, William. "Current Account Balances in Central America 1974-1984: External and Domestic Influences," *Journal of Latin American Studies* 19:1 (May 1987), 87-111.

365.   López, José Roberto. "Centroamérica: nuevas perspectivas de la integración económica regional en la década de los 80," *Estudios Sociales Centroamericanos* 13:39 (August-December 1984), 79-93.

366.   Lowenthal, Abraham F. "The United States and Central America: Reflections on the Kissinger Commission Report." In *The Central American Crisis: Sources of Conflict and the Failure of U.S. Policy,* edited by Kenneth M. Coleman and George C. Herring. Wilmington, DE: Scholarly Resources, 1985. pp. 205-215.

367.   Luers, William H. "European and Western Hemispheres Policies toward Central America," In *Central America: Human Rights and U.S. Foreign Policy,* edited by Dermot Keogh. Cork, Ireland: Cork University Press, 1985. pp. 81-111.

368.   Lungo, Mario. "Panorama histórico de las regiones fronterizas en Centroamérica: 6 tesis y 2 hipótesis," *Estudios Sociales Centroamericanos* 40 (January-April 1986), 19-32.

369.   McDonald, Ronald H. "Civil-Military Relations in Central America: The Dilemmas of Political Institutionalization." In *Rift and Revolution: The Central American Imbroglio,* edited by Howard J. Wiarda. Washington, DC: American Enterprise Institute, 1984. pp. 129-166.

370.   McDonald, Ronald H., and Nina Tamrowski. "Technology and Armed Conflict in Central America," *Journal of Inter-American Studies and World Affairs* 29:1 (Spring 1987), 93-108.

371.   MacLeod, Murdo J. "La situación legal de los indios en América Central durante la Colonia: teoría y práctica," *América Indígena* 45:3 (July-September 1985), 485-504.

372.   Millett, Richard. "The Central American Militaries." In *Armies and Politics in Latin America,*" edited by Abraham F. Lowenthal and Samuel Fitch. Rev. ed. New York: Holmes & Meier, 1986. pp. 204-223.

373.   Molina Chocano, Guillermo. "Estado y proceso de acumulación en Centroamérica," *Estudios Sociales Centroamericanos* 13:37 (January-April 1984), 91-106.

374.   Montgomery, Tommie Sue. "Liberation and Revolution: Christianity as a Subversive Activity in Central America." In *Trouble in Our Backyard: Central America and the United States in the Eighties,* edited by Martin Diskin. New York: Pantheon, 1983. pp. 75-99.

375.   Moore, John Norton. "The Secret War in Central American and the Future of World Order," *American Journal of International Law* 80:1 (January 1986), 43-127.

376.   Morales A., Miguel. "Crisis del Estado Nacional: los problemas fronterizos en Centroamérica," *Estudios Sociales Centroamericanos* 40 (January-April 1986), 33-46.

377.   Mujal-León, Eusebio. "European Socialism and the Crisis in Central America," *Orbis* 28:1 (Spring 1984), 53-81.

378.   Mujal-León, Eusebio. "El socialismo europeo y la crisis en Centro-américa," *Foro Internacional* 24:2 (October-December 1983), 155-198.

379.   Nations, James, and H. Jeffrey Leonard. "Grounds of Conflict in Central America." In *Bordering On Trouble: Resources and Politics in Latin America,* edited by Andrew Maguire and Janet Welsh Brown. Bethesda, MD: Adler & Adler, 1986. pp. 55-98.

380.   Oduber, Daniel. "Is Peace Possible in Central America?" In *The Central American Crisis: Sources of Conflict and the Failure of U.S. Policy,* edited by Kenneth M. Coleman and George C. Herring. Wilmington, DE: Scholarly Resources, 1985. pp. 193-204.

381.   Ortiz Rosales, Rolando Eliseo. "Rasgos sociales y económicos de la crisis centroamericana," *Foro Internacional* 26:1 (July-September 1985), 5-15.

382.   Paige, Jeffery M. "Coffee and Politics in Central America." In *Crises in the Caribbean Basin,* edited by Richard Tardanico. Beverly Hills, CA: Sage, 1987. pp. 141-190.

383.   Payeras, Mario. "In Central America," *Monthly Review* 37:10 (March 1986), 14-20.

384.   Paz Salinas, María Emilia. "Contadora: ?'impasse' o agotamiento?" *Revista Mexicana de Sociología* 47:2 (April-June 1985), 389-411.

385.   Pérez Brignoli, Héctor, assisted by Yolanda Baires Martínez. "Growth and Crisis in the Central American Economies, 1950-1980," *Journal of Latin American Studies* 15:2 (November 1983), 365-398.

386.   Petras, James F., and Morris H. Morley. "Economic Expansion, Political Crisis and U.S. Policy in Central America." In *Capitalist and Socialist Crises in the Late Twentieth Century,* by James F. Petras. Totowa, NJ: Rowman & Allenheld, 1984. 350p.

387.   Purcell, Susan Kaufman. "The Choice in Central America," *Foreign Affairs* 66:1 (Fall 1987), 109-128.

388.   Purcell, Susan Kaufman. "Demystifying Contadora," *Foreign Affairs* 64:1 (Fall 1985), 74-95.

389.   Richard, Pablo. "The Role of the Church in the Central American Revolutionary Process." In *Towards an Alternative for Central America and the Caribbean,* edited by George Irvin and Xabier Gorostiaga. London; Boston: Allen & Unwin, 1985. pp. 215-230.

390.   Romero, Anibal. "The Kissinger Commission: A Latin American Perspective." In *Central America: Human Rights and U.S. Foreign Policy,* edited by Dermot Keogh. Cork, Ireland: Cork University Press, 1985. 127-143.

391.   Rosenberg, Mark B. "Pequeños países y potencias hegemónicas: Centroamérica y el Caribe en el contexto global," *Estudios Sociales Centroamericanos* 43 (January-April 1987), 27-40.

392.   Rosenberg, Mark B. "Political Obstacles to Democracy in Central America." In *Authoritarians and Democrats: Regime Transition in Latin America,* edited by James M. Malloy and Mitchell A. Seligson. Pittsburgh, PA: Pittsburgh University Press, 1987. pp. 193-215.

393.   Rosenthal, Gert. "Central American Economic Integration." In *Latin404 American Prospects for the 1980s,* edited by Archibald R.M. Ritter and David H. Pollock. New York: Praeger, 1983. pp. 147-157.

394.   Sánchez, Nestor D. "The Communist Threat," *Foreign Policy* 52 (Fall 1983), 43-50.

395.   Schultz, Donald E. "Ten Theories in Search of Central American Reality." In *Revolution and Counterrevolution in Central America and the Caribbean,* edited by Donald E. Schultz and Douglas H. Graham. Boulder, CO: Westview, 1984. pp. 3-64.

396.   Seligson, Mitchell A. "Development, Democratization, and Decay: Central America at the Crossroads." In *Authoritarians and Democrats: Regime Transition in Latin America,* edited by James M. Malloy and Mitchell A. Seligson. Pittsburgh, PA: Pittsburgh University Press, 1987. pp. 167-192.

397.   Singer, Max. "Losing Central America," *Commentary* 82:1 (July 1986), 11-14.

398. Sol, Ricardo. "Nuevos sujetos políticos y comunicación," *Estudios Sociales Centroamericanos* 41 (May-August 1986), 104-123.

399. Stone, Samuel. "Production and Politics in Central America's Convulsions," *Journal of Latin American Studies* 15:2 (November 1983), 453-469.

400. Thrower, Mary M. "Background to Revolution: U.S. Intervention in Central America and the Caribbean," *Journal of Third World Studies* 3:2 (Fall 1986), 97-101.

401. Torres-Rivas, Edelberto. "Escenarios, sujetos, desenlaces," *Revista Mexicana de Sociología* 46:3 (July-September 1984), 5-26.

402. Valero, Ricardo. "Contadora: la búsqueda de la pacificación en Centroamérica," *Foro Internacional* 26:2 (October-December 1985), 125-156.

403. Vanderlaan, Mary. "The Dual Strategy Myth in Central American Policy," *Journal of Inter-American Studies and World Affairs* 26:2 (May 1984), 199-224.

404. van Young, Eric. "Recent Anglophone Scholarship on Mexico and Central American in the Age of Revolution, 1750-1850," *Hispanic American Historical Review* 65:4 (November 1985), 725-743.

405. Wallich, Henry C. "Central America: Monetary Policy and Economic Growth," *Journal of Inter-American Studies and World Affairs* 27:4 (Winter 1985-86), 111-115.

406. Webb, Michael A. "Economic Opportunity and Labor Markets in Central America." In *The Central American Crisis: Sources of Conflict and the Failure of U.S. Policy,* edited by Kenneth M. Coleman and George C. Herring. Wilmington, DE: Scholarly Resources, 1985. pp. 19-41.

407. Weeks, John, "An Interpretation of the Central American Crisis," *Latin American Research Review* 21:3 (1986), 31-53.

408. Whitehead, Laurence. "The Costa Rican Initiative in Central America," *Government and Opposition* 22:4 (Autumn 1987), 457-464.

409. Whitehead Laurence. "Explaining Washington's Central American Policies," *Journal of Latin American Studies* 15:2 (November 1983), 321-363.

410. Woods, James M. "Expansionism as Diplomacy: The Career of Solon Borland in Central America 1853-1854," *The Americas* 40:3 (January 1984), 399-415.

411. Woodward, Ralph Lee, Jr. "The Historiography of Modern Central America Since 1960," *Hispanic American Historical Review* 67:3 (August 1987), 461-496.

412. Woodward, Ralph Lee, Jr. "The Rise and Decline of Liberalism in Central America: Historical Perspectives on the Contemporary Crisis," *Journal of Inter-American Studies and World Affairs* 26:3

(August 1984), 291-312.

413.   Worrell, DeLisle. "Central America and the Caribbean: Adjustment in Small, Open Economies." In *Adjustment Crisis in the Third World*, edited by Richard E. Feinberg and Valeriana Kallab. Rutgers, NJ: Transaction, 1984. pp. 159-181.

LATIN AMERICA

Books and Monographs

414. Abel, Christopher, and Colin M. Lewis, eds. *Latin America, Economic Imperialism and the State: The Political Economy of the External Connection from Independence to the Present.* London; Dover, NH: Athlone, 1985. 540p.

415. Ames, Barry. *Political Survival: Politicians and Public Policy in Latin America.* Berkeley: University of California Press, 1987. 286p.

416. Anna, Timothy E. *Spain and the Loss of America.* Lincoln: University of Nebraska Press, 1983. 343p.

417. Archetti, Eduardo P., Paul Cammack, and Bryan Roberts, eds. *Latin America.* London: MacMillan, 1987. 357p.

418. Armstrong, Warwick, and T.G. McGee. *Theatres of Accumulation: Studies in Asian and Latin American Urbanization.* London; New York: Methuen, 1985. 269p.

419. Ascher, William. *Scheming for the Poor: The Politics of Redistribution in Latin America.* Cambridge, MA: Harvard University Press, 1984. 349p.

420. Bahbah, Bishara. *Israel and Latin America: The Military Connection.* New York: St. Martin's, 1986. 210p.

421. Balassa, Bela, Gerardo M. Bueno, Pedro-Pablo Kuczynski, and Mario Henrique Simonsen. *Toward Renewed Economic Growth in Latin America.* Mexico City: Colegio de México; Washington, DC: Institute for International Economics, 1986. 205p.

422. Ballesteros Gaibrois, Manuel, et al. *Cultura y religión de la América prehispánica.* Madrid, Spain: Biblioteca de Autores Cristianos, 1985. 346p.

423.   Balmori, Diana, Stuart F. Voss, and Miles Wortman. *Notable Family Networks in Latin America.* Chicago: University of Chicago Press, 1984. 290p.

424.   Baloyra, Enrique A., ed. *Comparing New Democracies; Transition and Consolidation in Mediterranean Europe and the Southern Cone.* Boulder, CO: Westview, 1987. 318p.

425.   Barbier, Jacques, and Allan J. Kuethe, eds. *The North American Role in the Spanish Imperial Economy, 1760-1819.* Manchester, England: Manchester University Press, 1984. 232p.

426.   Bark, Dennis L., ed. *The Red Orchestra: Instruments of Soviet Policy in Latin America and the Caribbean.* Stanford, CA: Hoover Institution Press, 1986. 140p.

427.   Barrett, Jeffrey. *The Impulse to Revolution in Latin America.* New York: Praeger, 1985. 357p.

428.   Beeson, Trevor, and Jenny Pearce, eds. *A Vision of Hope: The Churches and Change in Latin America.* Philadelphia, PA: Fortress, 1984. 290p.

429.   Bergquist, Charles. *Labor in Latin America: Comparative Essays on Chile, Argentina, Venezuela and Colombia.* Stanford, CA: Stanford University Press, 1986. 397p.

430.   Berryman, Phillip. *Liberation Theology: Essential Facts about the Revolutionary Movement in Latin America and Beyond.* Philadelphia, PA: Temple University Press, 1987. 231p.

431.   Bethell, Leslie, ed. *The Cambridge History of Latin America.* New York: Cambridge University Press, 5 vols.
       Vol. 1 and 2:   *Colonial Latin America,* 1984. 645p. 912p.
       Vol. 3:   *From Independence to c. 1870,* 1985. 945p.
       Vol. 4 and 5:   *c. 1870 to 1930,* 1986. 676p. 951p.

432.   Bingham, Majorie W., and Susan H. Gross. *Women in Latin America.* St. Louis Park, MN: Glenhurst, 1985. 2 vols.

433.   Bitar, Sergio, and Carlos J. Moneta. *Crisis Financiera e industrial en América Latina.* Buenos Aires: Grupo Editor Latinoamericano (dist. by Emece), 1985. 75p.

434.   Black, Jan Knippers. *Sentinels of Empire: The United States and Latin American Militarism.* Westport, CT: Greenwood, 1986. 240p.

435.   Black, Jan Knippers, ed. *Latin America, Its Problems and Its Promise: A Multidisciplinary Introduction.* Boulder, CO; Westview, 1984. 549p.

436.   Blakemore, Harold, and Cliffort T. Smith, eds. *Latin America: Geographical Perspectives.* 2d ed. London; New York: Methuen, 1983. 557p.

437.   Blasier, Cole. *The Giant's Rival: The USSR and Latin America.* Pittsburgh, PA: University of Pittsburgh Press, 1983. 213p.

438.   Blasier, Cole. *The Hovering Giant: U.S. Responses to Revolutionary*

Changes in Latin America, 1910-1985. Rev. ed. Pittsburgh, PA: University of Pittsburgh Press, 1985. 339p.

439. Brock, Colin, and Hugh Lawlor, eds. *Education in Latin America*. Dover, NH: Croom Helm, 1985. 196p.

440. Bronstein, Audrey. *The Triple Struggle: Latin American Peasant Women*. Boston, MA: South End, 1983. 268 p.

441. Browman, David L. *Arid Land Use Strategies and Risk Management in the Andes: A Regional Anthropological Perspective*. Boulder, CO: Westview 1986. 335p.

442. Brown, Cynthia, ed. *With Friends Like These: The Americas Watch Report on Human Rights and U.S. Policy in Latin America*. New York: Pantheon-Random House, 1985. 281p.

443. Brown, Janet W., and Andrew Maguire, eds. *Bordering on Trouble: Resources and Politics in Latin America*. Bethesda, MD: Adler & Adler, 1986. 448p.

444. Bruneau, Thomas C., Chester E. Gabriel, and Mary Mooney, eds. *The Catholic Church and Religions in Latin America*. Montreal, Canada: Centre for Developing Area Studies, McGill University, 1984. 279p.

445. Buergenthal, Thomas, Robert Norris, and Dinah Shelton. *Protecting Human Rights in the Americas: Selected Problems*. 2d ed. Arlington, VA: N.P. Engel, 1986. 389p.

446. Burns, E. Bradford. *Latin America: A Concise Interpretive History*. 4th ed. Englewood Cliffs, NJ: Prentice-Hall, 1986. 374p.

447. Caballero, Manuel. *Latin America and the Comintern, 1919-1943*. Cambridge, England; New York: Cambridge University Press, 1987. 213p.

448. Cardoso, Fernando Henrique, Bernardo Sorj, and Mauricio Font, eds. *Economia e movimentos sociais na América Latina*. São Paulo: Brasiliense, 1985. 323p.

449. Carmagnani, Marcello. *Estado y sociedad en América Latina, 1850-1930*. Barcelona, Spain: Crítica, 1984. 260p.

450. Caviedes, César L. *The Southern Cone: Realities of the Authoritarian State in South America*. Totowa, NJ: Rowman & Allanheld, 1984. 212p.

451. Cepeda Ulloa, Fernando, et al. *Democracia y desarrollo en América Latina*. Buenos Aires: Grupo Editor Latinoamericano (dist. by Emece), 1985. 273p.

452. Chilcote, Ronald H., and Joel C. Edelstein. *Latin America: Capitalist and Socialist Perspectives of Development and Underdevelopment*. Boulder, CO: Westview, 1985. 175p.

453. Child, Jack. *Geopolitics and Conflict in South America: Quarrels among Neighbors*. New York: Praeger; Stanford, CA: Hoover Institution

Press, 1985. 196p.

454.   Clayton, Lawrance A. *Grace: W.R. Grace and Company: The Formative Years, 1850-1930.* Ottawa, IL: Jameson, 1985. 403p.

455.   Cleary, Edward L. *Crisis and Change: The Church in Latin America Today.* Maryknoll, NY: Orbis, 1985. 202p.

456.   Cole, Jeffrey A., ed. *The Church and Society in Latin America.* New Orleans, LA: Center for Latin American Studies, Tulane University Press, 1984. 379p.

457.   Cortes, Mariluz, and Peter Bocock. *North-South Technology Transfer: A Case Study of Petrochemicals in Latin America.* Baltimore, MD: For the World Bank by Johns Hopkins University Press, 1984. 176p.

458.   Cortés Conde, Roberto, and Shane J. Hunt, eds. *The Latin American Economies: Growth and the Export Sector, 1880-1930.* New York: Holmes & Meier, 1985. 387p.

459.   Costelo, Michael P. *Response to Revolution: Imperial Spain and the Spanish American Revolutions, 1810-1840.* Cambridge, England; New York: Cambridge University Press, 1986. 272p.

460.   Czinkota, Michael R., ed. *U.S.-Latin American Trade Relations: Issues and Concerns.* New York: Praeger, 1983. 297p.

461.   Dean, Warren. *Diplomatic Claims: Latin American Historians View the United States.* Lanham, MD: University Press of America, 1985. 320p.

462.   Deere, Carmen Diana, and Magdalena León de Leal, eds. *Rural Women and State Policy: Feminist Perspective on Latin American Agricultural Development.* Boulder, CO: Westview, 1987. 282p.

463.   Denoon, Donald. *Settler Capitalism: The Dynamics of Dependent Development in the Southern Hemisphere.* New York: Oxford University Press, 1983. 280p.

464.   Drake, Paul W., and Eduardo Silva, eds. *Elections and Democratization in Latin America, 1980-85.* San Diego: Center for Iberian and Latin American Studies, University of California, San Diego, 1986. 335p.

465.   Duff, Ernest A. *Leader and Party in Latin America.* Boulder, CO: Westview, 1985. 177p.

466.   Durán, Esperanza. *European Interests in Latin America.* London: Royal Institute of International Affairs; Boston, MA: Routledge & Kegan Paul, 1985. 110p.

467.   Durán, Esperanza, ed. *Latin America and the World Recession.* Cambridge, England; New York: Cambridge University Press, 1985. 162p.

468.   Economic Commission for Latin America. *La crisis en América Latina: su evaluación y perspectivas.* Santiago, Chile; New York: United Nations, 1985. 119p.

469.   Economic Commission for Latin America. *Debt, Adjustment, and Renegotiation in Latin America: Orthodox and Alternative approaches.* Boulder, CO: Lynne Rienner, 1986. 171p.

470.   Economic Commission for Latin America. *El desarrollo de la seguridad social en América Latina.* Santiago, Chile: United Nations, 1985. 348p.

471.   Economic Commission for Latin America. *Five Studies of the Situation of Women in Latin America.* New York, 1983. 188p.

472.   Economic Commission for Latin America. *Políticas de promoción de exportaciones en algunos paises de América Latina.* Santiago, Chile; New York: United Nations, 1985. 304p.

473.   Economic Commission for Latin America and the Caribbean. *The Economic Crisis: Policies for Adjustment, Stabilization and Growth.* Santiago, Chile: United Nations, 1986. 132p.

474.   Economic Commission for Latin America and the Caribbean. *Economic Survey of Latin America and the Caribbean 1984.* Vol. 1: *The Latin American Economy in 1984.* Santiago, Chile; New York, 1986. 685p.

475.   Economic Commission for Latin America and the Caribbean. *External Debt in Latin America: Adjustment Policies and Renegotiation.* Boulder, CO: Lynne Rienner, 1985. 125p.

476.   English, Andrian J. *Armed Forces of Latin America: Their Histories, Development, Present Strength and Military Potential.* New York: Jane's, 1984. 490p.

477.   Falcoff, Mark. *Small Countries, Large Issues: Studies in U.S.-Latin American Asymmetries: Nicaragua, Cuba, Uruguay, El Salvador, Chile.* Washington, DC: American Enterprise Institute for Public Policy Research, 1984. 126p.

478.   Fauriol, Georges A., ed. *Latin American Insurgencies.* Washington, DC: Center for Strategic and International Studies and the National Defense University (dist. by the Government Printing Office), 1985. 214p.

479.   Ffrench-Davis, Ricardo. *Dos estudios sobre política arancelaria.* Santiago, Chile: United Nations, 1984. 96p.

480.   Ffrench-Davis, Ricardo, and Richard E. Feinberg, eds. *Mas allá de la crisis de la deuda: bases para un nuevo enfoque.* Santiago, Chile: CIEPLAN, 1986. 250p.

481.   Fisher, John. *Commercial Relations between Spain and Spanish America in the Era of Free Trade, 1778-1796.* Liverpool, England: Centre for Latin American Studies, University of Liverpool, 1985. 158p.

482.   Foxley, Alejandro. *Latin American Experiments in Neoconservative Economics.* Berkeley: University of California Press, 1983. 213p.

483.   Gauhar, Altaf, ed. *Regional Integration: The Latin American Experience.*

Boulder, CO; Westview, 1985. 282p.

484.   Ghosh, Pradip K., ed. *Developing Latin America: A Modernization Perspective.* Westport, CT: Greenwood, 1984. 416p.

485.   Gilderhus, Mark T. *Pan American Visions: Woodrow Wilson in the Western Hemisphere, 1913-1921.* Tucson: University of Arizona Press, 1986. 194p.

486.   Godio, Julio. *Sindicalismo y política en América Latina.* Caracas: ILDIS, 1983. 315p.

487.   González Cassanova, Pablo, ed. *Historia del movimiento obrero en América Latina.* Mexico City: Siglo Veintiuno, 1984. 4 vols.

488.   González Casanova, Pablo, ed. *No intervención: audodeterminación y democracia en América Latina.* Mexico City: Siglo Veintiuno, 1983. 338p.

489.   González Casanova, Pablo, coord. *Historia política de los campesinos latinoamericanos.* Mexico City: Siglo Veintiuno, 1984-85. 4 vols.

490.   Grabendorff, Wolf, and Riordan Roett, eds. *Latin America, Western Europe, and the United States: Reevaluating the Atlantic Triangle.* New York: Praeger, 1985. 295p.

491.   Griffith-Jones, Stephany. *International Finance and Latin America.* New York: St. Martin's, 1984. 113p.

492.   Griffith-Jones, Stephany, and Osvaldo Sunkel. *Debt and Development Crises in Latin America: The End of an Illusion.* New York: Oxford University Press, 1986. 201p.

493.   Grindle, Merilee S. *State and Countryside: Development Policy and Agrarian Politics in Latin America.* Baltimore, MD: Johns Hopkins University Press, 1986. 255p.

494.   Gwynne, Robert N. *Industrialization and Urbanization in Latin America.* Baltimore, MD: Johns Hopkins University Press, 1986. 259p.

495.   Haglund, David G. *Latin America and the Transformation of U.S. Strategic Thought, 1936-1940.* Albuquerque: University of New Mexico Press, 1984. 280p.

496.   Halperin-Donghi, Tulio. *Reforma y disolución de los imperios ibéricos, 1750-1850.* Madrid, Spain: Alianza, 1985. 383p. (*Historia de América Latina,* Vol. 3.)

497.   Harnecker, Marta. *La revolución social: Lenin y América Latina.* Mexico City: Siglo Veintiuno, 1986. 307p.

498.   Harrison, Lawrance E. *Underdevelopment is a State of Mind: The Latin American Case.* Lanham, MD: Center for International Affairs, Harvard University and University Press of America, 1985. 192p.

499.   Hartlyn, Jonathan, and Samuel A. Morley, eds. *Latin American Political Economy: Financial Crisis and Political Change.* Boulder, CO:

Westview, 1986, 386p.

500.   Hayes, Margaret Daly. *Latin America and the U.S. National Interest: A Basis for U.S. Foreign Policy.* Boulder, CO: Westview, 1984. 295p.

501.   Hirschman, Albert O. *Getting Ahead Collectively: Grassroots Experiences in Latin America.* New York: Pergamon, 1984. 101p.

502.   Hoberman, Louisa Schell, and Susan Migden Socolow, eds. *Cities and Society in Colonial Latin America.* Albuquerque: University of New Mexico Press, 1986. 350p.

503.   Hopkins, Jack W., ed. *Latin America: Perspectives on a Region.* New York: Holmes & Meier, 1987. 320p.

504.   Hughes, Steven W., and Kenneth J. Mijeski. *Politics and Public Policy in Latin America.* Boulder, CO: Westview, 1984. 256p.

505.   Hunter, John M., Robert Thomas, and Scott Whiteford, eds. *Population Growth and Urbanization in Latin America.* Cambridge, MA: Schenkman, 1983. 310p.

506.   Jenkins, Rhys Owen. *Transnational Corporations and the Latin American Automobile Industry.* Pittsburgh, PA: University of Pittsburgh Press, 1987. 270p.

507.   Johnson, John J., Peter J. Blakewell, and Meredith D. Dodge, eds. *Readings in Latin American History.* Durham, NC: Duke University Press, 1985.
        Vol. 1:   *The Formative Centuries,* 428p.
        Vol. 2:   *The Modern Experience,* 464p.

508.   Keen, Benjamin, ed. *Latin American Civilization: History and Society, 1492 to the Present.* 4th ed. Boulder, CO: Westview, 1986. 425p.

509.   Kim, Kwan S., and David F. Ruccio, eds. *Debt and Development in Latin America.* Notre Dame, IN: University of Notre Dame Press, 1985. 226p.

510.   Klarén, Peter F. and Thomas J. Bossert, eds. *Promise of Development: Theories of Change in Latin America.* Boulder, CO: Westview, 1986. 350p.

511.   Klein, Herbert S. *African Slavery in Latin America and the Caribbean.* New York: Oxford University Press, 1986. 311p.

512.   Kronish, Rich, and Kenneth S. Mericle, eds. *Political Economy of the Latin American Motor Vehicle Industry.* Cambridge, MA: M.I.T. Press, 1984. 314p.

513.   Kryzanek, Michael J. *U.S.-Latin American Relations.* New York: Praeger, 1985. 242p.

514.   La Belle, Thomas J. *Nonformal Education in Latin America and the Caribbean: Stability, Reform, or Revolution?* New York: Praeger, 1986. 367p.

515.   Langley, Lester D. *The Banama Wars: An Inner History of American Empire, 1900-1934.* Lexington: University Press of Kentucky, 1983. 255p.

516.   Lanning, John Tate. *The Royal Protomedicato: The Regulation of the Medical Professions in the Spanish Empire.* Edited by John Jay TePaske. Durham, NC: Duke University Press, 1985. 485p.

517.   Latin American Bureau. *The Poverty Brokers: The IMF in Latin America.* London: 1983. 138p.

518.   Levine, Daniel H., ed. *Religion and Political Conflict in Latin America.* Chapel Hill: University of North Carolina Press, 1986. 266p.

519.   Lincoln, Jennie K., and Elizabeth G. Ferris, eds. *The Dynamics of Latin American Foreign Policies: Challenges for the 1980s.* Boulder, CO: Westview, 1984. 325p.

520.   Liss, Peggy K. *Atlantic Empires: The Network of Trade and Revolution, 1713-1826.* Baltimore, MD: Johns Hopkins University Press, 1983. 348p.

521.   Liss, Sheldon B. *Marxist Thought in Latin America.* Berkeley: University of California Press, 1984. 374p.

522.   Lockhart, James, and Stuart B. Schwartz. *Early Latin America: A History of Colonial Spanish America and Brazil.* Cambridge, England; New York: Cambridge University Press, 1983. 480p.

523.   Lord, Montague J. *Commodity Export Prospects of Latin America.* Washington, DC: Inter-American Development Bank, 1985. 73p.

524.   Lowenthal, Abraham F. *Partners in Conflict: The United States and Latin America.* Baltimore, MD: Johns Hopkins University Press, 1987. 242p.

525.   Lowenthal, Abraham F., and Samuel Fitch, eds. *Armies and Politics in Latin America.* Rev. ed. New York: Holmes & Meier, 1986. 489p.

526.   McAlister, Lyle N. *Spain and Portugal in the New World, 1492-1700.* Minneapolis: University of Minnesota Press, 1984. 585p.

527.   MacDonald, Theodore Jr., ed. *Native Peoples and Economic Development: Six Case Studies from Latin America.* Cambridge, MA: Cultural Survival, 1985. 103p.

528.   McNeill, John Robert. *Atlantic Empires of France and Spain: Louisbourg and Havana, 1700-1763.* Chapel Hill: University of North Carolina Press, 1985. 329p.

529.   Maguire, Andrew, and Janet Welsh Brown, eds. *Bordering on Trouble: Resources and Politics in Latin America.* Bethesda, MD: Adler & Adler, 1986. 448p.

530.   Malloy, James M., and Mitchell A. Seligson, eds. *Authoritarians and Democrats: Regime Transition in Latin America.* Pittsburgh, PA: University of Pittsburgh Press, 1987. 268p.

531.   Maolain, Ciaran O., ed. *Latin American Political Movements.* New York: Facts on File, 1985. 287p.

532.   Maos, Jacob O. *The Spatial Organization of New Land Settlement in Latin America.* Boulder, CO: Westview, 1984. 179p.

533.   Martín del Campo, Julio Labastida, coord. *Hegemonía y alternativas políticas en América Latina.* Mexico City: Siglo Veintiuno, 1985. 486p.

534.   Martín del Campo, Julio Labastida, ed. *Dictaduras y dictadores.* Mexico City: Siglo Veintiuno, 1986. 239p.

535.   Mesa-Lago, Carmelo, ed. *The Crisis of Social Security and Health Care: Latin American Experiences and Lessons.* Pittsburgh, PA: Center for Latin American Studies, University of Pittsburgh, 1985. 365p.

536.   Middlebrook, Kevin J., and Carlos Rico, eds. *The United States and Latin America in the 1980's: Contending Perspectives on a Decade of Crisis.* Pittsburgh, PA: University of Pittsburgh Press, 1986. 648p.

537.   Molineu, Harold. *U.S. Policy toward Latin America: From Regionalism to Globalism.* Boulder, CO: Westview, 1986. 242p.

538.   Morade, Pedro. *Cultura y modernización en América Latina: ensayo sociológico acerca de la crisis del desarrollismo y de su superación.* Santiago: Instituto de Sociología de la Pontificia Universidad Católica de Chile, 1984. 181p.

539.   Moreno Fraginals, Manuel, ed. *Africa in Latin America: Essays on History, Culture, and Socialization.* Translated by Leonor Blum. New York: Holmes & Meier, 1984. 342p.

540.   Mörner, Magnus, in collaboration with Harold Sims. *Adventures and Proletarians: The Story of Migrants in Latin America.* Pittsburgh, PA: University of Pittsburgh Press, 1985. 178p.

541.   Mouzelis, Nicos P. *Politics in the Semi-Periphery: Early Parliamentarism and Late Industrialization in the Balkans and Latin America.* New York: St. Martin's, 1986. 284p.

542.   Munck, Ronaldo. *Politics and Dependency in the Third World: The Case of Latin America.* London: Zed (Totowa, NJ: Dist. by Biblio Distribution Center), 1984. 374p.

543.   Munck, Ronaldo. *Revolutionary Trends in Latin America.* Montreal, Canada: Centre for Developing Area Studies, McGill University, 1984. 154p.

544.   Muñoz, Heraldo, and Joseph S. Tulchin, eds. *Latin American Nations in World Politics.* Boulder, CO: Westview, 1984. 278p.

545.   Murra, John V., Nathan Wachtel, and Jacques Revel, eds. *The Anthropological History of Andean Politics.* New York: Cambridge University Press, 1986. 383p.

546.   Nash, June, and Helen I. Safa, eds. *Women and Change in Latin*

America. South Hadley, MA: Bergin & Garvey, 1986. 372p.

547. Nassif, Ricardo, Germán W. Rama, and Juan Carlos Tedesco. *El sistema educativo en América Latina.* Buenos Aires: Kapelusz, 1984. 139p.

548. Needler, Martin C. *The Problem of Democracy in Latin America.* Lexington, MA: Lexington, 1987. 190p.

549. Newfarmer, Richard, ed. *From Gunboats to Diplomacy: New U.S. Policies for Latin America.* Baltimore, MD: Johns Hopkins University Press, 1984. 254p.

550. Novak, Michael, and Michael P. Jackson, eds. *Latin America: Dependency or Interdependence?* Washington, DC: American Enterprise Institute, 1985. 186p.

551. Nunn, Frederick M. *Yesterday's Soldiers: European Military Professionalism in South America, 1890-1940.* Lincoln: University of Nebraska Press, 1983. 365p.

552. O'Brien, Philip J., and Paul Cammack, eds. *Generals in Retreat: The Crisis of Military Rule in Latin America.* Dover, NH: Manchester University Press, 1985. 208p.

553. Ocampo, José Antonio, ed. *La política económica en la encrucijada.* Bogotá: CEDE, 1984. 192p.

554. O'Donnell, Guillermo, Philippe C. Schmitter, and Laurence Whitehead, eds. *Transition from Authoritarian Rule.* Baltimore, MD: Johns Hopkins University Press, 1986. 244p.

555. Organization of American States. *The Economy of Latin America and the Caribbean: Analysis and Interpretations Prompted by the Financial Crisis.* Washington, DC, 1984. 100p.

556. Organization of American States. *Hemispheric Cooperation and Integral Development.* Washington, DC, 1986. 2 vols.

557. Orrego Vicuña, Francisco, ed. *The Exclusive Economic Zone: A Latin American Perspective.* Boulder, CO: Westview, 1984. 188p.

558. Pacini, Deborah, and Christine Franquemont, eds. *Coca and Cocaine: Effects on the People and Policies in Latin America.* Cambridge, MA: Cultural Survival, 1986. 169p.

559. Para Sandoval, Rodrigo, et al. *La educación popular en América Latina.* Buenos Aires: Kapelusz, 1984. 127p.

560. Parry, John H., and Robert G. Keith, with Michael Jiménez. *New Iberian World: A Documentary History of the Discovery and Settlement of Latin America to the Early 17th Century.* New York: Times Books, 1984. 5 vols.

561. Pastor, Manuel, Jr. *The International Monetary Fund and Latin America: Economic Stabilization and Class Conflict.* Boulder, CO: Westview, 1987, 228p.

562. Pastor, Robert A., ed. *Latin America's Debt Crisis: Adjusting to the Past or Planning for the Future?* Boulder, CO: Lynne Rienner, 1987. 176p.

563. Perry, William, and Peter Wehner, eds. *The Latin American Policies of U.S. Allies: Balancing Global Interests and Regional Concerns.* New York: Praeger, 1985. 185p.

564. Petras, James F., with Howard Brill, Dennis Engbarth, Edward S. Herman, and Morris H. Morley. *Latin America Bankers, Generals, and the Struggle for Social Justice.* Totowa, NJ: Rowman & Littlefield, 1986. 187p.

565. Philip, George. *The Military in South American Politics.* Dover, NH: Croom Helm, 1985. 394p.

566. Piñeiro, Martín, and Eduardo Trigo. *Technical Change and Social Conflict in Agriculture: Latin American Perspectives.* Boulder, CO: Westview, 1983. 248p.

567. Puig, Juan Carlos. *Integración latinoamericana y régimen internacional.* Caracas: University Simón Bolívar, 1987. 408p.

568. Puig, Juan Carlos, ed. *América Latina: políticas exteriores comparadas.* Buenos Aires: Grupo Editor Latinoamericano, 1984. 2 vols.

569. Ramsaran Ramesh F. *U.S. Investments in Latin America and the Caribbean.* New York: St. Martin's, 1985. 196p.

570. Ritter, Archibald R.M., and David H. Pollock, eds. *Latin American Prospects for the 1980s: Equity, Democratization and Development.* New York: Praeger, 1983. 330p.

571. Riviere, Peter. *Individual and Society in Guiana: A Comparative Study of Amerindian Social Organization.* Cambridge, England; New York: Cambridge University Press, 1984. 136p.

572. Roper, Christopher, and Jorge Silva, eds. *Science and Technology in Latin America.* London; New York: Longman, 1983. 363p.

573. Rouquié, Alain. *El estado militar en América Latina.* Translated by Daniel Zadunaisky. Buenos Aires: Emece, 1984. 433p.

574. Russell, Roberto, ed. *América Latina y la guerra del Atlántico sur: experiencias y desafíos.* Buenos Aires: Belgrano, 1984. 248p.

575. Sanderson, Steven E., ed. *The Americas in the New International Division of Labor.* New York: Holmes & Meier, 1985. 296p.

576. Sater, William F. *The Southern Cone Nations of Latin America.* Arlington Heights, IL: Forum, 1984. 99p.

577. Saulniers, Alfred H., ed. *The Public Sector in Latin America.* Austin: Institute of Latin American Studies, University of Texas, 1984. 235p.

578. Saunders, John V.D., ed. *Population Growth in Latin America and U.S.*

National Security. Winchester, MA: Allen & Unwin, 1986. 305p.

579.   Sauvant, Karl P. *Trade and Foreign Direct Investment in Data Services.* Boulder, CO: Westview, 1986. 223p.

580.   Schmink, Marianne, and Charles H. Wood, eds. *Frontier Expansion in Amazonia.* Gainesville: University of Florida Press, 1984. 502p.

581.   Schoultz, Lars. *National Security and United States Policy toward Latin America.* Princeton, NJ: Princeton University Press, 1987. 377p.

582.   Shane, Douglas R. *Hoofprints on the Forest: Cattle Ranching and the Destruction of Latin America's Tropical Forests.* Philadelphia, PA: ISHI, 1986. 159p.

583.   Sistema Económico Latinomericano. *América Latina/Estados Unidos: evolución de las relaciones económicas (1984-1985).* Mexico City: Siglo Veintiuno, 1986. 223p.

584.   Sistema Económico Latinoamericano. *América Latina y la Comunidad Económica Europea: problemas y perspectivas.* Caracas, Venezuela: Monte Avila, 1984. 187p.

585.   Sistema Económico Latinoamericano. *El FMI, el Banco Mundial y la crisis Latinoamericana.* Mexico City: Siglo Veintiuno, 1986. 474p.

586.   Sistema Económico Latinoamericano. *Latin American-U.S. Economic Relations, 1982-1983.* Boulder, CO: Westview, 1984. 115p.

587.   Sistema Económico Latinoamericano. *La política económica de Estados Unidos y su impacto en América Latina.* Mexico City: Siglo Veintiuno, 1985. 229p.

588.   Sistema Económico Latinoamericano. *Situación y perspectivas de las relaciones económicas entre América Latina y el Japón.* Buenos Aires: Flor, 1987. 93p.

589.   Skidmore, Thomas E., and Peter H. Smith. *Modern Latin America.* New York: Oxford University Press, 1984. 419p.

590.   Slater, David, ed. *New Social Movements and the State in Latin America.* Amsterdam: CEDLA (Cinnaminson, NJ: Dist. by Foris) 1985. 295p.

591.   Slatta, Richard W., ed. *Bandidos: The Varieties of Latin American Banditry.* Westport, CT: Greenwood, 1987. 218p.

592.   Sloan, John W. *Public Policy in Latin America: A Comparative Survey.* Pittsburgh, PA: University of Pittsburgh Press, 1984. 276p.

593.   Stockholm Institute of Latin American Studies. *The Debt Crisis in Latin America.* Stockholm, Sweden, 1986. 199p.

594.   Super, John C., and Thomas C. Wright, eds. *Food, Politics, and Society in Latin America.* Lincoln: University of Nebraska Press, 1985. 261p.

595.   Szekely, Francisco, ed. *Energy Alternatives in Latin America.* Dublin:

Tycooly, 1983. 168p.

596. Thorp, Rosemary. ed. *Latin America in the 1930s: The Role of the Periphery in World Crisis.* New York: St. Martin's, 1984. 344p.

597. Todorov, Tzvetan. *The Conquest of America.* Translated by Richard Howard. New York: Harper & Row, 1984. 274p.

598. Triska, Jan F. *Dominant Powers and Subordinate States: The United States in Latin America and the Soviet Union in Eastern Europe.* Durham, NC: Duke University Press, 1986. 504p.

599. Tulchin, Joseph S. *The United States and Latin America in the 1980s.* Montevideo: Centro de Informaciones y Estudios de Uruguay, 1985. 23p.

600. Tussie, Diana, ed. *Latin America in the World Economy: New Perspectives.* New York: St. Martin's, 1983. 238p.

601. United Nations. *Economic Survey of Latin America and the Caribbean 1982.* Santiago, Chile, 1984. 2 vols.

602. Vaky, Viron P., ed. *Governance in the Western Hemisphere.* New York: Praeger, 1983. 532p.

603. Varas, Augusto. *Militarization and the International Arms Race in Latin America.* Boulder, CO: Westview, 1985. 160p.

604. Varas, Augusto, ed. *Soviet-Latin American Relations in the 1980's.* Boulder, CO: Westview, 1987. 290p.

605. Viñas, David. *Anarquistas en América Latina.* Mexico City: Katun, 1983. 203p.

606. Wasserstrom, Robert, ed. *Grassroots Development in Latin America and the Caribbean: Oral Histories of Social Change.* New York: Praeger, 1985. 198p.

607. Watkins, Alfred J., ed. *Till Debt Do Us Part: Who Wins, Who Loses, and Who Pays for the International Debt Crisis.* Washington, DC: Roosevelt Center for American Policy Studies, 1986. 87p.

608. Weinberg, Gregorio. *Modelos educativos en la historia de América Latina.* Buenos Aires: Kapelusz 1984. 260p.

609. Welch, Claude E., Jr. *No Farewell to Arms? Military Disengagement from Politics in Africa and Latin America.* Boulder, CO: Westview, 1987. 224p.

610. Wesson, Robert G., ed. *The Latin American Military Institution.* New York: Praeger, 1986. 234p.

611. Wesson, Robert G., ed. *Politics, Policies, and Economic Development in Latin America.* Stanford, CA: Hoover Institution, 1984. 262p.

612. Wiarda, Howard J. *Latin America at the Crossroads: Debt, Development, and the Future.* Boulder, CO: Westview; Washington, DC: American

Enterprise Institute for Public Policy Research, 1987. 114p.

613.   Wiarda, Howard J. *In Search of Policy: The United States and Latin America.* Washington, DC: American Enterprise Institute, 1984. 147p.

614.   Wiarda, Howard J., ed. *The Iberian-Latin American Connection: Implications for U.S. Foreign Policy.* Boulder, CO: Westview; Washington, DC: American Enterprise Institute, 1986. 482p.

615.   Wiarda, Howard J., and Harvey F. Kline, eds. *Latin American Politics and Development.* 2d ed. Boulder, CO: Westview, 1985. 672p.

616.   Wionczek, Miguel S., ed. in collaboration with Luciano Tomassini. *Politics and Economics of External Debt Crisis: The Latin American Experience.* Boulder, CO: Westview, 1985. 482p.

617.   Wirth, John D., ed. *Latin American Oil Companies and the Politics of Energy.* Lincoln: University of Nebraska Press, 1985. 282p.

618.   Wood, Bryce. *The Dismantling of the Good Neighbor Policy.* Austin: University of Texas Press, 1986. 290p.

619.   Wood, Robert D. *"Teach Them Good Customs": Colonial Indian Education and Acculturation in the Andes.* Culver City, CA: Labyrinthos, 1986. 134p.

620.   Wynia, Gary W. *The Politics of Latin American Development.* 2d ed. New York: Cambridge University Press, 1984. 318p.

Articles and Chapters

621.   Abente, Diego. "The War of the Triple Alliance: Three Explanatory Models," *Latin American Research Review.* 22:2 (1987), 47-69.

622.   Aguiar, Neuma. "Research Guidelines: How to Study Women's Work in Latin America." In *Women and Change in Latin America,* edited by June Nash and Helen Safa. South Hadley, MA: Bergin & Garvey, 1986. pp. 22-33.

623.   Aguila, Juan M. del. "Soviet Activities and U.S. Interests in Latin America," *World Affairs* 149:2 (Fall 1986), 93-100.

624.   Alfonsín, Raúl. "How Can the Inter-American Community Consolidate Democracy in the Americas," *Journal of Third World Studies* 4:1 (Spring 1987), 139-147.

625.   Aliber, Robert Z. "The Debt Cycle in Latin America," *Journal of Inter-American Studies and World Affairs* 27:4 (Winter 1985-86), 117-124.

626.   Altimir, Oscar. "Poverty, Income Distribution and Child Welfare in Latin America: A Comparison of Pre- and Post-Recession Data," *World Development* 12:3 (March 1984), 261-282.

627.   Alzamora T, Carlos, and Enrique V. Iglesias. "Bases for a Latin American Response to the International Economic Crisis," *CEPAL*

Review 20 (August 1983), 17-46.

628.   Anderson, Thomas D. "Progress in the Democratic Revolution in Latin America: Country Assessments, 1987," *Journal of Inter-American Studies World Affairs* 29:1 (Spring 1987), 57-72.

629.   Andrews, George Reid. "Spanish American Independence: A Structural Analysis," *Latin American Perspectives* 12:1 (Winter 1985), 105-132.

630.   Andrieu, P.E. "El desarrollo del Tercer Mundo y de América Latina desde la posguerra: esperanzas, resultados y perspectivas," *International Review of Administrative Sciences* 50:1 (1984), 25-46.

631.   Angotti, Thomas. "Urbanization in Latin America: Toward a Theoretical Synthesis," *Latin American Perspectives* 14:2 (Spring 1987), 134-156.

632.   Archetti, Eduardo. "Rural Families and Demographic Behaviour: Some Latin American Analogies," *Comparative Studies in Society and History* 26:2 (April 1984), 251-279.

633.   Arida, Persio. "Macroeconomic Issues for Latin America," *Journal of Development Economics* 22:1 (June 1986), 171-208.

634.   Assael, Héctor. "El pensamiento de la CEPAL; un intento de evaluar algunas críticas a sus ideas principales," *El Trimestre Económico* 51:203 (July-September 1984), 545-558.

635.   Astori, Danilo. "La agricultura campesina en América Latina: sus relaciones con el crecimento urbano y la disponibilidad alimentaria," *Estudios Rurales Latinoamericanos* 6:2-3 (May-December 1983), 109-140.

636.   Bacal Roij, Azril. "Procesos de desarrollo rural en areas indígenas de América Latina: perspectivas, experiencias, reflexiones y sugerencias," *América Indígena* 44 (December 1984), 99-120.

637.   Bacha, Edmar L., and Richard E. Feinberg. "The World Bank and Structural Adjustment in Latin America," *World Development* 14:3 (March 1986), 333-346.

638.   Baer, Werner, and Melissa Birch. "The International Economic Relations of a Small Country," *Economic Development and Cultural Change* 35:3 (April 1987), 601-627.

639.   Bailey, Jessica M., and James H. Sood. "Banana Pricing Strategies for Exporting Countries," *Inter-American Economic Affairs* 39:2 (Autumn 1985), 45-62.

640.   Bailey, John J. "Politics and Agricultural Trade Policies in the Western Hemisphere: A Survey of Trends and Implications in the 1980s." In *Food, the State and International Political Economy,* edited by F. LaMond Tullis and W. Ladd Hollist. Lincoln: University of Nebraska Press, 1986. pp. 180-214.

641.   Balmori, Diana. "Family and Politics: Three Generations (1790-1890)," *Journal of Family History* 10:3 (Fall 1985), 247-257.

642.   Barabas, Alicia M. "Movimientos étnicos religiosos y seculares en América Latina: una aproximación a la construcción de la utopía india," *América Indígena* 46:3 (July-September 1986), 495-529.

643.   Bauer, Arnold J. "The Church in the Economy of Spanish America: *Censos* and *Depósitos* in the Eighteenth and Nineteenth Centuries," *Hispanic American Historical Review* 63:4 (November 1983), 707-733.

644.   Becker, David G. "Development, Democracy and Dependency in Latin America: A Post-Imperialist View," *Third World Quarterly* 6:2 (April 1984), 411-431.

645.   Behrman, Jere R. "Schooling in Latin America: What Are the Patterns and What Is the Impact? *Journal of Inter-American Studies and World Affairs* 27:4 (Winter 1985-86), 21-35.

646.   Berdichewsky, Bernardo. "Del indigenismo a la indianidad y el surgimiento de una ideología indígena en Andinoamérica," *América Indígena* 46:4 (October-December 1986), 643-658.

647.   Berry, Albert. "Predicting Income Distribution in Latin America during the 1980s." In *Latin American Prospects for the 1980s,* edited by Archibald R.M. Ritter and David H. Pollock. New York: Praeger, 1983. pp. 57-84.

648.   Berryman, Phillip. "Basic Christian Communities and the Future of Latin America," *Monthly Review* 36:3 (July-August 1984), 27-40.

649.   Bianchi, Andrés, Robert Devlin, and Joseph Ramos. "El proceso de ajuste en la América Latina, 1981-1986," *El Trimestre Económico* 54:216 (October-December 1987), 855-911.

650.   Biggs, Gonzalo. "Legal Aspects of the Latin American Public Debt: Relations with the Commercial Banks," *CEPAL Review* 25 (April 1985), 163-187.

651.   Bitar, Sergio. "Crisis financiera e industrialización de América Latina," *Desarrollo Económico* 25:98 (July-September 1985), 217-243.

652.   Bitar, Sergio. "La inversión norteamericana en el Grupo Andino," *El Trimestre Económico* 52:206 (April-June 1985), 313-326.

653.   Bitar, Sergio. "United States-Latin American Relations: Shifts in Economic Power and Implications for the Future," *Journal of Inter-American Studies and World Affairs* 26:1 (February 1984), 3-31.

654.   Blasier, Cole. "The United States and Democracy in Latin America." In *Authoritarians and Democrats: Regime Transition in Latin America,* edited by James M. Malloy and Mitchell A. Seligson. Pittsburgh, PA: University of Pittsburgh Press, 1987. pp. 219-233.

655.   Blasier, Cole, and Aldo C. Vacs. "América Latina frente a la Unión Soviética," *Foro Internacional* 24:2 (October-December 1983), 199-211.

656.   Bogdanowicz-Bindert, Christine A. "The Debt Crisis: The Baker Plan Revisited," *Journal of Inter-American Studies and World Affairs* 28:3

(Fall 1986), 33-45.

657.   Borsotti, Carlos A. "Development and Education in Rural Areas," *CEPAL Review* 21 (December 1983), 113-132.

658.   Brock, Philip L. "Financial Controls and Economic Liberalization in Latin America," *Journal of Inter-American Studies and World Affairs* 27:4 (Winter 1985-86), 125-139.

659.   Bronner, Fred. "Urban Society in Colonial Spanish America: Research Trends," *Latin American Research Review* 21:1 (1986), 7-72.

660.   Bryan, Lynne B. "Toward an Understanding of Latin American Problems: Communicating Across Cultural Barriers," *Journal of Third World Studies* 2:2 (Fall 1985), 34-41.

661.   Bunster-Burotto, Ximena. "Surviving Beyond Fear: Women and Torture in Latin America." In *Women and Change in Latin America,* edited by June Nash and Helen Safa. South Hadley, MA: Bergin & Garvey, 1986. pp. 297-325.

662.   Burstin, Luis. "A Few Home Truths about Latin America," *Commentary* 79:2 (February 1985), 46-53.

663.   Bushnell, David. "South America" *Hispanic American Historical Review* 65:4 (November 1985), 767-787.

664.   Cáceres. Luis René. "Ahorro, inversión, deuda externa y catástrofe," *El Trimestre Económico* 52:207 (July-September 1985), 683-704.

665.   Calderón G., Fernando, and Mario R. Dos Santos. "Lo político y lo social: bifurcación o síntesis en la crisis," *Revista Paraguaya de Sociología* 23:67 (September-December 1986), 163-174.

666.   Calvert, Peter. "Demilitarisation in Latin America," *Third World Quarterly* 7:1 (January 1985), 31-43.

667.   Cammack, Paul. "Democratisation: A Review of the Issues," *Bulletin of Latin American Research* 4:2 (1985), 39-46.

668.   Cammack, Paul "Resurgent Democracy: Threat and Promise," *New Left Review* 157 (May-June 1986), 121-128.

669.   Canak, William L. "The Peripheral State Debate: State Capitalist and Bureaucratic-Authoritarian Regimes in Latin America," *Latin American Research Review* 19:1 (1984), 3-36.

670.   Cardoso, Fernando Henrique. "Democracy in Latin America," *Politics and Society* 15:1 (1986-87), 23-41.

671.   Casas González, Antonio. "El potencial de las fuentes convencionales en el abastecimiento energético de la América Latina," *El Trimestre Económico* 50:200 (October-December 1983), 1995-2016.

672.   César, José Vicente. "Situação legal do indio durante o periodo colonial, 1500-1822," *América Indígena* 45:2 (April-June 1985), 391-425.

673.   Chaffee, Wilber A. "The Political Economy of Revolution and Democracy: Toward a Theory of Latin American Politics," *American Journal of Economics and Sociology* 43:4 (October 1984), 385-398.

674.   Chalmers, Douglas A., and Craig H. Robinson. "Why Power Contenders Choose Liberalization: Perspectives from South America." In *Armies and Politics in Latin America*, edited by Abraham H. Lowenthal and Samuel Fitch. Rev. ed. New York: Holmes & Meier, 1986. pp. 389-414.

675.   CLALI. "Sobre la cuestión étnico-nacional en América Latina," *Boletín de Antropología Americana* 7 (July 1983), 41-47.

676.   Clawson, David L. "Religious Allegiance and Economic Development in Rural Latin America," *Journal of Inter-American Studies and World Affairs* 26:4 (November 1984), 499-524.

677.   Cline, William R. "Debt, Macro Policy, and State Intervention: The Next Phase for Latin America," *Journal of Inter-American Studies and World Affairs* 27:4 (Winter 1985-86), 155-172.

678.   Cohen, Alvin, and Chris Duelfer. "Quantifiable Elements in Dependency Theory: Sources of Savings and Rates of Growth," *Inter-American Economic Affairs* 38:4 (Spring 1985), 41-58.

679.   Cohen, Youssef. "The Impact of Bureaucratic-Authoritarian Rule on Economic Growth," *Comparative Political Studies* 18:1 (April 1985), 123-136.

680.   Collins, Jane L. "Smallholder Settlement of Tropical South America: The Social Causes of Ecological Destruction," *Human Organization* 45:1 (Spring 1986), 1-10.

681.   Cooney, Jerry W. "Neutral Vessels and Platine Slavers: Building a Viceregal Merchant Marine," *Journal of Latin American Studies* 18:1 (May 1986), 25-39.

682.   Corvalán, Graziella. "El bilingüismo en América Latina," *Revista Paraguaya de Sociología* 21:59 (January-April 1984), 151-198.

683.   Couriel, Alberto. "Poverty and Underemployment in Latin America," *CEPAL Review* 24 (December 1984), 39-62.

684.   Craig, Richard B. "Illicit Drug Traffic: Implications for South American Source Countries," *Journal of Inter-American Studies and World Affairs* 29:2 (Summer 1987) 1-34.

685.   Cullen, Andrew. "Structural Economic Domination and World Trade with Reference to Latin America: A Marxist Approach," *Social and Economic Studies* 32:3 (September 1983), 35-82.

686.   Cunningham, S.M. "Multinationals and Restructuring in Latin America." In *Multinational Companies and the Third World*, edited by C. J. Dixon, David Drakakis-Smith and H.D. Watts. London: Croom Helm, 1986. pp. 39-65.

687.   Dallas, Roland. "Democracy and Debt in Latin America," *World Today*

40:4 (April 1984), 160-165.

688. Dallas, Roland. "Will Latin American Democracy Last?" *World Today* 43:4 (April 1987), 70-72.

689. Davis, Charles L., and Kenneth M. Coleman. "Labor and the State: Union Incorporation and Working-Class Politicization in Latin America," *Comparative Political Studies* 18:4 (January 1986), 395-417.

690. Davis, Harold Eugene. "Simón Bolívar: Political Idealist or Realist?" *Inter-American Review of Bibliography* 33:2 (1983), 161-170.

691. Davis, Harold Eugene. "Tradition and Traditionalists in Latin America," *Inter-American Review of Bibliography* 36:3 (1986), 298-314.

692. Deere, Carmen Diana. "Rural Women and State Policy: The Latin American Agrarian Reform Experience," *World Development* 13:9 (September 1985), 1037-1053.

693. Demetrius, F. Joseph, Edward J. Tregurtha, and Scott B. MacDonald. "A Brave New World: Debt, Default and Democracy in Latin America," *Journal of Inter-American Studies and World Affairs* 28:2 (Summer 1986), 17-38.

694. Dent, David W. "Past and Present Trends in Research on Latin American Politics, 1950-1980," *Latin American Research Review* 21:1 (1986), 139-151.

695. Devlin, Robert T. "Banca privada, deuda y capacidad negociadora de la periferia: teoría y práctica," *El Trimestre Económico* 51:203 (July-September 1984), 559-589.

696. Devlin, Robert T. "The Burden of Debt and the Crisis: Is It Time for a Unilateral Solution?" *CEPAL Review* 22 (April 1984), 107-120.

697. Devlin, Robert T. "External Debt and Crisis: The Decline of the Orthodox Procedures," *CEPAL Review* 27 (December 1985), 35-52.

698. Devlin, Robert T. "Renegotiation of Latin America's Debt: An Analysis of the Monopoly Power of Private Banks," *CEPAL Review* 20 (August 1983), 101-112.

699. DeWitt, R. Peter. "Policy Directions in International Lending, 1961-1984: The Case of the Inter-American Development Bank," *Journal of Developing Areas* 21:2 (April 1987), 277-284.

700. Dewitt, R. Peter. "The Management of International Debt in Latin America," *Journal of Social, Political and Economic Studies* 12:2 (Summer 1987), 185-201.

701. Dietz, Henry A., and Karl Schmitt. "Militarization in Latin America: For What? And Why?" *Inter-American Economic Affairs* 38:1 (Summer 1984), 44-64.

702. Dietz, James L. "Debt and Development: The Future of Latin America," *Journal of Economic Issues* 20:4 (December 1986), 1029-1051.

703.   Dietz, James L. "Destabilization and Intervention in Latin America and the Caribbean," *Latin American Perspectives* 11:3 (Summer 1984), 3-14.

704.   Dietz, James L. "The Latin American Economies and Debt: Institutional and Structural Response to Crisis," *Journal of Economic Issues* 21:2 (June 1987), 827-836.

705.   Di Filippo, Armando. "Social Use of the Surplus, Accumulation, Distribution and Employment," *CEPAL Review* 24 (December 1984), 117-134.

706.   Di Tella, Torcuato S. "'Partidos del pueblo' en América Latina: revisión teórica y reseña de tendencias históricas," *Desarrollo Económico* 22:88 (January-March 1983), 451-483.

707.   Di Tella, Torcuato S. "The Political and Social Outlook for Latin America," *CEPAL Review* 26 (August 1985), 89-99.

708.   Dixon, William J. "Progress in the Provision of Basic Human Needs: Latin America, 1960-1980," *Journal of Developing Areas* 21:2 (January 1987), 129-139.

709.   Dix, Robert H. "Incumbency and Electoral Turnover in Latin America," *Journal of Inter-American Studies and World Affairs* 26:4 (November 1984), 435-448.

710.   Dix, Robert H. "Populism: Authoritarian and Democratic," *Latin American Research Review* 20:2 (1985), 29-52.

711.   Domínguez, Jorge I. "Los conflictos internacionales en América Latina y la amenaza de guerra," *Foro Internacional* 25:1 (July-September 1984), 1-13.

712.   Dornbusch, Rudiger. "El problema mundial de la deuda," *El Trimestre Económico* 54:216 (October-December 1987), 805-825.

713.   Dourojeanni, A., and M. Molina. "The Andean Peasant, Water and the Role of the State," *CEPAL Review* 19 (April 1983), 145-166.

714.   Draper, Elaine. "Women's Work and Development in Latin America," *Studies in Comparative International Development* 20:1 (Spring 1985), 3-30.

715.   Droucopoulos, Vassilis. "The Changing Remittance Behaviour of U.S. Manufacturing Firms in Latin America," *World Development* 12:1 (January 1984), 97-100.

716.   Dunbar Ortiz, Roxanne. "The Indigenous Question." In *Towards an Alternative for Central America and the Caribbean,* edited by George Irvin and Xabier Gorostiaga. London; Boston: Allen & Unwin, 1985. pp. 231-250.

717.   Duncan, W. Raymond. "Soviet Interests in Latin America: New Opportunities and Old Constraints," *Journal of Inter-American Studies and World Affairs* 26:2 (May 1984), 163-198.

718.   Dunn, Marvin G. "Liberation Theology and Class Analysis: A Reassessment of Religion and Class," *Latin American Perspectives* 13:3 (Summer 1986), 59-70.

719.   Durán, Esperanza. "Latin America's External Debt: The Limits of Regional Cooperation," *World Today* 42:5 (May 1986), 84-88.

720.   ECLA Economic Projections Centre. "Latin American Development Problems and the World Economic Crisis," *CEPAL Review* 19 (April 1983), 51-83.

721.   Edwards, Sebastian, and Simón Teitel "Introduction to Growth, Reform, and Adjustment: Latin America's Trade and Macroeconomic Policies in the 1970s and 1980s," *Economic Development and Cultural Change* 34:3 (April 1986), 423-431.

722.   Eltis, David. "The Nineteenth-Century Trans-Atlantic Slave Trade: An Annual Time Series of Imports into the Americas Broken Down by Region," *Hispanic American Historical Review* 67:1 (February 1987), 109-138.

723.   Engstrand, Iris H.W. "The Enlightenment in Spain: Influences upon New World Policy," *The Americas* 41:4 (April 1985), 436-444.

724.   Epstein, Edward C. "Legitimacy, Institutionalization, and Opposition in Exclusionary Bureaucratic-Authoritarian Regimes: The Situation of the 1980s," *Comparative Politics* 17:1 (October 1984), 37-54.

725.   Esser, Klaus. "Modification of the Industrialization Model in Latin America," *CEPAL Review* 26 (August 1985), 101-113.

726.   Evanson, Robert K. "Soviet Economic and Military Trade in Latin America," *World Affairs* 149:2 (Fall 1986), 75-85.

727.   Evanson, Robert K. "Soviet Political Uses of Trade with Latin America," *Journal of Inter-American Studies and World Affairs* 27:2 (Summer 1985), 99-126.

728.   Executive Secretariat, ECLAC. "Crisis and Development in Latin America and the Caribbean," *CEPAL Review* 26 (August 1985), 9-56.

729.   Fagen, Patricia Weiss. "Latin American Refugees: Problems of Mass Migration and Mass Asylum." In *From Gunboats to Diplomacy: New U.S. Policies for Latin America,* edited by Richard Newfarmer. Baltimore, MD: Johns Hopkins University Press, 1984. pp. 228-243.

730.   Fairchild, Loretta G., and Kim Sosin. "Evaluating Differences in Technological Activity between Transnational and Domestic Firms in Latin America," *Journal of Development Studies* 22:4 (July 1986), 697-708.

731.   Faletto, Enzo. "Youth as a Social Movement in Latin America," *CEPAL Review* 29 (August 1986), 183-189.

732.   Farer, Tom J. "Human Rights and Human Welfare in Latin America," *Daedalus* 112:4 (Fall 1983), 139-170.

733.   Felix, David. "Alternative Outcomes of the Latin American Debt Crisis: Lessons from the Past," *Latin American Research Review* 22:2 (1987), 3-46.

734.   Fernández Baeza, Mario. "La intervención militar en la política en América Latina," *Revista de Estudios Políticos* 48 (November-December 1985), 197-220.

735.   Ffrench-Davis, Ricardo. "Una estrategia de apertura externa selectiva," *El Trimestre Económico* 51:203 (July-September 1984), 485-526.

736.   Ffrench-Davis, Ricardo, "Foreign Debt and Development Alternatives in Latin America," *International Journal of Political Economy* 17:1 (Spring 1987), 64-87.

737.   Ffrench-Davis, Ricardo. "Latin American Debt: Debtor-Creditor Relations," *Third World Quarterly* 9:4 (October 1987), 1167-1183.

738.   Ffrench-Davis, Ricardo. "Notas sobre el desarrollo económico y la deuda externa en América Latina, " *Desarrollo Económico* 25:100 (January-March 1986), 571-585.

739.   Filgueira, Carlos H. "To Educate or Not to Educate: Is That Question?" *CEPAL Review* 21 (December 1983), 57-80.

740.   Fisher, John. "The Imperial Response to 'Free Trade': Spanish Imports from Spanish America, 1778-1796," *Journal of Latin American Studies* 17:1 (May 1985), 35-78.

741.   Fisher, Julie. "Development from Below: Neighborhood Improvement Associations in the Latin American Squatter Settlements," *Studies in Comparative International Development* 19:1 (Spring 1984), 61-85.

742.   Fitzgerald, E.V.K. "Foreign Finance and Capital Accumulation in Latin America: A Critical Approach." In *Latin America, Economic Imperialism and the State,* edited by Christopher Abel and Colin M. Lewis. London; Dover, NH: Athlone, 1985. pp. 451-471.

743.   Flora, Cornelia Butler, and Blas Santos. "Women in Farming Systems in Latin America." In *Women and Change in Latin America,* edited by June Nash and Helen Safa. South Hadley, MA: Bergin & Garvey, 1986. pp. 208-228.

744.   Foroohar, Manzar. "Liberation Theology: The Response of Latin American Catholics to Socioeconomic Problems," *Latin American Perspectives* 13:3 (Summer 1986), 37-57.

745.   Fortín, Carlos. "Latin America in the 1980s: Issues, Trends and Prospects," *Boletín de Estudios Latinoamericanos y del Caribe* 34 (June 1983), 3-15.

746.   Foxley, Alejandro. "The Foreign Debt Problem: The View from Latin America," *International Journal of Political Economy* 17:1 (Spring 1987), 88-116.

747.   Frenkel, Roberto. "Salarios e inflación en América Latina: resultados de investigaciones recientes en la Argentina, Brasil, Colombia, Costa

Rica y Chile," *Desarrollo Económico* 25:100 (January-March 1986), 587-622.

748. Furtado, Celso. "Transnationalization and Monetarism," *International Journal of Political Economy* 17:1 (Spring 1987), 15-44.

749. Garavaglia, Juan Carlos. "Economic Growth and Regional Differentiations: The River Plate Region at the End of the Eighteenth Century," *Hispanic American Historical Review* 65:1 (February 1985), 51-89.

750. García, Noberto E. "Industria manufacturera y empleo: América Latina, 1950-1980," *El Trimestre Económico* 50:200 (October-December 1983), 2077-2121.

751. García, Noberto E., and Víctor Tokman. "Changes in Employment and the Crisis," *CEPAL Review* 24 (December 1984), 103-115.

752. Gartner, Gonzalo. "La inserción de la América Latina en la economía mundial: una visión del futuro," *El Trimestre Económico* 52:208 (October-December 1985), 1021-1048.

753. Gasiorowski, Mark J. "Dependency and Cliency in Latin America," *Journal of Inter-American Studies and World Affairs* 28:3 (Fall 1986), 47-65.

754. Giusti, Jorge. "Los programas DRI y el proceso de capitalización del agro en América Latina," *Estudios Rurales Latinoamericanos* 7:1 (April 1984), 5-22.

755. Glezakos, Constantine, and Jeffrey B. Nugent. "Price Instability and Inflation: The Latin American Case," *World Development* 12:7 (July 1984), 755-758.

756. Glezakos, Constantine, and Jeffrey B. Nugent. "The Relationship between the Rate of Inflation and Its Unpredictability in High Inflation Latin American Countries," *World Development* 15:2 (February 1987), 291-293.

757. Gligo, Nicolo. "Energy and the Prevailing Model of Agricultural Technology in Latin America," *CEPAL Review* 22 (April 1984), 121-136.

758. Goetze, Dieter. "De Medellín a Puebla: la evolución de las ideas integracionistas del CELAM," *América Indígena* 44:1 (January-March 1984), 157-181.

759. González, Heliodoro. "Bloc Voting at the United Nations or U.S. Foreign Aid? The Kasten Amendment," *Inter-American Economic Affairs* 38:1 (Summer 1984), 78-84.

760. González, Heliodoro. "The Deteriorating Relationship of the U.S. and Latin America at the UN: Will It Doom Economic Planning and Economic Development in Latin America," *Inter-American Economic Affairs* 37:3 (Winter 1983), 77-82.

761. González, Heliodoro. "Latin America at the United Nations: The Gathering Storm," *Inter-American Economic Affairs* 39:2 (Autumn 1985),

11-25.

762.   González, Heliodoro. "The Latin American Debt Crisis: The Bailout of the Banks," *Inter-American Economic Affairs* 39:3 (Winter 1985), 55-70.

763.   Gracia, Jorge J.E., and Iván A. Jaksic. "The Problem of Philosophical Identity in Latin America," *Inter-American Review of Bibliography* 34:1 (1984), 53-71.

764.   Graham-Yooll, Andrew. "The Wild Oats They Sowed: Latin American Exiles in Europe," *Third World Quarterly* 9:1 (January 1987), 246-253.

765.   Greenow, Linda. "Microgeographic Analysis as an Index to Family Structure and Networks," *Journal of Family History* 10:3 (Fall 1985), 272-283.

766.   Ground, Richard Lynn. "Orthodox Adjustment Programmes in Latin America: A Critical Look at the Policies of the International Monetary Fund," *CEPAL Review* (August 1984), 45-82.

767.   Guimarãea, Roberto P. "Co-operativism and Popular Participation: New Considerations Regarding an Old Subject," *CEPAL Review* 28 (April 1986), 187-201.

768.   Gurrieri, Adolfo, and Pedro Sáinz. "Is There a Fair and Democratic Way Out of the Crisis?" *CEPAL Review* 20 (August 1983), 127-148.

769.   Gwynne, R.N. "Multinational Corporations and the Triple Alliance in Latin America." In *Multinational Companies and the Third World,* edited by C.J. Dixon, David Drakakis-Smith and H.D. Watts. London: Croom Helm, 1986. pp. 118-136.

770.   Hahner, June E. "Researching the History of Latin American Women:" Past and Future Directions," *Inter-American Review of Bibliography* 33:4 (1983), 545-552.

771.   Hardoy, Jorge E. "Urban Cartography in Latin America during the Colonial Period," *Latin American Research Review* 18:3 (1983), 127-135.

772.   Hardoy, Jorge E., and Marta Savigliano. "La ciudad y los niños," *Revista Paraguaya de Sociología* 21:60 (May-August 1984), 159-181.

773.   Haubert, Maxine. "Adult Education and Grass-Roots Organizations in Latin America: The Contribution of the International Co-operative University," *International Labour Review* 125:2 (March-April 1986), 177-192.

774.   Hayes, Margaret Daly. "United States Policy toward Latin America: A Prospectus." In *Conflict in Central America: Aproaches to Peace and Security,* edited by Jack Child. London: C. Hurst, 1985. pp. 21-41.

775.   Heath, John Richard. "Reproducción y diferenciación de la economía campesina: esbozo de un nuevo enfoque y aplicación a tres casos latinoamericanos," *Estudios Rurales Latinoamericanos* 10:1 (January-

April 1987), 5-36.

776. Heller, Peter S., and Adrienne Cheasty. "Sectoral Adjustment in Government Expenditure in the 1970s: The Educational Sector in Latin America," *World Development* 12:10 (October 1984), 1039-1049.

777. Hermet, Guy. "Política francesa en América Latina," *Foro Internacional* 26:3 (January-March 1986), 385-398.

778. Herrera, Felipe. "Twenty-Five Years of the Inter-American Development Bank," *CEPAL Review* 27 (December 1985), 143-151.

779. Herrera, Felipe. "Vigencia de la integración latinoamericana," *Foro Internacional* 25:1 (July-September 1984), 77-88.

780. Hirabayashi, Lane Ryo. "The Migrant Village Association in Latin America: A Comparative Analysis," *Latin American Research Review* 21:3 (1986), 7-29.

781. Hirschman, Albert O. "La economía política del desarrollo latinoamericano: siete ejercicios en retrospectiva," *El Trimestre Económico* 54:216 (October-December 1987), 769-804.

782. Hirschman, Albert O. "The Political Economy of Latin American Development: Seven Exercises in Retrospection," *Latin American Research Review* 22:3 (1987), 7-36.

783. Huizer, Gerrit. "The Politics of Rural Development in Latin America: Constraints on Cooperatives and Popular Participation," *Boletín de Estudios Latinoamericanos y del Caribe* 35 (December 1983), 3-20.

784. Ibarra, David. "Crisis, Adjustment and Economic Policy in Latin America," *CEPAL Review* 26 (August 1985), 147-154.

785. Iglesias, Enrique V. "Latin America: Crisis and Development Options," *CEPAL Review* 23 (August 1984), 7-28.

786. Iglesias, Enrique V. "The Latin American Economy during 1984: A Preliminary Overview," *CEPAL Review* 25 April 1985), 7-44.

787. Iglesias, Enrique V. "A Preliminary Overview of the Latin American Economy during 1983," *CEPAL Review* 22 (April 1984), 7-38.

788. Iglesias, Enrique V. "Reflections on the Latin American Economy in 1982," *CEPAL Review* 19 (April 1983), 7-49.

789. Isuani, Ernesto. "Universalización de la seguridad social en América Latina: limites estructurales y cambios necesarios," *Desarrollo Económico* 25:97 (April-June 1985), 71-84.

790. Jameson, Kenneth P. "Latin American Structuralism: A Methodological Perspective," *World Development* 14:2 (February 1986), 223-232.

791. Jaramillo, Samuel, and Martha Schteingart. "Procesos sociales y producción de vivienda en América Latina: 1960-1980," *Revista Mexicana de Sociología* 45:1 (January-March 1983), 11-28.

792.   Jenkins, Rhys O. "Latin America and the New International Division of
        Labour: A Critique of Some Recent Views." In *Latin America,
        Economic Imperialism and the State,* edited by Christopher Abel and
        Colin M. Lewis. London; Dover, NH: Athlone, 1985. pp. 415-429.

793.   Johnson, John J. "One Hundred Years of Historical Writing on Modern
        Latin America by United States Historians," *Hispanic American
        Historical Review* 65:4 (November 1985), 745-765.

794.   Joint ECLAC/FAO Agricultural Division. "The Agriculture of Latin
        America: Changes, Trends and Outlines of Strategy," *CEPAL Review*
        27 (December 1985), 117-129.

795.   Joint ECLAC/UNIDO Industrial Development Division. "Thoughts on
        Industrialization, Linkage and Growth," *CEPAL Review* 28 (April
        1986), 49-66.

796.   Jordan, David C. "Soviet Strategy in Latin America," *World Affairs* 149:2
        (Fall 1986), 87-92.

797.   Jorge, Antonio, and Raúl Moncarz. "Aspectos teóricos de la inflación en
        la América Latina y el Caribe," *El Trimestre Económico* 51:204
        (October-December 1984), 871-883.

798.   Kärner, Hartmut. "La cuestión campesina y el subdesarrollo del
        Marxismo en Latinoamérica," *Estudios Rurales Latinoamericanos* 8:1
        (January-April 1985), 5-20.

799.   Katz, Jorge. "Technological Change in the Latin American Metalworking
        Industries: Results of a Programme of Case Studies," *CEPAL Review*
        19 (April 1983), 85-143.

800.   Kaztman, Rubén. "Sectoral Transformations in Employment in Latin
        America," *CEPAL Review* 24 (December 1984), 83-101.

801.   Kearney, Michael. "Religion, Ideology and Revolution in Latin America,"
        Latin American Perspectives 13:3 (Summer 1986), 3-12.

802.   Keen, Benjamin. "Main Currents in United States Writings on Colonial
        Spanish America, 1884-1984," *Hispanic American Historical Review*
        65:4 (November 1985), 657-682.

803.   Kicza, John E. "The Role of the Family in Economic Development in
        Nineteenth-Century Latin America," *Journal of Family History* 10:3
        (Fall 1985), 235-246.

804.   Kirsch, Henry. "University Youth as Social Protagonist in Latin
        America," *CEPAL Review* 29 (August 1986), 191-202.

805.   Klaveren, Alberto van. "Enfoques alternativos para el estudio del
        autoritarismo en América Latina," *Revista de Estudios Políticos* 51
        (May-June 1986), 23-52.

806.   König, Wolfgang. "Relación entre teoría, estrategia y praxis del
        desarrollo económico: la industrialización latinoamericana en el
        contexto internacional," *Foro Internacional* 25:4 (April-June 1985),
        372-381.

807. Kuczynski, Pedro-Pablo. "Latin American Debt: Act Two," *Foreign Affairs* 62:1 (Fall 1983), 17-38.

808. Kuczynski, Pedro-Pablo. "The Outlook for Latin American Debt," *Foreign Affairs* 66:1 (Fall 1987), 129-149.

809. Kuznesof, Elizabeth, and Robert Oppenheimer. "The Family and Society in Nineteenth-Century Latin America," *Journal of Family History* 10:3 (Fall 1985), 215-234.

810. LaFeber, Walter. "The Alliance in Retrospect." In *Bordering on Trouble: Resources and Politics in Latin America,* edited by Andrew Maguire and Janet Walsh Brown. Bethesda, MD: Adler and Adler, 1986. pp. 337-388.

811. Lagos E., Ricardo. "El precio de la ortodoxia," *El Trimestre Económico* 52:205 (January-March 1985), 37-52.

812. Lahera, Eugenio. "The Transnational Corporations and Latin America's International Trade," *CEPAL Review* 25 (April 1985), 45-65.

813. Lahera, Eugenio, and Hugo Nochteff. "Microelectronics and Latin American Development," *CEPAL Review* 19 (April 1983), 167-181.

814. Lazarte, Rolando. "Los migrantes en los mercados de trabajo metropolitano: líneas de abordaje del problema en América Latina," *Revista Paraguaya de Sociología* 23:67 (September-December 1986), 133-141.

815. Ledergerber-de-Kohli, Paulina. "Planteamientos para promover el desarrollo de la arqueología de rescate en América Latina," *Boletín de Antropología Americana* 10 (December 1984), 109-117.

816. Lee, Rensselaer W., III. "The Latin American Drug Connection," *Foreign Policy* 61 (Winter 1985-86), 142-159.

817. Leff, Nathaniel H., and Kazuo Sato. "Entrada de capital extranjero, ahorro interno e inversión en la América Latina: una historia negativa y precautoria," *El Trimestre Económico* 53:211 (July-September 1986), 561-584.

818. Le Guay, François. "The International Crisis and Latin American Development: Objectives and Instruments," *CEPAL Review* 26 (August 1985), 127-137.

819. LeoGrande, William M. "The United States and Latin America," *Current History* 85:507 (January 1986), 1-4.

820. Little, Walter. "International Conflict in Latin America," *International Affairs* 63:4 (Autumn 1987), 589-601.

821. Lizano, Eduardo. "Relaciones económicas externas de América Latina," *Foro Internacional* 24:2 (October-December 1983), 233-247.

822. Lomnitz, Larisa. "La antropología y el desarrollo latinoamericano," *América Indígena* 43:2 (April-June 1983), 247-260.

823.   Looney, Robert E., and Peter C. Frederiksen. "The Impact of Latin
        American Arms Production on Economic Performance," *Journal of
        Social, Political and Economic Studies* 12:3 (Fall 1987), 309-320.

824.   Lowenthal, Abraham F. "Change the Agenda," *Foreign Policy* 52 (Fall
        1983), 64-77.

825.   Lowenthal, Abraham F. "Rethinking U.S. Interests in the Western
        Hemisphere," *Journal of Inter-American Studies and World Affairs*
        29:1 (Spring 1987), 1-23.

826.   Lowenthal, Abraham F. "Ronald Reagan y Latinoamérica: enfrentamiento
        con la hegemonía declinante," *Foro Internacional* 24:1 (July-
        September 1983), 21-49.

827.   Lowenthal, Abraham F. "Threat and Opportunity in the Americas,"
        Foreign Affairs 64:3 (1985), 539-561.

828.   Lowy, Michael, and Eder Sader. "The Militarization of the State in
        Latin America," *Latin American Persepctives* 12:4 (Fall 1985), 7-40.

829.   Luard, Evan. "Superpowers and Regional Conflicts," *Foreign Affairs*
        64:5 (Summer 1986), 1006-1025.

830.   McCoy, Terry L. "Latin America at a Critical Juncture," *Journal of
        Third World Studies* 2:2 (Fall 1985), 31-33.

831.   McCoy, Terry L. "The Role of U.S. Business in the Third World: Lessons
        from Latin America," *Journal of Third World Studies* 1 (Fall 1984),
        10-19.

832.   McCreery, David J. "Latin Americna Economic Development: An
        Historical Overview," *Journal of Third World Studies* 3:1 (Spring
        1986), 77-89.

833.   MacEwan, Arthur. "The Current Crisis in Latin America and the Inter-
        national Economy," *Monthly Review* 36:9 (February 1985), 1-18.

834.   MacEwan, Arthur. "Latin America: Why Not Default?" *Monthly Review*
        38:4 (September 1986), 1-13.

835.   McFarlane, Anthony. "Civil Disorders and Popular Protests in Late
        Colonial New Granada," *Hispanic American Historical Review* 64:1
        (February 1984), 17-54.

836.   McIntyre, John R. "The Sovereign Debt Problem of Latin America: U.S.
        Policy Dilemmas," *Journal of Third World Studies* 3:1 (Spring 1986),
        90-94.

837.   Majal-León, Eusebio. "Spain and Latin America: The Quest for
        Partnership." In *The Iberian-Latin American Connection: Implica-
        tions for U.S. Foreign Policy,* edited by Howard J. Wiarda. Boulder,
        CO: Westview, 1986. pp. 375-407.

838.   McNelis, Paul D. "Indexing, Exchange Rate Policy and Inflationary
        Feedback Effects in Latin America," *World Development* 15:8
        (August 1987), 1107-1117.

839. Maldonado Lince, Guillermo. "Latin America and Integration: Options in the Crisis," *CEPAL Review* 27 (December 1985), 55-68.

840. Maldonado Lince, Guillermo, Eduardo Gana, and Armando Di Filippo. "Latin America: Crisis, Co-operation and Development," *CEPAL Review* 20 (August 1983), 75-100.

841. Mamalakis, Markos J. "Interamerican Economic Relations: The New Development View," *Journal of Inter-American Studies and World Affairs* 27:4 (Winter 1985-86), 1-8.

842. Mamalakis, Markos J. "A North-South Dilemma: The Need and Limits of Conditionalities in the Americas," *Journal of Inter-American Studies and World Affairs* 27:1 (February 1985), 103-121.

843. Mansilla, H.C.F. "Las metas generales de desarrollo en la conciencia colectiva latinoamérica," *Revista de Estudios Políticos* 51 (May-June 1986), 177-190.

844. Marcella, Gabriel. "Defense of the Western Hemisphere: Strategy for the 1990s," *Journal of Inter-American Studies and World Affairs* 27:3 (Fall 1985), 1-25.

845. Márquez, Patricio V., and Daniel J. Joly. "A Historical Overview of the Ministries of Public Health and the Medical Programs of the Social Security System in Latin America." *Journal of Public Health Policy* 7:3 (Autumn 1986), 378-394.

846. Martínez, Javier, and Eduardo Valenzuela. "Working Class Youth and Anomy," *CEPAL Review* 29 (August 1986), 171-181.

847. Martínez Moreno, Carlos. "Thinking about Youth," *CEPAL Review* 29 (August 1986), 153-170.

848. Martz, John D., III, and David J. Myers. "Understanding Latin American Politics: Analytic Models and Intellectual Traditions," *Polity* 16:2 (Winter 1983), 214-241.

849. Massad, Carlos. "The External Debt and the Financial Problems of Latin America," *CEPAL Review* 20 (August 1983), 149-166.

850. Massad, Carlos. "The Real Cost of the External Debt for the Creditor and for the Debtor," *CEPAL Review* 19 (April 1983), 183-195.

851. Maxwell, Philip. "Technical Change and Appropriate Technology: A Review of Some Latin America Case Studies." In *Macro Policies for Appropriate Technology in Developing Countries,* edited by Frances Stewart. Boulder, CO: Westview, 1987. pp. 248-270.

852. Meller, Patrício. "Remuneração e emprego das filiais manufactureiras norte-americanas na América Latina," *Revista Brasileira de Economia* 38:3 (July-September 1984), 253-274.

853. Merquior, J.G. "Power and Identity: Politics and Ideology in Latin America," *Government and Opposition* 19:2 (Spring 1984), 239-249.

854. Merrick, Thomas W., with PRB Staff. "Population Pressures in Latin

America," *Population Bulletin* 41:3 (July 1986), 1-50.

855.   Mesa-Lago, Carmelo. "Social Security and Development in Latin America," *CEPAL Review* 28 (April 1986), 135-150.

856.   Millett, Richard. "The United States and Latin America," *Current History* 83:490 (February 1984), 49-53.

857.   Miller, Francesca. "The International Relations of Women of the Americas, 1890-1928," *The Americas* 43:2 (October 1986), 171-182.

858.   Miller, Simon. "La agricultura capitalista en América Latina: el agricultor moderno y el pequeño propietario," *Boletín de Antropología* 8 (December 1983), 83-88.

859.   Moneta, Carlos J. "Energy Dimensions of Latin American-U.S.-Western European Relations." In *Latin America, Western Europe, and the United States: Reevaluating the Atlantic Triangle,* edited by Wolf Grabendorff and Riordan Roett. New York: Praeger, 1985. pp. 193-221.

860.   Moya, Ruth. "Educación bilingüe. "Para qué?" *Revista Paraguaya de Sociología* 23:67 (September-December 1986), 65-72.

861.   Mujal-León, Eusebio. "Soviet Strategic Perspectives on Latin America in the 1980s," *World Affairs* 149:2 (Fall 1986), 101-106.

862.   Muñoz, Heraldo. "Las relaciones entre Estados Unidos y América Latina bajo el gobierno de Reagan: divergencias y ajustes parciales," *Foro Internacional* 27:4 (April-June 1987), 501-522.

863.   Nash, June. "A Decade of Research of Women in Latin America." In *Women and Change in Latin America,* edited by June Nash and Helen Safa. South Hadley, MA: Bergin & Garvey, 1986. pp. 3-21.

864.   Navarrete, Jorge Eduardo. "Foreign Policy and International Financial Negotiations: The External Debt and the Cartagena Consensus," *CEPAL Review* 27 (December 1985), 7-25.

865.   Newson, Linda A. "Indian Population Patterns in Colonial Spanish America," *Latin American Research Review* 20:3 (1985), 41-74.

866.   Nun, José. "The Middle-Class Military Coup Revisited." In *Armies and Politics in Latin America,* edited by Abraham F. Lowenthal and Samuel Fitch. Rev. ed. New York: Holmes & Meier, 1986. pp. 59-95.

867.   Ocampo, José Antonio. "Una evaluación comparativa de cuatro planes antinflacionarios recientes," *El Trimestre Económico* 54:Special (September 1987), 7-51.

868.   Olivieri, Mabel. "Orígenes y evolución de la presencia militar en América Latina," *Revista de Estudios Políticos* 42 (November-December 1984), 163-188.

869.   Orlandi, Alberto. "Latin American Commodity Exports: The Case of Cotton Fibre," *CEPAL Review* 22 (April 1984), 137-158.

870.   Orlando, Frank and Simón Teitel. "Latin America's External Debt Problem: Debt-Servicing Strategies Compatible with Long-Term Economic Growth," *Economic Development and Cultural Change* 34:3 April 1986), 641-671.

871.   Osiel, Mark J. "Popular Culture in Latin America: A Lively Debate within the Left," *Dissent* (Winter 1984), 109-115.

872.   Ozlak, Oscar. "Public Policies and Political Regimes in Latin America," *International Social Science Journal* 38:2 (1986), 236-219.

873.   Pansters, Wil. "Urban Social Movements and Political Strategy in Latin America," *Boletín de Estudios Latinoamericanos* 41 (December 1986), 13-27.

874.   Parkinson, Fred. "Latin America, Her Newly Industrialising Countries and the New International Economic Order," *Journal of Latin American Studies* 16:1 (May 1984), 127-141.

875.   Pastor, Manuel, Jr. "The Effects of IMF Programs in the Third World: Debate and Evidence from Latin America," *World Development* 15:2 (February 1987), 249-262.

876.   Pastor, Robert A. "El gobierno de Carter y América Latina: principios a prueba," *Foro Internacional* 27:2 (October-December 1986), 197-233.

877.   Pastor, Robert A. "El gobierno de Reagan y América Latina: la búsqueda implacable de seguridad," *Foro Internacional* 27:1 (July-September 1986), 5-44.

878.   Pastor, Robert A. "Nurturing Democracy in the Americas: Seven Proposals," *Journal of Third World Studies* 4:2 (Fall 1987), 108-120.

879.   Pastor, Robert. A. "U.S. Immigration Policy and Latin America: In Search of the 'Special Relationship'," *Latin American Research Review* 19:3 (1984), 35-56.

880.   Pazos, Felipe. "Cincuenta años de pensamiento económico en la América Latina," *El Trimestre Económico* 50:200 (October-December 1983), 1915-1948.

881.   Pazos, Felipe. "Have Import Substitution Policies Either Precipitated or Aggravated the Debt Crisis?" *Journal of Inter-American Studies and World Affairs* 27:4 (Winter 1985-86), 57-73.

882.   Pazos, Felipe. "¿Qué modificaciones a su política económica deben hacer los países de la América Latina?" *El Trimestre Económico* 54:216 (October-December 1987), 827-853.

883.   Pearson, Ruth. "Latin American Women and the New International Division of Labour: A Reassessment," *Bulletin of Latin American Research* 5:2 (1986), 67-79.

884.   Pease G.Y., Franklin. "En busca de una imagen andina propia durante la colonia," *América Indígena* 45:2 (April-June 1985), 309-341.

885.   Pérez Salgado, Ignacio, and Bernardo Kliksberg. "Políticas de gestión

pública: el rol del Estado en la presente situación de América Latina y el Caribe," *International Review of Administrative Sciences* 51:3 (1985), 221-238.

886. Philip, George. "Autoritarismo militar en América del Sur: Brasil, Chile, Uruguay y Argentina," *Foro Internacioal* 25:1 (July-September 1984), 57-76.

887. Philip, George. "Military Rule in South America: The Dilemmas of Authoritarianism." In *The Political Dilemmas of Military Regimes,* edited by Christopher Clapham, Ian Campbell, and George Philip. Totowa, NJ: Rowman & Allanheld, 1985. pp. 128-150.

888. Pike, Fredrick B. "Latin America and the Inversion of United States Stereotypes in the 1920s and 1930s," *The Americas* 42:2 (October 1985), 131-162.

889. Piñeiro, Martín E., and James A. Chapman. "Cambio técnico y diferenciación en las economías campesinas: un análisis de seís estudios de caso en América Latina," *Estudios Rurales Latinoamericanos* 7:1 (April 1984), 27-57.

890. Pinto, Aníbal. "Metropolization and Tertiarization: Structural Distortions in Latin American Development," *CEPAL Review* 24 (December 1984), 17-38.

891. Pollin, Robert, and Eduardo Zepeda. "Latin American Debt: The Choices Ahead," *Monthly Review* 38:9 (February 1987), 1-16.

892. Portales Cifuentes, Diego. "Políticas nacionales de comunicación: la lucha por la utopía en el mercado," *Revista Paraguaya de Sociología* 23:66 (May-August 1986), 113-119.

893. Portes, Alejandro. "Latin American Class Structures: Their Composition and Change during the Last Decades," *Latin American Research Review* 20:3 (1985), 7-39.

894. Pourgerami, Abbas, and Keith E. Maskus. "The Effects of Inflation on the Predictability of Price Changes in Latin America: Some Estimates and Policy Implications," *World Development* 15:2 (February 1987), 287-290.

895. Prebisch, Raúl. "The Latin American Periphery in the Global Crisis of Capitalism," *CEPAL Review* 26 (August 1985), 63-88.

896. Puhle, Hans-Jürgen. "Nacionalismo en América Latina," *Revista Paraguaya de Sociología* 23:67 (September-December 1986), 119-131.

897. Purcell, Susan Kaufman. "Latin American Debt and U.S. Economic Policy," *Orbis* 27:3 (Fall 1983), 591-602.

898. Rama, Germán W. "Education in Latin America: Exclusion or Participation," *CEPAL Review* 21 (December 1983), 13-38.

899. Rama, Germán W. "Latin American Youth between Development and Crisis," *CEPAL Review* 29 (August 1986), 17-39.

900. Rama, Germán W., and Enzo Faletto. "Dependent Societies and Crisis in Latin America: The Challenges of Social and Political Transformation," *CEPAL Review* 25 (April 1985), 129-147.

901. Ramet, Pedro, and Fernando López-Alves. "Moscow and the Revolutionary Left in Latin America," *Orbis* 28:2 (Summer 1984), 341-363.

902. Ramos, Joseph. "Stabilization and Adjustment Policies in the Southern Cone, 1974-1983," *CEPAL Review* 25 (April 1985), 85-109.

903. Ramos, Joseph. "Urbanization and the Labour Market," *CEPAL Review* 24 (December 1984), 63-81.

904. Raw, Silvia, ed. "The Debt Crisis in Latin America," *International Journal of Political Economy* 17:1 (Spring 1987), entire issue.

905. Redclift, M.R. "'Urban Bias' and Rural Poverty: A Latin American Perspective," *Journal of Development Studies* 20:3 (April 1984), 123-138.

906. Reif, Linda L. "Women in Latin America Guerrilla Movements: A Comparative Perspective," *Comparative Politics* 18:2 (January 1986), 147-169.

907. Reilly, Charles A. "Latin America's Religious Populists." In *Religion and Political Conflict in Latin America,* edited by Daniel H. Levine. Chapel Hill: University of North Carolina Press, 1986. pp. 42-57.

908. Reisner, Marc, and Ronald H. McDonald. "The High Costs of High Dams." In *Bordering On Trouble: Resources and Politics in Latin America,* edited by Andrew Maguire and Janet Welsh Brown. Bethesda, MD: Adler & Adler, 1986. pp. 270-307.

909. Remmer, Karen L. "Evaluating the Policy Impact of Military Regimes in Latin America." In *Armies and Politics in Latin America,* edited by Abraham F. Lowenthal and Samuel Fitch. Rev. ed. New York: Holmes & Meier, 1986. pp. 367-385.

910. Remmer, Karen L. "The Politics of Economic Stabilization: IMF Standby Programs in Latin America, 1954-1984," *Comparative Politics* 19:1 (October 1986), 1-24.

911. Remmer, Karen L. "Redemocratization and the Impact of Authoritarian Rule in Latin America," *Comparative Politics* 17:3 (April 1985), 253-275.

912. Restrepo, José Luis. "Latin America: An Assessment of the Past and a Search for the Future," *Inter-American Economic Affairs* 39:3 (Winter 1985), 3-26.

913. Richards, Gordon. "Stabilization Crises and the Breakdown of Military Authoritarianism in Latin America," *Comparative Political Studies* 18:4 (January 1986), 449-485.

914. Richardson, William. "Soviet Policy toward Latin America: A Historical Outline," *World Affairs* 149:2 (Fall 1986), 61-66.

915.   Ridings, Eugene W. "Foreign Predominance among Overseas Traders in Nineteenth-Century Latin America," *Latin American Research Review* 20:2 (1985), 3-27.

916.   Rivera Urrutia, Eugenio. "Estado y regulación económica en América Latina," *Estudios Sociales Centroamericanos* 13:37 (January-April 1984), 49-70.

917.   Riz, Liliana de. "Política y partidos. Ejercicio de análisis comparado: Argentina, Chile, Brasil y Uruguay," *Desarrollo Económico* 25:100 (January-March 1986), 659-682.

918.   Roberts, Kenneth. "Democracy and the Dependent Capitalist State in Latin America," *Monthly Review* 37:5 (October 1985), 12-26.

919.   Roett, Riordan. "Democracy and Debt in South America: A Continent's Dilemma," *Foreign Affairs* 62:3 (1983), 695-720.

920.   Roett, Riordan. "Latin America's Response to the Debt Crisis," *Third World Quarterly* 7:2 (April 1985), 227-241.

921.   Rogers, William D. "The United States and Latin America," *Foreign Affairs* 63:3 (1984), 560-580.

922.   Romano, Ruggiero. "American Feudalism," *Hispanic American Historical Review* 64:1 (February 1984), 121-134.

923.   Ronfeldt, David F. "Rethinking the Monroe Doctrine," *Orbis* 28:4 (Winter 1985), 684-696.

924.   Rothenberg, Morris. "Latin America in Soviet Eyes," *Problems of Communism* 32:5 (September-October 1983), 1-18.

925.   Roxborough, Ian. "Unity and Diversity in Latin American History," *Journal of Latin American Studies* 16:1 (May 1984), 1-26.

926.   Rubenstein, Richard L. "The Political Significance of Latin American Liberation Theology," *World Affairs* 148:3 (Winter 1985-86), 159-167.

927.   Salazar, José Miguel. "On the Psychological Viability of Latin Americanism," *International Social Science Journal* 35:2 (1983), 295-808.

928.   Salazar-Carrillo, Jorge, and Irma Tirado de Alonso. "Comparaciones de productos reales y precios entre la América Latina y el resto del mundo," *El Trimestre Económico* 52:206 (April-June 1985), 357-377.

929.   Sanderson, Steven E. "The Emergence of the 'World Steer': International and Foreign Domination in Latin American Cattle Production." In *Food, the State and International Political Economy,* edited by F. LaMond Tullis and W. Ladd Hollist. Lincoln: University of Nebraska Press, 1986. pp. 123-148.

930.   Sanderson, Steven E. "Recasting the Politics of Inter-American Trade," *Journal of Inter-American Studies and World Affairs* 28:3 (Fall 1986), 87-124.

931.   Saulniers, Alfred H. "Public Enterprise in Latin America: Their Origins and Importance," *International Review of Administrative Sciences* 51:4 (1985), 327-348.

932.   Schejtman, Alejandro. "Análisis integral del problema alimentario y nutricional en América Latina," *Estudios Rurales Latinoamericanos* 6:2-3 (May-December 1983), 141-180.

933.   Schiefelbein, Ernesto. "Elementos para una evaluación de los estudios de recursos humanos en América Latina," *Revista Paraguaya de Sociología* 20:58 (September-December 1983), 37-58.

934.   Schwartz, Hugh. "The Industrial Sector and the Debt Crisis in Latin America," *Journal of Inter-American Studies and World Affairs* 27:4 (Winter 1985-86), 95-110.

935.   Scott, Alison MacEwen. "Women in Latin America: Stereotypes and Social Science," *Bulletin of Latin American Research* 5:2 (1986), 21-27.

936.   Scott, Christopher D. "Transnational Corporations and Asymetries in Latin American Food System," *Bulletin of Latin American Research* 3:1 (January 1984), 63-80.

937.   Scott, Christopher D. "Transnational Corporations, Comparative Advantage and Food Security in Latin America." In *Latin America, Economic Imperialism and the State,* edited by Christopher Abel and Colin M. Lewis. London; Dover, NH: Athlone, 1985. pp. 482-499.

938.   Segal, Aaron. "Latin America: Development with Siesta." In *Learning by Doing: Science and Technology in the Developing World,* by Aaron Segal, et al. Boulder, CO: Westview, 1987. pp. 33-54.

939.   Selcher, Wayne A. "Recent Strategic Developments in South America's Southern Cone." In *Latin American Nations in World Politics,* edited by Heraldo Muñoz and Joseph S. Tulchin. Boulder, CO: Westview, 1984. pp. 101-118.

940.   Sheehey, Edmund J. "Unanticipated Inflation, Devaluation and Output in Latin America," *World Development* 14:5 (May 1986), 665-671.

941.   Soares, João Clemente Baena. "A Different Perspective for the Financial Crisis in Latin America and the Carribean," *Journal of Inter-American Studies and World Affairs* 27:4 (Winter 1985-86), 9-20.

942.   Socolow, Susan M. "Recent Historiography of the Río de la Plata: Colonial and Early National Periods," *Hispanic American Historical Review* 64:1 (February 1984), 105-120.

943.   Spoerer, Sergio. "Las transformaciones del campo religioso en América Latina: un ensayo de interpretación," *Revista Paraguaya de Sociología* 23:67 (September-December 1986), 29-37.

944.   Stavenhagen, Rodolfo. "Los movimientos étnicos indígenas y el estado nacional en América Latina," *Revista Paraguaya de Sociología* 21:59 (January-April 1984), 7-22.

945.   Stepan, Alfred. "The New Professionalism of Internal Welfare and Military Role Expansion." In *Armies and Politics in Latin America,* edited by Abraham F. Lowenthal and Samuel Fitch. Rev. ed. New York: Holmes & Meier, 1986, pp. 134-147.

946.   Stoetzer, O. Carlos. "El espíritu de la legislación de Indias y la identidad latinamericana," *Revista de Estudios Políticos* 53 (September-October 1986), 101-123.

947.   Stoll, David. "Con qué derecho adoctrinan ustedes a nuestro indígenas? La polémica en torno al Instituto Lingüístico de Verano," *América Indígena* 44:1 (January-March 1984), 9-24.

948.   Stone, Carl. "Patterns of Insertion into the World Economy: Historial Profile and Contemporary Options," *Social and Economic Studies* 32:3 (September 1983), 1-33.

949.   Stoner K. Lynn. "Directions in Latin American Women's History, 1977-1984," *Latin American Research Review* 22:2 (1987), 101-134.

950.   Street, James H. "Intervención política y ciencia en el Cono Sur," *El Trimestre Económico* 50:200 (October-December 1983), 2373-2396.

951.   Suchlicki, Jaime. "Soviet Policy in Latin America: Some Implications for the United States," *Journal of Inter-American Studies and World Affairs* 29:1 (Spring 1987), 25-46.

952.   Sunkel, Osvaldo. "Past, Present and Future of the International Economic Crisis," *CEPAL Review* 22 (April 1984), 81-105.

953.   Syrquin, Moshé. "Growth and Structural Change in Latin America since 1960: A Comparative Analysis," *Economic Development and Cultural Change* 34:3 (April 1986), 433-454.

954.   Tavares, Maria da Conceição. "The Revival of American Hegemony," *CEPAL Review* 26 (August 1985), 139-146.

955.   Tedesco, Juan Carlos. "Pedagogical Model and School Failure," *CEPAL Review* 21 (December 1983), 133-146.

956.   Tedesco, Juan Carlos. "El problema de la enseñanza media en América Latina," *Revista Paraguaya de Sociología* 20:57 (May-August 1983), 75-92.

957.   Teitel, Simón. "Creación de tecnología en la América Latina," *El Trimestre Económico* 50:200 (October-December 1983), 2397-2417.

958.   Teitel, Simón. "Indicadores científico tecnológicos: la América Latina, países industrializados y otros países en vía de desarrollo," *El Trimestre Económico* 52:205 (January-March 1985), 95-119.

959.   Teitel, Simón and Francisco Colman Sercovich. "Exportación de tecnología latinoamericana," *El Trimestre Económico* 51:204 (October-December 1984), 811-841.

960.   Teitel, Simón, and Francisco Colman Sercovich. "Exports of Technology by Newly-Industrializing Countries: Latin America," *World Devel-*

opment 12:5-6 (May-June 1984), 645-660.

961.   Terra, Juan Pablo. "The Role of Education in Relation to Employment Problems," *CEPAL Review* 21 (December 1983), 81-111.

962.   Teubal, Miguel. "Internationalization of Capital and Agroindustrial Complexes: Their Impact on Latin American Agriculture," *Latin American Perspectives* 14:3 (Summer 1987), 316-364.

963.   Thoumi, Francisco E. "Intraregional Trade of the Least-Developed Members of Latin American Integration Systems," *Journal of Inter-American Studies and World Affairs* 27:4 (Winter 1985-86), 75-94.

964.   Tironi B., Ernesto. "A Reappraisal of the Role of Primary Exports in Latin America." In *Latin America, Economic Imperialism and the State,* edited by Christopher Abel and Colin M. Lewis. London; Dover, NH: Athlone, 1985. pp. 472-481.

965.   Tokman, Víctor E. "Adjustment and Employment in Latin America: The Current Challenge," *International Labour Review* 125:5 (September-October 1986), 533-543.

966.   Tokman, Víctor E. "Crisis, ajuste económico y costo social," *El Trimestre Económico* 53:209 (January-March 1986), 3-34.

967.   Tokman, Víctor E. "La crisis del empleo en América Latina," *Revista Paraguaya de Sociología* 23:67 (September-December 1986), 7-19.

968.   Tokman, Víctor E. "The Employment Crisis in Latin America," *International Labour Review* 123:5 (September-October 1984), 585-597.

969.   Tokman, Víctor E. "The Process of Accumulation and the Weakness of the Protagonists," *CEPAL Review* 26 (August 1985), 115-126.

970.   Tokman, Víctor E. "El sector informal: quince años después," *El Trimestre Económico* 54:215 (July-September 1987), 513-536.

971.   Tokman, Víctor E. "Wages and Employment in International Recessions: Recent Latin American Experience," *CEPAL Review* 20 (August 1983), 113-126.

972.   Tomassini, Luciano. "The International Scene and Latin America's External Debt," *CEPAL Review* 24 (December 1984), 135-146.

973.   Torres Zorrilla, Jorge, and Eduardo Gana. "Trade and Equilibrium among the ALADI Countries," *CEPAL Review* 27 (December 1985), 69-77.

974.   Touraine, Alain. "Las pautas de acción colectiva," *Revista Paraguaya de Sociología* 21:60 (May-August 1984), 7-32.

975.   Trigo, Eduardo, Martín Piñeiro, and Jorge F. Sábato. "La cuestión tecnológica y la organización de la investigación agropecuaria en América Latina," *Desarrollo Económico* 23:89 (April-June 1983), 99-119.

976.   Vaky, Viron P. "Political Change in Latin America: A Foreign Policy Dilemma for the United States," *Journal of Inter-American Studies*

and World Affairs 28:2 (Summer 1986), 1-15.

977.   Valenzuela, J. Samuel, and Arturo Valenzuela. "Modernization and Dependency: Alternative Perspectives in the Study of Latin American Underdevelopment." In *The Gap between Rich and Poor,* edited by Mitchell A. Seligson. Boulder, CO: Westview, 1984. pp. 105-118.

978.   Varas, August. "Concepts of Security in Latin America," *International Social Science Journal* 38:4 (1986), 563-574.

979.   Varas, Augusto. "Ideology and Politics in Latin American-Soviet Relations," *Problems of Communism* 33:1 (January-February 1984), 35-47.

980.   Vargas Valente, Virginia. "El aporte de la rebeldía de las mujeres," *Revista Paraguaya de Sociología* 23:66 (May-August 1986), 7-28.

981.   Verner, Joel G. "Budgetary Trade-offs between Education and Defense in Latin America: A Research Note," *Journal of Developing Areas* 18:1 October 1983), 77-91.

982.   Verner, Joel G. "The Independence of Supreme Courts in Latin America: A Review of the Literature," *Journal of Latin American Studies* 16:2 (November 1984), 463-506.

983.   Villa A., Manuel. "La forma intervencionista del Estado en América Latina," *Revista Mexicana de Sociología* 49:2 (April-June 1987), 145-163.

984.   von Lazar, Arpad, with Michele McNabb. "Inter-American Energy Policy: Prospects and Constraints," *Journal of Inter-American Studies and World Affairs* 27:1 (February 1985), 123-143.

985.   Waddell, D.A.G. "British Neutrality and Spanish-American Independence: The Problem of Foreign Enlistment," *Journal of Latin American Studies* 19:1 (May 1987), 1-18.

986.   Weinberg, Gregorio. "A Historical Perspective of Latin American Education," *CEPAL Review* 21 (December 1983), 39-55.

987.   Weitz, Richard. "Insurgency and Counterinsurgency in Latin America, 1960-1980," *Political Science Quarterly* 101:3 (1986), 397-413.

988.   Wesson, Robert. "The Soviet Way in Latin America," *World Affairs* 149:2 (Fall 1986), 67-74.

989.   Wiarda, Howard J. "Misreading Latin America — Again," *Foreign Policy* 65 (Winter 1986-87), 135-153.

990.   Wiarda, Howard J. "United States Policy in South America: A Maturing Relationship?" *Current History* 84:499 (February 1985), 49-52.

991.   Wiarda, Howard J. "United States Relations with South America," *Current History* 86:516 (January 1987), 1-4.

992.   Wiesner, Eduardo. "Latin American Debt: Lessons and Pending Issues,"

American Economic Review 75:2 (May 1985), 191-195.

993.   Wilson, Fiona. "Women and Agricultural Change in Latin America: Some Concepts Guiding Research," *World Development* 13:9 (September 1985), 1017-1035.

994.   Wise, Timothy. "The Current Food Crisis in Latin America: A Discussion of de Janvry's *The Agrarian Question,*" *Latin American Perspectives* 14:3 (Summer 1987), 298-315.

995.   Wolfe, Marshall. "Poverty in Latin America: Diagnoses and Prescription." In *Social Development in the Third World,* edited by Jos G.M. Hilhorst and Matty Klatter. London: Croom Helm, 1985. pp. 146-167.

996.   Wood, Richard E. "La sociolingüística actual en América Latina," *Revista Paraguaya de Sociología* 20:57 (May-August 1983), 111-122.

997.   Zabaleta, Marta. "Research on Latin American Women: In Search of Our Political Independence," *Bulletin of Latin American Research* 5:2 (1986), 97-103.

998.   Zschock, Dieter K. "Medical Care under Social Insurance in Latin America," *Latin American Research Review* 1:1 (1986), 99-122.

ARGENTINA

Books and Monographs

999. Abos, Alvaro. *Las organizaciones sindicales y el poder militar (1976-1983)*. Buenos Aires: Centro Editor de América Latina, 1984. 150p.

1000. Agulla, Juan Carlos. *Estudios sobre la sociedad argentina*. Buenos Aires: Belgrano, 1984. 290p.

1001. Ardito Barletta, Nicolas, Mario I. Blejer, and Luis Landau, eds. *Economic Liberalization and Stabilization Policies in Argentina, Chile and Uruguay: Applications of the Monetary Approach to the Balance of Payments*. Washington, DC: World Bank, 1984. 163p.

1002. Auza, Néstor T. *Corrientes sociales del catolicismo argentino*. Buenos Aires: Claretiana, 1984. 398p.

1003. Avellaneda, Andrés. *Censura, authoritarismo y cultura: Argentina, 1960-1983*. Buenos Aires: Centro Editor de América Latina, 1986. 2 vols.

1004. Barbero, María Inés, and Fernando Devoto. *Los nacionalistas*. Centro Editor de América Latina, 1983. 117p.

1005. Bengash, Perla, ed. *La introducción de la technología norteamericana e inglesa en Argentina*. Buenos Aires: Poligono, 1984. 4 vols.

1006. Biagini, Hugo E., comp. *El movimiento positivista argentino*. Buenos Aires: Belgrano, 1985. 590p.

1007. Bilsky, Edgardo. *La semana trágica*. Buenos Aires: Centro Editor de América Latina, 1984. 161p.

1008. Bittel, Deolindo F. *Que es el peronismo*. Buenos Aires: Sudamerica, 1983. 264p.

1009.   Bittel, Deolindo F., comp. *Peronismo y dictadura.* Buenos Aires: Movimiento, 1983. 167p.

1010.   Botana, Natalio R. *La tradición republicana: Alberdi, Sarmiento y las ideas políticas de su tiempo.* Buenos Aires: Sudamericana, 1984. 493p.

1011.   Burns, Robert Andrew. *Diplomacy, War and Parliamentary Democracy: Further Lessons from the Falklands or Advice from Academe.* Lanham, MD: University Press of America, 1985. 52p.

1012.   Bushnell, David. *Reform and Reaction in Platine Provinces, 1810-1852.* Gainesville: University Presses of Florida, 1983. 182p.

1013.   Campo, Hugo del. *Sindicalismo y peronismo: los comienzos de un vínculo perdurable.* Buenos Aires: Consejo Latinoamericano de Ciencias Sociales, 1983. 273p.

1014.   Cavarozzi, Marcelo. *Authoritarismo y democracia, 1955-1983.* Buenos Aires: Centro Editor de América Latina, 1983. 142p.

1015.   Cavarozzi, Marcelo. *Sindicatos y política en Argentina.* Buenos Aires: CEDES, 1984. 176p.

1016.   Ciria, Alberto. *Política y cultura popular: la Argentina peronista, 1946-1955.* Buenos Aires: Flor, 1983. 357p.

1017.   Coggiola, Osvaldo. *Historia del trotskismo argentino.* Buenos Aires: Centro Editor de América Latina, 1985. 159p.

1018.   Coll, Alberto R., and Anthony C. Arends, eds. *The Falklands War: Lessons for Strategy, Diplomacy and International Law.* Boston, MA: Allen & Unwin, 1985. 252p.

1019.   Corradi, Juan E. *The Fitful Republic: Economy, Society and Politics in Argentina.* Boulder, CO: Westview, 1985. 175p.

1020.   Crawley, Eduardo. *A House Divided: Argentina 1880-1980.* New York: St. Martin's, 1984. 472p.

1021.   Dabat, Alejandro, and Luis Lorenzano. *Argentina: The Malvinas and the End of Military Rule.* Translated by Ralph Johnstone. London: Verso, 1984. 205p.

1022.   Demitrópulos, Libertad. *Eva Perón.* Buenos Aries: Centro Editor de América Latina, 1984. 156p.

1023.   Deutsch, Sandra McGee. *Counterrevolution in Argentina, 1900-1932: The Argentine Patriotic League.* Lincoln: University of Nebraska Press, 1986. 319p.

1024.   Devoto, Fernando, and Gianfausto Rosoli, eds. *La inmigración italiana en la Argentina.* Buenos Aries: Biblos, 1985. 270p.

1025.   Di Tella, Guido. *Argentina under Peron, 1973-1976: The Nation's Experience with a Labor-Based Government.* Oxford, England: Macmillan, in association with St. Antony's College. 1983. 246p.

1026. Di Tella, Guido, and D.C.M. Platt. *The Political Economy of Argentina, 1880-1946.* New York: St. Martin's, 1986. 217p.

1027. Di Tella, Torcuato S. *Política y clase obrera.* 2d ed. Buenos Aires: Centro Editor de América Latina, 1983. 128p.

1028. Dorfman, Adolfo. *Cincuenta años de industrialización en la Argentina, 1930-1980.* Buenos Aries: Solar, 1983, 618p.

1029. Duncan, Tim, and John Fogarty. *Australia and Argentina: On Parallel Paths.* Melbourne, Australia: Melbourne University Press, 1984. 203p.

1030. Economic Commission for Latin America. *Empresas transnacionales en la industria de alimentos: el caso argentino, cereales y carne.* Santiago, Chile: United Nations, 1983. 93p.

1031. Escudé, Carlos. *La Argentina ¿Paria Internacional?* Buenos Aires: Belgrano, 1984. 165p.

1032. Escudé, Carlos. *La Argentina vs. las grandes potencias: el precio del desafío.* Buenos Aires: Belgrano, 1986. 273p.

1033. Etchepareborda, Roberto. *Biografía Yrigoyen.* Buenos Aires: Centro Editor de América Latina, 1983. 2 vols.

1034. Falcón, Ricardo. *Los orígenes del movimiento obrero, 1857-1899.* Buenos Aires: Centro Editor de América Latina, 1984. 129p.

1035. Fasano-Filho, Ugo. *Currency Substitution and Liberalization: The Case of Argentina.* Brookfield, VT: Gower, 1986. 194p.

1036. Feldman, Ernesto, and Juan Sommer. *Crisis financiera y endeudamiento externo en la Argentina.* Buenos Aires: Centro Editor de América Latina, 1986. 184p.

1037. Ferrer, Aldo. *Living within Our Means: An Examination of the Argentine Economic Crisis.* Translated by María Inés Alvarez and Nick Caistor. Boulder, CO: Westview, 1986. 98p.

1038. Friedman, Douglas. *The State of Underdevelopment in Spanish America: The Political Roots of Dependency in Peru and Argentina.* Boulder, CO: Westview, 1984. 236p.

1039. Gamba, Virginia. *The Falklands/Malvinas War: A Model for North-South Crisis Prevention.* Boston, MA: Allen & Unwin, 1987. 212p.

1040. García Heras, Raúl. *Automotores norteamericanos, caminos y modernización urbana en la Argentina, 1918-1939.* Buenos Aires: Libros de Hispanoamérica, 1985. 141p.

1041. García Molina, Fernando, and Carlos A. Mayo. *El General Uriburu y el petróleo.* Buenos Aires: Centro Editor de América Latina, 1985. 156p.

1042. Giussani, Pablo. *Los días de Alfonsín.* Buenos Aires: Legasa, 1986. 436p.

1043. Godio, Julio. *La Internacional Socialista en la Argentina.* Buenos Aires:

Centro Editor de América Latina, 1986. 218p.

1044.   Gravil, Roger. *The Anglo-Argentine Connection, 1900-1939.* Boulder, CO: Westview, 1984. 267p.

1045.   Hastings, Max, and Simon Jenkins. *The Battle for the Falklands.* New York: Norton, 1983. 384p.

1046.   Hilb, Claudia, and Daniel Lutzky. *La nueva izquierda argentina, 1960-1980: política y violencia.* Buenos Aires: Centro Editor de América Latina, 1984. 129p.

1047.   Hoffman, Fritz L., and Olga Mingo Hoffman. *Sovereignty in Dispute: The Falklands/Malvinas, 1493-1982.* Boulder, CO: Westview, 1984. 194p.

1048.   Jones, Rodney W., and Steven A. Hildreth. *Modern Weapons and Third World Powers.* Boulder, CO: Westview, 1984. 125p.

1049.   Katra, William H. *Domingo F. Sarmiento: Public Writer.* Tempe: Center for Latin American Studies, Arizona State University, 1985. 235p.

1050.   Kinsbruner, Jay. *Petty Capitalism in Spanish America: The Pulperos of Puebla, Mexico City, Caracas, and Buenos Aires.* Boulder, CO: Westview, 1987. 159p.

1051.   Koburger, Charles W., Jr. *Sea Power in the Falklands.* New York: Praeger, 1983. 186p.

1052.   Lattuada, Mario J. *La política agraria peronista, 1943-1983.* Buenos Aires: Centro Editor de América Latina, 1986. 2 vols.

1053.   Lewis, Colin M. *British Railways in Argentina, 1857-1914: A Case Study in Foreign Investment.* London: Athlone Press for the Institute of Latin American Studies, University of London, 1983. 259p.

1054.   Looney, Robert E. *The Political Economy of Latin American Defense Expenditures: Case Studies of Venezuela and Argentina.* Lexington, MA: Lexington, 1986. 325p.

1055.   Matsushita, Hiroshi. *Movimiento obrero argentino, 1930-1945.* Buenos Aires: Siglo Veinte, 1983. 347p.

1056.   Moneta, Charles J., Ernesto López, and Aníbal Romero. *La reforma militar.* Buenos Aires: Legasa, 1986. 234p.

1057.   Munck, Ronaldo, with Ricardo Falcón and Bernardo Galitelli. *Argentina from Anarchism to Peronism: Workers, Unions and Politics, 1855-1985.* London, Zed, 1987. 261p.

1058.   Page, Joseph. *Peron: A Biography.* New York: Random House, 1983. 594p.

1059.   Peralta-Ramos, Mónica, and Carlos H. Waisman, eds. *From Military Rule to Liberal Democracy in Argentina.* Boulder, CO: Westview, 1987. 175p.

1060.   Pereira, Luiz Carlos Bresser, and Yoshiaki Nakano. *The Theory of*

Inertial Inflation: The Foundation of Economic Reform in Brazil and Argentina. Translated by Colleen Reeks. Boulder, CO: Lynne Rienner, 1987. 206p.

1061.   Perina, Rubén M. *Onganía, Levingston, Lanusse: los militares en la política argentina.* Buenos Aires: Belgrano, 1983. 267p.

1062.   Platt, D.C.M., and Guido Di Tella. *Argentina, Australia and Canada: Studies in Comparative Development, 1870-1965.* London Macmillan, in association with St. Antony's College, Oxford, 1985. 237p.

1063.   Poneman, Daniel. *Argentina: Democracy on Trial.* New York: Paragon House, 1987. 238p.

1064.   Pont, Elena Susana. *Partido laborista: estado y sindícatos.* Buenos Aires: Centro Editor de América Latina, 1984. 157p.

1065.   Ramos, Joseph. *Neoconservative Economics in the Southern Cone of Latin America, 1973-1983.* Baltimore, MD: Johns Hopkins University Press, 1986. 200p.

1066.   Remmer, Karen L. *Party Competition in Argentina and Chile: Political Recruitment and Public Policy, 1890-1930.* Lincoln: University of Nebraska Press, 1984. 296p.

1067.   Rock, David. *Argentina 1516-1982: From Spanish Colonization to the Falklands War.* Berkeley: University of California Press, 1985. 478p.

1068.   Rodríguez, Leopoldo F. *Inmigración, nacionalismo y fuerzas armadas: antecedentes del golpismo en Argentina, 1870-1930.* Mexico City: Impresora Internacional, 1986. 120p.

1069.   Romero, José Luis, and Luis Alberto Romero, eds. *Buenos Aires: historia de cuatro siglos.* Buenos Aires: Abril, 1983. 2 vols.

1070.   Schoultz, Lars. *The Populist Challenge: Argentine Electoral Behavior in the Postwar Era.* Chapel Hill: University of North Carolina Press, 1983. 141p.

1071.   Senéz González, Santiago, with the collaboration of Ricardo Callo. *Diez años de sindicalismo argentino: de Perón al "proceso".* Buenos Aires: Corregidor, 1984. 225p.

1072.   Simpson, John. *The Disappeared and the Mothers of the Plaza: The Story of the 11,000 Argentinians Who Vanished.* New York: St. Martin's, 1985. 416p.

1073.   Simpson, John, and Jana Bennett. *The Disappeared: Voices from a Secret War.* London: Robson, 1985. 416p.

1074.   Tamarin, David. *The Argentine Labor Movement, 1930-1945: A Study in the Origins of Peronismo.* Albuquerque: University of New Mexico Press, 1985. 273p.

1075.   Torre, Juan Carlos. *Los sindicatos en el gobierno, 1973-1976.* Buenos Aires: Centro Editor de América Latina, 1983. 166p.

1076.   Vacs, Aldo César. *Discreet Partners: Argentina and the USSR since 1917.* Translated by Michael Joyce. Pittsburgh, PA: University of Pittsburgh Press, 1984. 154p.

1077.   Walter, Richard J. *The Province of Buenos Aries and Argentine Politics, 1912-1943.* Cambridge, England; New York: Cambridge University Press, 1985. 244p.

1078.   Watson, Bruce W., and Peter M. Dunn, eds. *Military Lessons of the Falkland Islands War: Views from the United States.* Boulder, CO: Westview, 1984. 181p.

1079.   Wynia, Gary W. *Argentina: Illusions and Realities.* New York: Holmes & Meier, 1986. 207p.

Articles and Chapters

1080.   Abreu, Mancelo de Paiva. "La Argentina y Brasil en los años treinta: efectos de la política económica internacional británica y estadounidense," *Desarrollo Económico* 24:96 (January-March 1985), 543-559.

1081.   Acevedo, Domingo, E. "The U.S. Measures against Argentina Resulting from the Malvinas," *American Journal of International Law* 78:2 (April 1984), 323-344.

1082.   Alhadeff, Peter. "Dependency, Historiography and Objectives to the Roca Pact." In *Latin America, Economic Imperialism, and the State,* edited by Christopher Abel and Colin M. Lewis. London; Dover, NH: Athlone, 1985. pp. 367-378.

1083.   Altimir, Oscar. "Estimaciones de la distribución del ingreso en la Argentina, 1953-1980," *Desarrollo Económico* 25:100 (January-March 1986), 521-566.

1084.   Amaral, Samuel. "El empréstito de Londres de 1824," *Desarrollo Económico* 23:92 (January-March 1984), 559-588.

1085.   Amaral, Samuel. "Public Expenditures Financing in the Colonial Treasury: An Analysis of the Real Caja de Buenos Aires Accounts, 1789-91," *Hispanic American Historical Review* 64:2 (May 1984), 287-295.

1086.   Arienza, Marisa, and Carlos A. Mallmann, "Argentina on the Road to Democracy: Comparisons with Chile and Uruguay," *International Social Science Journal* 37:1 (1985), 31-46.

1087.   Aspiazu, Daniel, Eduardo Basualdo, and Bernardo Kosacoff. "Transnational Corporations in Argentina, 1976-1983," *CEPAL Review* 28 (April 1986), 99-133.

1088.   Barrolomé, Leopoldo J. "Forced Resettlement and the Survival Systems of the Urban Poor," *Ethnology* 23:3 (July 1984), 177-192.

1089.   Bartolomé, Miguel Alberto. "La desindianización de la Argentina," *Boletín de Antropología Americana* 11 (July 1985), 39-50.

1090.   Beck, Peter J. "Britain's Antarctic Dimension," *International Affairs* 59:3 (Summer 1983), 429-444.

1091.   Beck, Peter J. "The Future of the Falkland Islands: A Solution Made in Hong Kong?" *International Affairs* 61:4 (Autumn 1985), 643-660.

1092.   Beck, Peter J. "Research Problems in Studying Britain's Latin American Past: The Case of the Falklands Dispute 1920-1950," *Bulletin of Latin American Research* 2:2 (May 1983), 3-16.

1093.   Benencia, Roberto. "Procesos políticos y movimientos campesinos: dos experiencias de organización en contextos históricos diferentes, " *Revista Paraguaya de Sociología* 23:67 (September-December 1986), 39-53.

1094.   Benencia, Roberto, and Floreal H. Forni. "Condiciones de trabajo y condiciones de vida de familias campesinas y asalariadas en un área rural en Argentina," *Estudios Rurales Latinoamericanos* 8:3 (September-December 1985), 281-303.

1095.   Biagini, Hugo E. "La Argentina y Ortega," *Revista de Estudios Políticos* 53 (September-October 1986), 191-197.

1096.   Blejer, Mario I. "Liberalization and Stabilization Policies in the Southern Cone Countries," *Journal of Inter-American Studies and World Affairs* 25:4 (November 1983), 431-444.

1097.   Bluth, Christoph. "The British Resort to Force in the Falkland/Malvinas Conflict," *Journal of Peace Research* 24:1 (March 1987), 5-20.

1098.   Braslavasky, Cecilia. "Youth in Argentina: Between the Legacy of the Past and the Construction of the Future," *CEPAL Review* 29 (August 1986), 41-54.

1099.   Brown, Jonathan C. "The Bondage of Old Habits in Nineteenth-Century Argentina," *Latin American Research Review* 21:2 (1986), 3-31.

1100.   Buchanan, Paul G. "State Corporatism in Argentina: Labor Adminitration under Perón and Onganía," *Latin American Research Review* 20:1 (1985), 61-95.

1101.   Caistor, Nick. "Argentina: Higher Education and Political Instability." In *Education in Latin America,* edited by Colin Brock and Hugh Lawlor. Dover, NH: Croom Helm, 1985. pp. 183-192.

1102.   Calvert, Peter. "Sovereignty and the Falklands Crisis," *International Affairs* 59:3 (Summer 1983), 405-413.

1103.   Calvo, Guillermo A. "Fractured Liberalism: Argentina under Martínez de Hoz," *Economic Development and Cultural Change* 34:3 (April 1986), 511-533.

1104.   Cantón, Darío, Jorge R. Jorrat, and Luis R. Acosta. "La consulta por el Beagle en la Capital Federal y La Matanza," *Desarrollo Económico* 25:97 (April-June 1985), 24-45.

1105.   Cara-Walker, Ana. "Cocoliche: The Art of Assimilation and Dissumulation among Italians and Argentines," *Latin American Research Review* 22:3 (1987), 37-67.

1106.   Carrera, Nicolás Iñgio. "Violence as Economic Power: The Role of the State in Creating the Conditions for a Productive Rural System," *Latin American Perspectives* 10:4 (Fall 1983), 97-113.

1107.   Cavarozzi, Marcelo. "Political Cycles in Argentina since 1955." In *Transition from Authoritarian Rule,* edited by Guillermo O'Donnell, Philippe C. Schmitter and Laurence Whitehead. Baltimore, MD: Johns Hopkins University Press, 1986. pp. 19-48.

1108.   Chehabi, Houchang Esfandiar. "Self-Determination, Territorial Integrity and the Falkland Islands," *Political Science Quarterly* 100:2 (Summer 1985), 215-225.

1109.   Chiaramonte, José Carlos. "Legalidad constitutional o caudillismo: el problema del orden social en el surgimiento de los estados autónomos del litoral argentino en la primera mitad del siglo XIX," *Desarrollo Económicos* 26:102 (July-September 1986), 175-196.

1110.   Chudnovsky, Daniel. "La difusión de tecnología de punta en la Argentina: el caso de las máquinas herramientas con control numérico, el CAD/CAM y los robots," *Desarrollo Económico* 24:96 (January-March 1985), 483-516.

1111.   Corbo, Vittorio, Jaime de Melo, and James Tybout. "What Went Wrong with the Recent Reforms in the Southern Cone," *Economic Development and Cultural Change* 34:3 (April 1986), 607-640.

1112.   Corradi, Juan E. "Two Cheers (and a Prayer) for Argentine Democracy," *Dissent* (Spring 1984), 203-206.

1113.   Cortés, Rosalía, and Adriana Marshall. "Salario real, composición del consumo y balanza comercial," *Desarrollo Económico* 26:101 (April-June 1986), 71-88.

1114.   Cortés Conde, Roberto. "The Export Economy of Argentina, 1880-1920." In *The Latin American Economies: Growth and the Export Sector, 1880-1930,* edited by Roberto Cortés Conde and Shane J. Hunt. New York: Holmes & Meier, 1985. 319-381.

1115.   Deutsch, Sandra McGee. "The Argentine Right and the Jews, 1919-1933," *Journal of Latin American Studies* 18:1 (May 1986), 113-134.

1116.   Diamand, Marcelo. "Overcoming Argentina's Stop-and-Go Economic Cycle." In *Latin American Political Economy: Financial Crisis and Political Change,* edited by Jonathan Hartlyn and Samuel A. Morley. Boulder, CO: Westview, 1986. pp. 129-164.

1117.   Diamand, Marcelo, and Daniel Naszewski. "Argentina's Foreign Debt: Its Origin and Consequences." In *Politics and Economics of External Debt Crisis: The Latin American Experience,* edited by Miguel S. Wionczek in collaboration with Luciano Tomassini. Boulder, CO: Westview, 1985. pp. 231-276.

1118.   Dieguez, Héctor L., and Pablo Gerchunoff. "La dinámica del mercado laboral urbano en la Argentina, 1976-1981," *Desarrollo Económico* 24:93 (April-June 1984), 3-40.

1119.   Di Tella, Guido. "La estrategia del desarrollo indirecto veinte años después," *Desarrollo Económico* 26:101 (April-June 1986), 51-70.

1120.   Di Tella, Torcuato S. "The October 1983 Elections in Argentina," *Government and Opposition* 19:2 (Spring 1984), 188-192.

1121.   Di Tella, Torcuato S. "The Popular Parties in Brazil and Argentina," *Government and Opposition* 19:2 (Spring 1984), 250-268.

1122.   Dorfman, Adolfo. "The Structural Crisis in Argentine Industry," *CEPAL Review* 23 (August 1984), 123-134.

1123.   Duncan, Tim. "La política fiscal durante el gobierno de Juárez Celman, 1866-1890: una audaz estrategia financiera internacional," *Desarrollo Económico* 23:89 (April-June 1983), 11-34.

1124.   Dunnett, Denzil. "Self-Determination and the Falklands," *International Affairs* 59:3 (Summer 1983), 415-428.

1125.   Epstein, Edward C. "Recent Stabilization Programs in Argentina, 1973-86," *World Development* 15:8 (August 1987), 991-1005.

1126.   Falcoff, Mark. "Is Peronism Finished?" *Commentary* 77:2 (February 1984), 60-65.

1127.   Falcoff, Mark. "Spain and the Southern Cone." In *The Iberian-Latin American Connection: Implications for U.S. Foreign Policy,* edited by Howard J. Wiarda. Boulder, CO: Westview, 1986. pp. 337-359.

1128.   Feldman, David Lewis. "The United States Role in the Malvinas Crisis, 1982: Misguidance and Misperception in Argentina's Decision to Go to War," *Journal of Inter-American Studies and World Affairs* 27:2 (Spring 1985), 1-22.

1129.   Fernández, Roque B. "La crisis financiera argentina: 1980-1982," *Desarollo Económico* 23:89 (April-June 1983), 79-97.

1130.   Fernández, Roque B. "The Expectations Management Approach to Stabilization in Argentina during 1976-1982," *World Development* 13:8 (August 1985), 871-892.

1131.   Fernández Berdaguer, M. Leticia. "Educación universitaria y desempeño profesional: el caso de las mujeres estudiantes de ciencias económicas de la Universidad de Buenos Aires," *Revista Paraguaya de Sociología* 20:56 (January-April 1983), 75-97.

1132.   Floria, Carlos Alberto. "Dilemmas of the Consolidation of Democracy in Argentina." In *Comparing New Democracies: Transition and Consolidation in Mediterranean Europe and the Southern Cone,* edited by Enrique A. Baloyra. Boulder, CO: Westview, 1987. pp. 153-178.

1133.   Foster, David William. "Argentine Sociopolitical Commentary, the Malvinas Conflict, and Beyond: Rhetoricizing a National Experience," *Latin American Research Review* 22:1 (1987), 7-34.

1134.   Frenkel, Roberto. "A dinâmica dos preços industriais na Argentina em 1966-82: um estudo econométrico." *Revista Brasileira de Economia* 38:1 (January-March 1984), 53-94.

1135.   Frenkel, Roberto, and José María Fanelli. "La Argentina y el Fondo en la década pasada," *El Trimestre Económico* 54:213 (January-March 1987), 75-131.

1136.   Frenkel, Roberto, and José María Fanelli. "El Plan Austral: un año y medio después," *El Trimestre Económico* 54:Special (September 1987), 55-117.

1137.   García Heras, Raúl. "Hostage Private Companies under Restraint: British Railways and Transport Coordination in Argentina during the 1930s," *Journal of Latin American Studies* 19:1 (May 1987), 41-67.

1138.   García Heras, Raúl. "World War II and the Frustrated Nationalization of the Argentine British-Owned Railways, 1939-1943," *Journal of Latin American Studies* 17:1 (May 1985), 135-155.

1139.   Garrett, James L. "The Beagle Channel: Confrontation and Negotiation in the Southern Cone," *Journal of Inter-American Studies and World Affairs* 27:3 (Fall 1985), 81-109.

1140.   Gaudio, Ricardo, and Jorge Pilone. "El desarrollo de la negociación colectiva durante la etapa de modernización industrial en la Argentina, 1935-1943," *Desarrollo Económico* 23:90 (July-September 1983), 255-286.

1141.   Gerchunoff, Pablo, and Carlos Bozzalla, "Posibilidades y límites de un programa de estabilización heterodoxo: el caso argentino," *El Trimestre Económico* 54:Special (September 1987), 119-154.

1142.   Ghadar, Fariborz. "Development of the Oil Industry in Argentina." In *The Petroleum Industry in Oil-Importing Developing Countries,* by Fariborz Ghadar. Lexington, MA: Lexington, 1983. pp. 105-129.

1143.   Gordillo, Agustín. "An Ombudsman for Argentina: Yes, but..." *International Review of Administrative Sciences* 50:3 (1984), 230-234.

1144.   Gordon, Dennis R. "Argentina's Foreign Policies in the Post-Malvinas Era." In *The Dynamics of Latin American Foreign Policies,* edited by Jeannie K. Lincoln and Elizabeth G. Ferris. Boulder, CO: Westview, 1984. pp. 85-100.

1145.   Graham-Yooll, Andrew. "Argentina: The State of Transition 1983-85," *Third World Quarterly* 7:3 (July 1985), 573-593.

1146.   Greenberg, Daniel J. "Sugar Depression and Agrarian Revolt: The Argentine Radical Party and the Tucumán Cañeros' Strike of 1927," *Hispanic American Historical Review* 67:2 (May 1987), 301-327.

1147.   Guadagni, Alieto A. "La programación de las inversiones eléctricas y las actuales prioridades energéticas," *Desarrollo Económico* 25:98 (July-September 1985), 179-216.

1148.   Gustafson, Lowell S. "The Principle of Self-Determination and the

Dispute about Sovereignty over the Falkland Islands," *Inter-American Economic Affairs* 37:4 (Spring 1984), 81-99.

1149.   Guy, Donna J. "Lower-Class Families, Women and the Law in Nineteenth-Century Argentina," *Journal of Family History* 10:3 (Fall 1985), 318-331.

1150.   Guy, Donna J. "Sugar Industries at the Periphery of the World Market: Argentina, 1860-1914." In *Crisis and Change in the International Sugar Economy, 1860-1914,* edited by Bill Albert and Adrian Graves. Edinburgh, Scotland: ISC Press, 1984.pp. 147-164.

1151.   Halperin Donghi, Tulio. "Canción de otoño en primavera: previsiones sobre la crisis de la agricultura cerealera argentina, 1894-1930," *Desarrollo Económico* 24:95 (October-December 1984), 367-386.

1152.   Halperin Donghi, Tulio. "Un cuarto de siglo de historiografía argentina, 1960-1985," *Desarrollo Económico* 25:100 (January-March 1986), 487-520.

1153.   Heymann, Daniel. "Inflation and Stabilization Policies," *CEPAL Review* 28 (April 1986), 67-98.

1154.   Hodge, John E. "The Formation of the Argentine Public Primary and Secondary School System," *The Americas* 44:1 (July 1987), 45-65.

1155.   Hodge, John E. "The Role of the Telegraph in the Consolidation and Expansion of the Argentine Republic," *The Americas* 41:1 (July 1984), 59-80.

1156.   Hopple, Gerald W. "Intelligence and Warning: Implications and Lessons of the Falkland Islands War," *World Politics* 36:3 (April 1984), 339-361.

1157.   Horowitz, Joel. "Occupational Community and the Creation of a Self-Styled Elite: Railroad Workers in Argentina," *The Americas* 42:1 (July 1985), 55-81.

1158.   Horowitz, Joel. "Los trabajadores ferroviarios en la Argentina, 1920-1943: la formación de una elite obrera," *Desarrollo Económico* 25:99 (October-December 1985), 421-446.

1159.   Jacobsson, Staffan. "Technical Change and Industrial Policy: The Case of Computer Numerically Controlled Lathes in Argentina, Korea and Taiwan," *World Development* 13:3 (March 1985), 353-370.

1160.   Jones, Charles A. "The State and Business Practice in Argentina, 1862-1914." In *Latin America, Economic Imperialism and the State,* edited by Christopher Abel and Colin M. Lewis. London; Dover, NH: Athlone, 1985. pp. 184-198.

1161.   Jones, Kristine L. "Nineteenth Century British Travel Accounts of Argentina," *Ethnohistory* 33:2 (May 1986), 195-212.

1162.   Jongkind, C. Fred. "Ethnic Solidarity and Social Stratification: Migrants' Organizations in Argentina and Peru," *Boletín de Estudios Latino-americanos y del Caribe* 40 (June 1986), 37-48.

1163. Jorrat, Jorge Raúl. "Las elecciones de 1983: ¿desviación o realine-amiento?" *Desarrollo Económico* 26:101 (April-June 1986), 89-120.

1164. Kapschutschenko, Ludmila. "José Martí y la Argentina," *Inter-American Review of Bibliography* 33:3 (1983), 383-388.

1165. Kaufman, Robert E. "Democratic and Authoritarian Responses to the Debt Issue: Argentina, Brazil, Mexico," *International Organization* 39:3 (Summer 1985), 473-503.

1166. Kilgore, William J. "Ideology in Argentina in the Post-Revolutionary Period," *Inter-American Review of Bibliography* 33:4 (1983), 553-561.

1167. Korn, Francis, and Lidia de la Torre. "La vivienda en Buenos Aires, 1887-1914," *Desarrollo Económico* 25:98 (July-September 1985), 245-258.

1168. Leiderman, Leonardo, and Mario I. Blejer. "The Term Structure of Interest Rates during a Financial Reform: Argentina 1977-81," *Journal of Development Economics* 25:2 (April 1987), 285-299.

1169. León, Carlos, Nora Prudkin, and Carlos Reboratti. "El conflicto entre producción, sociedad y medio ambiente: la expansión agricola en el sur de Salta," *Desarrollo Económico* 25:99 (October-December 1985), 399-420.

1170. Lewis, Colin M. "Railways and Industrialization: Argentina and Brazil, 1870-1929." In *Latin America, Economic Imperialism and the State,* edited by Christopher Abel and Colin M. Lewis. London; Dover, NH: Athlone, 1985. pp. 199-230.

1171. Little, Walter. "Civil-Military Relations in Contemporary Argentina," *Government and Opposition* 19:2 (Spring 1984), 207-224.

1172. Llach, Juan J. "El Plan Pinedo de 1940, su significado histórico y los orígenes de la economía política del peronismo," *Desarrollo Económico* 23:92 (January-March 1984), 415-558.

1173. Looney, Robert E., and P.C. Frederiksen. "Consequences of Military and Civilian Rule in Argentina: An Analysis of Central Government Budgetary Trade-Offs, 1961-1982," *Comparative Political Studies* 20:1 (April 1987), 34-46.

1174. MacDonald, Callum A. "The U.S., the Cold War and Perón." In *Latin America, Economic Imperialism and the State,* edited by Christopher Abel and Colin M. Lewis. London; Dover, NH: Athlone, 1985. pp. 405-414.

1175. McGee, Sandra F. "The Visible and Invisible Liga Patriotica Argentina, 1919-28: Gender Roles and the Right Wing," *Hispanic American Historical Review* 64:2 (May 1984), 233-258.

1176. McLynn, F.J. "Consequences for Argentina of the War of Triple Alliance 1865-1870," *The Americas* 41:1 (July 1984), 81-98.

1177. McLynn, F.J. "The Ideology of Peronism," *Government and Opposition*

19:2 (Spring 1984), 193-206.

1178. Mainwaring, Scott. "The State and the Industrial Bourgeoisie in Peron's Argentina, 1945-1955," *Studies in Comparative International Development* 21:3 (Fall 1986), 3-31.

1179. Mainwaring, Scott, and Eduardo J. Viola. "Transitions to Democracy: Brazil and Argentina in the 1980s," *Journal of International Affairs* 38:2 (Winter 1985), 193-219.

1180. Makin, Guillermo A. "Argentine Approaches to the Falklands/Malvinas: Was the Resort to Violence Forseeable?" *International Affairs* 59:3 (Summer 1983), 391-403.

1181. Makin, Guillermo A. "Argentina: The Authoritarian Impasse." In *The Political Dilemmas of Military Regimes,* edited by Christopher Clapham, Ian Campbell, and George Philip. Totowa, NJ: Rowman & Allanheld, 1985. pp. 151-170.

1182. Makin, Guillermo A. "The Argentine Process of Demilitarization: 1980-83," *Government and Opposition* 19:2 (Spring 1984), 225-238.

1183. Mann, Arthur J., and Carlos E. Sánchez. "Labor Market Responses to Southern Cone Stabilization Policies: The Cases of Argentina, Chile, Uruguay," *Inter-American Economic Affairs* 38:4 (Spring 1985), 19-39.

1184. Mann, Arthur J., and Jacques Delons. "The Buenos Aires Mini-Enterprise Sector," *Social and Economic Studies* 36:2 (June 1987), 41-67.

1185. Manzanal, Mabel, and Cesar A. Vapnarsky. "The Development of the Upper Valley of Rio Negro and Its Periphery within the Comahue Region, Argentina." In *Small and Intermediate Urban Centers,* edited by Jorge E. Hardoy and David Satterthwaite. Boulder, CO: Westview, 1986. pp. 18-79.

1186. Marshall, Adriana. "El 'salario social' en la Argentina," *Desarrollo Económico* 24:93 (April-June 1984), 41-70.

1187. Marshall, Adriana, and Dora Orlansky. "Inmigración de países limítrofes y demanda de mano de obra en la Argentina, 1940-1980," *Desarrollo Económico* 23:89 (April-June 1983), 35-58.

1188. Méndez, Jesús. "Church-State Relations in Argentina in the Twentieth Century: A Case Study of the Thirty-Second International Eucharistic Congress," *Journal of Church and State* 27:2 (Spring 1985), 223-243.

1189. Molyneux, Maxine. "No God, No Boss, No Husband: Anarchist Feminism in Nineteenth-Century Argentina," *Latin American Perspectives* 13:1 (Winter 1986), 119-145.

1190. Moneta, Carlos J. "Fuerzas armadas y gobierno constitutional después de las Malvinas hacia una nueva relación civil-militar," *Foro Internacional* 26:2 (October-December 1985), 190-213.

1191. Moneta, Carlos J. "The Malvinas Conflict: Analyzing the Argentine

Military Regime's Decision-Making Process." In *Latin American Nations in World Politics,* edited by Heraldo Muñoz and Joseph S. Tulchin. Boulder, CO: Westview, 1984. pp. 119-132.

1192.   Moreno, Martín Jorge. "La urbanización en la Provincia de Misiones," *Revista Paraguaya de Sociología* 23:65 (January-April 1986), 77-98.

1193.   Mouzelis, Nicos. "On the Rise of Postwar Military Dictatorships: Argentina, Chile and Greece," *Comparative Studies in Society and History* 28:1 (January 1986), 55-80.

1194.   Munck, Ronaldo. "Cycles of Class Struggle and the Making of the Working Class in Argentina, 1890-1920," *Journal of Latin American Studies* 19:1 (May 1987), 19-39.

1195.   Munck, Ronaldo. "Democratization and Demilitarization in Argentina, 1982-1985," *Bulletin of Latin American Research* 4:2 (1985), 85-93.

1196.   Munck, Ronaldo. "The 'Modern' Military Dictatorship in Latin America: The Case of Argentina (1976-1982)," *Latin American Perspectives* 12:4 (Fall 1985), 41-74.

1197.   Mustapic, Ana María. "Conflictos institucionales durante el primer gobierno radical: 1916-1922," *Desarrollo Económico* 24:93 (April-June 1984), 85-108.

1198.   Newton, Ronald C. "The Neutralization of Fritz Mandl: Notes on Wartime Journalism, the Arms Trade, and Anglo-American Rivalry in Argentina during World War II," *Hispanic American Historial Review* 66:3 (August 1986), 541-579.

1199.   Newton, Ronald C. "The United States, the German-Argentines, and the Myth of the Fourth Reich, 1943-1947," *Hispanic American Historical Review* 64:1 (February 1984), 81-103.

1200.   Nogués, Julio J. "Alternative Trade Strategies and Employment in the Argentine Manufacturing Sector," *World Development* 11:12 (December 1983), 1029-1042.

1201.   Nun, José. "Averiguación sobre algunos significados del peronismo," *Revista Mexicana de Sociología* 47:2 (April-June 1985), 251-286.

1202.   O'Connell, Arturo A. "La Argentina en la Depresión: los problemas de una economía abierta," *Desarrollo Económico* 23:92 (January-March 1984), 479-514.

1203.   O'Connell, Arturo A. "La fiebre aftosa, el embargo sanitario norte-americano contra las importaciones de carne y el triángulo Argentina-Gran Bretaña-Estados Unidos en el período entre las dos guerras mundiales," *Desarrollo Económico* 26:101 (April-June 1986), 21-50.

1204.   O'Donnell, Guillermo A. "Modernization and Military Coups: Theory, Comparisons, and the Argentine Case." In *Armies and Politics in Latin America,* edited by Abraham F. Lowenthal and Samuel Fitch. Rev. ed. New York: Holmes & Meier, 1986. pp. 96-133.

1205.   Orsatti, Alvaro. "La nueva distribución funcional del ingreso en la Argentina, *Desarrollo Económico* 23:91 (October-December 1983), 315-337.

1206.   Osiel, Mark. "The Making of Human Rights Policy in Argentina: The Impact of Ideas and Interests on a Legal Conflict," *Journal of Latin American Studies* 18:1 (May 1986), 135-180.

1207.   Oszlak, Oscar. "Política y organización estatal de las actividades científico-técnicas en la Argentina: crítica de modelos y prescripciones corrientes." In *The Public Sector in Latin America,* edited by Alfred H. Saulniers. Austin: Institute of Latin American Studies, University of Texas, 1984. pp. 165-209.

1208.   Pantelides, Edith Alejandra. "La transición demográfica argentina: un modelo no ortodoxo," *Desarrollo Económico* 22:88 (January-March 1983), 511-534.

1209.   Passanante, María Inés. "Tercera edad y política social: una reflexión sociológica," *Revista Paraguaya de Sociología* 21:61 (September-December 1984), 173-188.

1210.   Petrei, A. Humberto, and James Tybout. "Microeconomic Adjustments in Argentina during 1976-81: The Importance of Changing Levels of Financial Subsidies," *World Development* 13:8 (August 1985), 949-967.

1211.   Philip, George. "Democratization in Brazil and Argentina: Some Reflections," *Government and Opposition* 19:2 (Spring 1984), 269-276.

1212.   Philip, George. "The Fall of the Argentine Military," *Third World Quarterly* 6:3 (July 1984), 624-637.

1213.   Pion-Berlin, David. "The Fall of Military Rule in Argentina: 1976-1983," *Journal of Inter-American Studies and World Affairs* 27:2 (Summer 1985), 55-76.

1214.   Poneman, Daniel. "Nuclear Proliferation Prospects for Argentina," *Orbis* 27:4 (Winter 1984), 853-880.

1215.   Porth, Jacquelyn S. "Argentina." In *Arms Production in Developing Countries: An Analysis of Decision Making,* edited by James Everett Katz. Lexington, MA: Lexington, 1984. pp. 53-72.

1216.   Ranis, Peter. "The Dilemmas of Democratization in Argentina," *Current History* 85:507 (January 1986), 29-33.

1217.   Rapoport, Mario. "Argentina and the Soviet Union: History of Political and Commercial Relations, 1917-1955," *Hispanic American Historical Review* 66:2 (May 1986), 239-285.

1218.   Rock, David. "Intellectual Precursors of Conservative Nationalism in Argentina, 1900-27," *Hispanic American Historical Review* 67:2 (May 1987), 271-300.

1219.   Rofman, Alejandro. "Políticas alternativas de transformación en el medio rural minifundista: la acción de las ONG en el área del nordeste," *Revista Paraguay de Sociología* 23:66 (May-August 1986), 39-61.

1220.   Rouquié, Alain. "Argentina: The Departure of the Military: End of a Political Cycle or Just Another Episode?" *International Affairs* 59:4 (Autumn 1983), 575-586.

1221.   Sabato, Hilda. "La formación del mercado de trabajo en Buenos Aires, 1850-1880," *Desarrollo Económico* 24:96 (January-March 1985), 561-592.

1222.   Saeger, James Schofield. "Another View of the Mission as a Frontier Institution: The Guaycuruan Reductions of Santa Fe, 1743-1810," *Hispanic American Historical Review* 65:3 (August 1985), 493-517.

1223.   Saguier, Eduardo R. "Church and State in Buenos Aires in the Seventeenth Century," *Journal of Church and State* 26:3 (Autumn 1984), 491-514.

1224.   Saguier, Eduardo R. "The Social Impact of a Middleman Minority in a Divided Host Society: The Case of the Portuguese in Early Seventeenth-Century Buenos Aires," *Hispanic American Historical Review* 65:3 (August 1985), 467-491.

1225.   Salvatore, Ricardo D. "Control del trabajo y discriminación: el sistema de contratistas en Mendoza, Argentina, 1880-1920," *Desarrollo Económico* 26:102 (July-September 1986), 229-253.

1226.   Salvatore, Ricardo D., and Jonathan C. Brown. "Trade and Proletarianiza-tion in Late Colonial Banda Oriental: Evidence from the Estancia de las Vacas, 1791-1805," *Hispanic American Historical Review* 67:3 (August 1987), 431-459.

1227.   Santamaria, Daniel J. "Acceso tradicional a la fuerza de trabajo rural, política de tierras y desarrollo capitalista: el caso de la agricultura de caña de azúcar en el noroeste argentino," *Revista Paraguaya de Sociología* 21:60 (May-August 1984), 117-130.

1228.   Scarzanella, Eugenia. "'Corn Fever': Italian Tenant Farming Families in Argentina, 1895-1912," *Bulletin of Latin American Research* 3:1 (January 1984), 1-23.

1229.   Scheetz, Thomas. "Gastos militares en Chile, Perú y la Argentina," *Desarrollo Económico* 25:99 (October-December 1985), 315-328.

1230.   Schumacher, Edward. "Argentina and Democracy," *Foreign Affairs* 62:5 (Summer 1984), 1070-1095.

1231.   Schvarzer, Jorge. "Cambios en el liderazgo industrial argentino en el período de Martínez de Hoz," *Desarrollo Económico* 23:91 (October-December 1983), 395-422.

1232.   Selcher, Wayne A. "Brazilian-Argentine Relations in the 1980s: From Wary Rivalry to Friendly Competition," *Journal of Inter-American Studies and World Affairs* 27:2 (Summer 1985), 25-53.

1233.   Simonsen, Mario Henrique, and Rudiger Dornbusch. "Estabilização da inflação com o apoio de políticas de rendas: um exame da experiencia na Argentina, Brasil, e Israel," *Revista Brasiliera de Economia* 41:1 (January-March 1987), 3-50.

1234. Slatta, Richard W. "Images of Social Banditry on the Argentine Pampas." In *Bandidos: The Varieties of Latin American Banditry,* edited by Richard W. Slatta. Westport, CT: Greenwood, 1987. pp. 49-65.

1235. Slatta, Richard W. "'Llaneros' and gauchos: A Comparative View," *Inter-American Review of Bibliography* 35:4 (1985), 409-421.

1236. Smith, William C. "Reflections on the Political Economy of Authoritarian Rule and Capitalist Reorganization in Contemporary Argentina." In *Generals in Retreat: The Crisis of Military Rule in Latin America,* edited by Philip J. O'Brien and Paul Cammack. Dover, NH: Manchester University Press, 1985. pp. 37-88.

1237. Soifer, Ricardo J. "Exports of Technology by Newly-Industrializing Countries: Argentina," *World Development* 12:5-6 (May-June 1984), 625-644.

1238. Sotomayor Torres, Clivia M., and Wolfgang Rudig. "Nuclear Power in Argentina and Brazil," *Review of Radical Political Economics* 15:3 (Fall 1983), 67-82.

1239. Suárez, Waldino C. "Argentina: Political Transition and Institutional Weakness in Comparative Perspective." In *Comparing New Democracies: Transition and Consolidation in Mediterranean Europe and the Southern Cone,* edited by Enrique A. Baloyra. Boulder, CO: Westview, 1987. pp. 269-296.

1240. Taylor, Lance. "El Plan Austral (y otros choques heterodoxos): Fase II," *El Trimestre Económico* 54:Special (September 1987), 155-175.

1241. Teitel, Simón, and Francisco E. Thoumi. "From Import Substitution to Exports: The Manufacturing Exports Experience of Argentina and Brazil," *Economic Development and Cultural Change* 34:3 (April 1986), 455-490.

1242. Thompson, Ruth. "The Limitations of Ideology in the Early Argentine Labour Movement: Anarchism in the Trade Unions, 1890-1920," *Journal of Latin American Studies* 16:1 (May 1984), 81-99.

1243. Tiano, Susan. "Authoritarianism and Political Culture in Argentina and Chile in the Mid-1960s," *Latin American Research Review* 21:1 (1986), 73-98.

1244. Tokman, Víctor E. "Global Monetarism and Destruction of Industry," *CEPAL Review* 23 (August 1984), 107-121.

1245. Trask, Roger R. "Spruille Braden versus George Messersmith: World War II, the Cold War, and the Argentine Policy, 1945-1947," *Journal of Inter-American Studies and World Affairs* 26:1 (February 1984), 69-95.

1246. Tulchin, Joseph S. "Authoritarian Regimes and Foreign Policy: The Case of Argentina." In *Latin American Nations in World Politics,* edited by Heraldo Muñoz and Joseph S. Tulchin. Boulder, CO: Westview, 1984. pp. 186-199.

1247.   Vacs, Aldo C. "Authoritarian Breakdown and Redemocratization in Argentina." In *Authoritarians and Democrats: Regime Transition in Latin America,* edited by James M. Malloy and Mitchell A. Seligson. Pittsburgh, PA: University of Pittsburgh Press, 1987. pp. 15-42.

1248.   Vacs, Aldo C. "From Hostility to Partnership: The New Character of Argentine-Soviet Relations." In *Soviet-Latin American Relations in the 1980s,* edited by Augusto Varas. Boulder, CO: Westview, 1987. pp. 174-196.

1249.   Vannucci, Albert P. "The Influence of Latin American Governments on the Shaping of United States Foreign Policy: The Case of U.S.-Argentine Relations, 1943-1948," *Journal of Latin American Studies* 18:2 (November 1986), 355-382.

1250.   Varas, Augusto. "The Soviet Union in the Foreign Relations of the Southern Cone." In *Latin American Nations in World Politics,* edited by Heraldo Muñoz and Joseph S. Tulchin. Boulder, CO: Westview, 1984. pp. 243-259.

1251.   Vasena, Adalbert Krieger, and Enrique Szewach. "Inflation and Indexation: Argentina." In *Inflation and Indexation: Argentina, Brazil, and Israel,* edited by John Williamson. Washington, DC: Institute for International Economics (dist. by M.I.T. Press), 1985. pp. 7-22.

1252.   Waisman, Carlos H. "Argentina: Economic and Political Implications." In *The Implications of Third World Military Industrialization,* edited by James Everett Katz. Lexington, MA: Lexington, 1986. pp. 93-102.

1253.   Walter, Richard J. "Politics, Parties, and Elections in Argentina's Province of Buenos Aires, 1912-42," *Hispanic American Historical Review* 64:4 (November 1984), 707-735.

1254.   Watson, Cynthia Ann. "Will Argentina Go to the Bomb after the Falklands?" *Inter-American Economic Affairs* 37:4 (Spring 1984), 63-80.

1255.   Wogart, Jan Peter. "Combining Price Stabilization with Trade and Financial Liberalization Policies: The Argentine Experience, 1976-1981," *Journal of Inter-American Studies and World Affairs* 25:4 (November 1983), 445-476.

1256.   Wynia, Gary W. "Argentina: Rebuilding the Relationship." In *From Gunboats to Diplomacy: New U.S. Policies for Latin America,* edited by Richard Newfarmer. Baltimore, MD: Johns Hopkins University Press, 1984. pp. 162-175.

1257.   Wynia, Gary W. "Democracy in Argentina," *Current History* 84:499 (February 1985), 53-56.

1258.   Wynia, Gary W. "The Frustation of Ungovernability." In *Politics, Policies, and Economic Development in Latin America,* edited by Robert G. Wesson. Stanford, CA: Hoover Institution Press, 1984. pp. 14-37.

1259.   Wynia, Gary W. "Readjusting to Democracy in Argentina," *Current*

History 86:516 (January 1987), 5-8.

1260. Zalazar, Daniel E. "De 'Facundo' a 'Conflicto y armonías de las razas en América'," *Inter-American Review of Bibliography* 35:2 (1985), 191-200.

1261. Zalazar, Daniel E. "Las oposiciones dualistas en el 'Facundo'," *Inter-American Review of Bibliography* 33:1 (1983), 3-12.

1262. Ziccardi, Alicia. "El tercer gobierno peronista y las villas miseria de la ciudad de Buenos Aires, 1973-1976," *Revista Mexicana de Sociología* 46:4 (October-December 1984), 145-172.

1263. Ziccardi, Alicia. "Villas miserias y favelas: sobre las relaciones entre las instituciones del Estado y la organización social en las democracias de los años sesenta," *Revista Mexicana de Sociología* 45:1 (January-March 1983), 45-67.

BARBADOS

Books and Monographs

1264. Dann, Graham. *The Quality of Life in Barbados.* London, Macmillan Caribbean, 1984. 290p.

1265. Duncan, Neville, and Kenneth O'Brien. *Women and Politics in Barbados, 1948-1981.* Cave Hill, Barbados: Institute of Social and Economic Research, University of West Indies, 1983. 68p.

1266. Fischer, Lawrence E. *Colonial Madness: Mental Health in the Barbadian Social Order.* New Brunswick, NJ: Rutgers University Press, 1985. 275p.

1267. Massiah, Joycelin. *Employed Women in Barbados: A Demographic Profile.* Cave Hill, Barbados: Institute of Social and Economic Research, University of West Indies, 1984. 131p.

1268. Puckrein, Gary A. *Little England: Plantation Society and Anglo-Barbadian Politics 1627-1700.* New York: New York University Press, 1984. 235p.

1269. Richardson, Bonham C. *Panama Money in Barbados, 1900-1920.* Knoxville: University of Tennessee Press, 1985. 283p.

Articles and Chapters

1270. Barrow, Christine. "Finding the Support: Strategies for Survival," *Social and Economic Studies* 35:2 (June 1986), 131-176.

1271. Barrow, Christine. "Male Images of Women in Barbados," *Social and Economic Studies* 35:3 (September 1986), 51-64.

1272.   Barrow, Christine. "Ownership and Control of Resources in Barbados: 1834 to the Present," *Social and Economic Studies* 32:3 (September 1983), 83-120.

1273.   Beckles, Hilary McD. "Rebels without Heroes: Slave Politics in Seventeenth Century Barbados," *Journal of Caribbean History* 18:2 (November 1983), 1-21.

1274.   Beckles, Hilary McD. "The Slave-Drivers' War: Bussa and the 1916 Barbados Slave Rebellion," *Boletín de Estudios Latinoamericanos y del Caribe* 39 (December 1985), 85-110.

1275.   Beckles, Hilary McD., and Andrew Downes. "The Economics of Transition to the Black Labor System in Barbados, 1630-1680," *Journal of Interdisciplinary History* 23:2 (Autumn 1987), 225-247.

1276.   Boamah, Daniel. "Wage Formation, Employment and Output in Barbados," *Social and Economic Studies* 34:4 (December 1985), 199-218.

1277.   Butler, Mary. "Mortality and Labour on the Codrington Estates, Barbados," *Journal of Caribbean History* 19:1 (May 1984), 48-67.

1278.   Codrington, Harold. "An Explanation of Short Term Capital Movements in Barbados," *Social and Economic Studies* 34:4 (December 1985), 45-57.

1279.   Downes, Andrew S. "Inflation in Barbados: An Econometric Investigation," *Economic Development and Cultural Change* 34:3 (April 1985), 532-521.

1280.   Gmelch, George. "Work, Innovation, and Investment: The Impact of Return Migrants in Barbados," *Human Organization* 46:2 (Summer 1987), 131-140.

1281.   Handler, Jerome. "Freedman and Slaves in the Barbados Militia," *Journal of Caribbean History* 19:1 (May 1984), 1-25.

1282.   Handler, Jerome S., and Robert S. Corruccini. "Plantation Slave Life in Barbados: A Physical Anthropological Analysis," *Journal of Interdisciplinary History* 14:1 (Summer 1983), 65-90.

1283.   Karch, Cecilia A. "The Transport and Communications Revolution in the West Indies: Imperial Policy and Barbadian Response, 1870-1914," *Journal of Caribbean History* 18:2 (November 1983), 22-42.

1284.   Long, Frank. "Industrialization and the Role of Industrial Development Corporations in a Caribbean Economy: A Study of Barbados, 1960-80," *Inter-American Economic Affairs* 37:3 (Winter 1983), 33-56.

1285.   Marshall, Dawn I. "Vincentian Contract Labour Migration to Barbados: The Satisfaction of Mutual Needs?" *Social and Economic Studies* 33:3 (September 1984), 63-92.

1286.   Sackey, James A., and Thywill E. Sackey. "Secondary School Employment Aspirations and Expectations and the Barbados Labour Market," *Social and Economic Studies* 34:3 (September 1984), 211-258.

1287.   Whitewall, Peter. "Profit Variation in the Barbados Manufacturing Sector," *Social and Economic Studies* 35:4 (December 1986), 67-91.

BELIZE

Books and Monographs

1288.   Belize. Ministry of Foreign Affairs and Economic Development. *Five Year Macro-Economic Plan for Belize, 1985-1989.* Belmopan, 1985. 48p.

1289.   Bolland, O. Nigel. *Belize: A New Nation in Central America.* Boulder, CO: Westview, 1986. 157p.

1290.   Bolland, O. Nigel. *A History of Belize: A Nation in the Making.* 2d rev. ed. Edited by Jessica G. Gordon. Belize City: Sunshine, 1984. 79p.

1291.   Hammond, Norman. *Nohmul: A Prehistoric Maya Community in Belize: Excavations, 1973-1983.* Oxford, England: British Archeological Reports, 1985. 2 vols.

1292.   Johnson, Wallace R. *A History of Christianity in Belize: 1776-1838.* Lanham, MD: University Press of America, 1985. 279p.

1293.   MacKie, Euan Wallace. *Excavations at Xunatunich and Pomona, Belize, in 1959-60: A Ceremonial Centre and Earthen Mound of the May Classic.* Oxford, England: British Archeological Reports, 1985. 216p.

1294.   Robertson, Robin A., and David A. Freidel, eds. *Archaeology at Cerros, Belize, Central America.* Dallas, TX: Southern Methodist University Press, 1986. 173p.

1295.   Sutherland, Anne. *Caye Caulker: Economic Success in a Belizean Fishing Village.* Boulder, CO: Westview, 1986. 153p.

1296.   Turner, B.L., II., and Peter D. Harrison, eds. *Pulltrouser Swamp, Ancient Maya Habitat, Agriculture and Settlement in Northern Belize.* Austin: University of Texas Press, 1983. 294p.

1297.   World Bank. *Belize: Economic Report.* Washington, DC, 1984. 111p.

Articles and Chapters

1298.   Bolland, O. Nigel. "Alcaldes and Reservations: British Policy towards the Maya in Late Nineteenth Century Belize," *América Indígena* 47:1 (January-March 1987), 33-75.

1299.   Broad, Dave. "Belize: On the Rim of the Cauldron," *Monthly Review* 35:9 (February 1984), 38-47.

1300.   Brockman, C. Thomas. "El sistema de fiestas en el noroeste de Belice," *América Indígena* 47:1 (January-March 1987), 121-138.

1301.   Brockmann. C. Thomas. "Women and Development in Northern Belize," *Journal of Developing Areas* (July 1985), 501-513.

1302.   Davidson, William V. "The Amerindians of Belize: An Overview," *América Indígena* 47:1 (January-March 1987), 9-22.

1303.   Everitt, John C. "The Growth and Development of Belize City," *Journal of Latin American Studies* 18:1 (May 1986), 75-112.

1304.   Fursman, Noël. "Belice: balance de los dos primeros años de vida independiente," *Foro Internacional* 24:2 (October-December 1983), 131-152.

1305.   González, Nancie L. "Una mayor recompensa en el cielo: actividades de misioneros metodistas entre los amerindios de Belice," *América Indígina* 47:1 (January-March 1987), 139-168.

1306.   Green, William A. "The Perils of Comparative History: Belize and the British Sugar Colonies after Slavery," *Comparative Studies in Society and History* 26:1 (January 1984), 112-119.

1307.   Jantzen, Carl R. "From the Maya to the Mennonites: Intercommunity Relationships in West-Central Belize," *América Indígena* 47:1 (January-March 1987), 169-192.

1308.   Joefield-Napier, Wallace. "External Public Debt and Public Finances in OECS Member Countries and Belize: 1977-82," *Social and Economic Studies* 34:4 (December 1985), 59-89.

1309.   Nelkin-Terner, Antoinette. "Belice: tiempos y espacios," *América Indígena* 47:1 (January-March 1987), 23-31.

1310.   Palacio, Joseph O. "Age As Source of Differentiation Within a Garifuna Village in Southern Belize," *América Indígena* 47:1 (January-March 1987), 97-119.

1311.   Pearce, Douglas G. "Planning for Tourism in Belize," *Geographical Review* 74:3 (July 1984), 291-303.

1312.   Philip, George. "Belize: The Troubled Regional Context," *World Today* 40:8-9 (August-September 1984), 370-376.

1313.   Thorndike, Tony. "The Conundrum of Belize: An Anatomy of a Dispute," *Social and Economic Studies* 32:2 (June 1983), 65-102.

1314.   Wilk, Richard R. "The Search for Tradition in Southern Belize: A Personal Narrative," *América Indígena* 47:1 (January-March 1987), 77-95.

BOLIVIA

Books and Monographs

1315. Bakewell, Peter. *Miners of the Red Mountain: Indian Labor in Potosí, 1545-1650.* Albuquerque: University of New Mexico Press, 1984. 213p.

1316. Bieber, León Enrique. *Las relaciones económicas de Bolivia con Alemania, 1880-1920.* Berlin, West Germany: Colloquium Verlag, 1984. 134p.

1317. Calderón, Fernando, and Jorge Dandler, comps. *Bolivia: la fuerza histórico del campesinado.* Cochabamba, Bolivia: Centro de Estudios de la Realidad Economia y Social, 1984. 625p.

1318. Cole, Jeffrey A. *The Potosí Mita, 1573-1700: Compulsory Indian Labor in the Andes.* Stanford, CA: Stanford University Press, 1985. 206p.

1319. Dunkerley, James. *Rebellion in the Veins: Political Struggle in Bolivia, 1952-1982.* London: Verso, 1984. 385p.

1320. Economic Commission for Latin America. *Los Bancos transnacionales, el estado y el endeudamiento externo en Bolivia.* Santiago, Chile; New York: United Nations, 1983. 282p.

1321. Gill, Lesley. *Peasants, Entrepreneurs, and Social Change: Frontier Development in Lowland Bolivia.* Boulder, CO: Westview, 1987. 246p.

1322. Havet, José. *Diffusion of Power: Rural Elites in a Bolivian Province.* Ottawa: University of Ottawa Press, 1985. 156p.

1323. Healy, Kevin. *Caciques y patrones: una experiencia de desarrollo rural en el sud de Bolivia.* Cochabamba, Bolivia: Buitre, 1984. 431p.

1324. Jordán Pando, Roberto. *De Bolivar a la revolución boliviana.* Buenos Aires: Legasa, 1984. 162p.

1325.   Knudson, Jerry W. *Bolivia, Press and Revolution, 1932-1964.* Lanham, MD: University Press of America, 1986. 488p.

1326.   Larson, Brooke. *Explotación agraria y resistencia campesina: cinco ensayos historicos sobre Cochabamba, siglos XVI-XIX.* 2d ed. Cochabamba, Bolivia: Centro de Estudios de la Realidad Economica y Social, 1984. 214p.

1327.   Mörner, Magnus. *The Andean Past: Land, Societies and Conflicts.* New York: Columbia University Press, 1985. 300p.

1328.   Stearman, Allyn McLean. *Camba and Kolla: Migration and Development in Santa Cruz, Bolivia.* Gainesville: University of Central Florida Press, 1985. 227p.

1329.   Zavaleta Mercado, Rene. *Lo nacional-popular en Bolivia.* Mexico City: Siglo Veintiuno, 1986. 273p.

Articles and Chapters

1330.   Alexander, Robert J. "Bolivia's Democratic Experiment, *Current History* 84:499 (February 1985), 73-76.

1331.   Ardaya Salinas, Gloria. "The Barzolas and the Housewives Committee." In *Women and Change in Latin America,* edited by June Nash and Helen Safa. South Hadley, MA: Bergin & Garvey, 1986. pp. 326-343.

1332.   Bailey, Jennifer L., and Torbjørn L. Knutsen. "Surgery without Anesthesia: Bolivia's Response to Economic Chaos," *World Today* 43:3 (March 1987), 47-51.

1333.   Buechler, Judith-Maria. "Trade and Market in Bolivia before 1953: An Ethnologist in the Garden of Ethnohistory," *Ethnohistory* 30:2 (Spring 1983), 107-119.

1334.   Buechler, Judith-Maria. "Women in Petty Commodity Production in La Paz, Bolivia." In *Women and Change in Latin America,* edited by June Nash and Helen Safa. South Hadley, MA: Bergin & Garvey, 1986. pp. 165-188.

1335.   Carter, William E. "Religion in the Andes." In *The Catholic Church and Religions in Latin America,* edited by Thomas C. Bruneau, Chester E. Gabriel and Mary Mooney. Montreal, Canada: Centre for Developing Area Studies, McGill University Press, 1984. pp. 88-118.

1336.   Crandon, Libbet. "Medical Dialogue and the Political Economy of Medical Pluralism: A Case from Rural Highland Bolivia," *American Ethnologist* 13:3 (August 1986), 463-478.

1337.   Dandler, Jorge. "El desarrollo de la agricultura, políticas estatales y el proceso de acumulación en Bolivia," *Estudios Rurales Latino-americanos* 7:2 (May-August 1984), 81-149.

1338.   Delgado P., Guillermo. "Industrial Stagnation and Women's Strategies for Survival at the Siglo XX and Unica Mines." In *Miners and Mining in the Americas,* edited by Thomas Greaves and William Culver.

Manchester, England; Dover, NH: Manchester University Press, 1985. pp. 162-170.

1339.   Dunkerley, James. "The Bolivian Crisis," *New Left Review* 155 January-February 1986), 86-106.

1340.   Eastwood, D.A., and H.J. Pollard. "The Development of Colonization in Lowland Bolivia: Objectives and Evaluation," *Boletín de Estudios Latinoamericanos y del Caribe* 38 (June 1985), 61-82.

1341.   Eckstein, Susan, and Frances Hagopian. "The Limits of Industrialization in the Less Developed World: Bolivia," *Economic Development and Cultural Change* 32:1 (October 1983), 63-95.

1342.   Fox, David J. "Bolivian Mining: A Crisis in the Making." In *Miners and Mining in the Americas,* edited by Thomas Greaves and William Culver. Manchester, England; Dover, NH: Manchester University Press, 1985. pp. 108-133.

1343.   Gill, Lesley. "Frontier Expansion and Settlement in Lowland Bolivia," *Journal of Peasant Studies* 14:3 (April 1987), 380-398.

1344.   Godoy, Ricardo A. "Entrepreneurial Risk Management in Peasant Mining: The Bolivian Experience." In *Miners and Mining in the Americas,* edited by Thomas Greaves and William Culver. Manchester, England; Dover, NH: Manchester University Press, 1985. pp. 136-161.

1345.   Godoy, Ricardo A. "Technical and Economic Efficiency of Peasant Miners in Bolivia," *Economic Development and Cultural Change* 34:1 (October 1985), 103-120.

1346.   Greaves, Thomas C., Xavier Albo, and Godofredo Sandoval S. "Becoming a Tin Miner." In *Miners and Mining in the Americas,* edited by Thomas Greaves and William Culver. Manchester, England; Dover, NH: Manchester University Press, 1985. pp. 171-191.

1347.   Hillman, John. "The Emergence of the Tin Industry in Bolivia," *Journal of Latin American Studies* 16:2 (November 1984), 403-437.

1348.   Kohl, James V. "National Revolution to Revolution of Restoration: Arms and Factional Politics in Bolivia," *Inter-American Economic Affairs* 39:1 (Summer 1985), 3-31.

1349.   Ladman, Jerry R. "Loan-Transactions Costs, Credit Rationing, and Market Structure: The Case of Bolivia." In *Undermining Rural Development with Cheap Credit,* edited by Dale W. Adams, Douglas H. Graham, and J.D. Von Pischke. Boulder, CO: Westview, 1984. pp. 104-119.

1350.   Langer, Erick D. "Andean Banditry and Peasant Community Organization, 1882-1930." In *Bandidos: The Varieties of Latin American Banditry,* edited by Richard W. Slatta. Westport, CT: Greenwood, 1987. pp. 113-130.

1351.   Langer, Erick D. "Franciscan Missions and Chuiriguano Workers: Colonization Acculturation and Indian Labor in Southeastern Bolivia," *The Americas* (January 1987), 305-322.

1352.   Langer, Erick D. "Labor Strikes and Reciprocity on Chuquisaca Haciendas," *Hispanic American Historical Review* 65:2 (May 1985), 255-277.

1353.   Léons, Madeline Barbara. "Political Penetration and Conflict Resolution in the Bolivian Yungas," *Journal of Developing Areas* 18:4 (July 1984), 465-480.

1354.   Lindert, Paul van. "Collective Consumption and the State in La Paz, Bolivia," *Boletín de Estudios Latinoamericanos y del Caribe* 41 (December 1986), 71-93.

1355.   Lora T., Eduardo. "Una nota sobre la hiperinflación boliviana," *El Trimestre Económico* 54:Special (September 1987), 213-220.

1356.   Malloy, James. "Bolivia's Economic Crisis," *Current History* 86:516 (January 1987), 9-12.

1357.   Malloy, James M., and Eduardo A. Gamarra. "The Transition to Democracy in Bolivia." In *Authoritarians and Democrats: Regime Transition in Latin America,* edited by James M. Malloy and Mitchell A. Seligson. Pittsburgh, PA: Pittsburgh University Press, 1987. pp. 93-119.

1358.   Mansilla, H.C.F. "La influencia de la tradición hispano-católica sobre las pautas de comportamiento sociopolítico en Bolivia," *Revista de Estudios Políticos* 53 (September-October 1986), 151-160.

1359.   Mendelberg, Uri. "The Impact of the Bolivian Agrarian Reform on Class Formation," *Latin American Perspectives* 12:3 (Summer 1985), 45-58.

1360.   Miller, Calvin J., and Jerry R. Ladman. "Factors Impeding Credit Use in Small-Farm Households in Bolivia," *Journal of Development Studies* 19:4 (July 1983), 522-538.

1361.   Morales Anaya, Juan Antonio. "Estabilización y nueva política económica en Bolivia," *El Trimestre Económico* 54:Special (September 1987), 179-211.

1362.   Nelson, Susan Rosales. "Bolivia: Continuity and Conflict in Religious Discourse." In *Religion and Political Conflict in Latin America,* edited by Daniel H. Levine. Chapel Hill: University of North Carolina Press, 1986. pp. 218-235.

1363.   Painter, Michael. "Unequal Exchange: The Dynamics of Settler Impoverishment and Environmental Destruction in Lowland Bolivia." In *Lands at Risk in the Third World: Local-Level Perspectives,* edited by Peter D. Little and Michael M. Horowitz. Boulder, CO: Westview, 1987. pp. 164-191.

1364.   Queiser Morales, Waltraud. "Bolivian Foreign Policy: The Struggle for Sovereignty." In *The Dynamics of Latin American Foreign Policies,* edited by Jennie K. Lincoln and Elizabeth G. Ferris. Boulder, CO: Westview, 1984. pp. 171-191.

1365.   Redclift, Michael. "Sustainability and the Market: Survival Strategies on the Bolivian Frontier," *Journal of Development Studies* 23:1

(October 1986), 93-105.

1366.   Rondinelli, Dennis A., and Hugh Evans. "Integrated Regional
          Development Planning: Linking Urban Centres and Rural Areas in
          Bolivia," *World Development* 11:1 (January 1983), 31-53.

1367.   Sage, Colin. "Intensification of Commodity Relations: Agricultural
          Specialization and Differentiation in the Cochabamba *Serranía,
          Bolivia*," *Bulletin of Latin American Research* 3:1 (January 1984),
          81-97.

1368.   Sandoval S., Godofredo. "Los migrantes de origen campesino en la
          ciudad de La Paz, Bolivia," *Estudios Rurales Latinoamericanos* 8:3
          (September-December 1985), 305-315.

1369.   Stearman, Allyn MacLean. "The Yukuí Connection: Another Look at
          Sirionó Deculturation," *American Anthropologist* 86:3 (September
          1984), 630-650.

1370.   Tandeter, Enrique, and Nathan Wachtel. "Precios y producción agraria:
          Potosí y Charcas en el siglo XVIII," *Desarrollo Económico* 23:90
          (July-September 1983), 197-232.

1371.   Whitehead, Laurence. "Bolivia's Failed Democratization, 1977-1980." In
          Transition from Authoritarian Rule, edited by Guillermo O'Donnell,
          Philippe C. Schmitter and Laurence Whitehead. Baltimore, MD: Johns
          Hopkins University Press, 1986. pp. 49-71.

BRAZIL

Books and Monographs

1372. Alves, Maria Helena Moreira. *State and Opposition in Military Brazil.* Austin: University of Texas Press, 1985. 352p.

1373. Alves, Rubem. *Protestantism and Repression: A Brazilian Case Study.* Translated by John Drury. Maryknoll, NY: Orbis, 1985. 215p.

1374. Anderson, Dole. *Management Education in Developing Countries: The Brazilian Experience.* Boulder, CO: Westview, 1987. 205p.

1375. Anglade, Christian, and Carlos Fortín, eds. *The State and Capital Accumulation in Latin America.* Vol. 1: *Brazil, Chile, Mexico.* Pittsburgh, PA: University of Pittsburgh Press, 1985. 254p.

1376. Barzelay, Michael. *The Politicized Market Economy: Alcohol in Brazil's Energy Strategy.* Berkeley: University of California Press, 1986. 289p.

1377. Branford, Sue, and Oriel Glock. *The Last Frontier: Fighting over Land in the Amazon.* London: Zed (Totowa, NJ: Dist. by Biblio Distribution Center), 1985. 182p.

1378. Bunker, Stephen G. *Underdeveloping the Amazon: Unequal Exchange and the Failure of the Modern State.* Chicago: University of Illinois Press, 1985. 279p.

1379. Camargo, Aspásia, Eduardo Raposo, and Sérgio Flaksman. *O Nordeste e a política: diálogo com José Américo de Almeida.* Rio de Janeiro: Nova Fronteira, 1984. 579p.

1380. Cardoso, Gerald. *Negro Slavery in the Sugar Plantations of Veracruz and Pernambuco 1550-1680: A Comparative Study.* Lanham, MD: University Press of America, 1983. 211p.

1381.   Carneiro, Maria Luiza Tucci. *Preconceito racial no Brasil-Colônia: os Cristãos-Novos.* São Paulo: Brasiliense, 1983. 264p.

1382.   Cignolli, Alberto. *Estado e força de trabalho: introdução à política social no Brasil.* São Paulo: Brasiliense, 1985. 120p.

1383.   Conrad, Robert Edgar, comp. *Children of God's Fire: A Documentary History of Black Slavery in Brazil.* Princeton, NJ: Princeton University Press, 1983. 515p.

1384.   Costa, Emília Viotti da. *The Brazilian Empire: Myths and Histories.* Revised translation of *Da monarquia à república.* Chicago: University of Chicago Press, 1985. 287p.

1385.   Crocker, Jon Christopher. *Vital Souls: Bororo Cosmology, Natural Symbolism, and Shamanism.* Tucson: University of Arizona Press, 1985. 380p.

1386.   Dassin, Joan, ed. *Torture in Brazil: A Report by the Archdiocese of São Paulo.* Translated by Jaime Wright. New York: Vintage, 1986. 238p.

1387.   Dean. Warren. *Brazil and the Struggle for Rubber: A Study in Environmental History.* Cambridge, England; New York: Cambridge University Press, 1987. 234p.

1388.   Dulles, John W. F. *Brazilian Communism, 1935-1945.* Austin: University of Texas Press, 1983, 289p.

1389.   Dulles, John W. F. *The São Paulo Law School and the Anti-Vargas Resistance, 1938-1945.* Austin: University of Texas Press, 1986. 262p.

1390.   Economic Commission for Latin America. *Dos estudios sobre empresas transnacionales en Brasil.* Santiago, Chile: United Nations, 1983. 141p.

1391.   Economic Commission for Latin America and the Caribbean. *Trade Relations between Brazil and the United States.* Santiago, Chile; 1985. 154p.

1392.   Fausto, Boris. *Crime e Cotidiano: a criminalidade em São Paulo (1880-1924).* São Paulo: Brasiliense, 1984. 294p.

1393.   Foot, Francisco. *Nem pátria, nem patrão: vida operária e cultura anarquista no Brasil.* São Paulo: Brasiliense, 1983. 199p.

1394.   Griggs, William Clark. *The Elusive Eden: Frank McMullan's Confederate Colony in Brazil.* Austin: University of Texas Press, 1987. 218p.

1395.   Hahner, June E. *Poverty and Politics: The Urban Poor in Brazil, 1870-1920.* Albuquerque: University of New Mexico Press, 1986. 415p.

1396.   Huggins, Martha Knisely. *From Slavery to Vagrancy in Brazil: Crime and Social Control in the Third World.* New Brunswick, NJ: Rutgers University Press, 1984. 183p.

1397.   Jatobá, Jorge, ed. *Emprego no Nordeste, 1950-1980: modernização e heterogeneidade, um estudo para uma política de emprego.* Recife,

Brazil: Fundação Joaquim Nabuco; Massangara, 1983. 535p.

1398. Jones, Rodney W., and Steven A. Hildreth. *Modern Weapons and Third World Powers.* Boulder, CO: Westview, 1984. 125p.

1399. Kowarick, Lúcio. *The Subjugation of Labour: The Constitution of Capitalism in Brazil.* Providence, RI: Foris, 1987. 114p.

1400. Kuznesof, Elizabeth Anne. *Household Economy and Urban Development: São Paulo, 1765-1836.* Boulder, CO: Westview, 1986. 216p.

1401. Lesbaupin, Ivo. *As classes populares e os Direitos Humanos.* Petrópolis, Brazil: Vozes, 1984. 195p.

1402. Lewin, Linda. *Politics and Parentela in Paraiba: A Case Study of Family-Based Oligarchy in Brazil.* Princeton, NJ: Princeton University Press, 1987. 497p.

1403. Lockhart, James, and Stuart B. Schwartz. *Early Latin America: A History of Colonial Spanish America and Brazil.* Cambridge, England; New York: Cambridge University Press, 1983. 480p.

1404. Macaulay, Neill. *Dom Pedro: The Struggle for Liberty in Brazil and Portugal, 1798-1834.* Durham, NC: Duke University Press, 1986. 361p.

1405. Mainwaring, Scott. *The Catholic Church and Politics in Brazil, 1916-1985.* Stanford, CA: Stanford University Press, 1986. 328p.

1406. Mattoso, Kátia M. de Queirós. *To Be a Slave in Brazil, 1550-1888.* Translated by Arthur Goldhammer. New Brunswick, NJ: Rutgers University Press, 1986. 250p.

1407. Mendonça, Sonia Regina de. *Estado e economia no Brasil: opções de desenvolvimento.* Rio de Janeiro: Graal, 1986. 106p.

1408. Meyers, Kenneth, and F. Desmond McCarthy. *Brazil: Medium-Term Policy Analysis.* Washington, DC: World Bank, 1985. 102p.

1409. Moreira, Maria Helena. *State and Opposition in Military Brazil.* Austin: University of Texas Press, 1985. 368p.

1410. Novaes e Cruz, Adelina Maria Alves, Célia Maria Leite Costa, Maria Celina Soares D'Araújo, and Suely Braga da Silva, eds. *Impasse na Democracia Brasileira 1951-1955: Coletânea de Documentos.* Rio de Janeiro: Fundação Getúlio Vargas, 1983. 477p.

1411. Pereira, Luiz Carlos Bresser. *Development and Crisis in Brazil, 1930-1983.* Translated by Monica Van Dyke. Boulder, CO: Westview, 1984. 241 p.

1412. Pereira, Luiz Carlos Bresser, and Yoshiaki Nakano. *The Theory of Inertial Inflation: The Foundation of Economic Reform in Brazil and Argentina.* Translated by Colleen Reeks. Boulder, CO: Lynne Rienner, 1987. 206p.

1413. Reis, João José. *Rebelião escrava no Brasil: a história do levante dos malês, 1835.* São Paulo: Brasiliense, 1986. 293p.

1414. Roett, Riordan. *Brazil: Politics in a Patrimonial Society.* 3d ed. New York: Praeger, 1984. 218p.

1415. Rothman, Harry, Rod Greenshields, and Francisco Rosillo Calle. *Energy from Alcohol: The Brazilian Experience.* Lexington: University of Kentucky Press, 1983. 188p.

1416. Salazar-Carrillo, Jorge, and Roberto Fendt, Jr., eds. *The Brazilian Economy in the Eighties.* New York: Pergamon, 1985. 191p.

1417. Santos, Corcino Medeiros dos. *Economia e sociedade do Rio Grande do Sul: Século XVIII.* São Paulo: Nacional, 1984. 216p.

1418. Schwartz, Stuart B. *Sugar Plantations in the Formation of Brazilian Society: Bahia, 1550-1835.* New York: Cambridge University Press, 1985. 616p.

1419. Seckinger, Ron. *The Brazilian Monarchy and the South American Republics, 1822-1831: Diplomacy and State Building.* Baton Rouge: Louisiana State University Press, 1984. 187p.

1420. Seitenfus, Ricardo Antônio Silva. *O Brasil de Getúlio Vargas e a formação dos blocos, 1930-1942: o processo do envolvimento brasileiro na II Guerra Mundial.* São Paulo: Nacional, 1985. 488p.

1421. Selcher, Wayne A., ed. *Political Liberalization in Brazil: Dynamics, Dilemmas, and Future Prospects.* Boulder, CO: Westview, 1986. 272p.

1422. Silva, Maria Beatriz Nizza da. *Sistema de casamento no Brasil colonial.* São Paulo: Editora da Universidade de São Paulo, 1984. 264p.

1423. Sorj, Bernardo, and Maria Herminia Tavares de Almeida, comps. *Sociedade e política no Brasil pós-64.* São Paulo: Brasiliense, 1983. 261p.

1424. Suzigan, Wilson. *Indústria brasileira: origem e desenvolvimento.* São Paulo: Brasiliense, 1986. 403p.

1425. Tigre, Paulo Bastos. *Technology and Competition in the Brazilian Computer Industry.* New York: St. Martin's, 1983. 186p.

1426. Topik, Steven. *The Political Economy of the Brazilian State, 1889-1930.* Austin: University of Texas Press, 1987. 241p.

1427. Trebat, Thomas J. *Brazil's State-Owned Enterprises: A Case Study of the State as Entrepreneur.* Cambridge, England; New York: Cambridge University Press, 1983. 294p.

1428. Weinstein, Barbara. *The Amazon Rubber Boom, 1850-1920.* Stanford, CA: Stanford University Press, 1983. 356p.

1429. Wirth, John D., Edson de Oliveira Nunes, and Thomas E. Bogenschild. *State and Society in Brazil: Continuity and Change.* Boulder, CO: Westview, 1987. 349p.

Articles and Chapters

1430. Abreu, Marcelo de Paiva. "Anglo-Brazilian Economic Relations and the Consolidation of American Preeminence in Brazil, 1930-1945." In *Latin America, Economic Imperialism and the State*, edited by Christopher Abel and Colin M. Lewis. London; Dover, NH: Athlone, 1985. 379-393.

1431. Abreu, Marcelo de Paiva. "Argentina e Brasil na década de 30: o impacto das políticas econômicas internacionais da Grã-Bretanha e dos EUA," *Revista Brasileira de Economia* 38:4 (October-December 1984), 309-326.

1432. Abreu, Marcelo de Paiva, and Winston Fritsh. "Lessons of History: 1929-33 and 1979-8?," *International Journal of Political Economy* 17:1 (Spring 1987), 45-63.

1433. Accioli, Wilson. "O colégio eleitoral do Presidente da República," *Revista Brasileira de Estudos Políticos* 57 (July 1983), 217-234.

1434. Adler, Emanuel. "Ideological 'guerrillas' and the Quest for Technological Autonomy: Brazil's Domestic Computer Industry," *International Organization* 40:3 (Summer 1986), 673-705.

1435. Aguiar, Marco Antônio de Souza, Marcos Arruda, and Parsifal Flores. "Economic Dictatorship versus Democracy in Brazil," *Latin American Perspectives* 11:1 (Winter 1984), 13-25.

1436. Alden, Dauril. "El indio desechable en el estado de Maranhão durante los siglos XVII y XVIII," *América Indígena* 45:2 (April-June 1985), 427-446.

1437. Alden, Dauril, and Joseph C. Miller. "Out of Africa: The Slave Trade and the Transmission of Smallpox to Brazil, 1560-1831," *Journal of Interdisciplinary History* 18:2 (Autumn 1987), 195-224.

1438. Alves, Maria Helena Moreira. "Grassroots Organization, Trade Unions and the Church: A Challenge to the Controlled Abertura in Brazil," *Latin American Perspective* 11:1 (Winter 1984), 73-102.

1439. Alves, Maria Helena Moreira. "Mechanisms of Social Control of the Military Governments in Brazil, 1964-80." In *Latin American Prospects for the 1980s*, edited by Archibald R.M. Ritter and David H. Pollock. New York: Praeger, 1983. 240-303.

1440. Alves, Maria Helena Moreira. "The PT and the New Republic," *Bulletin of Latin American Research* 4:2 (1985), 95-98.

1441. Ames, Barry. "The Congressional Connection: The Structure of Politics and the Distribution of Public Expenditures in Brazil's Competitive Period," *Comparative Politics* 19:2 (January 1987), 147-171.

1442. Andrade, Thompson Almeida. "Custos de urbanização: os enfoques financeiro, de eficiência e de equidade social," *Revista Brasileira de Economia* 37:2 (April-June 1983), 131-146.

1443. Arida, Persio, and André Lara-Resende. "Inertial Inflation and Monetary

Reform: Brazil." In *Inflation and Indexation: Argentina, Brazil, and Israel,* edited by John Williamson. Washington, DC: Institute for International Economics (dist. by M.I.T. Press), 1985. 27-45.

1444.   Azzoni, Carlos Roberto. "Teoria econômica versus evidência empírica: o caso da localização industrial em São Paulo," *Revista Brasileira de Economia* 37:2 (April-June 1983), 177-206.

1445.   Bacchus, Wilfred A. "Long-Term Military Rulership in Brazil: Ideologic Consensus and Dissensus, 1963-1983," *Journal of Political and Military Sociology* 13:1 (Spring 1985), 99-123.

1446.   Bacha, Edmar L. "External Shocks and Growth Prospects: The Case of Brazil, 1973-89," *World Development* 14:8 (August 1986), 919-936.

1447.   Baer, Werner. "Political Determinants of Development." In *Politics, Policies, and Economic Development in Latin America,* edited by Robert G. Wesson. Stanford, CA: Hoover Institution Press, 1984. 53-73.

1448.   Baer, Werner. "The Resurgence of Inflation in Brazil, 1974-86," *World Development* 15:8 (August 1987), 1007-1034.

1449.   Baer, Werner, Manuel A.R. da Fonseca, and Joaquim J.M. Guilhoto. "Structural Changes in Brazil's Industrial Economy, 1960-80," *World Development* 15:2 (February 1987), 275-286.

1450.   Baer, Werner, Richard Newfarmer, and Thomas Trebat. "On State Capitalism in Brazil: Some New Issues and Questions." In *The Public Sector in Latin America,* edited by Alfred H. Saulniers. Austin: Institute of Latin American Studies, University of Texas, 1984. 3-18.

1451.   Bak, Joan L. "Political Centralization and the Building of the Interventionist State in Brazil: Corporatism, Regionalism and Interest Group Politics in Rio Grande do Sul, 1930-1937," *Luso-Brazilian Review* 22:1 (Summer 1985), 9-25.

1452.   Baracho, José Alfredo de Oliveira. "Novos rumos do federalismo," *Revista Brasileira de Estudos Políticos* 56 (January 1983), 97-134.

1453.   Baracho, José Alfredo de Oliveira. "O projeto político brasileiro e as eleições nacionais," *Revista Brasileira de Estudos Políticos* 57 (July 1983), 29-145.

1454.   Barros, Alexandre de Souza Costa. "Back to the Barracks: An Option for the Brazilian Military," *Third World Quarterly* 7:1 (January 1985), 63-77.

1455.   Barros, Alexandre de Souza Costa. "Brazil." In *Arms Production in Developing Countries: An Analysis of Decision Making,* edited by James Everett Katz. Lexington, MA: Lexington, 1984. 73-87.

1456.   Barros, Alexandre de Souza Costa. "The Formulation and Implementation of Brazilian Foreign Policy: Itamaraty and the New Actors." In *Latin American Nations in World Politics,* edited by Heraldo Muñoz and Joseph S. Tulchin. Boulder, CO: Westview, 1984. 30-44.

1457.   Barros, Alexandre de Souza Costa. "Política exterior brasileña y el mito de Barón," *Foro Internacional* 24:1 (July-September 1983), 1-20.

1458.   Batista, Paulo Nogueira, Jr. "Rescheduling Brazil's Foreign Debt: Recent Developments and Prospects." In *Politics and Economics of External Debt Crisis: The Latin American Experience,* edited by Miguel S. Wionczek in collaboration with Luciano Tomassini. Boulder, CO: Westview, 1985. pp. 277-293.

1459.   Beiguelman, Paula. "The Destruction of Modern Slavery: The Brazilian Case," *Review* 6:3 (Winter 1983), 305-320.

1460.   Bills, David B., and Archibald O. Haller. "Socioeconomic Development and Social Stratification: Reassessing the Brazilian Case," *Journal of Developing Areas* 19:1 (October 1984), 59-69.

1461.   Birdsall, Nancy. "Public Inputs and Child Schooling in Brazil," *Journal of Development Economics* 18:1 (May-June 1985), 67-86.

1462.   Birdsall, Nancy, and M. Louise Fox. "Why Males Earn More: Location and Training of Brazilian School Teachers," *Economic Development and Cultural Change* 34:3 (April 1985), 533-556.

1463.   Boddewyn, J. J. "Developed Advertising Self-Regulation in a Developing Country: The Case of Brazil's CONAR," *Inter-American Economic Affairs* 38:3 (Winter 1984), 75-93.

1464.   Braga, Helson C., and José W. Rossi. "Mensuração da eficiência técnica na indústria brasileira: 1980," *Revista Brasileira de Economia* 40:1 (January-March 1986), 89-118.

1465.   Braverman, Avishay, Jeffrey S. Hammer, and Antônio Salazar P. Brandão. "Análise econômica das políticas agrícolas no Brasil: os casos do trigo e da soja," *Revista Brasileira de Economia* 41:1 (January-March 1987), 51-80.

1466.   Brigagão, Clóvis. "The Brazilian Arms Industry," *Journal of International Affairs* 40:1 (Summer 1986). 101-114.

1467.   Brito, Angela Neves-Xavier de. "Brazilian Women in Exile: The Quest for an Identity," *Latin American Perspectives* 13:2 (Spring 1986), 58-80.

1468.   Brito, Fausto. "O estado tutelar: o INDI e a industrialização na década de 70," *Revista Brasileira de Estudos Políticos* 58 (January 1984), 241-257.

1469.   Brito, Luiz Navarro de. "As eleições de novembro e suas consequências," *Revista Brasileira de Estudos Políticos* 57 (July 1983), 147-164.

1470.   Brooke, Nigel. "The Diversification of Secondary Education in Latin America: The Case of Brazil." In *Education in Latin America,* edited by Colin Brock and Hugh Lawlor. Dover, NH: Croom Helm, 1985. 146-162.

1471.   Browder, John O. "Brazil's Export Promotion Policy, 1980-1984: Impacts on the Amazon's Industrial Wood Sector," *Journal of Developing Areas* 21:3 (April 1987), 285-304.

1472.   Brown, Diana. "Religion as an Adaptive Institution: Umbanda in Brazil."
         In *The Catholic Church and Religions in Latin America,* edited by
         Thomas C. Bruneau, Chester E. Gabriel and Mary Mooney. Montreal,
         Canada: Centre for Developing Area Studies, McGill University
         Press, 1984. 119-152.

1473.   Bruce, David. "Brazil Plays the Japan Card," *Third World Quarterly* 5:4
         (October 1983), 848-860.

1474.   Bruneau, Thomas C. "Brazil: The Catholic Church and Basic Christian
         Communities." In *Religion and Political Conflict in Latin America,*
         edited by Daniel H. Levine. Chapel Hill: University of North
         Carolina Press, 1986. 106-123.

1475.   Bruneau, Thomas C. "Church and Politics in Brazil: The Genesis of
         Change," *Journal of Latin American Studies* 17:2 (November 1985),
         271-293.

1476.   Bruneau, Thomas C. "Church, State and Religion in Brazil." In *The
         Catholic Church and Religions in Latin America,* edited by Thomas
         C. Bruneau, Chester E. Gabriel, and Mary Mooney. Montreal,
         Canada: Centre for Developing Areas, McGill University, 1984. 13-
         40.

1477.   Bruneau, Thomas C. "Consolidating Civilian Brazil," *Third World
         Quarterly* 7:4 (October 1985), 973-987.

1478.   Bunker, Stephen G. "Modes of Extraction, Unequal Exchange, and the
         Progressive Underdevelopment of an Extreme Periphery: The
         Brazilian Amazon, 1600-1980," *American Journal of Sociology* 89:5
         (March 1984), 1017-1060.

1479.   Caldeira, Teresa P.R. "Electoral Struggles in a Neighborhood on the
         Periphery of São Paulo," *Politics and Society* 15:1 (1986-87), 43-66.

1480.   Camargo, José Márcio, and Franklin Serrano. "Os dois mercados: homens
         e mulheres na indústria brasileira," *Revista Brasileira de Economia*
         37:4 (October-December 1983), 435-447.

1481.   Carneiro, Dionisio Dias. "El Plan Cruzado: una temprana evaluación
         después de diez meses," *El Trimestre Económico* 54:Special
         (September 1987), 251-274.

1482.   Carrion, Eduardo K.M. "Representação proporcional e voto distrital,"
         Revista Brasileira de Estudos Políticos 56 (January 1983), 135-146.

1483.   Castro, Antônio Barros de. "Ajuste por adaptación estructural: la
         experiencia brasileña," *El Trimestre Económico* 52:207 (July-
         September 1985), 705-719.

1484.   Chacon, Vamireh. "A revolução pelo voto," *Revista Brasileira de Estudos
         Políticos* 59 (July 1984), 71-121.

1485.   Chandler, Billy Jaynes. "Brazilian *Cangaceiros* as Social Bandits: A
         Critical Appraisal." In *Bandidos: The Varieties of Latin American
         Banditry,* edited by Richard W. Slatta. Westport, CT: Greenwood,
         1987. 97-112.

1486.   Chilcote, Ronald H. "Reflections on Brazilian Political Thought and the
         Crisis of the Intellectual," *Luso-Brazilian Review* 22:2 (Winter 1985),
         111-121.

1487.   Chilcote, Ronald H. "Toward the Democratic Opening in Latin America:
         The Case of Brazil," *Monthly Review* 35:9 (February 1984), 15-24.

1488.   Clements, Benedict J. "Foreign Trade Strategies and Their Impact on
         Employment: The Case of Brazil," *Bulletin of Latin American
         Research* 6:2 (1987), 183-195.

1489.   Cohen, Youssef. "Democracy from Above: The Political Origins of
         Military Dictatorship in Brazil," *World Politics* 40:1 (October 1987),
         30-54.

1490.   Dassin, Joan R. "The Brazilian Press and the Politics of Abertura,"
         Journal of Inter-American Studies and World Affairs 26:3 (August
         1984), 385-414.

1491.   Delson, Roberta M. "Sugar Production for the Nineteenth Century
         British Market: Rethinking the Roles of Brazil and the British West
         Indies." In *Crisis and Change in the International Sugar Economy,
         1860-1914,* edited by Bill Albert and Adrian Graves. Edinburgh,
         Scotland: ISC Press, 1984. 59-82.

1492.   Denslow, David, Jr., and William Tyler. "Perspectives on Poverty and
         Income Inequality in Brazil," *World Development* 12:10 (October
         1984), 1019-1028.

1493.   Diniz, Clélio Campolina. "Economia e planejamento em Minas Gerais,"
         Revista Brasileira de Estudos Políticos 58 (January 1984), 259-295.

1494.   Diniz, Eli. "The Political Transition in Brazil: A Reappraisal of the
         Dynamics of the Political Opening," *Studies in Comparative
         International Development* 21:2 (Summer 1986), 63-73.

1495.   Di Tella, Torcuato S. "The Popular Parties in Brazil and Argentina,"
         Government and Opposition 19:2 (Spring 1984), 250-268.

1496.   Dressler, William W., José Ernesto Dos Santos, Philip N. Gallagher, Jr.,
         and Fernando E. Viteri. "Arterial Blood Pressure and Modernization
         in Brazil," *American Anthropologist* 89:2 (June 1987), 398-409.

1497.   Drobny, Andres, and John Wells. "Wages, Minimum Wages, and Income
         Distribution in Brazil: Results from the Construction Industry,"
         Journal of Development Economics 13:3 (December 1983), 305-330.

1498.   Druckman, Daniel, and Elaine Vaurio. "Regimes and Selection of
         Political and Military Leaders: Brazilian Cabinet Ministers and
         Generals," *Journal of Political and Military Sociology* 11:2 (Fall
         1983), 301-324.

1499.   D'Souza, Herbert, "Return Ticket to Brazil," *Third World Quarterly* 9:1
         (January 1987), 203-211.

1500.   Duncan Baretta, Silvio R., and John Markoff. "Brazil's *Abertura*: A
         Transition from What to What?" In *Authoritarians and Democrats:*

Regime Transition in Latin America, edited by James M. Malloy and Mitchell A. Seligson. Pittsburgh, PA: University of Pittsburgh Press, 1987. 43-65.

1501.   Eakin, Marshall C. "Business Imperialism and British Enterprise in Brazil: The St. John d'el Rey Mining Company, Limited, 1830-1960," *Hispanic American Historical Review* 66:4 (November 1986), 697-741.

1502.   Eakin, Marshall C. "Race and Identity: Sílvio Romero, Science, and Social Thought in Late 19th Century Brazil," *Luso-Brazilian Review* 22:2 (Winter 1985), 151-174.

1503.   Eakin, Marshall C. "The Role of British Capital in the Development of Brazilian Gold Mining." In *Miners and Mining in the Americas,* edited by Thomas Greaves and William Culver. Manchester, England; Dover, NH: Manchester University Press, 1985. 10-28.

1504.   Ebinger, Charles K. "The Brazilian Energy Sector." In *Banks, Petrodollars, and Sovereign Debtors,* edited by Penelope Hartland-Thunberg and Charles K. Ebinger. Boulder, CO: Westview, 1986. 131-153.

1505.   Erber, Fabio Stefano. "The Development of the 'Electronic Complex' and Government Policies in Brazil," *World Development* 13:3 (March 1985), 293-309.

1506.   Evans, Peter B. "State, Capital, and the Transformation of Dependence: The Brazilian Computer Case," *World Development* 14:7 (July 1986), 791-808.

1507.   Evans, Peter B. "State, Local and Multinational Capital in Brazil: Prospects for the Stability of the 'Triple Alliance' in the Eighties." In *Latin America in the World Economy: New Perspectives,* edited by Diana Tussie. New York: St. Martin's, 1983. 139-168.

1508.   Evans, Peter B. "Three Views of Regime Change and Party Organization in Brazil," *Politics and Society* 15:1 (1986-87), 1-21.

1509.   Evers, Tilman. "Labor-Force Reproduction and Urban Movements: Illegal Subdivision of Land in São Paulo," *Latin American Perspectives* 14:2 (Spring 1987), 187-203.

1510.   Fearnside, Philip M. "Agricultural Plans for Brazil's Grande Carajás Program: Lost Opportunity for Sustainable Local Development?" *World Development* 14:3 (March 1986), 385-409.

1511.   Fendt, Roberto Jr. "Bilateral and Multilateral Aspects of Brazilian Foreign Policy." In *Latin America, Western Europe, and the United States: Reevaluating the Atlantic Triangle,* edited by Wolf Grabendorff and Riordan Roett. New York: Praeger, 1985. 135-146.

1512.   Ferreira, Léo da Rocha, and Ronaldo Serôa da Motta. "Reavaliação econômica e novos ajustamentos do Proálcool," *Revista Brasileira de Economia* 41:1 (January-March 1987), 117-133.

1513.   Ferreira, Manoel Gonçalves Filho. "As eleições de novembro e o 'equilíbrio federativo'," *Revista Brasileira de Estudos Políticos* 57

(July 1983), 181-186.

1514.   Fishlow, Albert. "Brazil: The Case of the Missing Relationship." In *From Gunboats to Diplomacy: New U.S. Policies for Latin America,* edited by Richard Newfarmer. Baltimore, MD: Johns Hopkins University Press, 1984. 147-161.

1515.   Fleischer, David V. "Constitutional and Electoral Engineering in Brazil: A Double-Edged Sword, 1964-1982," *Inter-American Economic Affairs* 37:4 (Spring 1984), 3-36.

1516.   Fleischer, David V. "'Ingenieras' política en Suramérica: Brasil en perspectiva comparada," *Revista de Estudios Políticos* 36 (November-December 1983), 61-105.

1517.   Font, Mauricio A. "Coffee Planters, Politics, and Development in Brazil," *Latin American Research Review* 22:3 (1987), 69-90.

1518.   Forbes, Geraldo de F. "How Not to Do It, or the Brazilian Renegotiation Affair," *Journal of International Affairs* 38:1 (Summer 1984), 81-89.

1519.   Franco, Gustavo H.B. "Taxa de câmbio e oferta de moeda, 1880-1897: uma análise econométrica," *Revista Brasileira de Economia* 40:1 (January-March 1986), 63-88.

1520.   Frieden, Jeffry A. "The Brazilian Borrowing Experience: From Miracle to Debacle and Back," *Latin American Research Review* 22:1 (1987), 95-131.

1521.   Frieden, Jeffry A. "Third World Indebted Industrialization: International Finance and State Capitalism in Mexico, Brazil, Algeria, and South Korea." In *Postimperialism: International Capitalism and Development in the Late Twentieth Century,* edited by David G. Becker, Jeff Frieden, Sayer P. Schatz and Richard L. Sklar. Boulder, CO: Lynne Rienner, 1987. 131-159.

1522.   Furtado, Celso. "Rescuing Brazil, Reversing Recession," *Third World Quarterly* 6:3 (July 1984), 604-623.

1523.   Gabriel, Chester E. "Spiritism in Manaus: The Cults and Catholicism." In *The Catholic Church and Religions in Latin America,* edited by Thomas C. Bruneau, Chester E. Gabriel and Mary Mooney. Montreal, Canada: Centre for Developing Areas, McGill University, 1984. 153-187.

1524.   García, Brígida, Humberto Muñoz, and Orlandina de Oliveira. "Mercados de trabajo y familia: una comparación de dos ciudades brasileñas," *Revista Mexicana de Sociología* 45:1 (January-March 1983), 235-261.

1525.   Gerschman, Silvia. "O voto na favela," *Revista Brasileira de Estudos Políticos* 56 (January 1983), 155-177.

1526.   Góes, Walder de. "Brazil Turns to Western Europe: Changing Perspectives." In *Latin America, Western Europe, and the United States: Reevaluating the Atlantic Triangle,* edited by Wolf Grabendorff and Riordan Roett. New York: Praeger, 1985. 95-123.

1527.   Gomes, Eduardo Rodrigues. "Campo contra cidade: o ruralismo e a crise oligárquica no pensamento político brasileiro, 1910-1935," *Revista Brasileira de Estudos Políticos* 56 (January 1983), 49-96.

1528.   Gomes, Gustavo Maia. "Monetaristas, neostructuralistas e inflación brasileña en 1985," *El Trimestre Económico* 53:210 (April-June 1986), 283-313.

1529.   Gonçalves, Reinaldo. "Brazil's Search for Stabilization," *Third World Quarterly* 7:2 (April 1985), 279-300.

1530.   Graham, Douglas H., Howard Gauthier, and José Roberto Mendonça de Barros. "Thirty Years of Agricultural Growth in Brazil: Crop Performance, Regional Profile, and Recent Policy Review," *Economic Development and Cultural Change* 36:1 (October 1987), 1-34.

1531.   Greenfield, Gerald Michael. "Migrant Behavior and Elite Attitudes: Brazil's Great Drought, 1877-1879," *The Americas* 43:1 (July 1986), 69-85.

1532.   Guimarães, Edson P. "Uma nota sobre a influência da estrutura industrial na exportação de manufaturados brasileiros," *Revista Brasileira de Economia* 38:1 (January-March 1984), 95-110.

1533.   Hagopian, Frances, and Scott Mainwaring. "Democracy in Brazil: Problems and Prospects," *World Policy Journal* 4:3 (Summer 1987), 485-514.

1534.   Hahner, June E. "Recent Research on Women in Brazil," *Latin American Research Review* 20:3 (1985), 163-179.

1535.   Hakkert, Ralph. "Who Benefits from Economic Development? The Brazilian Income Distribution Controversy Revisited," *Boletín de Estudios Latinoamericanos y del Caribe* 36 (June 1984), 83-103.

1536.   Hall, Anthony. "Agrarian Crisis in Brazilian Amazonia: The Grande Carajás Programme," *Journal of Development Studies* 23:4 (July 1987), 522-552.

1537.   Hall, John R. "World-System Holism and Colonial Brazilian Agriculture: A Critical Case Analysis," *Latin American Research Review* 19:2 (1984), 43-69.

1538.   Hall, Lana L. "United States Food Aid and the Agricultural Development of Brazil and Colombia, 1954-73." In *Food, Politics, and Society in Latin America,* edited by John C. Super and Thomas C. Wright. Lincoln: University of Nebraska Press, 1985. 133-149.

1539.   Hanson, Carl A. "The European 'Renovation' and the Luso-Atlantic Economy, 1560-1715," *Review* 6:4 (Spring 1983), 475-530.

1540.   Hartland-Thunberg, Penelope. "Brazil's Interrupted Economic Miracle." In *Banks, Petrodollars, and Sovereign Debtors,* edited by Penelope Hartland-Thunberg and Charles K. Ebinger. Boulder, CO: Westview, 1986. 99-130.

1541.   Hewitt, W. E. "The Influence of Social Class on Activity Preferences of

Communidades Eclesiais de Base (CEBs) in the Archdiocese of São Paulo," *Journal of Latin American Studies* 19:1 (May 1987), 141-156.

1542. Higgs, David. "Unbelief and Politics in Rio de Janeiro during the 1790s," *Luso-Brazilian Review* 21:1 (Summer 1984), 13-31.

1543. Hill, Jonathan D. "Los misioneros y las fronteras," *América Indígena* 44:1 (January-March 1984), 183-190.

1544. Hilton, Stanley E. "The Argentine Factor in Twentieth-Century Brazilian Foreign Policy," *Political Science Quarterly* 100:1 (Spring 1985), 27-51.

1545. Hilton, Stanley E. "Brazil's International Economic Strategy, 1945-1960: Revival of the German Option," *Hispanic American Historical Review* 66:2 (May 1986), 287-318.

1546. Hilton, Stanley E. "The Overthrow of Getúlio Vargas in 1945: Diplomatic Intervention, Defense of Democracy, or Political Retribution?" *Hispanic American Historical Review* 67:1 (February 1987), 1-37.

1547. Hirst, Monica. "Democratic Transition and Foreign Policy: The Experience of Brazil." In *Latin American Nations in World Politics,* edited by Heraldo Muñoz and Joseph S. Tulchin. Boulder, CO: Westview, 1984. 216-229.

1548. Homem de Melo, Fernando. "Unbalanced Technological Change and Income Disparity in a Semi-open Economy: The Case of Brazil." In *Food, the State and International Political Economy,* edited by F. LaMond Tullis and W. Ladd Hollist. Lincoln: University of Nebraska Press, 1986. 262-275.

1549. Horta, Raul Machado. "Constituição e direitos individuais," *Revista Brasileira de Estudos Políticos* 59 (July 1984), 41-68.

1550. Horta, Raul Machado. "Reflexões sobre a constituinte," *Revista Brasileira de Estudos Políticos* 62 (January 1986), 4-42.

1551. Humphrey, John. "The Growth of Female Employment in Brazilian Manufacturing Industry in the 1970s," *Journal of Development Studies* 20:4 (July 1984), 224-247.

1552. Hurrell, Andrew. "Brazil, the United States and the Debt," *World Today* 41:3 (March 1985), 62-64.

1553. Jackson, Jean E. "The Impact of the State on Small-Scale Societies," *Studies in Comparative International Development* 19:2 (Summer 1984), 3-32.

1554. Jacobi, Pedro Roberto. "São Paulo: las luchas de los excluidos de la ciudad por el derecho a la ciudadanía, 1970-1982," *Revista Mexicana de Sociología* 46:4 (October-December 1984), 191-209.

1555. Jaguaribe, Helio. "La posición de Brasil en los grandes conflictos de nuestro tiempo," *Foro Internacional* 25:4 (April-June 1985), 362-371.

1556. Jaguaribe, Helio. "Principales opciones brasileñas para el fin del decenio," *El Trimestre Económico* 53:212 (October-December 1986), 793-811.

1557. Jaguaribe, Helio. "Raza, cultura y clase en la integración de las sociedades," *El Trimestre Económico* 53:209 (January-March 1986), 81-103.

1558. Kaufman, Robert R. "Democratic and Authoritarian Responses to the Debt Issue: Argentina, Brazil, Mexico," *International Organization* 39:2 (Summer 1985), 473-503.

1559. Keck, Margaret E. "Democratization and Dissension: The Formation of the Workers' Party," *Politics and Society* 15:1 (1986-87), 67-95.

1560. Keck, Margaret. "Update on the Brazilian Labor Movement," *Latin American Perspectives* 11:1 (Winter 1984), 27-34.

1561. Kelly, Philip. "Geopolitical Themes in the Writings of General Carlos de Meira Mattos of Brazil," *Journal of Latin American Studies* 16:2 (November 1984), 439-461.

1562. Kinzo, Maria d'Alva G. "Opposition Politics in Brazil: The Electoral Performance of the PMDB in São Paulo," *Bulletin of Latin American Research* 3:2 1984), 29-45.

1563. Kowarick, Lucio. "Los caminos de encuentro: reflexiones sobre las luchas sociales en São Paulo," *Revista Mexicana de Sociología* 46:4 (October-December 1984), 67-83.

1564. Kowarick, Lucio, and Nabil Bounduky. "São Paulo. Espacio urbano y espacio político: del populismo a la redemocratización," *Estudios Sociales Centroamericanos* 44 (May-August 1987), 45-61.

1565. Krane, Dale. "Opposition Strategy and Survival in Praetorian Brazil, 1964-79," *Journal of Politics* 45:1 (February 1983), 28-63.

1566. Krischke, Paulo J. "The Role of the Church in a Political Crisis: Brazil, 1964," *Journal of Church and State* 27:3 (Autumn 1985), 403-427.

1567. Lafer, Celso. "The Brazilian Political System: Trends and Perspectives," *Government and Opposition* 19:2 (Spring 1984), 178-187.

1568. Lafer, Celso. "As eleições de novembro e a política exterior do Brasil," *Revista Brasileira de Estudos Políticos* 57 (July 1983), 7-28.

1569. Lamounier, Bolivar. "Will the Brazilian Case Become a Paradigm," *Government and Opposition* 19:2 (Spring 1984), 167-177.

1570. Lamounier, Bolivar, and Alkimar R. Moura. "Economic Policy and Political Opening in Brazil." In *Latin American Political Economy: Financial Crisis and Political Change,* edited by Jonathan Hartlyn and Samuel A. Morley. Boulder, CO: Westview, 1986. 165-196.

1571. Lamounier, Bolivar, and Rachel Meneguello. "Los partidos políticos y la consolidación democrática: el caso brasileno," *Revista Mexicana de Sociología* 47:2 (April-June 1985), 353-388.

1572.   Largman, Ester Regina, and Robert M. Levine. "Jews in the Tropics: Bahian Jews in the Early Twentieth Century," *The Americas* 43:2 (October 1986), 159-170.

1573.   Lawlor, Hugh. "Education and National Development in Brazil." In *Education in Latin America,* edited by Colin Brock and Hugh Lawlor. Dover, NH: Croom Helm, 1985. 130-145.

1574.   Leff, Nathaniel H. "El gobierno y el desarrollo económico del Brasil en el siglo XIX," *El Trimestre Económico* 50:200 (October-December 1983), 2193-2225.

1575.   Lemos, Maurício Borges. "Natureza e perspectiva da indústria de bens de capital em Minas Gerais," *Revista Brasileira de Estudos Políticos* 58 (January 1984), 121-164.

1576.   Levine, Robert M. "Elite Intervention in Urban Popular Culture in Modern Brazil", *Luso-Brazilian Review* 21:2 (Winter 1984), 9-22.

1577.   Levinson, Marc. "Alcohol Fuels Revisited: The Costs and Benefits of Energy Independence in Brazil," *The Journal of Developing Areas* 21:3 (April 1987), 243-257.

1578.   Lewin, Linda. "The Oligarchical Limitations of Social Banditry in Brazil: The Case of the 'Good' Thief Antônio Silvino." In *Bandidos: The Varieties of Latin American Banditry,* edited by Richard W. Slatta. Westport, CT: Greenwood, 1987. 67-96.

1579.   Lewis, Colin M. "Railways and Industrialization: Argentina and Brazil, 1870-1929." In *Latin America, Economic Imperialism and the State,* edited by Christopher Abel and Colin M. Lewis. London; Dover, NH: Athlone, 1985. 199-230.

1580.   Locatelli, Ronaldo Lamounier. "Relações intersetoriais e estratégia de desenvolvimento: o caso brasileiro reexaminado," *Revista Brasileira de Economia* 37:4 (October-December 1983), 415-433.

1581.   Love, Joseph L., and Bert J. Barickman. "Rulers and Owners: A Brazilian Case Study in Comparative Perspective," *Hispanic American Historical Review* 66:4 (November 1986), 743-769.

1582.   Lowy, Michael. "A New Type of Party: The Brazilian PT," *Latin American Perspectives* 14:4 (Fall 1987), 453-464.

1583.   McBeth, Michael C. "Brazilian Generals, 1822-1865: A Statistical Study of Their Career," *The Americas* 44:2 (October 1987), 125-141.

1584.   McCann, Frank D. "The Formative Period of Twentieth-Century Brazilian Army Thought, 1900-1922, *Hispanic American Historical Review* 64:4 (November 1984), 737-765.

1585.   Macedo, Roberto. "Brazilian Children and the Economic Crisis: Evidence from the State of São Paulo," *World Development* 12:3 (March 1984), 203-221.

1586.   Macedo, Roberto. "Diferenciais de salários entre empresas privadas e estatais no Brasil," *Revista Brasileira de Economia* 39:4 (October-

December 1985), 437-448.

1587.   Machado, J. Teixeira, Júnior. "Regionalização ou municipalização do Brasil?" *Revista Brasileira de Estudos Políticos* 63-64 (July 1986-January 1987), 171-183.

1588.   Madeira, Felicia Reicher. "Youth in Brazil: Old Assumptions and New Approaches," *CEPAL Review* 29 (August 1986), 55-78.

1589.   Mainwaring, Scott. "Brazil: The Catholic Church and the Popular Movement in Nova Iguaçu, 1974-1985." In *Religion and Political Conflict in Latin America,* edited by Daniel H. Levine. Chapel Hill: University of North Carolina Press, 1986. 124-155.

1590.   Mainwaring, Scott. "The Catholic Church, Popular Education, and Political Change in Brazil," *Journal of Inter-American Studies and World Affairs* 26:1 (February 1984), 97-124.

1591.   Mainwaring, Scott. "The Transition to Democracy in Brazil," *Journal of Inter-American Studies and World Affairs* 28:1 (Spring 1986), 149-179.

1592.   Mainwaring, Scott. "Urban Popular Movements, Identity, and Democratization in Brazil," *Comparative Political Studies* 20:2 (July 1987), 131-159.

1593.   Mainwaring, Scott, and Eduardo J. Viola. "Transitions to Democracy: Brazil and Argentina in the 1980s," *Journal of International Affairs* 38:2 (Winter 1985), 193-219.

1594.   Markoff, John, and Silvio R. Duncan Baretta. "Professional Ideology and Military Activism in Brazil: Critique of a Thesis of Alfred Stepan," *Comparative Politics* 17:2 (January 1985), 175-191.

1595.   Marques, Maria Silvia Bastos. "A aceleração inflacionária no Brasil: 1973-83," *Revista Brasileira de Economia* 39:4 (October-December 1985), 343-384.

1596.   Martins, Luciano. "The 'Liberalization' of Authoritarian Rule in Brazil." In *Transition from Authoritarian Rule,* edited by Guillermo O'Donnell, Philippe C. Schmitter and Laurence Whitehead. Baltimore, MD: Johns Hopkins University Press, 1986. 72-94.

1597.   Martins, Roberto Borges, and Maria do Carmo Salazar Martins. "As exportações de Minas Gerais no século XIX," *Revista Brasileira de Estudos Políticos* 58 (January 1984), 105-120.

1598.   Mauro, Frédéric. "Recent Works on the Political Economy of Brazil in the Portuguese Empire," *Latin American Research Review* 19:1 (1984), 87-105.

1599.   Meller, Patricio. "Apreciaciones globales y específicas en torno del Plan Cruzado," *El Trimestre Económico* 54: Special (September 1987), 275-292.

1600.   Mello, João Manoel Cardoso de, and Maria da Conceição Tavares. "The Capitalist Export Economy in Brazil, 1884-1930." In *The Latin*

American Economies: Growth and the Export Sector, 1880-1930, edited by Roberto Cortés Conde and Shane J. Hunt. New York: Holmes & Meier, 1985. 82-136.

1601.   Mello e Souza, Alberto de, and Nelson do Valle Silva. "Mobilidade intersetorial e homogeneidade do setor informal: o caso brasileiro," *Revista Brasileira de Economia* 38:4 (October-December 1984), 327-356.

1602.   Mendes, Candido. "The 1982 Elections in Brazil," *Government and Opposition* 19:2 (Spring 1984), 152-156.

1603.   Metcalf, Alida C. "Fathers and Sons: The Politics of Inheritance in a Colonial Brazilian Township," *Hispanic American Historical Review* 66:3 (August 1986), 455-484.

1604.   Milton, Katharine. "Protein and Carbohydrate Resources of the Maku Indians of Northwestern Amazonia," *American Anthropologist* 86:1 (March 1984), 7-27.

1605.   Modiano, Eduardo Marco. "Consequências macroeconômicas da restrição exterior de 1983: simulações com um modelo econométrico para a economia brasileira," *Revista Brasileira de Economia* 37:3 (July-September 1983), 313-335.

1606.   Modiano, Eduardo Marco. "El Plan Cruzado: bases teóricas y limitaciones prácticas," *El Trimestre Económico* 54:Special (September 1987), 223-250.

1607.   Moldau, Juan Hersztajn. "O custo dos recursos domésticos como critério para avaliar a eficiência na produção de exportáveis, aplicado ao caso brasileiro no início da década de 70," *Revista Brasileira de Economia* 39:2 (April-June 1985), 145-174.

1608.   Moreira, Marcilio Marques. "Political Liberalization and Economic Crisis," *Government and Opposition* 19:2 (Spring 1984), 157-166.

1609.   Mueller, Charles C. "Gênese de estratégia agrícola no Brasil: uma interpretação," *Revista Brasileira de Economia* 38:1 (January-March 1984), 3-24.

1610.   Musalem, Alberto Roque. "Política comercial e distribuição no Brasil," *Revista Brasileira de Economia* 37:2 (April-June 1983), 245-260.

1611.   Myers, David J. "Brazil: Reluctant Pursuit of the Nuclear Option," *Orbis* 27:4 (Winter 1984), 881-911.

1612.   Nabuco, Maria Regina. "Agricultura, Estado e desenvolvimento regional em Minas Gerais, 1950-1980," *Revista Brasileira de Estudos Políticos* 58 (January 1984), 165-239.

1613.   Naro, Nancy P. "Rio Studies Rio: Ongoing Research on the First Republic in Rio de Janeiro," *The Americas* 43:4 (April 1987), 429-440.

1614.   Nazario, Olga. "Brazil's Rapproachement with Cuba: The Process and the Prospect," *Journal of Inter-American Studies and World Affairs* 28:3

(Fall 1986), 67-86.

1615.   Needell, Jeffrey D. *"The Revolta Contra Vacina* of 1904: The Revolt against 'Modernization' in *Belle-Epoque* Rio de Janeiro," *Hispanic American Historical Review* 67:2 (May 1987), 233-269.

1616.   Norris, William P. "Patron-Client Relationships in the Urban Social Structure: A Brazilian Case Study," *Human Organization* 43:1 (Spring 1984), 16-26.

1617.   Nunberg, Barbara. "Structural Change and State Policy: The Politics of Sugar in Brazil since 1964," *Latin American Research Review* 21:2 (1986), 53-92.

1618.   Nunes, Francisco Vidal, and Iraci del Nero da Costa. "Demografia histórica de Minas Gerais," *Revista Brasileira de Estudos Políticos* 58 (January 1984), 15-62.

1619.   O'Donnell, Guillermo. "Brazil's Failure: What Future for Debtors' Cartels?" *Third World Quarterly* 9:4 (October 1987), 1157-1166.

1620.   Oliveira, João do Carmo. "Trade Policy, Market Distortions and Agriculture in the Process of Economic Development: Brazil, 1950-1974," *Journal of Development Economics* 24:1 (November 1986), 91-109.

1621.   Oliveira, João Pacheco de Filho. "Terras indígenas no Brasil: uma tentativa de abordagem sociológica," *América Indígena* 43:3 (July-September 1983), 655-682.

1622.   Oliveira, Maria Helena de. "Evidências empíricas de comércio intra-indústria," *Revista Brasileira de Economia* 43:3 (July-September 1986), 211-232.

1623.   Oliven, Rubén George. "The Production and Consumption of Culture in Brazil," *Latin American Perspectives* 11:1 (Winter 1984), 103-115.

1624.   Pang, Eul-Soo, and Laura Jarnagin. "Brazilian Democracy and the Foreign Debt," *Current History* 83:490 (February 1984), 63-67.

1625.   Pang, Eul-Soo, and Laura Jarnagin. "Brazil's Cruzado Plan," *Current History* 86:516 (January 1987), 13-16.

1626.   Pang, Eul-Soo, and Laura Jarnagin. "A Requiem for Authoritarianism in Brazil," *Current History* 84:499 (February 1985), 61-64.

1627.   Paoli, Maria Célia. "Working-Class São Paulo and Its Representations, 1900-1940," *Latin American Perspectives* 14:2 (Spring 1987), 204-225.

1628.   Paula, João Antônio de. "Os limites da industrialização em Minas Gerais no século XVIII," *Revista Brasileira de Estudos Políticos* 58 (January 1984), 63-104.

1629.   Pereira, Luiz C. Bresser. "Inertial Inflation and the Cruzado Plan," *World Development* 15:8 (August 1987), 1035-1044.

1630.   Pereira, Luiz C. Bresser. "Six Interpretations of the Brazilian Social

Formation," *Latin American Perspectives* 11:1 (Winter 1984), 35-72.

1631.   Pérez Llana, Carlos. "Brazil and Western Europe in a Global Context." In *Latin America, Western Europe, and the United States: Reevaluating the Atlantic Triangle,* edited by Wolf Grabendorff and Riordan Roett. New York: Praeger, 1985. 124-134.

1632.   Perry, William. "The Fabric of Luso-Brazilian Relations." In *The Iberian-Latin American Connection: Implications for U.S. Foreign Policy,* edited by Howard J. Wiarda. Boulder, CO: Westview, 1986. 408-423.

1633.   Perry, William, and Juan Carlos Weiss. "Brazil." In *The Implications of Third World Military Industrialization,* edited by James Everett Katz. Lexington, MA: Lexington, 1986. 103-117.

1634.   Petersen, Dwight E. "Sweet Success: Some Notes on the Founding of a Brazilian Sugar Dynasty, The Pais Barreto Family of Pernambuco," *The Americas* 40:3 (January 1984) 325-348.

1635.   Petras, James. "The Anatomy of State Terror: Chile, El Salvador and Brazil," *Science and Society* 51:3 (Fall 1987), 314-338.

1636.   Pfeffermann, Guy P., and Richard Webb. "Pobreza e distribuição de renda no Brasil: 1960-1980," *Revista Brasileira de Economia* 37:2 (April-June 1983), 147-175.

1637.   Philip, George. "Democratization in Brazil and Argentina: Some Reflections," *Government and Opposition* 19:2 (Spring 1984), 269-276.

1638.   Pinto, Humberto da Costa, Jr. "Trading Companies: The Brazilian Experience." In *U.S.-Latin American Trade Relations,* edited by Michael R. Czinkota. New York: Praeger, 1983. 244-252.

1639.   Pinto Vallejos, Julio. "Slave Control and Slave Resistance in Colonial Minas Gerais, 1700-1750," *Journal of Latin American Studies* 17:1 (May 1985), 1-34.

1640.   Pope, Clara. "Human Rights and the Catholic Church in Brazil, 1970-1983: The Pontifical Justice and Peace Commission of the São Paulo Archdiocese," *Journal of Church and State* 27:3 (Autumn 1985), 429-452.

1641.   Porto, Walter da Costa. "Partidos, programas e as eleições de 82," *Revista Brasileira de Estudos Políticos* 57 (July 1983), 165-179.

1642.   Posey, Darrell A., John Frechione, John Eddins, and Luiz Francelino da Silva. "Ethnoecology as Applied Anthropology in Amazonian Development," *Human Organization* 43:2 (Summer 1984), 95-107.

1643.   Price, David. "La pacificación de los Mambiquara," *América Indígena* 43:3 (July-September 1983), 601-628.

1644.   Ramamurti, Ravi. "High Technology Exports by State Enterprises in LDCs: The Brazilian Aircraft Industry," *Developing Economies* 23:3 (September 1985), 254-280.

1645.   Ramos, Donald. "Community, Control and Acculturation: A Case Study of Slavery in Eighteenth Century Brazil," *The Americas* 42:4 (April 1986), 419-451.

1646.   *Revista Brasileira de Estudos Políticos*. "Número especial sobre temas constitucionais," 60-61 (January-July 1985).

1647.   Rezende, Gervásio Castro de. "A agricultura e a reforma do crédito rural," *Revista Brasileira de Economia* 39:2 (April-June 1985), 185-206.

1648.   Rios, José Arthur. "As eleições de 82 e os pequenos partidos," *Revista Brasileira de Estudos Políticos* 57 (July 1983), 187-216.

1649.   Rodrigues, Maria Cecília Prates. "Subsídios de equalização de custos ao açúcar e álcool," *Revista Brasileira de Economia* 43:3 (July-September 1986), 285-295.

1650.   Rodríguez Silvero, Ricardo. "Los acreedores de Itaipú: un análisis descriptivo," *Revista Paraguaya de Sociología* 21:60 (May-August 1984), 131-158.

1651.   Roett, Riordan. "Brazil and the United States: Beyond the Debt Crisis," *Journal of Inter-American Studies and World Affairs* 27:1 (February 1985), 1-15.

1652.   Roett, Riordan. "Brazil's Debt Crisis." In *Adjustment Crisis in the Third World,* edited by Richard E. Feinberg and Valeriana Kallab. Rutgers, NJ: Transaction, 1984. 139-146.

1653.   Roett, Riordan, and Scott D. Tollefson. "The Transition to Democracy in Brazil," *Current History* 85:507 (January 1986), 21-24.

1654.   Roniger, Luis. "Caciquismo and Coronelismo: Contextual Dimensions of Patron Brokerage in Mexico and Brazil," *Latin American Research Review* 22:2 (1987), 71-99.

1655.   Roniger, Luis. "Coronelismo, Caciquismo, and Oyabun-Kobun Bonds: Divergent Implications of Hierarchical Trust in Brazil, Mexico and Japan," *British Journal of Sociology* 38:3 (September 1987), 310-330.

1656.   Rosa, J. Eliseo da. "Economics, Politics, and Hydroelectric Power: The Paraná River Basin," *Latin American Research Review* 18:3 (1983), 77-107.

1657.   Rosenblüth, Guillermo. "Los nuevos estilos de desarrollo y la política habitacional," *Revista Paraguaya de Sociología* 20:56 (January-April 1983), 7-40.

1658.   Rossi, J. W. "Distribuição de renda pessoal no Brasil: 1970 e 1980," *Revista Brasileira de Economia* 40:2 (April-June 1986), 133-143.

1659.   Roxborough, Ian. "State, Multinationals and the Working Class in Brazil and Mexico," In *Latin America, Economic Imperialism and the State,* edited by Chrostopher Abel and Colin M. Lewis. London; Dover, NH: Athlone, 1985. 430-450.

1660.   Russell-Wood, A.J.R. "United States Scholarly Contributions to the Historiography of Colonial Brazil," *Hispanic American Historical Review* 65:4 (November 1985), 683-723.

1661.   Sader, Emir. "The Workers' Party in Brazil," *New Left Review* 165 (September-October 1987), 93-102.

1662.   Saffioti, Heleieth I.B. "Technological Change in Brazil: Its Effect on Men and Women in Two Firms." In *Women and Change in Latin America*, edited by June Nash and Helen Safa. South Hadley, MA: Bergin & Garvey, 1986. 109-135.

1663.   Sampaio de Sousa, Maria da Conceição. "Proteção, crescimento e distribuição de renda no Brasil: uma abordagem de equilíbrio geral," *Revista Brasileira de Economia* 41:1 (January-March 1987), 99-116.

1664.   Sandoval, Salvador Antonio, and Sonia María de Avelar. "Conciencia obrera y la negociación colectiva en Brasil," *Revista Mexicana de Sociología* 45:3 (July-September 1983), 1027-1047.

1665.   Sant'Ana, José Antonio. "The Role of Foreign Capital in Recent Brazilian Development." In *The Industrialization of Less Developed Contries*, edited by Colin H. Kirkpatrick and Frederick I. Nixson. Manchester, England; Dover, NH: Manchester University Press, 1983. 172-195.

1666.   Sayad, João. "Rural Credit and Positive Real Rates of Interest: Brazil's Experience with Rapid Inflation." In *Undermining Rural Development with Cheap Credit*, edited by Dale W. Adams, Douglas H. Graham, and J.D. Von Pischke. Boulder, CO: Westview, 1984. 146-160.

1667.   Schmink, Marianne. "Women and Urban Industrial Development in Brazil." In *Women and Change in Latin America*, edited by June Nash and Helen Safa. South Hadley, MA: Bergin & Garvey, 1986. 136-164.

1668.   Schmink, Marianne, and Charles H. Wood. "The 'Political Ecology' of Amazonia." In *Lands at Risk in the Third World: Local-Level Perspectives*, edited by Peter D. Little and Michael M. Horowitz. Boulder, CO: Westview, 1987. 38-57.

1669.   Seiblitz, Zelia. "Umbanda e 'potencial contestador' da religião," *América Indígena* 45:4 (October-December 1985), 669-690.

1670.   Seitenfus, Ricardo Silva. "Ideology and Diplomacy: Italian Fascism and Brazil, 1935-38," *Hispanic American Historical Review* 64:3 (August 1984), 503-534.

1671.   Selcher, Wayne A. "Brazilian-Argentine Relations in the 1980s: From Wary Rivalry to Friendly Competition," *Journal of Inter-American Studies and World Affairs* 27:2 (Summer 1985), 25-53.

1672.   Selcher, Wayne A. "Brazil's Foreign Policy: More Actors and Expanding Agendas." In *The Dynamics of Latin American Foreign Policies*, edited by Jennie K. Lincoln and Elizabeth G. Ferris. Boulder, CO: Westview, 1984. 101-123.

1673. Selcher, Wayne A. "Brazil's Relations with Latin America: A Pattern of Bilateral Cooperation," *Journal of Inter-American Studies and World Affairs* 28:2 (Summer 1986), 67-99.

1674. Sercovich, Francisco Colman. "Exports of Technology of Newly-Industrializing Countries: Brazil," *World Development* 12:5-6 (May-June 1984), 575-599.

1675. Shapiro, Judith. "From Tupã to the Land without Evil: The Christianization of Tupi-Guarani Cosmology," *American Ethnologist* 14:1 (February 1987), 126-139.

1676. Share, Donald, and Scott Mainwaring. "Transiciones vía transacción: la democratización en Brasil y en España," *Revista de Estudios Políticos* 49 (January-February 1986), 87-135.

1677. Silva, Ednaldo Araquem da. "Measuring the Incidence of Rural Capitalism: An Analysis of Survey Data from North-East Brazil," *Journal of Peasant Studies* 12:1 (October 1984), 65-75.

1678. Silva, José F. Graziano da. "Capitalist 'Modernization' and Employment in Brazilian Agriculture, 1960-1975: The Case of the State of São Paulo," *Latin American Perspectives* 11:1 (Winter 1984), 117-136.

1679. Silva, José F. Graziano da, Angela A. Kageyama, Devancyr A. Ramão, José A. Wagner Neto, and Lucia C. Guedes Pinto. "Tecnología y campesinado: consideraciones sobre el caso de Brazil," *Estudios Rurales Latinoamericanos* 8:2 (May-August 1985), 165-197.

1680. Silva, Luis Antônio Machado da, and Paulo Magalhães. "Mata Machado: aspectos de las luchas sociales en una favela carioca," *Revista Mexicana de Sociología* 46:4 (October-December 1984), 173-189.

1681. Simonsen, Mario Henrique, and Rudiger Dornbusch. "Estabilização da inflação com o apoio de políticas de rendas: um exame da experiência na Argentina, Brasil, e Israel," *Revista Brasileira de Economia* 41:1 (January-March 1987), 3-50.

1682. Skidmore, Thomas E. "Brazil's American Illusion: From Dom Pedro II to the Coup of 1964," *Luso-Brazilian Review* 23:2 (Winter 1986), 71-84.

1683. Sloan, John W. "Comparative Public Policy in Cuba and Brazil," *Studies in Comparative International Development* 18:3 (Fall 1983), 50-76.

1684. Smith, Russell E. "Indexación salarial, rotación de personal y variaciones de los salarios nominales en la industria manufacturera brasileña, 1966-1976," *Desarrollo Económico* 26:102 (July-September 1986), 269-288.

1685. Smith, William C. "El parto de la democracia brasileña," *Revista Mexicana de Sociología* 49:2 (April-June 1987), 89-126.

1686. Smith, William C. "The Political Transition in Brazil: From Authoritarian Liberalization and Elite Conciliation to Democratization." In *Comparing New Democracies: Transition and Consolidation in Mediterranean Europe and the Southern Cone,* Edited by Enrique A. Baloyra. Boulder, CO: Westview, 1987. 179-240.

1687.   Smith, William C. "The Travail of Brazilian Democracy in the 'New Republic', "*Journal of Inter-American Studies and World Affairs* 28:4 (Winter 1986-87), 39-74.

1688.   Soares, Glaucio Ary Dillon. "The Rise of the Brazilian Military Regime," *Studies in Comparative International Development* 21:2 (Summer 1986), 34-62.

1689.   Soares, Glaucio Ary Dillon, and Nelson do Valle Silva. "Urbanization, Race, and Class in Brazilian Politics," *Latin American Research Review* 22:2 (1987), 155-176.

1690.   Sotomayor Torres, Clivia M., and Wolfgang Rudig. "Nuclear Power in Argentina and Brazil," *Review of Radical Political Economics* 15:3 (Fall 1983), 67-82.

1691.   Souza, Amaury de, Olavo Brasil de Lima, and Marcus Figueiredo. "Brizola y las elecciones de 1982 en Rio de Janeiro," *Revista Mexicana de Sociología* 49:2 (April-June 1987), 233-281.

1692.   Süssekind, Arnaldo. "The Influence of International Labour Standards in Brazilian Legislation," *International Labour Review* 123:4 (July-August 1984), 441-456.

1693.   Szuchman, Mark D. "Disorder and Social Control in Buenos Aires, 1810-1860," *Journal of Interdisciplinary History* 15:1 (Summer 1984), 83-110.

1694.   Szuchman, Mark D. "Household Structure and Political Crisis: Buenos Aires, 1810-1860," *Latin American Research Review* 21:3 (1986), 55-93.

1695.   Szulc, Tad. "Brazil's Amazonian Frontier," In *Bordering On Trouble: Resources and Politics in Latin America,* edited by Andrew Maguire and Janet Welsh Brown. Bethesda, MD: Adler & Adler, 1986. 191-234.

1696.   Taniura, Taeko. "Economic Development Effects of an Integrated Iron and Steel Works: A Case Study of Minas Gerais Steel in Brazil," *Developing Economies* 24:2 (June 1986), 169-193.

1697.   Tanner, Christopher. "Malnutrition and the Development of Rural Households in the Agreste of Paraiba State, Northeast Brazil," *Journal of Development Studies* 23:2 (January 1987), 242-264.

1698.   Tanzer, Michael. "Stealing the Third World's Nonrenewable Resources: Lessons from Brazil," *Monthly Review* 35:11 (April 1984), 26-35.

1699.   Taylor, Kenneth I. "Las necesidades de Tierra de los Yanomami," *América Indígena* 43:3 (July-September 1983), 629-654.

1700.   Taylor, Timothy G., H. Evan Drummond, and Aloisie T. Gomes. "Agricultural Credit Programs and Production Efficiency: An Analysis of Traditional Farming in Southeastern Minas Gerais, Brazil," *American Journal of Agricultural Economics* 68:1 (February 1986), 110-119.

1701.   Teitel, Simón, and Francisco E. Thoumi. "From Import Substitution to Exports: The Manufacturing Exports Experience of Argentina and Brazil," *Economic Development and Cultural Change* 34:3 (April 1986), 455-490.

1702.   Teubal, Morris. "The Role of Technological Learning in the Exports of Manufactured Goods: The Case of Selected Capital Goods in Brazil," *World Development* 12:8 (August 1984), 849-865.

1703.   Thomas, Vinod. "Differences in Income and Poverty within Brazil," *World Development* 15:2 (February 1987), 262-273.

1704.   Thomas, Vinod. "Evaluating Pollution Control: The Case of São Paulo, Brazil," *Journal of Development Economics* 19:1-2 (September-October 1985), 133-146.

1705.   Topic, Steven. "State Autonomy in Economic Policy: Brazil's Experience 1822-1930," *Journal of Inter-American Studies and World Affairs* 26:4 (November 1984), 449-476.

1706.   Topik, Steven. "The State's Contribution to the Development of Brazil's Internal Economy, 1850-1930," *Hispanic American Historical Review* 65:2 (May 1985), 203-228.

1707.   Turrent, Isabel. "Brazil and the Soviet Union: A Low-Profile Relationship." In *Soviet-Latin American Relations in the 1980's,* edited by Augusto Varas. Boulder, CO: Westview, 1987. 230-249.

1708.   Turrent, Isabel. "La Unión Soviética en América Latina: el caso de Brasil," *Foro Internacional* 27:1 (July-September 1986), 75-101.

1709.   Tyler, William G. "Effective Incentives for Domestic Market Sales and Exports: A View of Anti-Export Biases and Commercial Policy in Brazil, 1980-81," *Journal of Development Economics* 18:2-3 (August 1985), 219-242.

1710.   Tyler, William G. "A incidência regional de políticas não-espaciais de incentivos no Brasil," *Revista Brasileira de Economia* 38:3 (July-September 1984), 183-204.

1711.   Tyler, William G. "Stabilization, External Adjustment, and Recession in Brazil: Perspectives on the Mid-1980s," *Studies in Comparative International Development* 21:2 (Summer 1986), 5-33.

1712.   Urban, Greg. "Developments in the Situation of Brazilian Tribal Populations from 1976 to 1982," *Latin American Research Review* 20:1 (1985), 7-25.

1713.   Urban, Greg. "Interpretations of Inter-Cultural Contact: The Shokleng and Brazilian National Society, 1914-1916," *Ethnohistory* 32:3 (November 1985), 224-244.

1714.   Valladares, Licia, and Ademir Figueiredo. "Housing in Brazil: An Introduction to Recent Literature," *Bulletin of Latin American Research* 2:2 (May 1983), 69-91.

1715.   Varas, Augusto. "The Soviet Union in the Foreign Relations of the

Southern Cone." In *Latin American Nations in World Politics,* edited by Heraldo Muñoz and Joseph S. Tulchin. Boulder, CO: Westview, 1984. 243-259.

1716. Vélez Rodríguez, Ricardo. "La historia de pensamiento filosófico brasileño, siglos XVII a XIX: problemas y corrientes," *Inter-American Review of Bibliography* 35:3 (1985), 279-288.

1717. Vianna, Sérgio Besserman. "As relações Brasil-Estados Unidos e a política econômica do segundo governo Vargas," *Revista Brasileira de Economia* 43:3 (July-September 1986), 193-210.

1718. Wadsted, Otto G. "O clima e a economia: análise de algumas culturas no Estado de São Paulo," *Revista Brasileira de Economia* 37:2 (April-June 1983), 225-244.

1719. Weis, W. Michael. "The Fundação Getúlio Vargas and the New Getúlio," *Luso-Brazilian Review* 24:2 (Winter 1987), 49-60.

1720. Welch, John H., Carlos Alberto Primo Braga, and Paulo de Tarso Alfonso de André. "The Brazilian Public Sector Disequilibrium," *World Development* 15:8 (August 1987), 1045-1052.

1721. Werneck, Rogério L. Furquim. "Uma análise do financiamento e dos investimentos das empresas estatais federais no Brasil, 1980-83," *Revista Brasileira de Economia* 39:1 (January-March 1985), 3-26.

1722. Werneck, Rogério L. Furquim. "Empresas estatais, controle de preços e contenção de importações," *Revista Brasileira de Economia* 40:1 (January-March 1986), 37-62.

1723. Werner, Dennis. "Psycho-Social Stress and the Construction of a Flood-Control Dam in Santa Catarina, Brazil," *Human Organization* 44:2 (Summer 1985), 161-167.

1724. Westman, John. "Modern Dependency: A 'Crucial Case' Study of Brazilian Government Policy in the Minicomputer Industry," *Studies in Comparative International Development* 20:2 (Spring 1985), 25-47.

1725. Wight, Jonathan. "The Efficiency of Producing Alcohol for Energy in Brazil," *Economic Development and Cultural Change* 33:4 (July 1985), 851-856.

1726. Williams, Gary W., and Robert L. Thompson. "Brazilian Soybean Policy: The International Effects of Intervention," *American Journal of Agricultural Economics* 66:4 (November 1984), 488-498.

1727. Willmore, Larry N. "The Comparative Performance of Foreign and Domestic Firms in Brazil," *World Development* 14:4 (April 1986), 489-502.

1728. Wright, Robin M. "Lucha y supervivencia en el Noroeste de la Amazonía," *América Indígena* 43:3 (July-September 1983), 537-554.

1729. Wright, Robin M., and Jonathan D. Hill. "History, Ritual, and Myth: Nineteenth Century Millenarian Movements in Northwest Amazon," *Ethnohistory* 33:1 (January 1986), 31-54.

1730.   Ziccardi, Alicia. "Villas miserias y favelas: Sobre las relaciones entre las institutciones del Estado y la organización social en las democracias de los años sesenta," *Revista Mexicana de Sociología* 45:1 (January-March 1983), 45-67.

1731.   Zirker, Daniel "Civilianization and Authoritarian Nationalism in Brazil: Ideological Opposition within a Military Dictatorship," *Journal of Political and Military Sociology* 14:2 (Fall 1986), 263-276.

1732.   Zottman, Luiz. "Problemas e soluções do Plano Cruzado como processo," *Revista Brasileira de Economia* 40:2 (April-June 1986), 145-163.

CHILE

Books and Monographs

1733. Anglade, Christian, and Carlos Fortín, eds. *The State and Capital Accumulation in Latin America* Vol. 1: *Brazil, Chile, Mexico.* Pittsburgh, PA: University of Pittsburgh Press, 1985. 254p.

1734. Ardito Barletta, Nicolas, Mario I. Blejer, and Luis Landau, eds. *Economic Liberalization and Stabilization Policies in Argentina, Chile and Uruguay: Applications of the Monetary Approach to the Balance of Payments.* Washington, DC: World Bank, 1984. 163p.

1735. Arellano, José Pablo. *Políticas sociales y desarrollo, Chile 1924-1984.* Santiago, Chile, CIEPLAN, 1985. 329p.

1736. Bermúdez Miral, Oscar. *Historia del salitre desde la Guerra del Pacifico hasta la Revolución de 1891.* Santiago, Chile: Pampa Desnuda, 1984. 337p.

1737. Bitar, Sergio. *Chile: Experiment in Democracy.* Translated by Sam Sherman. Philadelphia, PA: ISHI, 1985. 243p.

1738. Böhm, Günter. *Historia de los judíos en Chile.* Vol. 1: *Período colonial.* Santiago, Chile: Andrés Bello, 1984. 441p.

1739. Bouvier, Virginia Maria. *Alliance or Compliance: Implications of the Chilean Experience for the Catholic Church in Latin America.* Syracuse, NY: Foreign and Comparative Studies, Syracuse University, 1983. 105p.

1740. Campero, Guillermo and José A. Valenzuela. *El movimiento sindical en el regimen militar chileno: 1973-1981.* Santiago, Chile: Instituto Latinoamericano de Estudios Transnacionales, 1984. 380p.

1741.   Chavkin, Samuel. *Storm over Chile: The Junta under Siege.* Rev. ed. Westport, CT: L. Hill, 1984. 303p.

1742.   Davis, Nathaniel. *The Last Two Years of Salvador Allende.* Ithaca, NY: Cornell University Press, 1985. 480p.

1743.   DeShazo, Peter. *Urban Workers and Labor Unions in Chile, 1902-1927.* Madison: University of Wisconsin Press, 1983. 351p.

1744.   Dooner, Patricio. *Cambios sociales y conflicto político: el conflicto político nacional durante el gobierno de Eduardo Frei (1964-1970).* Santiago: Instituto Chileno de Estudios Humanísticos, 1984. 240p.

1745.   Edwards, Sebastian, and Alejandra Cox Edwards. *Monetarism and Liberalization: The Chilean Experiment.* Cambridge, MA: Ballinger, 1987. 233p.

1746.   Farrell, Joseph P. *The National United School in Allende's Chile: The Role of Education in the Destruction of a Revolution.* Vancouver: University of British Columbia Press in association with the Centre for Research on Latin America and the Caribbean, York University, 1986. 268p.

1747.   Fermandois, Joaquin. *Chile y el mundo, 1970-1973: la política exterior del gobierno de la Unidad Popular y el sistema internacional.* Santiago: Ediciones de la Universidad Católica de Chile, 1985. 444p.

1748.   Fernández, Jilberto A.E. *Dictadura militar y oposición política en Chile 1973-1981.* Amsterdam: CEDLA (Cinnaminson, NJ: Dist. by Foris), 1985. 455p.

1749.   Fleet, Michael. *The Rise and Fall of Chilean Christian Democracy.* Princeton, NJ: Princeton University Press, 1985. 274p.

1750.   Flusche, Della M., and Eugene H. Korth. *Forgotten Females: Women of African and Indian Descent in Colonial Chile, 1535-1800.* Detroit, MI: Blaine Ethridge, 1983. 112p.

1751.   Foxley, Alejandro. *Para una democracia estable.* Santiago, Chile: Aconcagua; CIEPLAN, 1985. 266p.

1752.   Furci, Carmelo. *The Chilean Communist Party and the Road to Socialism.* London: Zed (Totowa, NJ: Dist. by Biblio Distribution Center), 1984. 204p.

1753.   Gatica Barros, Jaime. *Deindustrialization in Chile.* Boulder, CO: Westview, 1987. 120p.

1754.   Goldberg, Joyce S. *The Baltimore Affair.* Lincoln: University of Nebraska Press, 1986. 207p.

1755.   Hojman, David E., ed. *Chile after 1973: Elements for the Analysis of Military Rule.* Liverpool, England: Centre for Latin American Studies, University of Liverpool, 1985. 152p.

1756.   Jarvis, Lovell S. *Chilean Agriculture under Military Rule: From Reform to Reaction, 1973-80.* Berkeley: Institute of International Studies,

University of California, 1985. 210p.

1757.   Knudson, Jerry W. *The Chilean Press during the Allende Years, 1970-73.* Buffalo: State University of New York, 1987. 90p.

1758.   Mayo, John. *British Merchants and Chilean Development, 1851-1886.* Boulder, CO: Westview, 1987. 272p.

1759.   Mericq, Luis S. *Antartica: Chile's Claim.* Washington, DC: National Defense University Press (dist. by the Government Printing Office), 1987. 125p.

1760.   Muñoz, Heraldo. *Las relaciones exteriores del gobierno militar chileno.* Santiago, Chile: Ornitorrinco y PROSPELCERC, 1986. 325p.

1761.   Muñoz Gomá, Oscar. *Chile y su industrialización: pasado, crisis y opciones.* Santiago, Chile: CIEPLAN, 1986. 323p.

1762.   O'Brien, Philip, ed. *Chile, the Pinochet Decade: The Rise and Fall of the Chicago Boys.* London: Latin American Bureau, 1983. 118p.

1763.   Pollack, Benny, and Hernan Rosenkranz. *Revolutionary Social Democracy: The Chilean Socialist Party.* New York: St. Martin's, 1986. 234p.

1764.   Ramos, Joseph. *Neoconservative Economics in the Southern Cone of Latin America, 1973-1983.* Baltimore, MD: Johns Hopkins University Press, 1986. 200p.

1765.   Rigoberto, García G., ed. *Chile 1973-1984.* Stockholm, Sweden: Institute of Latin American Studies, 1985. 223p.

1766.   Remmer, Karen L. *Party Competition in Argentina and Chile: Political Recruitment and Public Policy, 1890-1930.* Lincoln: University of Nebraska Press, 1984. 296p.

1767.   Sater, William F. *Chile and the War of the Pacific.* Lincoln: University of Nebraska Press, 1986. 343p.

1768.   Sater, William F. *The Revolutionary Left and Terrorist Violence in Chile.* Santa Monica, CA: Rand, 1986. 19p.

1769.   Turrent, Isabel. *La Unión Soviética en América Latina: el caso de la Unidad Popular Chilena, 1970-1973.* Mexico City: Centro de Estudios Internacionales, Colegio de México, 1984. 270p.

1770.   Valenzuela, J. Samuel, and Arturo Valenzuela, eds. *Military Rule in Chile: Dictatorship and Oppositions.* Baltimore, MD: Johns Hopkins University Press, 1986. 331p.

1771.   Winn, Peter. *Weavers of Revolution: The Yarur Workers and Chile's Road to Socialism.* New York: Oxford University Press, 1986. 328p.

1772.   Zeitlin, Maurice, *The Civil Wars in Chile (Or the Bourgeois Revolutions That Never Were).* Princeton, NJ: Princeton University Press, 1984. 265p.

Articles and Chapters

1773. Aedo-Richmond, Ruth, Ines Noguera, and Mark Richmond. "Changes in the Chilean Educational System during Eleven Years of Military Government: 1973-1984." In *Education in Latin America,* edited by Colin Brock and Hugh Lawlor. Dover, NH: Croom Helm, 1985. pp. 163-182.

1774. Angell, Alan, "Pinochet's Chile: The Beginning of the End?" *World Today* 41:2 (February 1985), 27-30.

1775. Angell, Alan. "Why Is the Transition to Democracy Proving so Difficult in Chile," *Bulletin of Latin American Research* 5:1 (1986), 25-40.

1776. Angell, Alan, and Susan Carstairs. "The Exile Question in Chilean Politics," *Third World Quarterly* 9:1 (January 1987), 148-167.

1777. Arellano, José Pablo. "De la liberación a la intervención: el mercado de capitales en Chile 1974-1983," *El Trimestre Económico* 52:207 (July-September 1985), 721-772.

1778. Arellano, José Pablo. "Social Policies in Chile: An Historical Review," *Journal of Latin American Studies* 17:2 (November 1985), 397-418.

1779. Barril, Alex, and Jaime Crispi. "Alcances y limitaciones de la tecnología campesina en el contexto de Chile," *Estudios Rurales Latino-americanos* 9:2 (May-August 1986), 49-57.

1780. Bell, Peter D. "Democracy and Double Standards: The View from Chile," *World Policy Journal* 2:4 (Fall 1985), 711-730.

1781. Bengoa, José. "Cuestiones de desarrollo rural alternativo," *Estudios Rurales Latinoamericanos* 8:2 (May-August 1985), 125-146.

1782. Bitar, Sergio. "Monetarism and Ultraliberalism, 1973-80," *International Journal of Politics* 12:4 (Winter 1982-83), 10-47.

1783. Blakemore, Harold. "Back to the Barracks: The Chilean Case," *Third World Quarterly* 7:1 (January 1985), 44-62.

1784. Blejer, Mario J. "Liberalization and Stabilization Policies in the Southern Cone Countries," *Journal of Inter-American Studies and World Affairs* 25:4 (November 1983), 431-444.

1785. Boeninger, Edgardo. "The Chilean Road to Democracy," *Foreign Affairs* 64:4 (Spring 1986), 812-832.

1786. Borzutzky, Silvia T. "The Pinochet Regime: Crisis and Consolidation." In *Authoritarians and Democrats: Regime Transition in Latin America,* edited by James M. Malloy and Mitchell A. Seligson. Pittsburgh, PA: Pittsburgh University Press, 1987. pp. 67-89.

1787. Boyle, Catherine M. "Images of Women in Contemporary Chilean Theatre," *Bulletin of Latin American Research* 5:2 (1986), 81-96.

1788. Boyle, Catherine M., and David E. Hojman. "Economic Policies and Political Strategies: Middle Sectors in Contemporary Chile," *Boletín de Estudios Latinoamericanos y del Caribe* 38 (June 1985), 15-45.

1789.   Campaña, Pilar, and María Soledad Lago. "La mujer en el argo chileno: un camino de esfuerzo y creación," *Estudios Rurales Latinoamericanos* 7:1 (April 1984), 79-92.

1790.   Cariola, Carmen, and Osvaldo Sunkel. "The Growth of the Nitrate Industry and Socioeconomic Change in Chile, 1880-1930." In *The Latin American Economies: Growth and the Export Sector, 1880-1930*, edited by Roberto Cortés Conde and Shane J. Hunt. New York: Holmes & Meier, 1985. pp. 137-254.

1791.   Constable, Pamela. "Pinochet's Grip on Chile," *Current History* 86:516 (January 1987), 17-20.

1792.   Constable, Pamela, and Arturo Valenzuela. "Is Chile Next?" *Foreign Policy* 63 (Summer 1986), 58-75.

1793.   Corbo, Vittorio. "Reforms and Macroeconomic Adjustments in Chile during 1974-84," *World Development* 13:8 (August 1985), 893-916.

1794.   Corbo, Vittorio, Jaime de Melo, and James Tybout. "What Went Wrong with the Recent Reforms in the Southern Cone," *Economic Development and Cultural Change* 34:3 (April 1986), 607-640.

1795.   Cortázar, René. "Chile: resultados distributivos 1973-1982," *Desarrollo Económico* 23:91 (October-December 1983), 369-394.

1796.   Cortés Douglas, Hernán. "El efecto de las recesiones internacionales en la economía chilena: una visión histórica, 1926-1982," *El Trimestre Económico* 52:208 (October-December 1985), 1075-1095.

1797.   Cortés Douglas, Hernán. "Opening Up and Liberalizing the Chilean Economy: The 1970s." In *Export-Oriented Development Strategies,* edited by Vittorio Corbo, Anne Krueger and Fernando Ossa. Boulder, CO: Westview, 1985. pp. 155-186.

1798.   Crispi, Jaime. "Agro, Estado y acumulación en Chile: un recuento histórico," *Estudios Rurales Latinoamericanos* 7:3 (September-December 1984), 155-198.

1799.   Culver, William W., and Cornel J. Reinhart. "The Decline of a Mining Region and Mining Policy: Chilean Copper in the Nineteenth Century." In *Miners and Mining in the Americas,* edited by Thomas Greaves and William Culver. Manchester, England; Dover, NH: Manchester University Press, 1985. pp. 68-81.

1800.   Deere, Carmen Diana. "Rural Women and Agrarian Reform in Peru, Chile, and Cuba." In *Women and Change in Latin America,* edited by June Nash and Helen Safa. South Hadley, MA: Bergin & Garvey, 1986. pp. 189-207.

1801.   Dick, Hermann, Egbert Gerken, Thomas Mayer, and David Vincent. "Stabilization Strategies in Primary Commodity Exporting Countries: A Case Study of Chile," *Journal of Development Economics* 15:1-3 (June-August 1984), 47-75.

1802.   Dorfman, Ariel. "The Chilean State Today and the Intellectual: Reflections on Some Urgent Problems," *International Journal of Politics* 12:4 (Winter 1982-83), 69-87.

1803.   Drobny, Andres. "The Influence of Minimum Wage Rates on the Level and Distribution of Real Wages in Chile, 1960-1972," *Bulletin of Latin American Research* 2:2 (May 1983), 17-38.

1804.   Durán Pérez, Teresa. "Identidad mapuche: un problema de vida y de concepto," *América Indígena* 46:4 (October-December 1986), 691-722.

1805.   Edwards, Sebastian. "Monetarism in Chile, 1973-1983: Some Economic Puzzles," *Economic Development and Cultural Change* 34:3 (April 1986), 535-559.

1806.   Edwards, Sebastian. "Stabilization with Liberalization: An Evaluation of Ten Years of Chile's Experiment with Free-Market Policies, 1973-1983," *Economic Development and Cultural Change* (January 1985), 223-254.

1807.   Falcoff, Mark. "Chile: Pinochet, the Opposition, and the United States," *World Affairs* 149:4 (Spring 1987), 183-194.

1808.   Falcoff, Mark. "Chile: The Dilemma for U.S. Policy," *Foreign Affairs* 64:4 (Spring 1986), 833-848.

1809.   Falcoff, Mark. "Spain and the Southern Cone." In *The Iberian-Latin American Connection: Implications for U.S. Foreign Policy,* edited by Howard J. Wiarda. Boulder, CO: Westview, 1986. pp. 337-359.

1810.   Ffrench-Davis, Ricardo. "El experimento monetarista en Chile: una sintesis critica," *Desarrollo Económico* 23:90 (July-September 1983), 163-196.

1811.   Ffrench-Davis, Ricardo. "The External Debt, Financial Liberalization, and Crisis in Chile." In *Politics and Economics of External Debt Crisis: The Latin American Experience,* edited by Miguel S. Wionczek in collaboration with Luciano Tomassini. Boulder, CO: Westview, 1985. pp. 348-382.

1812.   Ffrench-Davis, Ricardo. "The Monetarist Experiment in Chile: A Critical Survey," *World Development* 11:11 (November 1983), 905-926.

1813.   Ffrench-Davis, Ricardo. "Orígenes y efectos del endeudamiento externo en Chile," *El Trimestre Económico* 54:213 (January-March 1987), 159-178.

1814.   Fortín, Carlos. "The Failure of Repressive Monetarism: Chile, 1973-83," *Third World Quarterly* 6:2 (April 1984), 310-326.

1815.   Foxley, Alejandro. "Las alternativas para la política posautoritaria," *Desarrollo Económico* 25:98 (July-September 1985), 155-178.

1816.   Foxley, Alejandro, and Dagmar Raczynski. "Vulnerable Groups in Recessionary Situations: The Case of Children and the Young in Chile," *World Development* 12:3 (March 1984), 223-246.

1817. Frank, Volker. "Political Developments in Chile under the Pinochet Regime," *Journal of Third World Studies* 4:1 (Spring 1987), 128-138.

1818. Galvez, Julio, and James Tybout. "Microeconomic Adjustments in Chile during 1977-81: The Importance of Being a *Grupo,*" *World Development* 13:8 (August 1985), 969-994.

1819. Garretón, Manuel Antonio. "Chile: In Search of Lost Democracy." In *Latin American Political Economy: Financial Crisis and Political Change,* edited by Jonathan Hartlyn and Samuel A. Morley. Boulder, CO: Westview, 1986. pp. 197-216.

1820. Garretón, Manuel Antonio. "The Political Evolution of the Chilean Military Regime and Problems in the Transition to Democracy." In *Transition from Authoritarian Rule,* edited by Guillermo O'Donnell, Phillipe C. Schmitter and Laurence Whitehead. Baltimore, MD: Johns Hopkins University Press, 1986. pp. 95-122.

1821. Garrett, James L. "The Beagle Channel: Confrontation and Negotiation in the Southern Cone," *Journal of Inter-American Studies and World Affairs* 27:3 (Fall 1985), 81-109.

1822. Goldberg, Joyce S. "Consent to Ascent: The Baltimore Affair and the U.S. Rise to World Power Status," *The Americas* 41:1 (July 1984), 21-35.

1823. Grugel, Jean. "Nationalist Movements and Fascist Ideology in Chile," *Bulletin of Latin American Research* 4:2 (1985), 109-122.

1824. Gwynne. R.N. "The Deindustrialization of Chile, 1974-1984," *Bulletin of Latin American Research* 5:1 (1986), 1-23.

1825. Harberger, Arnold C. "Observations on the Chilean Economy, 1973-1983," *Economic Development and Cultural Change* 34:3 (April 1985), 451-462.

1826. Hojman, David E. "From Mexican Plantations to Chilean Mines: The Theoretical and Empirical Relevance of Enclave Theories in Contemporary Latin America," *Inter-American Economic Affairs* 39:3 (Winter 1985), 27-53.

1827. Hojman, David E. "Minimum Wage Rates and Real Earnings in the Chilean Labour Market: An Alternative Approach," *Bulletin of Latin American Research* 4:1 (1985), 49-60.

1828. Huneeus, Carlos. "La dinámica de los 'nuevos autoritarismos': Chile en una perspectiva comparada," *Revista de Estudios Políticos* 54 (November-December 1986), 105-166.

1829. Huneeus, Carlos. "From Diarchy to Polyarchy: Prospects for Democracy in Chile." In *Comparing New Democracies: Transition and Consolidation in Mediterranean Europe and the Southern Cone,* edited by Enrique A. Baloyra. Boulder, CO: Westview, 1987. pp. 109-152.

1830. Jaksic, Iván. "Philosophy and University Reform at the University of Chile: 1842-1973," *Latin American Research Review* 19:1 (1984), 57-86.

1831. Joseph, William A. "China's Relations with Chile under Allende: A Case Study of Chinese Foreign Policy in Transition," *Studies in Comparative Communism* 18:2-3 (Summer-Autumn 1985), 125-150.

1832. Kay, Cristóbal. "The Monetarist Experiment in the Chilean Countryside," *Third World Quarterly* 7:2 (April 1985), 301-322.

1833. Kirkwood, Julieta. "Women and Politics in Chile," *International Social Science Journal* 35:4 (1983), 625-637.

1834. Korth, Eugene H., and Della M. Flusche. "Dowry and Inheritance in Colonial Spanish America: Peninsular Law and Chilean Practice," *The Americas* 43:4 (April 1987), 395-410.

1835. Kusnetzoff, Fernando. "Democratización del Estado, gobiernos locales y cambio social: experiencias comparativas en Chile y Nicaragua," *Revista Mexicana de Sociología* 45:1 (January-March 1983), 191-219.

1836. Kusnetzoff, Fernando. "Urban and Housing Policies under Chile's Military Dictatorship: 1973-1985," *Latin American Perspectives* 14:2 (Spring 1987), 157-186.

1837. Lagos, Ricardo. "The Emergent Bourgeoisie," *International Journal of Politics* 12:4 (Winter 1982-83), 48-68.

1838. Latorre, Carmen Luz. "The Chilean Crisis: A Note on the Consequences of Liberal Policies towards the Private Sector," *Developing Economies* 22:3 (September 1984), 289-308.

1839. Leiva, Fernando Ignacio, and James Petras. "Chile: New Urban Movements and the Transition to Democracy," *Monthly Review* 39:3 (July-August 1987), 109-124.

1840. Leiva, Fernando Ignacio, and James Petras. "Chile's Poor in the Struggle for Democracy," *Latin American Perspectives* 13:4 (Fall 1986), 5-25.

1841. Levy, Daniel C. "Chilean Universities under the Junta: Regime and Policy," *Latin American Research Review* 21:3 (1986), 95-128.

1842. Loveman, Brian. "Military Dictatorship and Political Opposition in Chile, 1973-86," *Journal of Inter-American Studies and World Affairs* 28:4 (Winter 1986-87), 1-38.

1843. Mann, Arthur J., and Carlos E. Sánchez. "Labor Market Responses to Southern Cone Stabilization Policies: The Cases of Argentina, Chile, Uruguay," *Inter-American Economic Affairs* 38:4 (Spring 1985), 19-39.

1844. Martínez, Javier, and Eduardo Valenzuela. "Chilean Youth and Social Exclusion," *CEPAL Review* 29 (August 1986), 93-105.

1845. Martner, Gonzalo. "La vía pacífica al socialismo," *El Trimestre Económico* 51:204 (October-December 1984), 761-809.

1846. Mayo, John. "Commerce, Credit and Control in Chilean Copper Mining before 1880." In *Miners and Mining in the Americas,* edited by Thomas Greaves and William Culver. Manchester, England; Dover,

NH: Manchester University Press, 1985. pp. 29-46.

1847. Meacham, Carl E. "Changing of the Guard: New Relations between Church and State in Chile," *Journal of Church and State* 29:3 (Autumn 1987), 411-433.

1848. Meller, Patricio, and Andrés Solimano. "A Simple Macro Model for a Small Open Economy Facing a Binding External Constraint: Chile," *Journal of Development Economics* 26:1 (June 1987), 25-35.

1849. Menanteau-Horta, Darío. "Algunos antecedentes sobre la esterilización de la mujer en Chile: resultados de una encuesta," *Revista de Ciencias Sociales* 24:12 (January-July 1985), 231-248.

1850. Monteón, Michael. "Chile under the Dictator," *Socialist Review* 16:3-4 (May-August 1986), 99-118.

1851. Morande, Felipe G. "Domestic Prices of Importable Goods in Chile and the Law of One Price: 1975-1982," *Journal of Development Economics* 21:1 (April 1986), 131-147.

1852. Mouzelis, Nicos. "On the Rise of Postwar Military Dictatorships: Argentina, Chile and Greece," *Comparative Studies in Society and History* 28:1 (January 1986), 55-80.

1853. Muñoz, Heraldo. "The International Policy of the Socialist Party and Foreign Relations of Chile," In *Latin American Nations in World Politics,* edited by Heraldo Muñoz and Joseph S. Tulchin. Boulder, CO: Westview, 1984. pp. 150-167.

1854. Muñoz, Heraldo. "La política exterior chilena: la crisis continúa," *Foro Internacional* 26:2 (October-December 1985), 229-266.

1855. Nef, Jorge. "Economic Liberalism and Political Repression in Chile." In *Latin American Prospects for the 1980s,* edited by Archibald R.M. Ritter and David H. Pollack. New York: Praeger, 1983. pp. 304-324.

1856. North, Liisa, "The Military in Chilean Politics." In *Armies and Politics in Latin America,* edited by Abraham F. Lowenthal and Samuel Fitch. Rev. ed. New York: Holmes & Meier, 1986. pp. 167-199.

1857. Nunn, Frederick M. "One Year in the Life of Augusto Pinochet: Gulag of the Mind," *The Americas* 42:2 (October 1985), 197-206.

1858. O'Brien, Philip J. "Authoritarianism and Monetarism in Chile, 1973-1983," *Socialist Review* 14:5 (September-October 1984), 45-79.

1859. O'Brien, Philip J. "Authoritarianism and the New Orthodoxy: The Political Economy of the Chilean Regime, 1973-1982." In *Generals in Retreat: The Crisis of Military Rule in Latin America,* edited by Philip J. O'Brien and Paul Cammack. Dover, NH: Manchester University Press, 1985. pp. 144-183.

1860. Oppenheim, Lois. "Democracy and Social Transformation in Chile: The Debate Within the Left," *Latin American Perspectives* 12:3 (Summer 1985), 59-76.

1861.   Ortega, Luis. "Economic Policy and Growth in Chile from Independence to the War of the Pacific." In *Latin America, Economic Imperialism and the State,* edited by Christopher Abel and Colin M. Lewis. London; Dover, NH: Athlone, 1985. pp. 147-171.

1862.   Ortega, Luis. "Nitrates, Chilean Entrepreneurs and the Origins of the War of the Pacific," *Journal of Latin American Studies* 16:2 (November 1984), 337-380.

1863.   Osiel, Mark, and Eliza Willis. "Is Chile Headed for a Showdown?" *Dissent* (Spring 1984), 207-214.

1864.   Palma, Gabriel. "External Disequilibrium and Internal Industrialization: Chile, 1914-1935." In *Latin America, Economic Imperialism and the State,* edited by Christopher Abel and Colin M. Lewis. London; Dover, NH: Athlone, 1985. pp. 318-338.

1865.   Parot, Rodrigo. "Las expectativas en el ajuste inflacionario Chile, 1973-1978," *El Trimestre Económico* 54:213 (January-March 1987), 133-158.

1866.   Petras, James. "The Anatomy of State Terror: Chile, El Salvador and Brazil," *Science and Society* 51:3 (Fall 1987), 314-338.

1867.   Petras, James. "Death in Chile: On the Murder of a Journalist and Long-Time Friend," *Monthly Review* 38:6 (November 1986), 56-59.

1868.   Pinto S.C., Aníbal. "Estado y empresa privada: una visión retrospectiva de la experiencia chilena," *El Trimestre Económico* 53:209 (January-March 1986), 105-148.

1869.   Pion-Berlin, David. "The Defiant State: Chile in the Post-Coup Era." In *Armies and Politics in Latin America,* edited by Abraham F. Lowenthal and Samuel Fitch. Rev. ed. New York: Holmes & Meier, 1986. pp. 317-334.

1870.   Pittman, Howard. "Chilean Foreign Policy: The Pragmatic Pursuit of Geopolitical Goals." In *The Dynamics of Latin American Foreign Policies,* edited by Jennie K. Lincoln and Elizabeth G. Ferris. Boulder, CO: Westview, 1984. pp. 125-135.

1871.   Rivera, Rigoberto. "Desarrollo capitalista y medierías en Chile, " *Estudios Rurales Latinoamericanos* 10:1 (January-April 1987), 37-54.

1872.   Rivera, Rigoberto, and Jaime Crispi. "Bienes, salarios y agricultura capitalista en Chile," *Revista Paraguaya de Sociología* 23:66 (May-August 1986), 63-85.

1873.   Rivera, Rigoberto, and Raúl Molina. "Estrategias campesinas versus estrategias de supervivencia," *Revista Paraguaya de Sociología* 20:57 (May-August 1983), 93-110.

1874.   Rosenblüth, Guillermo. "Los nuevos estilos de desarrollo y la política habitacional," *Revista Paraguaya de Sociología* 20:56 (January-April 1983), 7-40.

1875.   Scheetz, Thomas. "Gastos militares en Chile, Perú y la Argentina,"

Desarrollo Económico 25:99 (October-December 1985), 315-328.

1876. Scheetz, Thomas. "Public Sector Expenditures and Financial Crisis in Chile," *World Development* 15:8 (August 1987), 1053-1075.

1877. Schneider Chaigneau, Antonio. "La crisis financiera chilena," *El Trimestre Económico* 52:208 (October-December 1985), 1049-1074.

1878. Sigmund, Paul E. "Free-Market Authoritarianism." In *Politics, and Economic Development in Latin America,* edited by Robert G. Wesson. Stanford, CA: Hoover Institution Press, 1984. pp. 1-13.

1879. Smith, Brian H. "Chile: Deepening the Allegiance of Working-Class Sectors to the Church in the 1970s." In *Religion and Political Conflict in Latin America,* edited by Daniel H. Levine. Chapel Hill: University of North Carolina Press, 1986. pp. 156-186.

1880. Somervell, Philip. "Naval Affairs in Chilean Politics, 1910-1932," *Journal of Latin American Studies* 16:2 (November 1984), 381-402.

1881. Tiano, Susan. "Authoritarianism and Political Culture in Argentina and Chile in the Mid-1960s," *Latin American Research Review* 21:1 (1986), 73-98.

1882. Tokman, Víctor E. "Global Monetarism and Destruction of Industry," *CEPAL Review* 23 (August 1984), 107-121.

1883. Uthoff, Andras W. "Changes in Earnings Inequality and Labour Market Segmentation: Metropolitan Santiago 1969-78," *Journal of Development Studies* 22:2 (January 1986), 300-326.

1884. Valenzuela, Arturo. "Chile's Political Instability," *Current History* 83:490 (February 1984), 68-72.

1885. Valenzuela, Arturo. "Prospects for the Pinochet Regime in Chile," *Current History* 84:499 (February 1985), 77-80.

1886. Valenzuela, Arturo, and Robert Kaufman. "Chile: From Democracy to Authoritarianism." In *From Gunboats to Diplomacy: New U.S. Policies for Latin America,* edited by Richard Newfarmer. Baltimore, MD: Johns Hopkins University Press, 1984. pp. 176-190.

1887. Varas, Augusto. "The Soviet Union in the Foreign Relations of the Southern Cone." In *Latin American Nations in World Politics,* edited by Heraldo Muñoz and Joseph S. Tulchin. Boulder, CO: Westview, 1984. pp. 243-259.

1888. Wilhelmy, Manfred. "Politics, Bureaucracy, and Foreign Policy in Chile." In *Latin American Nations in World Politics,* edited by Heraldo Muñoz and Joseph S. Tulchin. Boulder, CO: Westview, 1984. pp. 45-62.

1889. Yeager, Gertrude M. "Women's Roles in Nineteenth-Century Chile: Public Education Records, 1843-1883," *Latin American Research Review* 18:3 (1983), 149-156.

1890. Yocelevzky R., Ricardo A. "La Democracia Cristiana chilena: trayectoria de un proyecto," *Revista Mexicana de Sociología* 47:2 (April-June 1985), 287-352.

1891.   Yocelevzky R., Ricardo A. "La izquierda chilena en 1982," *Revista Mexicana de Sociología* 45:3 (July-September 1983), 981-1025.

1892.   Yocelevzky R., Ricardo A. "El Partido Socialista de Chile bajo la dictadura militar," *Foro Internacional* 27:1 (July-September 1986), 102-131.

1893.   Zahler, Roberto. "Recent Southern Cone Liberalization Reforms and Stabilization Policies: The Chilean Case, 1974-1982," *Journal of Inter-American Studies and World Affairs* 25:4 (November 1983), 509-562.

1894.   Zapata, Francisco. "Crisis económica y movilización social en Chile, 1981-1984," *Foro Internacional* 26:2 (October-December 1985), 214-228.

1895.   Zapata, Francisco. "Nationalisation, Copper Miners and the Military Government in Chile." In *Miners and Mining in the Americas,* edited by Thomas Greaves and William Culver. Manchester, England; Dover, NH: Manchester University Press, 1985. pp. 257-276.

COLOMBIA

Books and Monographs

1896. Berry, Albert, ed. *Essays on Industrialization in Colombia.* Tempe: Center for Latin American Studies, Arizona State University, 1983. 329p.

1897. Braun, Herbert. *The Assassination of Gaitán: Public Life and Urban Violence in Colombia.* University of Wisconsin Press, 1986. 282p.

1898. Colombia. Misión de Finanzas Intergubernamentales. *Intergovernmental Finance in Colombia: Final Report of the Mission on Intergovernmental Finance.* Cambridge, MA: International Tax Program, Law School of Harvard, 1984. 414p.

1899. Díaz de Zuluaga, Zamira. *Guerra y economía en las haciendas: Popayán, 1780-1830.* Bogotá: Banco Popular, 1983. 123p. *(Sociedad y economía en el Valle de Cauca,* Vol. 2)

1900. Dix, Robert H. *The Politics of Colombia.* New York: Praeger, 1986. 247p.

1901. Economic Commission for Latin American and the Caribbean. *La empresas transnacionales en el desarrollo colombiano.* Santiago, Chile; New York: United Nations, 1986. 218p.

1902. Escorcia, José. *Desarrollo político, social y económico, 1800-1845.* Bogotá: Banco Popular, 1983. 153p. *(Sociedad y economía en el Valle de Cauca,* Vol. 3.)

1903. Fals Borda, Orlando. *Historia doble de la costa.* Bogotá: Carlos Valencia.
Vol. 3: *Resistencia en el San Jorge,* 1984. 212p.
Vol. 4: *Retorno a la tierra,* 1986. 234p.

1904.   Gilbert, Alan, and Peter M. Ward. *Housing, the State and the Poor: Policy and Practice in Three Latin American Cities.* Cambridge, England; New York: Cambridge University Press, 1985. 319p.

1905.   González, Margarita. *Ensayos de historia colonial colombiana.* 2d ed. Bogotá: Ancora 1984. 329p.

1906.   Hanson, E. Mark. *Educational Reform and Administrative Development: The Cases of Colombia and Venezuela.* Stanford, CA: Hoover Institution Press, 1986. 246p.

1907.   Hartwig, Richard E. *Roads to Reason: Transportation, Administration, and Rationality in Colombia.* Pittsburgh, PA: University of Pittsburgh Press, 1983. 276p.

1908.   Helg, Aline. *Civiliser le peuple et former les élites: l'éducation en Colombie, 1918-1957.* Paris: L'Harmattan, 1984. 344p.

1909.   Helmsing, A.H.J. *Firms, Farms, and the State in Colombia: A Study of Rural, Urban, and Regional Dimensions of Change.* Winchester, MA: Allen & Unwin, 1986. 297p.

1910.   Henderson, James D. *Las ideas de Laureano Gómez.* Bogotá: Tercer Mundo, 1985. 279p.

1911.   Henderson, James D. *When Colombia Bled: A History of Violence in Tolima.* University: University of Alabama Press, 1985. 352p.

1912.   Hernández, Deborah. *Resource Development and Indigenous People: The El Cerrejón Coal Project in Guajira, Colombia.* Cambridge, MA: Cultural Survival, 1984. 52p.

1913.   Hopkins, Michael. *Alternatives to Unemployment and Underdevelopment: The Case of Colombia.* Boulder, CO: Westview, 1985. 129p.

1914.   Hyland, Richard Preston. *El crédito y la economía, 1851-1880.* Translated by Germán Colmenares. Bogotá: Banco Popular, 1983. 233p. *(Sociedad y economía en el Valle del Cauca.* Vol. 4.)

1915.   Johnson, David Church. *Santander, Siglo XIX: cambios socioeconómicos.* Bogotá: Carlos Valencia, 1984. 309p.

1916.   Kofas, Jon V. *Dependence and Underdevelopment in Colombia.* Tempe: Center for Latin American Studies, Arizona State University, 1986. 201p.

1917.   LeGrand, Catherine. *Frontier Expansion and Peasant Protest in Colombia, 1850-1936.* Albuquerque: University of New Mexico Press, 1986. 302p.

1918.   Marsh, Robin Ruth. *Development Strategies in Rural Colombia: The Case of Caqueta.* Los Angeles: Latin American Center, University of California, 1983. 241p.

1919.   Medhurst, Kenneth N. *The Church and Labour in Colombia.* Manchester, England: Manchester University Press, 1984. 233p.

1920.   Mohan, Rakesh. *An Anatomy of the Distribution of Urban Income: A Tale of Two Cities in Colombia.* Washington, DC: World Bank, 1984. 133p.

1921.   Mohan, Rakesh, and Nancy Hartline. *The Poor in Bogotá: Why They Are, What They Do, and Where They Live.* Washington, DC: World Bank, 1984. 85p.

1922.   Ocampo. José Antonio. *Colombia y la economía mundial, 1830-1910.* Mexico: Siglo Veintiuno, 1984. 456p.

1923.   Park, James William. *Rafael Núñez and the Politics of Colombian Regionalism, 1863-1886.* Baton Rouge; London: Louisiana State University Press, 1985. 304p.

1924.   Pedraja Tomán, René de la. *Historia de la energía en Colombia, 1537-1930.* Bogotá: Áncora, 1985. 231p.

1925.   Peeler, John A. *Latin American Democracies: Colombia, Costa Rica, Venezuela.* Chapel Hill: University of North Carolina Press, 1985, 193p.

1926.   Rausch, Jane M. *A Tropical Plains Frontier: The Llanos of Colombia, 1531-1831.* Albuquerque: University of New Mexico Press, 1984. 317p.

1927.   Rojas, G., José María. *Empresarios y tecnología en la formación del sector azucarero en Colombia, 1860-1980.* Bogatá: Banco Popular, 1983. 212p. *(Sociedad y economía en el Valle del Cauca.* Vol. 5)

1928.   Savage, Charles H., Jr. and George F.F. Lombard. *Sons of the Machine: Case Studies of Social Change in the Workplace.* Cambridge, MA: M.I.T. Press, 1986. 313p.

1929.   Thomas, Vinod, et al. *Linking Macroeconomics and Agricultural Policies for Adjustment with Growth: The Colombian Experience.* Baltimore, MA: Published for the World Bank by Johns Hopkins University Press, 1985. 252p.

1930.   Tirado, Thomas. *Alfonso López Pumarejo, el Conciliador: su contribución a la páz política en Colombia.* Bogotá: Planeta Colombiana, 1986. 289p.

1931.   Uribe Celis, Carlos. *Los años veinte en Colombia: ideología y cultura.* Bogotá: Aurora, 1985. 206p.

1932.   Urrutia, Miguel. *Winners and Losers in Colombia's Economic Growth in the 1970s.* New York: Oxford University Press for the World Bank, 1985. 142p.

1933.   Vásquez Carrizosa, Alfredo. *Betancur y la crisis nacional.* Bogotá: Aurora, 1986. 287p.

1934.   Vásquez Carrizosa, Alfredo. *Las relaciones de Colombia y Venezuela: la historia atormentada de dos naciones.* Bogotá: Tercer Mundo, 1983. 451p.

1935.   Wallace, Brian F. *Ownership and Development: A Comparison of Domestic and Foreign Firms in Colombian Manufacturing.* Athens: Ohio State University Press, 1987. 176p.

1936.   Zamosc, Leon. *The Agrarian Question and the Peasant Movement in Colombia: Struggles of the National Peasant Association 1967-1981.* Cambridge, England; New York: Cambridge University Press, 1986. 289p.

Articles and Chapters

1937.   Acevedo C., María Nelly. "La pobreza en Colombia: una medida estadística," *El Trimestre Económico* 53:210 (April-June 1986), 315-340.

1938.   Anrup, Roland. " Changing Forms of Disposition on an Andean Estate," *Economy and Society* 14:1 (February 1985), 28-54.

1939.   Anrup, Roland. "Trabajo y tierra en una hacienda andina colombiana," *Estudios Rurales Latinoamericanos* 9:1 (January-April 1986), 63-98.

1940.   Ardila, Ruben. "The Psychological Impact of the Nuclear Threat on the Third World: The Case of Colombia," *Journal of Public Health Policy* 8:2 (Summer 1987), 242-250.

1941.   Ashby, Jacqueline A. "The Social Ecology of Soil Erosion in a Colombian Farming System," *Rural Sociology* 50:3 (Fall 1985), 377-396.

1942.   Avellaneda, José Ignacio. "The Men of Nikolaus Federmann: Conquerors of the New Kingdom of Granada," *The Americas* 43:4 (April 1987), 385-394.

1943.   Bagley, Bruce Michael. "Colombian Politics: Crisis or Continuity?" *Current History* 86:516 (January 1987), 21-24.

1944.   Bagley, Bruce Michael. "National Front and Economic Development." In *Politics, Policies, and Economic Development,* edited by Robert G. Wesson. Stanford, CA: Hoover Institution Press, 1984. pp. 124-160.

1945.   Bagley, Bruce Michael, and Juan Gabriel Totkatlian. "Colombian Foreign Policy in the 1980s: The Search for Leverage," *Journal of Inter-American Studies and World Affairs* 27:3 (Fall 1985), 27-62.

1946.   Barrera, Cristina. "La migración femenina internacional: el caso Colombia-Venezuela," *Estudios Rurales Latinoamericanos* 9:3 (September-December 1986), 69-80.

1947.   Blanco, Armando. "Producción campesina y capitalismo en Colombia," *Estudios Rurales Latinoamericanos* 9:2 (May-August 1986), 59-81.

1948.   Braun, Dorit. "Transnational Corporations and Development: The Pharmaceutical Industry in Colombia." In *The Industrialisation of Less Developed Countries,* edited by Colin H. Kirkpatrick and Frederick I. Nixson. Manchester, England; Dover, NH: Manchester University Press, 1983. pp. 111-137.

1949.   Burgess, Rod. "The Political Integration of Urban Demands in Colombia,"

Boletín de Estudios Latinoamericanos y del Caribe 41 (December 1986), 29-52.

1950.   Butler Flora, Cornelia. "Religiosity among Working Class Catholic Colombians." In *The Catholic Church and Religions in Latin America,* edited by Thomas C. Bruneau, Chester E. Gabriel and Mary Mooney. Montreal, Canada: Centre for Developing Area Studies, McGill University, 1984. pp. 67-87.

1951.   Delpar, Helen. "Renegade or Regenator? Rafael Núñez as Seen by Colombian Historians," *Inter-American Review of Bibliography* 35:1 (1985), 25-37.

1952.   Dufour, Darna L. "Insects as Food: A Case Study from the Northwest Amazon," *American Anthropologist* 89:2 (June 1987), 383-397.

1953.   Edwards, Sebastian. "Coffee, Money and Inflation in Colombia," *World Development* 12:11-12 (November-December 1984), 1107-1117.

1954.   Escobar, Cristina. "La ANUC y el movimiento campesino durante los años setenta en Colombia," *Estudios Rurales Latinoamericanos* 8:3 (September-December 1985), 317-334.

1955.   Friedeman, Nina S. de. *"Troncos* among Black Miners in Colombia." In *Miners and Mining in the Americas,* edited by Thomas Greaves and William Culver. Manchester, England; Dover, NH: Manchester University Press, 1985. pp. 204-225.

1956.   García Castro, Mary. "Work versus Life: Colombian Women in New York." In *Women and Change in Latin America,* edited by June Nash and Helen Safa. South Hadley, MA: Bergin & Garvey, 1986. pp. 231-255.

1957.   Gros, Christian. "Luchas indígenas y prácticas autogestionarias: algunas reflexiones a partir de tres estudios de caso," *Estudios Rurales Latinoamericanos* 10:1 (January-April 1987), 55-69.

1958.   Grunwald, Joseph. "Restructuración de la industria maquiladora," *El Trimestre Económico* 50:200 (October-December 1983), 2123-2152.

1959.   Hall, Lana L. "United States Food Aid and the Agricultural Development of Brazil and Colombia, 1954-73." In *Food, Politics, and Society in Latin America,* edited by John C. Super and Thomas C. Wright. Lincoln: University of Nebraska Press, 1985. pp. 133-149.

1960.   Hansen, Elizabeth de G.R. "Let Them Eat Rice?" In *Bordering on Trouble: Resources and Politics in Latin America,* edited by Andrew Maguire and Janet Welsh Brown. Bethesda, MD: Adler & Adler, 1986. pp. 101-151.

1961.   Hartlyn, Jonathan. "The Impact of Patterns of Industrialization and of Popular Sector Incorporation on Political Regime Type: A Case Study of Colombia," *Studies in Comparative International Development* 19:1 (Spring 1984), 29-60.

1962.   Hartlyn, Jonathan. "Military Governments and the Transition to Civilian Rule: The Colombian Experience of 1957-1958," *Journal of Inter-*

American Studies and World Affairs 26:2 (May 1984), 245-281.

1963.   Hartlyn, Jonathan. "Producer Associations, the Political Regime, and Policy Processes in Contemporary Colombia," *Latin American Research Review* 20:3 (1985), 111-138.

1964.   Hazleton, William A. "The Foreign Policies of Venezuela and Colombia: Collaboration, Competition, and Conflict." In *The Dynamics of Latin American Foreign Policies,* edited by Jennie K. Lincoln and Elizabeth G. Ferris. Boulder, CO: Westview, 1984. pp. 151-170.

1965.   Hill, Jonathan D. "Los misioneros y las fronteras," *América Indígena* 44:1 (January-March 1984), 183-190.

1966.   Jackson, Jean E. "The Impact of the State on Small-Scale Societies," *Studies in Comparative International Development* 19:2 (Summer 1984), 3-32.

1967.   Jackson, Jean E. "Traducciones competitivas del evangelio en el Vaupés, Colombia," *América Indígena* 44:1 (January-March 1984), 49-94.

1968.   Jimeno, Miriam. "La descomposición de la colonización campesina en Colombia," *Estudios Rurales Latinoamericanos* 6:1 (January-April 1983), 65-76.

1969.   Kamas, Linda. "Dutch Disease Economics and the Colombian Export Boom," *World Development* 14:9 (September 1986), 1177-1198.

1970.   Keremitsis, Dawn. "Latin American Women Workers in Transition: Sexual Division of the Labor Force in Mexico and Colombia in the Textile Industry," *The Americas* 40:4 (April 1984), 491-499.

1971.   Kline, Harvey F. "New Directions in Colombia?" *Current History* 84:499 (February 1985), 65-68.

1972.   LeGrand, Catherine. "Colombian Transformations: Peasants and Wage-Labourers in the Santa Marta Banana Zone," *Journal of Peasant Studies* 11:4 (July 1984), 178-200.

1973.   LeGrand, Catherine. "Labor Acquisition and Social Conflict on the Colombian Frontier, 1850-1936," *Journal of Latin American Studies* 16:1 (May 1984), 27-49.

1974.   León, Magdalena. "Políticas agrarias en Colombia y discusión sobre la política para la mujer campesina," *Estudios Rurales Latino-americanos* 10:1 (January-April 1987), 71-93.

1975.   Levine, Daniel H. "Colombia: The Institutional Church and the Popular." In *Religion and Political Conflict in Latin America,* edited by Daniel H. Levine. Chapel Hill: University of North Carolina Press, 1986. pp. 187-217.

1976.   Levine, Daniel H. "Continuities in Colombia," *Journal of Latin American Studies* 17:2 (November 1985), 295-317.

1977.   McFarlane, Anthony. "The Transition from Colonialism in Colombia, 1819-1875." In *Latin America, Economic Imperialism and the State,* edited by Christopher Abel and Colin M. Lewis. London; Dover, NH: Athlone, 1985. pp. 101-124.

1978.   McGreevey, William Paul. "The Transition to Economic Growth in Colombia." In *The Latin American Economies: Growth in the Export Sector, 1880-1930,* edited by Roberto Cortés Conde and Shane J. Hunt. New York: Holmes & Meier, 1985. pp. 23-81.

1979.   Medellín Lozano, Fernando. "Religiones populares contra la emancipación," *América Indígena* 45:4 (October-December 1985), 625-646.

1980.   Mortimore, Michael. "The Subsidiary Role of Direct Foreign Investment in Industrialization: The Colombian Manufacturing Sector," *CEPAL Review* 25 (April 1985), 67-84.

1981.   Mosquera Torres, Gilma. "El movimiento de los destechados colombianos en la décade de los años 70," *Revista Mexicana de Sociología* 46:4 (October-December 1984), 127-144.

1982.   Murillo Castaño, Gabriel. "Effects of Emigration and Return on Sending Countries: The Case of Colombia," *International Social Science Journal* 36:3 (1984), 453-467.

1983.   Ocampo, José Antônio. "O mercado mundial do café e o surgimento da Colômbia como un país cafeicultor," *Revista Brasileira de Economia* 37:4 (October-December 1983), 449-481.

1984.   Park, James W. "Regionalism as a Factor in Colombia's 1875 Election," *The Americas* 42:4 (April 1986), 453-472.

1985.   Parra Sandoval, Rodrigo. "The Missing Future: Colombian Youth," *CEPAL Review* 29 (August 1986), 79-92.

1986.   Perrone, Mario Eduardo. "La tierra de los arhaucos: aspectos de la colonización y la lucha por la tierra en la Sierra Nevadade Santa Marta, Colombia, en el presente siglo," *Estudios Rurales Latinoamericanos* 6:2-3 (May-December 1983), 219-236.

1987.   Ramírez de Jara, María Clemencia, and Carlos Ernesto Pinzón C. "Los hijos del bejuco solar y la campana celeste: el yajé en la cultura popular urbana," *América Indígena* 46:1 (January-March 1986), 163-168.

1988.   Rappaport, Joanne. "History, Myth, and the Dynamics of Territorial Maintenance in Tierradentro, Colombia," *American Ethnologist* 12:1 (February 1985), 27-45.

1989.   Rappaport, Joanne. "Las misiones protestantes y la resistencia indígena en el sur de Colombia," *América Indígena* 44:1 (January-March 1984), 111-126.

1990.   Rappaport, Joanne. "Mythic Images, Historical Thought, and Printed Texts: The Páez and the Written Word," *Journal of Anthropological Research* 43:1 (Spring 1987), 43-61.

1991.   Rausch, Jane M. "Frontiers in Crisis: The Breakdown of the Missions in Far Northern Mexico and New Granada, 1821-1849," *Comparative*

Studies in Society and History 29:2 (April 1987), 340-359.

1992. Rausch, Jane M. "The Taming of a Colombian Caudillo: Juan Nepomuceno Moreno of Casanare," *The Americas* 42:3 (January 1986), 275-288.

1993. Reinhardt, Nola. "The Consolidation of the Import-Export Economy in Nineteenth-Century Colombia: A Political-Economic Analysis," *Latin American Perspectives* 13:1 (Winter 1986), 75-98.

1994. Reinhardt, Nola. "Modernizing Peasant Agriculture: Lessons from El Palmar, Colombia," *World Development* 15:2 (February 1987), 221-247.

1995. Revéiz, Edgar, and María José Pérez. "Colombia: Moderate Economic Growth, Political Stability, and Social Welfare." In *Latin American Political Economy: Financial Crisis and Political Change,* edited by Jonathan Hartlyn and Samuel A. Morley. Boulder, CO: Westview, 1986. pp. 265-291.

1996. Rubbo, Anna, and Michael Taussig. "Up Off Their Knees: Servanthood in Southwest Colombia," *Latin American Perspectives* 10:4 (Fall 1983), 5-23.

1997. Sánchez, Gonzalo. "La Violencia in Colombia: New Research, New Questions," *Hispanic American Historical Review* 65:4 (November 1985), 789-807.

1998. Sarmiento, Eduardo. "The Imperfections of the Capital Market," *CEPAL Review* 27 (December 1985), 97-111.

1999. Sheahan, John. "Aspects of Planning and Development in Colombia." In *The Public Sector in Latin America,* edited by Alfred H. Saulniers. Austin: Institute of Latin American Studies, University of Texas, 1984. pp. 213-235.

2000. Sowell, David. "'La teoría i la realidad': The Democratic Society of Artisans of Bogotá, 1847-1854," *Hispanic American Historical Review* 67:4 (November 1987), 611-630.

2001. Tardanico, Richard. "State Responses to the Great Depression, 1929-1934: Toward a Comparative Analysis of 'Revolutionary' Mexico and 'Non-revolutionary' Colombia." In *Crises in the Caribbean Basin,* edited by Richard Tardanico. Beverly Hills, CA: Sage, 1987. pp. 113-140.

2002. Thoumi, Francisco E. "Some Implications of the Growth of the Underground Economy in Colombia," *Journal of Inter-American Studies and World Affairs* 29:2 (Summer 1987), 35-53.

2003. Torres, Ricardo and Alvara Balcázar. "Evaluación del cambio tecnológico en la agricultura colombiana," *Estudios Rurales Latinoamericanos* 8:1 (January-April 1985), 101-117.

2004. Truelove, Cynthia. "The Informal Sector Revisited: The Case of the Talleres Rurales Mini-Maquilas in Colombia." In *Crises in the Caribbean Basin,* edited by Richard Tardanico. Beverly Hills, CA: Sage, 1987. pp. 95-110.

2005.   Vellinga, M., and D. Kruijt. "The State, Regional Development, and Regional Bourgeoisie in Latin America: Case Studies of Peru and Colombia," *Inter-American Economic Affairs* 37:3 (Winter 1983), 3-31.

2006.   Vogel, Robert C., and Donald W. Larson. "Illusion and Reality in Allocating Agricultural Credit: The Example of Colombia." In *Undermining Rural Development with Cheap Credit,* edited by Dale W. Adams, Douglas H. Graham, and J.D. Von Pischke. Boulder, CO: Westview, 1984. pp. 49-58.

2007.   Wade, Peter. "Patterns of Race in Colombia," *Bulletin of Latin American Research* 5:2 (1986), 1-19.

COSTA RICA

Books and Monographs

2008. Andic, Faut M. *What Price Equity? A Macroeconomic Evaluation of Government Policies in Costa Rica* Rio Piedras: Institute of Caribbean Studies, University of Puerto Rico, 1984. 70p.

2009. Bird, Leonard. *Costa Rica: The Unarmed Democracy.* London: Sheppard, 1984. 224p.

2010. Bourgois, Phillippe. *Ethnic Diversity on a Corporate Plantation: Guyamí Labor on a United Brands Subsidiary in Costa Rica and Panama.* Cambridge, MA: Cultural Survival, 1985. 52p.

2011. Esquivel, Francisco. *El desarrollo del capital en la industria de Costa Rica, 1950-1970.* Heredia, Costa Rica: Editorial de la Universidad Nacional, 1985. 197p.

2012. Fallas Monge, Carlos Luis. *El movimiento obrero en Costa Rica, 1830-1902.* San José, Costa Rica: Editorial Universidad Estatal a Distancia, 1983. 438p.

2013. Fonseca, Elizabeth. *Costa Rica colonial: la tierra y el hombre.* San José, Costa Rica: EDUCA, 1983. 387p.

2014. Gudmundson, Lowell. *Costa Rica before Coffee: Society and Economy on the Eve of the Export Boom.* Baton Rouge: Louisiana State University Press, 1986. 204p.

2015. Hall, Carolyn. *Costa Rica: A Geographical Interpretation in Historical Perspective.* Boulder, CO: Westview, 1985. 348p.

2016. Jacobstein, Helen L. *The Process of Economic Development in Costa Rica, 1948-1970: Some Political Factors.* New York: Garland, 1987. 338p.

2017.   Jonas, Susanne. *La ideología social demócrata en Costa Rica.* San José: EDUCA, 1984. 110p.

2018.   Montero Mejia, Alvaro. *La impagable deuda externa de Costa Rica.* San José, Costa Rica: Pensamiento Revolucionario, 1986. 86p.

2019.   Mora Corrales, Hernán. *La organización cooperativa en Costa Rica.* San José, Costa Rica: Editorial Universidad Estatal a Distancia, 1985. 259p.

2020.   Peeler, John A. *Latin American Democracies: Colombia, Costa Rica, Venezuela.* Chapel Hill: University of North Carolina, 1985. 193p.

2021.   Quiroz Martín, Teresa, et al. *La mujer en Costa Rica y su participación política-económica en el desarrollo del país.* San José: Instituto de Investigaciones Sociales, Facultad de Ciencias Sociales, Universidad de Costa Rica, 1984. 118p.

2022.   Rowles, James P. *Law and Agrarian Reform in Costa Rica.* Boulder, CO: Westview, 1985. 230p.

2023.   Sanders, Sol W. *The Costa Rican Laboratory.* New York: Priority, 1986. 72p.

2024.   Sojo, Ana. *Estado empresario y lucha política en Costa Rica.* San José, Costa Rica: EDUCA, 1984. 297p.

Articles and Chapters

2025.   Asociación Pablo Presbere. "Una experiencia de organización indígena en Costa Rica," *América Indígena* 43:1 (January-March 1983), 9-14.

2026.   Augelli, John P. "Costa Rica's Frontier Legacy," *Geographical Review* 77:1 (January 1987), 1-16.

2027.   Barlett, Peggy F., and Polly F. Harrison. "Poverty in Rural Costa Rica: A Conceptual Model." In *Social Impact Analysis and Development Planning in the Third World, edited by William Derman and Polly F. Harrison.* Boulder, CO: Westview, 1985. pp. 141-159.

2028.   Blachman, Morris J., and Ronald G. Hellman. "Costa Rica."In *Confronting Revolution: Security through Diplomacy in Central America,* edited by Morris J. Blachman, William M. Leogrande and Kenneth E. Sharpe. New York: Pantheon, 1986. pp. 156-182.

2029.   Booth, John A. "Representative Constitutional Democracy in Costa Rica: Adaptation to Crisis in the Turbulent 1980s." In *Central America: Crisis and Adaptation,* edited by Steve C. Ropp and James A. Morris. Albuquerque: University of New Mexico Press, 1984. pp. 153-188.

2030.   Borge Carvajal, Carlos. "Importancia de la Cacería en las poblaciones indígenas del suroeste del Valle de Talamanca," *América Indígena* 43:1 (January-March 1983), 87-95.

2031.   Bourgois Irwin, Philippe. "Etnicidad y lucha clases en una subsidiaria de la United Fruit Company en Costa Rica y Panamá," *Boletín de Antropología Americana* 8 (December 1983), 63-74.

2032. Centro de Estudios para la Acción Social. "Condiciones de vida y dinámica organizativa en un asentamiento urbano de Costa Rica," *Estudios Sociales Centroamericanos* 44 (May-August 1987), 112-121.

2033. Constenla Umaña, Adolfo. "Anotaciones sobre la religión tradicional Guatusa," *América Indígena* 43:1 (January-March 1983), 97-124.

2034. Feinberg, Richard E. "Costa Rica: The End of the Fiesta." In *From Gunboats to Diplomacy: New U.S. Policies for Latin America,* edited by Richard Newfarmer. Baltimore, MD: Johns Hopkins University Press, 1984. pp. 102-115.

2035. Franco, Rolando, and Arturo León. "El impacto redistributivo de la política social: los programas de vivienda en Costa Rica," *Revista Paraguaya de Sociología* 21:61 (September-December 1984), 207-223.

2036. Furlong, William L. "Costa Rica: Caught between Two Worlds," *Journal of Inter-American Studies and World Affairs* 29:2 (Summer 1987), 119-154.

2037. Garnier, Leonardo. "Industria, estado y desarrollo en Costa Rica: perspectivas y propuestas," *Estudios Sociales Centroamericanos* 13:37 (January-April 1984), 163-185.

2038. Gayle, Dennis J. "Democratic Pluralism and Economic Growth: Reflections on the Costa Rican Case," *Journal of Social, Political and Economic Studies* 8:4 (Winter 1983), 355-371.

2039. Goertzel, Ted G. "Costa Rica: Democracy and Antimilitarism," *Dissent* (Summer 1984), 333-337.

2040. González-Vega, Claudio. "Fear of Adjusting: The Social Costs of Economic Policies in Costa Rica in the 1970s." In *Revolution and Counterrevolution in Central America and the Caribbean,* edited by Donald E. Schulz and Douglas H. Graham. Boulder, CO: Westview, 1984. pp. 351-383.

2041. Granados, Carlos, and Liliana Quezeda. "Los intereses geopolíticos y el desarrollo de la zona nor-atlántica costarricense," *Estudios Sociales Centroamericanos* 40 (January-April 1986), 47-65.

2042. Gudmundson, Lowell. "El conflicto entre estabilidad y neutralidad en Costa Rica," *Foro Internacional* 26:1 (July-September 1985), 37-54.

2043. Gudmundson, Lowell. "Costa Rica before Coffee: Occupational Distribution, Wealth, Inequality, and Elite Society in the Village Economy of the 1840s," *Journal of Latin American Studies* 15:2 (November 1983), 427-452.

2044. Gudmundson, Lowell. "Costa Rica's Arias at Midterm," *Current History* 86:524 (December 1987), 417-420.

2045. Hall, Carolyn. "Regional Inequalities in Well-Being in Costa Rica," *Geographical Review* 74:1 (January 1984), 48-62.

2046.   Ibarra, David. "Cost Rica: política, política económica y política salarial," *Foro Internacional* 24:2 (October-December 1983), 117-130.

2047.   Lincoln, Jennie K. "Neutrality Costa Rican Style," *Current History* 84:500 (March 1985), 118-121.

2048.   Meehan, Peter M., and Michael B. Whiteford. "Expansion of Commercial Cattle Production and Its Effects on Stratification and Migration: The Costa Rican Case." In *Social Impact Analysis and Development Planning in the Third World,* edited by William Derman and Scott Whiteford. Boulder, CO: Westview, 1985. pp. 178-195.

2049.   Meléndez Chaverri, Carlos. "Primera etapa de la encomienda de indios de Nicoya, 1524-1545," *América Indígena* 43:1 (January-March 1983), 187-204.

2050.   Mora, Jorge, and Angela Arias. "Estado, planificación y acumulación de capital en Costa Rica 1974-1982," *Estudios Sociales Centroamericanos* 13:37 (January-April 1984), 187-209.

2051.   Morgan, Lynn M. "Health without Wealth? Costa Rica's Health System under Economic Crisis," *Journal of Public Health Policy* 8:1 (Spring 1987), 86-105.

2052.   Murillo, M., María Eugenia. "La Reproducción de la fuerza de trabajo en la comunidad de Salitre," *América Indígena* 43:1 (January-March 1983), 39-56.

2053.   Murillo Chaverri, Carmen, and Omar Hernández Cruz. "La relación etnica-clase entre los indígenas Cabécares de Chirripó," *América Indígena* 43:1 (January-March 1983), 15-24.

2054.   Ocampo S., Rafael Angel. "La comunidad de Telire en equilibrio con la naturaleza," *América Indígena* 43:1 (January-March 1983), 205-213.

2055.   Purcell, Trevor W. "Dependency and Responsibility: A View from West Indians in Costa Rica," *Caribbean Quarterly* 31:3-4 (September-December 1985), 1-15.

2056.   Reding, Andrew. "Democratic Model in Jeopardy," *World Policy Journal* 3:2 (Spring 1986), 301-315.

2057.   Rojas Aravena, Francisco. "Costa Rica, 1978-1982: ¿Una política internacional tercermundista?" *Foro Internacional* 24:2 (October-December 1983), 212-232.

2058.   Rojas Aravena, Francisco. "Costa Rica y Honduras: a similares problemas soluciones distintas," *Estudios Sociales Centroamericanos* 43 (January-April 1987), 49-61.

2059.   Rojas Aravena, Francisco. "Diplomatic, Economic, and Cultural Linkages between Costa Rica and the Soviet Union." In *Soviet-Latin American Relations in the 1980s,* edited by Augusto Varas. Boulder, CO: Westview, 1987. 250-269.

2060.   Romero, Carmen María. "Las transformaciones recientes del estado costarricense y las políticas reformistas," *Estudios Sociales Centro-*

americanos 13:38 (May-August 1984), 41-53.

2061. Sewastynowicz, James. "'Two-Step' Migration and Upward Mobility on the Frontier: The Safety Valve Effect in Pejibaye, Costa Rica," *Economic Development and Cultural Change* 34:4 (July 1986), 731-753.

2062. Smith W., David A. "La frontera Panamá-Costa Rica: relaciones económicas y sociales," *Estudios Sociales Centroamericanos* 40 (January-April 1986), 77-85.

2063. Sojo, Ana. "Morfología de la política estatal en Costa Rica y crisis económica," *Estudios Sociales Centroamericanos* 13:37 (January-April 1984), 139-162.

2064. Suárez Garcés, Gerardo Octavio. "Estructura de poder en la comunidad de Amubri, Talamanca," *América Indígena* 43:1 (January-March 1983), 25-37.

2065. Torres Rivas, Edelberto, and Mario Ramírez Boza. "Modalidades de la transición al capitalismo agrario en Costa Rica," *Estudios Rurales Latinoamericanos* 6:1 (January-April 1983), 23-50.

2066. Trejos París, María Eugeria. "Un sector de economía laboral en Costa Rica," *Estudios Sociales Centroamericanos* 13:37 (January-April 1984), 211-230.

2067. Trupp, L. Ann. "Políticas gubernamentales sobre el uso de plaguicidas: los casos en Costa Rica y Nicaragua," *Estudios Sociales Centroamericanos* 42 (September-December 1986), 59-75.

2068. Valverde O., Luis A. "Participación popular en el desarrollo comunal costarricense e intervención estatal," *Estudios Sociales Centroamericanos* 13:39 (August-December 1984), 63-77.

2069. Vega C. José Luis. "Inmigrantes centroamericanos en Costa Rica," *Estudios Sociales Centroamericanos* 40 (January-April 1986), 87-98.

2070. Vogel, Robert C. "The Effect of Subsidized Agricultural Credit on Income Distribution in Costa Rica." In *Undermining Rural Development with Cheap Credit,* edited by Dale W. Adams, Douglas H. Graham and J.D. Von Pischke. Boulder, CO: Westview, 1984. 133-145.

2071. Wesson, Robert G. "Problems of Social Democracy." In *Politics, Policies and Economic Development in Latin America,* edited by Robert G. Wesson. Stanford, CA: Hoover Institution Press, 1984. pp. 213-233.

2072. Whiteford, Michael B. "The Social Epidemiology of Nutritional Status among Costa Rican Children: A Case Study," *Human Organization* 44:3 (Fall 1985), 241-250.

CUBA

Books and Monographs

2073. Abel, Christopher, and Nissa Torrents, eds. *Jose Martí: Revolutionary Democrat.* Durham, NC: Duke University Press, 1986. 238p.

2074. Aguila, Juan M. del. *Cuba: Dilemmas of a Revolution.* Boulder, CO: Westview, 1984. 193p.

2075. Araujo Bernal, Leopoldo, and José Llorens Figueroa, eds. *La lucha por la salud en Cuba.* Mexico City: Siglo Veintiuno, 1985. 382p.

2076. Benjamin, Medea, Joseph Collins, and Michael Scott. *No Free Lunch: Food and Revolution in Cuba Today.* San Francisco: Institute for Food and Development Policy, 1984. 240p.

2077. Betancourt, Enrique C. *Apuntes para historia; radio, televisión y farándula en la Cuba de ayer.* Miami, FL: Universal, 1986. 457p.

2078. Bourne, Peter G. *Fidel: A Biography of Fidel Castro.* New York: Dodd, Mead, 1986. 332p.

2079. Brundenius, Claes. *Revolutionary Cuba: The Challenge of Economic Growth with Equity.* Boulder, CO; London: Westview, 1984. 224p.

2080. Castro, Fidel. *Fidel and Religion: Castro Talks on Revolution and Religion with Frei Betto.* Translated by the Cuban Center for Translation and Interpretation. New York: Simon and Schuster, 1987. 314p.

2081. Castro, Fidel. *Fidel Castro: Nothing Can Stop the Course of History.* Interview by Jeffrey M. Elliot and Mervyn M. Dymally. New York: Pathfinder, 1986. 258p.

2082.   Castro, Fidel. *War and Crisis in the Americas: Speeches 1984-85.* Edited by Michael Taber. New York: Pathfinder, 1985. 249p.

2083.   Clark, Juan. *Religious Repression in Cuba.* Coral Gables, FL: North-South Center, University of Miami, 1986. 115p.

2084.   Córdova, Efrén. *Castro and the Cuban Labor Movement: Statecraft and Society in a Revolutionary Period, 1959-1961.* Lanham, MD: University Press of America, 1987. 341p.

2085.   Cortada, James N., and James W. Cortada. *U.S. Foreign Policy in the Caribbean, Cuba and Central America.* New York: Praeger, 1985. 251p.

2086.   Cuban American National Foundation, *Castro and the Narcotics Connection: The Cuban Government's Use of Narcotic Trafficking to Finance and Promote Terrorism.* Washington, DC: 1983. 83p.

2087.   Cuban American National Foundation. *Cuba's Financial Crisis: The Secret Report from Banco Nacional de Cuba.* Washington, DC: 1985. 64p.

2088.   Díaz-Briquets, Sergio. *The Health Revolution in Cuba.* Austin: University of Texas Press, 1983. 227p.

2089.   Duncan, W. Raymond. *The Soviet Union and Cuba: Interests and Influence.* New York: Praeger, 1985. 220p.

2090.   Edquist, Charles. *Capitalism, Socialism, and Technology: A Comparative Study of Cuba and Jamaica.* London: Zed (Totowa, NJ: Dist. by Biblio Distribution Center), 1985. 182p.

2091.   Erisman, H. Michael. *Cuba's International Relations: The Anatomy of a Nationalistic Foreign Policy.* Boulder: Westview, 1985. 203p.

2092.   Falk, Pamela S. *Cuban Foreign Policy: Caribbean Tempest.* Lexington, MA: 1985. 336p.

2093.   Franqui, Carlos. *Family Portrait with Fidel: A Memoir.* Translated by Alfred MacAdam. New York: Random House, 1984. 262p.

2094.   Frederick, Howard H. *Cuban-American Radio Wars: Ideology in International Telecommunications.* Norwood, NJ: Ablex, 1986. 200p.

2095.   González, Edward, and David Ronfeldt. *Castro, Cuba and the World.* Santa Monica, CA: Rand Corporation, 1986. 133p.

2096.   Green, Gil. *Cuba: The Continuing Revolution.* 2d ed. New York: International Publishers, 1985. 120p.

2097.   Guevara, Che. *Guerilla Warfare.* Introduction and Case Studies by Brian Loveman and Thomas M. Davies. Lincoln: University of Nebraska Press, 1985. 440p.

2098.   Halebsky, Sandor, and John M. Kirk, eds. *Cuba: Twenty-Five Years of Revolution, 1959-1984.* New York: Praeger, 1985. 446p.

2099.   Harnecker, Marta. *Fidel Castro's Political Strategy: From Moncada to Victory.* New York: Pathfinder, 1987. 157p.

2100.   Hart, Armando. *Changing the Rules of the Game.* Havana: Letras Cubanas, 1983. 111p.

2101.   Horowitz, Irving Louis, ed. *Cuban Communism.* 6th ed. New Brunswick, NJ: Transaction, 1987. 743p.

2102.   Judson, C. Fred. *Cuba and the Revolutionary Myth: The Political Education of the Cuban Rebel Army, 1953-1963.* Boulder, CO: Westview, 1984. 294p.

2103.   Kirk, John M. *José Martí: Mentor of the Cuban Nation.* Tampa: University Presses of Florida, 1983. 201p.

2104.   Kuethe, Allan J. *Cuba 1753-1818: Crown, Military and Society.* Knoxville: University of Tennessee Press, 1986. 213p.

2105.   Latin American Center, UCLA. *José Martí and the Cuban Revolution Retraced.* Proceedings of a conference held at University of California-Los Angeles, March, 1985. Los Angeles, 1986. 76p.

2106.   Leahy, Margaret E. *Development Strategies and the Status of Women: A Comparative Study of the United States, Mexico, the Soviet Union and Cuba.* Boulder, CO: Lynne Rienner, 1986. 167p.

2107.   Liss, Sheldon B. *Roots of Revolution: Radical Thought in Cuba.* Lincoln: University of Nebraska, 1987. 269p.

2108.   McNeill, John Robert. *Atlantic Empires of France and Spain: Louisbourg and Havana, 1700-1763.* Chapel Hill: University of North Carolina, 1985. 329p.

2109.   Medea, Benjamin, Joseph Collins, and Michael Scott. *No Free Lunch: Food and Revolution in Cuba Today.* San Francisco: Institute for Food and Development Policy, 1985. 240p.

2110.   Mesa-Lago, Carmelo, and Jorge Pérez-López. *A Study of Cuba's Material Product System, Its Conversion to the System of National Accounts, and Estimation of Gross Domestic Product per Capital and Growth Rates.* Washington, DC: World Bank, 1985. 104p.

2111.   Montaner, Carlos Alberto. *Cuba, Castro and the Caribbean: The Cuban Revolution and the Crisis in Western Conscience.* Translated by Nelson Duran. New Brunswick, NJ: Transaction, 1985. 116p.

2112.   Montaner, Carlos Alberto. *Fidel Castro y la revolución cubana.* Barcelona, Spain: Plaza & James, 1984. 280p.

2113.   Marrero, Leví. *Cuba: economía y sociedad.* Vol. 4: *Azúcar, ilustración y conciencia, 1763-1868.* Madrid, Spain: Playor, 1985. 416p.

2114.   Pérez, Louis A., Jr. *Cuba between Empires 1878-1920.* Pittsburgh, PA: University of Pittsburgh Press, 1983. 490p.

2115.   Pérez, Louis A., Jr. *Cuba under the Platt Amendment, 1902-1934.*

Pittsburgh, PA: University of Pittsburgh Press, 1986. 410p.

2116.   Pérez-López, Jorge F. *Measuring Cuban Economic Performance.* Austin: University of Texas Press, 1987. 202p.

2117.   Ratliff, William E., ed. *The Selling of Fidel Castro: The Media and the Cuban Revolution.* New Brunswick, NJ: Transaction, 1987. 197p.

2118.   Riesgo, Rodolfo. *Cuba: el movimiento obrero y su retorno socio-político, 1865-1983.* Miami, FL: Saeta, 1985. 251p.

2119.   Ripoll, Carlos. *Harnessing the Intellectuals: Censoring Writers and Artists in Today's Cuba.* Washington, DC: Cuban American National Foundation, 1985. 59p.

2120.   Ripoll, Carlos. *The Heresy of Words in Cuba: Freedom of Expression and Information.* New York: Freedom House, 1985. 55p.

2121.   Ripoll, Carlos. *José Martí: The United States and the Marxist Interpretation of Cuban History.* Rutgers, NJ: Transaction, 1984. 80p.

2122.   Robbins, Carla Anne. *The Cuban Threat.* Philadelphia, PA: ISHI, 1985. 355p.

2123.   Scott, Rebecca J. *Slave Emancipation in Cuba: The Transition to Free Labor, 1860-1899.* Princeton, NJ: Princeton University Press, 1985. 319p.

2124.   Smith, Wayne S. *The Closest of Enemies: A Personal and Diplomatic Account of U.S.-Cuban Relations Since 1957.* New York: Norton, 1987. 308p.

2125.   Stubbs, Jean. *Tobacco on the Periphery: A Case Study of Cuban Labour History, 1860-1958.* New York: Cambridge University Press, 1985. 203p.

2126.   Suchlicki, Jaime. *Cuba: From Columbus to Castro.* 2d ed. Elmsford, NY: Pergamon-Brassey's, 1986. 231p.

2127.   Szulc, Tad. *Fidel: A Critical Portrait.* New York: William Morrow, 1986. 703p.

2128.   Taber, Michael, ed. *Fidel Castro Speeches.* Vol. 2: *Building Socialism in Cuba.* New York: Pathfinder, 1983. 368p.

2129.   Thomas, Hugh S., Georges A. Fauriol, and Juan Carlos Weiss. *The Cuban Revolution: Twenty-Five Years Later.* Boulder, CO: Westview, 1984. 69p.

2130.   Tokatlian, Juan G., ed. *Cuba y Estados Unidos: un debate para la convicencia.* Buenos Aires: Grupo Editor Latinoamérica, 1984. 247p.

2131.   Turton, Peter. *José Martí: Architect of Cuba's Freedom.* London: Zed, 1986. 157p.

2132.   Valladares, Armando. *Against All Hope: The Prison Memoirs of Armando Valladares.* Translated by Andrew Hurley. New York: Knopf (dist. by

Random House), 1986. 380p.

2133.   Welch, Richard E., Jr. *Response to Revolution: The United States and the Cuban Revolution, 1959-1961*. Chapel Hill, University of North Carolina Press, 1985. 243p.

Articles and Chapters

2134.   Aguila, Juan M. del. "Cuba's Declining Fortunes," *Current History* 86:524 (December 1987), 425-428.

2135.   Aguila, Juan M. del. "Cuba's Foreign Policy in Central America and the Caribbean." In *The Dynamics of Latin American Foreign Policies*, edited by Jennie K. Lincoln and Elizabeth G. Ferris. Boulder, CO: Westview, 1984. pp. 251-266.

2136.   Aguila, Juan M. del. "Cuba's Revolution After Twenty-Five Years," *Current History* 84:500 (March 1985), 122-126.

2137.   Aguila, Juan M. del. "Political Developments in Cuba," *Current History* 85:507 (January 1986), 12-15.

2138.   Aguila, Juan M. del. "The Politics of Confrontation: U.S. Policy toward Cuba." In *The Caribbean Challenge: U.S. Policy in a Volatile Region*, edited by H. Michael Erisman. Boulder, CO: Westview, 1984. pp. 95-116.

2139.   Aguirre, B.E. "The Conventionalization of Collective Behavior in Cuba," *American Journal of Sociology* 90:3 (November 1984), 541-566.

2140.   Ameringer, Charles D. "The Auténtico Party and the Political Opposition in Cuba, 1952-57," *Hispanic American Historical Review* 65:2 (May 1985), 327-351.

2141.   Bach, Robert L. "The Cuban Exodus: Political and Economic Motivations" In *The Caribbean Exodus*, edited by Barry B. Levine. New York: Praeger, 1987. pp. 106-130.

2142.   Baloyra Herp, Enrique. "Internationalism and the Limits of Autonomy: Cuba's Foreign Relations." In *Latin American Nations in World Politics*, edited by Heraldo Muñoz and Joseph S. Tulchin. Boulder, CO: Westview, 1984. pp. 168-185.

2143.   Benítez Rojo, Antonio. "La cultura caribena en Cuba: continuidad versus ruptura," *Cuban Studies* 14:1 (Winter 1984), 1-16.

2144.   Benítez Rojo, Antonio. "Power/Sugar/Literature: Toward a Reinterpretation of Cubanness," *Cuban Studies* 16 (1986), 9-31.

2145.   Bergad, Laird, W. "Slave Prices in Cuba, 1840-1875," *Hispanic American Historical Review* 67:4 (November 1987), 631-655.

2146.   Blight, James G., Joseph S. Nye, Jr., and David A. Welch. "The Cuban Missile Crisis Revisited," *Foreign Affairs* 66:1 (Fall 1987), 170-188.

2147.   Brundenius, Claes. "Development and Prospects of Capital Goods

Production in Revolutionary Cuba," *World Development* 15:1 (January 1987), 95-112.

2148. Brundenius, Claes. "Some Notes on the Development of the Cuban Labor Force 1970-80," *Cuban Studies* 13:2 (Summer 1983), 65-77.

2149. Crahan, Margaret E. "Cuba: Religion and Revolutionary Institutionalization," *Journal of Latin American Studies* 17:2 (November 1985), 319-340.

2150. Cuddy, Edward. "America's Cuban Obsession: A Case Study in Diplomacy and Psycho-History," *The Americas* 43:2 (October 1986), 183-196.

2151. Deere, Carmen Diana. "Rural Women and Agrarian Reform in Peru, Chile, and Cuba." In *Women and Change in Latin America,* edited by June Nash and Helen Safa. South Hadley, MA: Bergin & Garvey, 1986. pp. 189-207.

2152. Dilla Alfonso, Haroldo. "Cuba's Role in the Caribbean Basin." In *Conflict in Central America: Approaches to Peace and Security,* edited by Jack Child. London: C. Hurst, 1985. pp. 42-47.

2153. Domínguez, Jorge I. "The Civic Soldier in Cuba." In *Armies and Politics in Latin America,* edited by Abraham F. Lowenthal and Samuel Fitch. Rev. ed. New York: Holmes & Meier, 1986. pp. 262-314.

2154. Domínguez, Jorge I. "Cuba's Relations with Caribbean and Central American Countries," *Cuban Studies* 13:2 (Summer 1983), 79-112.

2155. Domínguez, Jorge I. "Seeking Permission to Build a Nation: Cuban Nationalism and U.S. Response under the First Machado Presidency," *Cuban Studies* 16 (1986), 33-48.

2156. Domínguez, Jorge I. "U.S.-Cuban Relations in the mid-1980s: Issues and Policies," *Journal of Inter-American Studies and World Affairs* 27:1 (February 1985), 17-34.

2157. Duncan, W. Raymond. "Castro and Gorbachëv: Politics of Accommodation," *Problems of Communism* 35:2 (March-April 1986), 45-57.

2158. Eckstein, Susan. "The Impact of the Cuban Revolution: A Comparative Perspective," *Comparative Studies in Society and History* 28:3 (July 1986), 502-534.

2159. Eckstein, Susan. "Restratification after Revolution: The Cuban Experience." In *Crises in the Caribbean Basin,* edited by Richard Tardanico. Beverly Hills, CA: Sage, 1987. pp. 217-240.

2160. Edquist, Charles. "Mechanization of Sugarcane Harvesting in Cuba," *Cuban Studies* 13:2 (Summer 1983), 41-64.

2161. Falk, Pamela S. "Cuba in Africa," *Foreign Affairs* 66:5 (Summer 1987), 1077-1096.

2162. Fernández, Susan. "The Sanctity of Property: American Responses to Cuban Expropriations, 1959-1984," *Cuban Studies* 14:2 (Summer

1984), 21-34.

2163.   Feuer, Carl Henry. "The Performance of the Cuban Sugar Industry, 1981-85," *World Development* 15:1 (January 1987), 67-81.

2164.   Forster, Nancy, and Howard Handelman. "Food Production and Distribution in Cuba: The Impact of the Revolution." In *Food, Politics, and Society in Latin America*, edited by John C. Super and Thomas C. Wright. Lincoln: University of Nebraska Press, 1985. pp. 174-198.

2165.   Fuller, Linda. "Changes in the Relationship among the Unions, Administration, and the Party at the Cuban Workplace, 1959-1982," *Latin American Perspectives* 13:2 (Spring 1986), 6-32.

2166.   Fuller, Linda. "Power at the Workplace: The Resolution of Worker, Management Conflict in Cuba," *World Development* 15:1 (January 1987), 139-152.

2167.   Furtak, Robert K. "Cuba: un cuarto de siglo de política exterior revolucionaria," *Foro Internacional* 25:4 (April-June 1985), 343-361.

2168.   Gonzalez, Edward. "An Alternative Perspective on Radio Martí," *Cuban Studies* 14:2 (Summer 1984), 47-54.

2169.   Gordon, Antonio M., Jr. "The Nutriture of Cubans: Perspective and Nutritional Analysis," *Cuban Studies* 13:2 (Summer 1983), 1-34.

2170.   Gutiérrez Muniz, José, José Camarós Fabián, José Cobas Manriquez, and Rachelle Hertenberg. "The Recent Worldwide Economic Crisis and the Welfare of Children: The Case of Cuba," *World Development* 12:3 (March 984), 247-260.

2171.   Hennessy, Alistair. "Spain and Cuba: An Enduring Relationship." In *The Iberian-Latin American Connection: Implications for U.S. Foreign Policy*, edited by Howard J. Wiarda. Boulder, CO: Westview, 1986. pp. 360-374.

2172.   Insulza, José Miguel."Cuban-Soviet Relations in the New International Setting." In *Soviet-Latin American Relations in the 1980s*, edited by Augusto Varas. Boulder, CO: Westview, 1987. pp. 127-143.

2173.   Jiménez, Alexis C. "Worker Incentives in Cuba," *World Development* 15:1 (January 1987), 127-138.

2174.   Jorge, Antonio. "Growth with Equity: The Failure of the Cuban Case," *Inter-American Review of Bibliography* 35:1 (1985), 48-62.

2175.   Kuethe, Allan J. "Guns, Subsidies, and Commercial Privilege: Some Historical Factors in the Emergence of the Cuban National Character, 1763-1815," *Cuban Studies* 16 (1986), 123-138.

2176.   Landau, Saul. "Understanding Revolution: A Guide for Critics," *Monthly Review* 39:1 (May 1987), 1-13.

2177.   Larguia, Isabel, and John Dumoulin. "Women's Equality and the Cuban Revolution." In *Women and Change in Latin America*, edited by June

Nash and Helen Safa. South Hadley, MA: Bergin & Garvey, 1986. pp. 344-368.

2178.   Latell, Brian. "Cuba after the Third Party Congress," *Current History* 85:515 (December 1986), 425-428.

2179.   Lebow, Richard Ned. "The Cuban Missile Crisis: Reading the Lessons Correctly," *Political Science Quarterly* 98:3 (Fall 1983), 431-458.

2180.   Leiken, Robert S. "Soviet and Cuban Policy in the Caribbean Basin." In *Revolution and Counterrevolution in Central America and the Caribbean,* edited by Donald E. Schulz and Douglas H. Graham. Boulder, CO: Westview, 1984. pp. 447-477.

2181.   LeoGrande, William M. "Cuba." In *Confronting Revolution: Security through Diplomacy in Central America,* edited by Morris J. Blachman, William M. LeoGrande and Kenneth E. Sharpe. New York: Pantheon, 1986. pp. 229-255.

2182.   LeoGrande, William M. "Cuba: Going to the Source." In *From Gunboats to Diplomacy: New U.S. Policies for Latin America,* edited by Richard Newfarmer. Baltimore, MD: Johns Hopkins University Press, 1984. pp. 135-146.

2183.   McColm, R. Bruce. "The Cuban and Soviet Dimension." In *Crisis and Opportunity: U.S. Policy in Central America and the Caribbean,* edited by Mark Falcoff and Robert Royal. Washington, DC: Ethics and Public Policy Center, 1984. pp. 51-78.

2184.   Maingot, Anthony P. "Perceptions as Realities: The United States, Venezuela and Cuba in the Caribbean." In *Latin American Nations in World Politics,* edited by Heraldo Muñoz and Joseph S. Tulchin. Boulder, CO: Westview, 1984. pp. 63-82.

2185.   Mesa-Lago, Carmelo. "Cuba's Centrally Planned Economy: An Equity Trade-off for Growth." In *Latin American Political Economy: Financial Crisis and Political Change,* edited by Jonathan Hartlyn and Samuel A. Morley. Boulder, CO: Westview, 1986. pp. 292-318.

2186.   Messmer, William. "Cuban Agriculture and Personnel Recruitment Policy," *Studies in Comparative International Development* 19:1 (Spring 1984), 3-28.

2187.   Morley, Morris H. "Reinterpreting the State-Class Relationship: American Corporations and U.S. Policy toward Cuba, 1959-1960," *Comparative Politics* 16:1 (October 1983), 67-83.

2188.   Morley, Morris H. "The United States and the Global Economic Blockade of Cuba: A Study in Political Pressures on America's Allies," *Canadian Journal of Political Science* 17:1 (March 1984), 25-48.

2189.   Nazario, Olga. "Brazil's Rapproachment with Cuba: The Process and the Prospect," *Journal of Inter-American Studies and World Affairs* 28:3 (Fall 1986), 67-86.

2190.   Nichols, John Spicer. "A Communication Perspective on Radio Martí,"

Cuban Studies 14:2 (Summer 1984), 35-46.

2191. O'Brien, Philip. "'The Debt Cannot Be Paid': Castro and the Latin American Debt," *Bulletin of Latin American Research* 5:1 (1986), 41-63.

2192. Oostindie, Gert J. "La burguesía cubana y sus caminos de hierro, 1830-1868," *Boletín de Estudios Latinoamericanos ye del Caribe* 37 (December 1984), 99-115.

2193. Packenham, Robert A. "Capitalist vs. Socialist Dependency: The Case of Cuba," *Journal of Inter-American Studies and World Affairs* 28:1 (Spring 1986), 59-92.

2194. Pérez, Lisandro. "The Political Contexts of Cuban Population Censuses, 1899-1981," *Latin American Research Review* 19:2 (1984), 143-161.

2195. Pérez, Louis A., Jr. "Aspects of Hegemony: Labor, State, and Capital in Plattist Cuba," *Cuban Studies* 16 (1986), 49-69.

2196. Pérez, Louis A., Jr. "'La Chambelona': Political Protest, Sugar, and Social Banditry in Cuba, 1914-1917." In *Bandidos: The Varieties of Latin American Banditry,* edited by Richard W. Slatta. Westport, CT: Greenwood, 1987. pp. 131-149.

2197. Pérez, Louis A., Jr. "Dollar Diplomacy, Preventive Intervention, and the Platt Amendment in Cuba, 1909-1912," *Inter-American Economic Affairs* 38:2 (Autumn 1984), 22-44.

2198. Pérez, Louis A., Jr. "Insurrection, Intervention, and the Transformation of Land Tenure Systems in Cuba, 1895-1902," *Hispanic American Historical Review* 65:2 (May 1985), 229-254.

2199. Pérez, Louis A., Jr. "Politics, Peasants, and People of Color: The 1912 'Race War' in Cuba Reconsidered," *Hispanic American Historical Review* 66:3 (August 1986), 509-539.

2200. Pérez, Louis A., Jr. "The Pursuit of Pacification: Banditry and the United States' Occupation of Cuba, 1889-1902," *Journal of Latin American Studies* 18:2 (November 1986), 313-332.

2201. Pérez, Louis A., Jr. "Toward a New Future, From a New Past: The Enterprise of History in Socialist Cuba," *Cuban Studies* 15:1 (Winter 1985), 1-14.

2202. Pérez-López, Jorge F. "Cuban Economy in the 1980s," *Problems of Communism* 35:5 (September-October 1986), 16-34.

2203. Pérez-López, Jorge F. "Nuclear Power in Cuba after Chernobyl," *Journal of Inter-American Studies and World Affairs* 29:2 (Summer 1987), 79-117.

2204. Pérez-López, Jorge F. "Real Economic Growth in Cuba, 1965-1982," *Journal of Developing Areas* 20:2 (January 1986), 151-172.

2205. Petras, James F., Miguel E. Correa, and Roberto P. Korzeniewicz. "The Crises in Market, Collectivist and Mixed Economies: Puerto Rico,

Cuba, and Jamaica." In *Capitalist and Socialist Crises in the Late Twentieth Century,* by James F. Petras. Totowa, NJ: Rowman & Allanheld, 1984. pp. 296-318.

2206.   Pollitt, Brian H. "The Cuban Sugar Economy and the Great Depression," *Bulletin of Latin American Research* 3:2 (1984), 3-28.

2207.   Poyo, Gerald E. "The Anarchist Challenge to the Cuban Independence Movement, 1885-1890," *Cuban Studies* 15:1 (Winter 1985), 29-42.

2208.   Radell, Willard W., Jr. "Cuban-Soviet Sugar Trade, 1960-1976: How Great Was the Subsidy," *Journal of Developing Areas* 17:3 (April 1983), 365-381.

2209.   Richmond, Mark. "Education and Revolution in Socialist Cuba: The Promise of Democratisation." In *Education in Latin America,* edited by Colin Brock and Hugh Lawlor. Dover, NH: Croom Helm, 1985. pp. 9-49.

2210.   Ritter, Archibald R.M. "The Authenticity of Participatory Democracy in Cuba." In *Latin American Prospects for the 1980s,* edited by Archibald R.M. Ritter and David H. Pollock. New York: Praeger, 1983. pp. 182-213.

2211.   Robbins, Carla A. "The 'Cuban Threat' in Central America." In *Political Change in Central America: Internal and External Dimensions,* edited by Wolf Grabendorff, Heinrich-W. Krumwiede and Jörg Todt. Boulder, CO: Westview, 1984. pp. 216-227.

2212.   Rodríguez, José L. "Agricultural Policy and Development in Cuba," *World Development* 15:1 (January 1987), 23-39.

2213.   Rojas, Iliana, Jorge Hernández, and Mariana Ravenet. "Reforma agraria y desarrollo rural en Cuba," *Estudios Rurales Latinoamericanos* 8:3 (September-December 1985), 265-280.

2214.   Santana, Sarah M. "The Cuban Health Care System: Responsiveness to Changing Population Needs and Demands," *World Development* 15:1 (January 1987), 113-125.

2215.   Santí, Enrico Mario. "José Martí and the Cuban Revolution," *Cuban Studies* 16 (1986), 139-150.

2216.   Scott, Rebecca J. "Class Relations in Sugar and Political Mobilization in Cuba, 1868-1899," *Cuban Studies* 15:1 (Winter 1985), 15-28.

2217.   Scott, Rebecca J. "Explaining Abolition: Contradiction, Adaptation, and Challenge in Cuban Slave Society, 1860-1886," *Comparative Studies in Society and History* 26:1 (January 1984), 83-111.

2218.   Scott, Rebecca J. "The Transformation of Sugar Production in Cuba after Emancipation, 1880-1900: Planters, Colonos and Former Slaves." In *Crisis and Change in the International Sugar Economy, 1860-1914,* edited by Bill Albert and Adrian Graves. Edinburgh, Scotland: ISC Press, 1984. pp. 111-120.

2219.   Sims, Harold D. "Cuban Labor and the Communist Party, 1937-1958,"

Cuban Studies 15:1 (Winter 1985), 43-58.

2220. Slater, David. "Socialismo, democracia y el imperativo territorial: elementos para una comparación de las experiencias cubana y nicaragüense," *Estudios Sociales Centroamericanos* 44 (May-August, 1987), 20-40.

2221. Sloan, John W. "Comparative Public Policy in Cuba and Brazil," *Studies in Comparative International Development* 18:3 (Fall, 1983), 50-76.

2222. Smith, John T. "Sugar Dependency in Cuba: Capitalism versus Socialism." In *The Gap Between Rich and Poor,* edited by Mitchell A. Seligson. Boulder, CO: Westview, 1984, pp. 366-378.

2223. Smith, Wayne S. "We Should Talk with Castro." In *Crisis and Opportunity: U.S. Policy in Central America and the Caribbean,* edited by Mark Falcoff and Robert Royal. Washington, DC: Ethics and Public Policy Center, 1984. pp. 159-164.

2224. Stuart, Angelica. "Impressions of the Cuban Revolution," *Latin American Perspectives* 11:3 (Summer 1984), 141-148.

2225. Stubbs, Jean. "Gender Issues in Contemporary Cuban Tobacco Farming," *World Development* 15:1 (January 1987), 41-65.

2226. Thomas, Hugh. "Cuba: The United States and Batista, 1952-58," *World Affairs* 149:4 (Spring 1987), 169-175.

2227. Turits, Richard. "Trade, Debt, and the Cuban Economy," *World Development* 15:1 (January 1987), 163-180.

2228. Wessman, James. "Sugar and Demography: Population Dynamics in the Spanish Antilles during the Nineteenth and Twentieth Centuries." In *Crisis and Change in the International Sugar Economy, 1860-1914,* edited by Bill Albert and Adrian Graves. Edinburgh, Scotland ISC Press, 1984. pp. 95-110.

2229. White, Gordon. "Cuban Planning in the Mid-1980s: Centralization, Decentralization and Participation," *World Development* 15:1 (January 1987), 153-161.

2230. Wilde, Kathleen L. "The Cuban and Nicaraguan Revolutions: Viewpoints of a Peace and Social Justice Activist," *Journal of Third World Studies* 3:2 (Fall 1986), 111-116.

2231. Yopo H., Boris. "Soviet Military Assistance to Cuba and Nicaragua, 1980-1984." In *Soviet-Latin American Relations in the 1980s,* edited by Augusto Varas. Boulder, CO: Westview, 1987. pp. 105-126.

2232. Zimbalist, Andrew. "Cuban Industrial Growth, 1965-84," *World Development* 15:1 (January 1987), 83-93.

2233. Zimbalist, Andrew, and Susan Eckstein. "Patterns of Cuban Development: The First Twenty-Five Years," *World Development* 15:1 (January 1987), 5-22.

DOMINICAN REPUBLIC

Books and Monographs

2234.   Black Jan Knippers. *The Dominican Republic: Politics and Development in an Unsovereign State.* Winchester, MA: Allen & Unwin, 1986. 164p.

2235.   Calder, Bruce J. *The Impact of Intervention: The Dominican Republic during the U.S. Occupation of 1916-1924.* Austin: University of Texas Press, 1984. 334p.

2236.   Ceara Hatton, Miguel. *Tendencias estructurales y coyuntura de la economía dominicana, 1968-1983.* Santo Domingo, Dominican Republic: Departmento de Investigaciones Económicas y Sociales, Fundación Friedrich Ebert, 1984. 265p.

2237.   Cross Beras, Julio A. *Sociedad y desarrollo en República Dominicana, 1844-1899.* Santo Domingo: Instituto Tecnológico de Santo Domingo, 1984. 262p.

2238.   Díaz Santana, Miriam, and Martin F. Murphy. *The 1982 National Elections in the Dominican Republic: A Sociological and Historical Interpretation.* Rio Piedras: Institute of Caribbean Studies, University of Puerto Rico, 1983. 76p.

2239.   Ferreras, Ramón Alberto. *Enfoques de la intervención military norteamericana a la República Dominicana, 1916-1924.* Santo Domingo, Dominican Republic: Nordeste, 1984. 368p.

2240.   Herman, Edward S., and Frank Brodhead. *Demonstration Elections: U.S.-Staged Elections in the Dominican Republic, Vietnam and El Salvador.* Boston, MA: South End, 1984. 270p.

2241.   Lora Medrano, Luis Eduardo. *Petán: la voz dominicana, su gente, sus cosas y sus cuentos.* Santo Domingo, Dominican Republic: Tele-3, 1984. 305p.

2242.   McCarthy, F. Desmond. *Macroeconomic Policy Alternatives in the Dominican Republic: An Analytical Framework.* Washington, DC: World Bank, 1984. 64p.

2243.   Moreno Ceballos, Nelson. *El estado dominicano: origen, evolución y su forma actual, 1844-1982.* Santo Domingo, Dominican Republic: Punto y Aparte, 1983. 351p.

2244.   Vedovato, Claudio. *Politics, Foreign Trade and Economic Development: A Study of the Dominican Republic.* New York: St. Martin's, 1986. 191p.

2245.   Vega, Bernardo. *Nazismo, fascismo y falangismo en la República Dominicana.* Santo Domingo, Dominican Republic: Fundación Cultural Dominicana, 1985. 415p.

2246.   Vega, Bernardo, ed. *Los Estados Unidos y Trujillo: collección de documentos del Departamento de Estado y de las fuerzas armadas norteamericanas. Año, 1947.* Santo Domingo, Dominican Republic: Fundación Cultural Dominicana, 1984. 2 vols.

2247.   World Bank. *Dominican Republic: Economic Prospects and Policies to Renew Growth.* Washington, DC: 1985. 174p.

Articles and Chapters

2248.   Abel, Christopher. "Politics and the Economy of the Dominican Republic, 1890-1930." In *Latin America, Economic Imperialism and the State,* edited by Christopher Abel and Colin M. Lewis. London; Dover, NH: Athlone, 1985. pp. 339-366.

2249.   Baud, Michiel. "The Origins of Capitalist Agriculture in the Dominican Republic," *Latin American Research Review* 22:2 (1987), 135-154.

2250.   Brands, H.W., Jr. "Decisions on American Armed Intervention: Lebanon, Dominican Republic, and Grenada," *Political Science Quarterly* 102:4 (Winter 1987-88), 607-624.

2251.   Bray, David B. "The Dominican Exodus: Origins, Problems, Solutions." In *The Caribbean Exodus,* edited by Barry B. Levine. New York: Praeger, 1987. pp. 152-170.

2252.   Bray, David B. "Industrialization, Labor Migration and Employment Crises: A Comparison of Jamaica and the Dominican Republic." In *Crises in the Caribbean Basin,* edited by Richard Tardanico. Beverly Hills, CA: Sage, 1987. pp. 79-93.

2253.   Chardon, Roland. "Sugar Plantations in the Dominican Republic," *Geographical Review* 74:4 (October 1984), 441-454.

2254.   Grasmuck, Sherri. "The Consequences of Dominican Urban Outmigration for National Development: The Case of Santiago ." In *The Americas in the New International Division of Labor,* edited by Steven E. Sanderson. New York: Holmes & Meier, 1985. pp. 145-176.

2255.   Murphy, Martin F. "The International Monetary Fund and Contemporary

Crisis in the Dominican Republic." In *Crises in the Caribbean Basin,* edited by Richard Tardanico. Beverly Hills, CA: Sage, 1987. pp. 241-259.

2256.   Musgrove, Philip. "Distribución del ingreso familiar en la República Dominicana 1976-1977: la encuesta nacional de ingresos y gastos familiares," *El Trimestre Económico* 53:210 (April-June 1986), 341-392.

2257.   Musgrove, Philip. "Household Food Consumption in the Dominican Republic: Effects of Income, Price, and Family Size," *Economic Development and Cultural Change* 34:1 (October 1985), 83-101.

2258.   Van Tassell, G. Lane. "American-Dominican Economic Linkages: External Financing and Domestic Politics Surrounding the 1965 U.S. Intervention," *Journal of Third World Studies* 4:2 (Fall 1987), 121-131.

2259.   Veloz, Alberto, Douglas Southgate, Fred Hitzhusen, and Robert Macgregor. "The Economics of Erosion Control in a Sub-Tropical Watershed: A Dominican Case," *Land Economics* 61:2 (May 1985), 145-155.

ECUADOR

Books and Monographs

2260.　Barriga López, Franklin. *Ecuador: la patria y la cultura*. Quito: Instituto Ecuatoriano de Credito Educativo y Becas, Universidad Central Del Ecuador, 1984. 289p.

2261.　Dávila Aldas, Francisco R. *Las luchas por la hegemonía y la consolidación política de la burguesia en Ecuador, 1972-1978*. Mexico City: Universidad Autónoma de México, 1984. 247p.

2262.　Economic Commission for Latin America. *La presencia de las empresas transcionales en la economía ecuatoriana*. Santiago, Chile: United Nations, 1984. 77p.

2263.　Hurtado, Osvaldo. *Political Power in Ecuador*. 2d ed. Translated by Nick D. Mills. Boulder, CO: Westview, 1985. 398p.

2264.　Luzuriaga C., Carlos, and Clarence Zuvekas, Jr. *Income Distribution and Poverty in Rural Ecuador: 1950-1979, A Survey of the Literature*. Tempe: Center for Latin American Studies, Arizona State University, 1983. 240p.

2265.　Martz, John D. *Politics and Petroleum in Ecuador*. New Brunswick, NJ: Transaction, 1987. 432p.

2266.　Mörner, Magnus. *The Andean Past: Land, Societies and Conflict*. New York: Columbia University Press, 1985. 300p.

2267.　Rodríguez, Linda Alexander. *The Search for Public Policy: Regional Politics and Government Finances in Ecuador, 1830-1940*. Berkeley: University of California Press, 1985. 281p.

2268.　Rodríguez de Troya, Ludmila. *Examen y evaluación de la década de la mujer en el Ecuador, 1976-1985*. Quito: Comité Ecuatoriano de Cooperación con la Comisión Interamericana de Mujeres, 1984. 253p.

2269.   Salomon, Frank. *Native Lords of Quito in the Age of the Incas: The Political Economy of North-Andean Chiefdoms.* New York: Cambridge University Press, 1986. 274p.

2270.   Schodt, David W. *Ecuador: An Andean Enigma.* Boulder, CO: Westview, 1987. 188p.

2271.   Whitten, Norman E., Jr. *Sicuanga Runa: The Other Side of Development in Amazonian Ecuador.* Urbana: University of Illinois Press, 1984. 314p.

2272.   World Bank. *Ecuador: An Agenda for Recovery and Sustained Growth.* Washington, DC, 1985. 183p.

Articles and Chapters

2273.   Archetti, Eduardo P. "Estructura agraria y diferenciación campesina en la sierra ecuatoriana," *Estudios Rurales Latinoamericanos* 9:1 (January-April 1986), 17-42.

2274.   Avery, William P. "Origins and Consequences of the Border Dispute between Ecuador and Peru," *Inter-American Economic Affairs* 38:1 (Summer 1984), 65-77.

2275.   Belote, Linda Smith, and Jim Belote. "Drain from the Bottom: Individual Ethnic Identity Change in Southern Ecuador," *Social Forces* 63:1 (September 1984), 25-50.

2276.   Black, Jan Knipers. "Ten Paradoxes of Rural Development: An Ecuadorian Case Study," *Journal of Developing Areas* 19:4 (July 1985), 527-555.

2277.   Bocco, Arnaldo M. "Ecuador: política económica y estilos de desarrollo en la fase de auge petrolero, 1972-78," *Desarrollo Económico* 22:88 (January-March 1983), 485-510.

2278.   Bottasso, Juan. "Las misiones y la aculturación de los Shuar," *América Indígena* 44:1 (January-March 1984), 143-155.

2279.   Chiriboga Vega, Manuel. "El análisis de las formas tradicionales: el caso de Ecuador," *América Indígena* 43 (December 1983), 37-99.

2280.   Chiriboga Vega, Manuel. "Estado, agro y acumulación en el Ecuador: una perspectiva histórica," *Estudios Rurales Latinoamericanos* 7:2 (May-August 1984), 35-80.

2281.   Conaghan, Catherine M. "Party Politics and Democratization in Ecuador." In *Authoritarians and Democrats: Regime Transition in Latin America,* edited by James M. Malloy and Mitchell A. Seligson. Pittsburgh, PA: University of Pittsburgh Press, 1987. pp. 145-163.

2282.   Corkill, David. "Democratic Politics in Ecuador, 1979-1984," *Bulletin of Latin American Research* 4:2 (1985), 63-74.

2283.   Descola, Philippe. "Cambios en la territorialidad y en la apropiación de al tierra entre los Achur," *Américan Indígena* 43:2 (April-June

1983), 299-318.

2284.   Fitch, J. Samuel. "The Military Coup d'Etat as a Political Process: A General Framework and the Ecuadorian Case." In *Armies and Politics in Latin America,* edited by Abraham F. Lowenthal and Samuel Fitch. Rev. ed. New York: Holmes & Meier, 1986. pp. 151-164.

2285.   Gros, Christian. "Luchas indígenas y prácticas autogestionarias: algunas reflexiones a partir de tres estudios de caso," *Estudios Rurales Latinoamericanos* 10:1 (January-April 1987), 55-69.

2286.   Jara, Carlos, and Roberto Mizrahi. "Alimentos: dimensión estratégica del desarrollo nacional ecuatoriano: un planteo metodológico para encarar su tratamiento," *Estudios Rurales Latinoamericanos* 6:2-3 (May-December 1983), 181-199.

2287.   Knapp, Gregory. "Una perspective de la irrigación en los Andes del Norte," *América Indígena* 46:2 (April-June 1986), 349-355.

2288.   Lehmann, David. "Sharecropping and the Capitalist Transition in Agriculture: Some Evidence from the Highlands of Ecuador," *Journal of Development Economics* 23:2 (October 1986), 333-354.

2289.   Levy, James, and Nick D. Mills, Jr. "The Challenge to Democratic Reformism in Ecuador," *Studies in Comparative International Development* 18:4 (Winter 1983), 3-33.

2290.   Lipski, John M. "The Chota Valley: Afro-Hispanic Language in Highland Ecuador," *Latin American Research Review* 22:1 (1987), 155-170.

2291.   Llovet, Ignacio D. "Algunas consideraciones acerca de las peculiaridades de diferenciación campesina en el Ecuador," *Boletín de Estudios Latinoamericanos y del Caribe* 38 (June 1985), 47-59.

2292.   Llovet, Ignacio D. "Capitalism and Social Differentiation: The Case of Ecuador's Rural Population," *Latin American Perspectives* 13:4 (Fall 1986), 60-85.

2293.   MacDonald, Theodore. "Tierras indígenas en Ecuador: un estudio de caso," *América Indígena* 43:3 (July-September 1983), 555-568.

2294.   Martz, John D. "Ecuador: The Right Takes Command," *Current History* 84:499 (February 1985), 69-72.

2295.   Martz, John D. "Populist Leadership and the Party Caudillo: Ecuador and the CFP, 1962-81," *Studies in Comparative International Development* 18:3 (Fall 1983), 22-49.

2296.   Naranjo, Plutarco. "El ayahuasca en la arqueología ecuatoriana," *América Indígena* 46:1 (January-March 1986), 117-127.

2297.   Nickelsburg, Gerald. "Inflation, Expectations and Qualitative Government Policy in Ecuador, 1970-82," *World Development* 15:8 (August 1987), 1077-1085.

2298.   North, Liisa L. "Problems of Democratization in Peru and Ecuador." In

Latin American Prospects for the 1980s, edited by Archibald R.M. Ritter and David H. Pollock. New York: Praeger, 1983. pp. 214-239.

2299. Pérez Sáinz, J.P. "Clase obrera y reproducción de la fuerza de trabajo en Ecuador: el caso de los obreros textiles en Quito," *Revista Paraguaya de Sociología* 23:66 (May-August 1986), 87-112.

2300. Pérez Sáinz, J.P. "Industrialización y fuerza de trabajo en Ecuador," *Boletín de Estudios Latinoamericanos y de Caribe* 37 (December 1984), 19-43.

2301. Preston, Rosemary. "Popular Education in Andean America: The Case of Ecuador." In *Education in Latin America,* edited by Colin Brock and Hugh Lawlor. Dover, NH: Croom Helm, 1985. pp. 92-108.

2302. Salomon, Frank. "A North Andean Status Trader Complex under the Inka Rule," *Ethnohistory* 34:1 (Winter 1987, 63-77.

2303. Salomon, Frank, and Sue Grosboll. "Names and Peoples in Incaic, Quito: Retrieving Undocumented Historic Processes through Anthroponymy and Statistics," *American Anthropologist* 88:2 (June 1986), 387-399.

2304. Santana, Roberto. "La cuestión étnica y la democracia en Ecuador," *Revista Mexicana de Sociología* 49:2 (April-June 1987), 127-144.

2305. Vos, Rob. "El modelo de desarrollo y el sector agrícola en Ecuador, 1965-1982," *El Trimestre Económico* 52:208 (October-December 1985), 1097-1140.

2306. Weiss, Wendy A. "The Social Organization of Property and Work: A Study of Migrants from the Rural Ecuadorian Sierra," *American Ethnologist* 12:3 (August 1985), 468-488.

EL SALVADOR

Books and Monographs

2307. Bonner, Raymond, *Weakness and Deceit: U.S. Policy and El Salvador.* New York: Times Books, 1984. 408p.

2308. Buckley, Tom. *Violent Neighbors: El Salvador, Central America, and the U.S.A.* New York: Times Books, 1984. 358p.

2309. Cabarrús P., Carlos Rafael. *Génesis de una revolución: análisis del surgimiento y desarrollo de la organización campesina en El Salvador.* Mexico City: Centro de Investigaciones y Estudios Superiores en Antropología Social, 1983. 411p.

2310. Castro Morán, Mariano. *Función política de ejército salvadoreño en el presente siglo.* San Salavdor: EDUCA, 1984. 455p.

2311. Clements, Charles. *Witness to War: An American Doctor in El Salvador.* Toronto; New York: Bantam, 1984. 268p.

2312. Demarest, Arthur A. *The Archaeology of Santa Leticia and the Rise of Maya Civilization.* New Orleans, LA: Middle American Research Institute, Tulane University, 1986. 272p.

2313. Duarte, José Napoleón with Diana Page. *Duarte: My Story.* New York: Putnam, 1986. 284p.

2314. Herman, Edward S., and Frank Brodhead. *Demonstration Elections: U.S.-Staged Elections in the Dominican Republic, Vietnam and El Salvador.* Boston, MA: South End, 1984. 270p.

2315. Kaufman, Daniel, and David L. Lindauer. *Income Transfers within Extended Families to Meet Basic Needs: The Evidence from El Salvador.* Washington, DC: World Bank, 1984. 60p.

2316.   McClintock, Michael. *The American Connection.* Vol. 1: *State Terror and Popular Resistance in El Salvador.* London, Zed (Totowa, NJ: Dist. by Biblio Distribution Center), 1985. 400p.

2317.   Pearce, Jenny. *Promised Land: Peasant Rebellion in Chalatenango, El Salvador.* London: Latin American Bureau (New York: Dist. by Monthly Review Foundation), 1986. 324p.

2318.   Russell, Philip L. *El Salvador in Crisis.* Austin, TX: Colorado River, 1984. 168p.

2319.   Schmidt, Steffen Walter. *El Salvador: America's Next Vietnam?* Salisbury, NC: Documentary Publications, 1983. 217p.

2320.   Sheets, Payson, D., ed. *Archaeology and Volcanism in Central America: The Zapotitán Valley of El Salvador.* Austin: University of Texas Press, 1984. 307p.

2321.   Thomson, Marilyn. *The Women of El Salvador: The Price of Freedom.* Philadelphia, PA: ISHI, 1986. 165p.

Articles and Chapters

2322.   Anderson, Thomas P. "El Salvador's Dim Prospect," *Current History* 85:507 (January 1986), 9-11.

2323.   Arnesen, Eric. "El Salvador: Reminders of War," *Monthly Review* 38:5 (October 1986), 20-28.

2324.   Arnson, Cynthia J. "The Salvadoran Military and Regime Transformation." In *Political Change in Central America: Internal and External Dimensions,* edited by Wolf Grabendorff, Heinrich-W Krumwiede and Jörg Todt. Boulder, CO: Westview, 1984. pp. 97-113.

2325.   Baktiari, Bahman. "Revolution and the Church in Nicaragua and El Salvador," *Journal of Church and State* 28:1 (Winter 1986), 14-42.

2326.   Baloyra, Enrique A. "Dilemmas of Political Transition in El Salvador," *Journal of International Affairs* 38:2 (Winter 1985), 221-242.

2327.   Baloyra, Enrique A. "Negotiating War in El Salvador: The Politics of Endgame," *Journal of Inter-American Studies and World Affairs* 28:1 (Spring 1986), 123-147.

2328.   Baloyra, Enrique A. "Political Change in El Salvador?" *Current History* 83:490 (February 1984), 54-58.

2329.   Baloyra, Enrique A. "Reactionary Despostism in El Salvador: An Impediment to Democratic Transition." In *Trouble in Our Backyard: Central America and the United States in the Eighties,* edited by Martin Diskin. New York: Pantheon, 1983. pp. 101-123.

2330.   Baloyra, Enrique A. "The Seven Plagues of El Salvador, *Current History* 86:524 (December 1987), 413-416.

2331.   Barry, Tom, and Deb Preusch. "The War in El Salvador; A Reassessment," *Monthly Review* 38:11 (April 1987), 29-44.

2332.   Berryman, Phillip. "El Salvador: From Evangelization to Insurrection." In *Religion and Political Conflict in Latin America,* edited by Daniel H. Levine. Chapel Hill: University of North Carolina Press, 1986. pp. 58-78.

2333.   Blachman, Morris J., and Kenneth Sharpe. "El Salvador: The Policy That Failed." In *From Gunboats to Diplomacy: New U.S. Policies for Latin America,* edited by Richard Newfarmer. Baltimore, MD: Johns Hopkins University Press, 1984. pp. 72-88.

2334.   Booth, John A. "The Evolution of U.S. Policy toward El Salvador: The Politics of Repression." In *The Caribbean Challenge: U.S. Policy in a Volatile Region,* edited by H. Michael Erisman. Boulder, CO: Westview, 1984. pp. 117-140.

2335.   Brockman, James R. "Oscar Romero: Sheperd of the Poor," *Third World Quarterly* 6:2 (April 1984), 446-457.

2336.   Browing, David. "Agrarian Reform in El Salvador," *Journal of Latin American Studies* 15:2 (November 1983), 399-426.

2337.   Burns, E. Bradford. "The Modernization of Underdevelopment: El Salvador, 1858-1931," *Journal of Developing Areas* 18:3 (April 1984), 293-316.

2338.   Chitnis, Pratap C. "Observing El Salvador: The 1984 Elections," *Third World Quarterly* 6:4 (October 1984), 963-980.

2339.   Comisión Político-Diplomática, FMLN-FDR. "Análisis del nuevo gobierno salvadoreño y de su contexto internacional," *Revista Mexicana de Sociología* 46:3 (July-September 1984), 111-141.

2340.   Deogh, Dermot. "The United States and the Coup d'Etat in El Salvador, 15 October 1979: A Case Study in American Foreign Policy Perceptions and Decision-Making." In *Human Rights and U.S. Foreign Policy,* edited by Dermot Keogh. Cork, Ireland: Cork University Press, 1985. pp. 21-69.

2341.   Department of Social Sciences, Universidad de El Salvador. "An Analysis of the Correlation of Forces in El Salvador," *Latin American Perspectives* 14:4 (Fall 1987), 426-452.

2342.   Diskin, Martin, and Kenneth E. Sharpe. "El Salvador." In *Confronting Revolution: Security through Diplomacy in Central America,* edited by Morris J. Blachman, William M. LeoGrande and Kenneth E. Sharpe. New York: Pantheon, 1986. pp. 50-87.

2343.   Eguizábal, Cristina. "La política exterior de la administración Duarte en El Salvador," *Estudios Sociales Centroamericanos* 43 (January-April 1987), 75-86.

2344.   Equipo de Trabajo del Departmento de Letras de la UCA. "Los medios de comunicación un arma más en la contienda," *Estudios Sociales Centroamericanos* 41 (May-August 1986), 61-86.

2345.   Ferguson, Anne. "Marketing Medicines: Pharmaceutical Services in a Salvadoran Community," *Latin American Perspectives* 10:4 (Fall 1983), 40-58.

2346.   Fundación Salvadoreña de Desarrollo y Vivienda Mínima. "Exploración preliminar sobre las condiciones de vida en los tugurios de San Salvador," *Estudios Sociales Centroamericanos* 44 (May-August 1987), 79-89.

2347.   García, José Z. "El Salvador: A Glimmer of Hope," *Current History* 85:515 (December 1986), 409-412.

2348.   García, José Z. "El Salvador: Legitimizing the Government," *Current History* 84:500 (March 1985), 101-104.

2349.   Herring, George C. "Vietnam, El Salvador, and the Uses of History." In *The Central American Crisis: Sources of Conflict and the Failure of U.S. Policy,* edited by Kenneth M. Coleman and George C. Herring. Wilmington, DE: Scholarly Resources, 1985. pp. 97-110.

2350.   Hutson, Heyward G. "Are the Salvadoran Armed Forces Ready to Fold," *World Affairs* 146:3 (Winter 1983-84), 263-271.

2351.   IIE, Universidad Centroamericana. "Hacia una economía de guerra: El Salvador 1982-1983," *Revista Mexicana de Sociología* 46:3 (July-September 1984), 155-184.

2352.   Jung, Harald. "The Civil War in El Salvador." In *Political Change in Central America: Internal and External Dimensions,* edited by Wolf Grabendorff, Heinrich-W. Krumwiede and Jörg Todt. Boulder, CO: Westview, 1984. pp. 82-96.

2353.   Karl, Terry Lynn. "The Prospects for Democratization in El Salvador," *World Policy Journal* 2:2 (Spring 1985), 305-330.

2354.   Kincaid, A. Douglas. "Peasants into Rebels: Community and Class in Rural El Salvador," *Comparative Studies in Society and History* 29:3 (July 1987), 466-494.

2355.   Kuhn, Gary G. "Church and State Conflict in El Salvador as a Cause of the Central American War of 1863," *Journal of Church and State* 27:3 (Autumn 1985), 455-462.

2356.   Luhan, J. Michael. "AIFLD's Salvador Labor Wars," *Dissent* (Summer 1986), 340-350.

2357.   Mason, T. David. "Land Reform and the Breakdown of Clientelist Politics in El Salvador," *Comparative Political Studies* 18:4 (January 1986), 487-516.

2358.   Montgomery, Tommie Sue. "El Salvador: The Roots of Revolution." In *Central America: Crisis and Adaptation,* edited by Steve C. Ropp and James A. Morris. Albuquerque: University of New Mexico Press, 1984. pp. 67-118.

2359.   Mooney, Joseph P. "Was It a WORSENING of Economic and Social Conditions That Brought Violence and Civil War to El Salvador?"

Inter-American Economic Affairs 38:2 (Autumn 1984), 61-69.

2360. Petras, James F. "The Anatomy of State Terror: Chile, El Salvador and Brazil," *Science and Society* 51:3 (Fall 1987), 314-338.

2361. Petras, James F., and Morris H. Morley. "Supporting Repression: U.S. Policy and the Demise of Human Rights in El Salvador, 1979-1981." In *Capitalist and Socialist Crises in the Late Twentieth Century* by James F. Petras. Totowa, NJ: Rowman & Allanheld, 1984. pp. 44-68.

2362. Ptacek, Kerry. "Misconceptions about the Role of the Church." In *Crisis and Opportunity: U.S. Policy in Central America and the Caribbean,* edited by Mark Falcoff and Robert Royal. Washington, DC: Ethics and Public Policy Center, 1984. pp. 263-278.

2363. Radu, Michael. "The Structure of the Salvadoran Left," *Orbis* 28:4 (Winter 1985), 673-684.

2364. Reinhardt, Nola. "Agro-Exports and the Peasantry in the Agrarian Reforms of El Salvador and Nicaragua," *World Development* 15:7 (July 1987), 941-959.

2365. Schulz, Donald E. "El Salvador: Revolution and Counterrevolution in the Living Museum." In *Revolution and Counterrevolution in Central American and the Caribbean,* edited by Donald E. Schulz and Douglas H. Graham. Boulder, CO: Westview, 1984. pp. 189-268.

2366. Shapiro, Charles S. "U.S. Policy in Central America: The Case of El Salvador," *Journal of Third World Studies* 2:1 (Spring 1985), 1-6.

2367. Sharpe, Kenneth E. "Why Duarte Is in Trouble," *World Policy Journal* 3:3 (Summer 1986), 473-494.

2368. Sharpe, Kenneth E., and Martin Diskin. "Facing Facts in El Salvador: Reconciliation or War," *World Policy Journal* 1:3 (Spring 1984), 517-547.

2369. Shugart, Matthew Soberg. "States, Revolutionary Conflict and Democracy: El Salvador and Nicaragua in Comparative Perspective," *Government and Opposition* 22:1 (Winter 1987), 13-22.

2370. Ungo, Guillermo M. "Causas y perspectivas de la guerra civil en El Salvador," *Revista Mexicana de Sociología* 46:3 (July-September 1984), 143-154.

2371. Ungo, Guillermo M. "The People's Struggle," *Foreign Policy* 52 (Fall 1983), 51-63.

2372. Verner, Joel G., and Marge M. Thoennes. "Los salvadoreños y el asilo político en Estados Unidos," *Foro Internacional* 26:1 (July-September 1985), 55-84.

2373. Zaid, Gabriel. "Salvadorans Go to the Ballot Box," *Dissent* (Fall 1984), 453-458.

GRENADA

Books and Monographs

2374. Ambrusley, Fitzroy, and James Dunkerley. *Grenada: Whose Freedom?* London: Latin American Bureau, 1984. 128p.

2375. Bishop, Maurice. *In Nobody's Backyard. Maurice Bishop's Speeches, 1979-1983: A Memorial Volume.* London: Zed, 1984. 260p.

2376. Bishop, Maurice. *Maurice Bishop Speaks: The Grenada Revolution, 1979-1983.* Edited by Bruce Marcus and Michael Taber. New York: Pathfinder, 1984. 352p.

2377. Brizan, George. *Grenada: Island of Conflict - From Amerindians to People's Revolution,* 1948-1979. London: Zed, 1984. 381p.

2378. Carew, Jan. *Grenada: The Hour Will Strike Again.* Chicago: Imported Publications, 1986. 278p.

2379. Cox, Edward L. *Free Coloreds in the Slave Societies of St. Kitts and Grenada, 1763-1833.* Knoxville: University of Tennessee Press, 1984. 197p.

2380. Davidson, Scott. *Grenada: A Study in Politics and the Limits of International Law.* Brookfield, VT: Gower, 1987. 196p.

2381. Dunn, Peter M., and Bruce W. Watson, eds. *American Intervention in Grenada: The Implications of Operation "Urgent Fury".* Boulder, CO: Westview, 1985. 185p.

2382. Gilmore, William C. *The Grenada Intervention: Analysis and Documentation.* Berlin: A. Spitz, 1984. 116p.

2383. Lewis, David E. *Reform and Revolution in Grenada, 1950 to 1981.* Havana, Cuba: Casa de las Américas, 1984. 264p.

2384.   Lewis, Gordon K. *Grenada: The Jewel Despoiled.* Baltimore, MD: Johns Hopkins University Press, 1987. 239p.

2385.   Mandle, Jay R. *Big Revolution, Small Country: The Rise and Fall of the Grenada Revolution.* Lanham, MD: North-South, 1985. 107p.

2386.   Payne, Anthony, Paul Sutton, and Tony Thorndike. *Grenada: Revolution and Invasion.* New York: St. Martin's, 1984. 233p.

2387.   Pryor, Fredric L. *Revolutionary Grenada: A Study in Political Economy.* New York: Praeger, 1986. 395p.

2388.   Sandford, Gregory. *The New Jewel Movement: Grenada's Revolution, 1979-1983.* Edited by Diane B. Bendahmane. Washington, DC: Foreign Service Institute, U.S. Department of State, 1985. 215p.

2389.   Sandford, Gregory, and Richard Vigilante. *Grenada: The Untold Story.* Lanham, MD: Madison, 1984. 180p.

2390.   Schoenhals, Kai P., and Richard A. Melanson. *Revolution and Intervention in Grenada: The New Jewel Movement, the United States, and the Caribbean.* Boulder, CO: Westview, 1985. 211p.

2391.   Seabury, Paul, and Walter A. McDougall, eds. *The Grenada Papers.* San Francisco: ICS, 1984. 346p.

2392.   Searle, Chris. *Grenada: The Struggle against Destabilization.* London: Writers & Readers (Norton, NY: Dist. by Norton), 1983. 164p.

2393.   Searle, Chris. *Words Unchained: Language and Revolution in Grenada.* London: Zed, 1984. 260p.

2394.   Thorndike, Tony. *Grenada: Politics, Economics and Society.* Boulder, CO: Lynne Rienner, 1985. 206p.

2395.   Valenta, Jiri, and Herbert J. Ellison, eds. *Grenada and Soviet/Cuban Policy: Internal Crisis and U.S./OECS Intervention.* Boulder, CO: Westview, 1986. 512p.

Articles and Chapters

2396.   Bell, Wendell. "The Invasion of Grenada: A Note on False Prophecy," *Yale Review* 75:4 (October 1986), 564-586.

2397.   Boodhoo, Ken I. "Violence and Militarization in the Eastern Caribbean: The Case of Grenada.: In *Militarization in the Non-Hispanic Caribbean,* edited by Alma H. Young and Dion E. Phillips. Boulder, CO: Lynne Rienner, 1986. pp. 65-89.

2398.   Brands, H.W., Jr. "Decisions on American Armed Intervention: Lebanon, Dominican Republic, and Grenada," *Political Science Quarterly* 102:4 (Winter 1987-88), 607-624.

2399.   Castro, Fidel. "On Grenada," *Monthly Review* 35:8 (January 1984), 11-29.

2400.   Connell-Smith, Gordon. "The Grenada Invasion in Historical Perspective:

From Monroe to Reagan," *Third World Quarterly* 6:2 (April 1984), 432-445.

2401. Henfrey, Colin. "Between Populism and Leninism: The Grenadian Experience." *Latin American Perspectives* 11:3 (Summer 1984), 15-36.

2402. Joyner, Christopher C. "The United States Action in Grenada: Reflections on the Lawfulness of Invasion," *American Journal of International Law* (January 1984), 131-144.

2403. Kenworthy, Eldon. "Grenada as Theater," *World Policy Journal* 1:3 (Spring 1984), 635-651.

2404. LaDuke, Betty. "Women, Art, and Culture in New Grenada," *Latin American Perspectives* 11:3 (Summer 1984), 37-52.

2405. MacDonald, Scott B. "The Future of Foreign Aid in the Caribbean after Grenada: Finlandization and Confrontation in the Eastern Tier," *Inter-American Economic Affairs* 38:4 (Spring 1985), 59-74.

2406. Moore, John N. "Grenada and the International Double Standard," *American Journal of International Law* 78:1 (January 1984), 145-168.

2407. Motley, James Berry. "Grenada: Low-Intensity Conflict and the Use of U.S. Military Power," *World Affairs* 146:3 (Winter 1983-84), 221-238.

2408. Pastor, Robert A. "Does the United States Push Revolutions to Cuba? The Case of Grenada," *Journal of Inter-American Studies and World Affairs* 28:1 (Spring 1986), 1-34.

2409. Reding, Andrew A. "Backing Democracy and Development," *World Policy Journal* 1:3 (Spring 1984), 653-667.

2410. Shearman, Peter. "The Soviet Union and Grenada under the New Jewel Movement," *International Affairs* 61:4 (Autumn 1985), 661-673.

2411. Thorndike, Tony. "The Grenada Crisis," *World Today* 39:12 (December 1983), 468-476.

2412. Thorndike, Tony. "Grenada: The New Jewel Revolution." In *Dependency under Challenge: The Political Economy of the Commonwealth Caribbean,* edited by Anthony Payne and Paul Sutton. Dover, NH: Manchester University Press, 1984. pp. 105-130.

2413. Waters, Maurice. "The Invasion of Grenada, 1983 and the Collapse of Legal Norms," *Journal of Peace Research* 23:3 (September 1986), 230-246.

GUATEMALA

Books and Monographs

2414. Bizarro Ujpan, Ignacio. *Campesino: The Diary of a Guatemalan Indian.* Translated and edited by James D. Sexton. Tucson: University of Arizona Press, 1985. 448p.

2415. Black, George, with Milton Jamail and Norma Stoltz Chinchilla. *Garrison Guatemala.* New York: Monthly Review Press, 1984. 198p.

2416. Bossen, Laurel Herbenar. *The Redivision of Labor: Woman and Economic Choice in Four Guatemalan Communities.* Albany: State University of New York Press, 1984. 396p.

2417. Calvert, Peter. *Guatemala: A Nation in Turmoil.* Boulder, CO: Westview, 1985. 239p.

2418. Cambranes, Julio Castellanos. *Café y campesinos en Guatemala, 1853-1897.* Guatemala City: Editorial Universitaria de Guatemala, 1985. 629p.

2419. Feldman, Lawrence H. *A Tumpline Economy: Production and Distribution Systems in Sixteenth-Century Eastern Guatemala.* Culver City, CA: Labyrinthos, 1985. 146p.

2420. Handy, Jim. *The Gift of the Devil: A History of Guatemala.* Boston, MA: South End, 1985. 319p.

2421. Hawkins, John. *Inverse Images: The Meaning of Culture, Ethnicity, and Family in Postcolonial Guatemala.* Albuquerque: University of New Mexico Press, 1984. 470p.

2422. Herrera Cálix, Tomás. *Guatemala: revolución de octubre.* Guatemala City: EDUCA, 1986, 146p.

2423. Hirth, Kenneth G., ed. *Trade and Exchange in Early Mesoamerica.* Albuquerque: University of New Mexico Press, 1984. 338p.

2424.   Jonas, Susanne, Ed McCaughan, and Elizabeth Sutherland Martínez, eds. and trans. *Guatemala: Tyranny on Trial. Testimony of the Permanent People's Tribunal.* San Francisco: Synthesis, 1984. 301p.

2425.   Lovell, W. George. *Conquest and Survival in Colonial Guatemala: A Historical Geography of the Cuchumatán Highlands, 1500-1821.* Kingston, Quebec: McGill-Queen's University Press, 1985. 254p.

2426.   McClintock, Michael. *The American Connection.* Vol. 2: *State Terror and Popular Resistance in Guatemala.* London: Zed (Totowa, NJ: Dist. by Biblio Distribution Center), 1985. 336p.

2427.   McCreery, David. *Development and the State in Reforma Guatemala, 1871-1885.* Athens: Center for International Studies, Ohio University, 1983. 120p.

2428.   Mathewson, Kent. *Irrigation Horticulture in Highland Guatemala: The Tablón System of Panajachel.* Boulder, CO: Westview, 1984. 180p.

2429.   Menchu, Rigoberta. *I...Rigoberta Menchu: An Indian Woman in Guatemala.* Edited by Elisabeth Burgos-Debray. Translated by Ann Wright. London: Verso (New York: Dist. in the U.S. and Canada by Schocker Books), 1984. 251p.

2430.   Morley, Sylvanus G., and George W. Brainerd. *The Ancient Maya.* 4th ed. Revised by Robert J. Sharer. Stanford, CA: Stanford University Press, 1983. 708p.

2431.   Orellana, Sandra L. *The Tzutujil Mayas: Continuity and Change, 1250-1630.* Norman: University of Oklahoma Press, 1984. 287p.

2432.   Payeras, Mario. *Days of the Jungle: The Testimony of a Guatemalan Guerrillero, 1972-1976.* New York: Monthly Review Press, 1983. 94p.

2433.   Schlesinger, Stephen, and Stephen Kinzer. *Bitter Fruit: The Untold Story of the American Coup in Guatemala.* 2d ed. Garden City, NY: Anchor/Doubleday, 1983. 320p.

2434.   Sexton, James D., ed. and trans. *Campesino: The Diary of a Guatemalan Indian.* Tucson: University of Arizona Press, 1985. 448p.

2435.   Steltzer, Ulli. *Health in the Guatemalan Highlands.* Seattle: University of Washington Press, 1983. 80p.

2436.   Study Group on United States-Guatemalan Relations. *Report on Guatemala.* Boulder, CO: Westview; Washington, DC: Foreign Policy Institute, School of Advanced International Studies, Johns Hopkins University, 1985. 74p.

2437.   Urban, Patricia A., and Edward M. Schortman, eds. *The Southeast Maya Periphery.* Austin: University of Texas Press, 1986. 399p.

2438.   van Oss, Adriaan C. *Catholic Colonialism: A Parish History of Guatemala, 1524-1821.* New York: Cambridge University Press, 1986. 248p.

2439.   Vargas Forondo, Jacobo. *Guatemala: sus recursos naturales, el militarismo y el imperialismo.* Mexico City: Claves Latinoamericanas, 1984. 173p.

Articles and Chapters

2440.   Aguilera, Gabriel. "El nuevo sujeto de la lucha en Guatemala," *Revista Mexicana de Sociología* 46:3 (July-September 1984), 211-240.

2441.   Amerlinck de Bontempo, Marijose. "Los Mayas de la Audiencia de Guatemala: una crítica de libros recientes," *Inter-American Review of Bibliography* 34:2 (1984), 289-301.

2442.   Arias, Arturo. "Cultura popular, culturas indígenas, genocidio y etnocidio en Guatemala, *Boletín de Antropología American*a 7 (July 1983), 57-77.

2443.   Bowen, Gordon L. "Guatemala: The Origins and Development of State Terrorism." In *Revolution and Counterrevolution in Central America and the Caribbean,* edited by Donald E. Schulz and Douglas H. Graham. Boulder, CO: Westview, 1984. pp. 269-300.

2444.   Brockett, Charles. "Malnutrition, Public Policy, and Agrarian Change in Guatemala," *Journal of Inter-American Studies and World Affairs* 26:4 (November 1984), 477-497.

2445.   Cambranes, Julio Catellanos. "Origins of the Crisis of the Established Order in Guatemala." In *Central America: Crisis and Adaptation,* edited by Steve C. Ropp and James A. Morris. Albuquerque: University of New Mexico Press, 1984. pp. 119-152.

2446.   Castillo G., Miguel Angel. "Algunos determinantes y principales transformaciones recientes de la migración guatemalteca a la frontera sur de México," *Estudios Sociales Centroamericanos* 40 (January-April 1986), 67-75.

2447.   Castro, Floria. "La política exterior de Guatemala: 1982-1986," *Estudios Sociales Centroamericanos* 43 (January-April 1987), 63-73.

2448.   Centro de Estudios Urbanos y Regionales, Universidad de San Carlos de Guatemala. "Reivindicación y condiciones de vida en un asentamiento popular en ciudad de Guatemala," *Estudios Sociales Centroamericanos* 44 (May-August 1987), 98-111.

2449.   Cojti, Demetrio. "La penetración de la radiofonía en las communidades tradicionales mayances," *Estudios Sociales Centroamericanos* 41 (May-August 1986), 87-103.

2450.   Davis, Shelton H. "State Violence and Agrarian Crisis in Guatemala: The Roots of the Indian-Peasant Rebellion." In *Trouble in Our Backyard: Central America and the United States in the Eighties,* edited by Martin Diskin. New York: Pantheon, 1983. pp. 155-171.

2451.   Early, John D. "Some Ethnographic Implications of an Ethnohistorical Perspective of the Civil-Religious Hierarchy," *Ethnohistory* 30:4 (1983), 185-202.

2452.   Frundt, Hank. "To Buy the World a Coke: Implications of Trade Union Redevelopment in Guatemala," *Latin American Perspectives* 14:3 (Summer 1987), 381-416.

2453.   Gleijeses, Piero. "Guatemala: Crisis and Response." In *The Future of Central America,* edited by Richard R. Fagen and Olga Pellicer. Stanford, CA: Stanford University Press, 1983. pp. 187-212.

2454.   Gleijeses, Piero. "Perspectives of a Regime Transformation in Guatemala." In *Political Change in Central America: Internal and External Dimensions,* edited by Wolf Grabendorff, Heinrich-W. Krumwiede and Jörg Todt. Boulder, CO: Westview, 1984. pp. 127-138.

2455.   Gonzalez, Nancie L. "Rethinking the Consanguineal Household and Matrifocality," *Ethnology* 23:1 (January 1984), 1-12.

2456.   Green, Sara E., Thomas A. Rich, and Edgar G. Nesman. "Beyond Individual Literacy: The Role of Shared Literacy for Innovation in Guatemala," *Human Organization* 44:4 (Winter 1985), 313-321.

2457.   Handy, Jim. "Resurgent Democracy and the Guatemalan Military," *Journal of Latin American Studies* 18:2 (November 1986), 383-408.

2458.   Hintermeister, Alberto. "Modernización de la agricultura y pobreza rural en Guatemala," *Estudios Rurales Latinoamericanos* 8:1 (January-April 1985), 41-79.

2459.   Hoy, Don R., and Francois J. Belisle. "Environmental Protection and Economic Development in Guatemala's Western Highlands," *Journal of Developing Areas* 18:2 (January 1984), 161-176.

2460.   Jonas, Susanne. "Contradictions of Revolution and Intervention in Central American in the Transnational Era: The Case of Guatemala." In *Revolution and Intervention in Central America,* edited by Marlene Dixon and Susanne Jonas. Rev. ed. San Francisco: Synthesis, 1983. pp. 281-329.

2461.   Lovell, W. George, Christopher H. Lutz, and William R. Swezey. "The Indian Population of Southern Guatemala, 1549-1551: An Analysis of López de Cerrato's *Tasaciones de Tributos.*" *The Americas* 40:4 (April 1984), 459-477.

2462.   McCreery, David. "Debt Servitude in Rural Guatemala, 1876-1936," *Hispanic American Historical Review* 63:4 (November 1983), 735-759.

2463.   McCreery, David. "'This Life of Misery and Shame': Female Prostitution in Guatemala City, 1880-1920," *Journal of Latin American Studies* 182:2 (November 1986), 333-353.

2464.   McCreery, David. "'An Odious Feudalism': *Mandamiento* Labor and Commercial Agriculture in Guatemala, 1858-1920," *Latin American Perspectives* 13:1 (Winter 1986), 99-117.

2465.   Millett, Richard. "Guatemala: Progress and Paralysis," *Current History* 84:500 (March 1985), 109-113.

2466.   Millett, Richard. "Guatemala's Painful Progress," *Current History* 85:515
         (December 1986), 413-416.

2467.   Power, Jonathan. "Guatemala: Stirrings of Change," *World Today* 42:2
         (February 1986), 31-35.

2468.   Reyes Illescas, Miguel Angel. "Guatemala: en el camino del indio nuevo,"
         Boletín de Antropología Americana 11 (July 1985), 51-73.

2469.   Rice, Don S., Prudence M. Rice, and Edward S. Deevey. "El impacto de
         los Mayas en el ambiente tropical de la cuenca de los lagos Yaxhá
         y Sacnab, el Petén, Guatemala," *América Indígena* 43:2 (April-June
         1983), 261-297.

2470.   Santley, Robert S., Thomas Killion, and Mark Lycett. "On the Maya
         Collapse," *Journal of Anthropological Research* 42:2 (Summer 1986),
         123-159.

2471.   Schöultz, Lars. "Guatemala: Social Change and Political Conflict." In
         *Trouble in Our Backyard: Central America and the United States in
         the Eighties,* edited by Martin Diskin. New York: Pantheon, 1983.
         pp. 173-202.

2472.   Schwartz, Norman B. "Colonization of Northern Guatemala: The Petén,"
         Journal of Anthropological Research 43:2 (Summer 1987), 163-183.

2473.   Smith, Carol A. "Does a Commodity Economy Enrich the Few While
         Ruining the Masses? Differentiation among Petty Commodity
         Producers in Guatemala," *Journal of Peasant Studies* 11:3 (April
         1984), 60-95.

2474.   Smith, Carol A. "Local History in Global Context: Social and Economic
         Transitions in Western Guatemala," *Comparative Studies in Society
         and History* 26:2 (April 1984), 193-228.

2475.   Tedlock, Barbara, and Dennis Tedlock. "Text and Textile: Language and
         Technology in the Arts of the Quiche Maya," *Journal of Anthro-
         pological Research* 41:2 (Summer 1985), 121-146.

2476.   Torres Rivas, Edelberto. "Problemas de la contrarevolución y la
         democracia en Guatemala," *Estudios Sociales Centroamericanos* 13:38
         (May-August 1984), 127-142.

2477.   Torres Rivas, Edelberto. "Problems of Democracy and Counterrevolution
         in Guatemala." In *Political Change in Central America: Internal and
         External Dimensions,* edited by Wolf Grabendorff, Heinrich-W.
         Krumwiede and Jörg Todt. Boulder, CO: Westview, 1984. pp. 114-
         126.

2478.   Trudeau, Robert H. "Guatemala: The Long-Term Costs of Short-Term
         Stability." In *From Gunboats to Diplomacy: New U.S. Policies for
         Latin America,* edited by Richard Newfarmer. Baltimore, MD: Johns
         Hopkins University Press, 1984. pp. 54-71.

2479.   Trudeau, Robert H., and Lars Schoultz. "Guatemala." In *Confronting
         Revolution: Security through Diplomacy in Central America,* edited
         by Morris J. Blachman, William M. LeoGrande and Kenneth E.

Sharpe. New York: Pantheon, 1986. pp. 23-49.

2480.   Webster, David. "Surplus, Labor, and Stress in Late Classic Maya Society," *Journal of Anthropological Research* 41:4 (Winter 1985), 375-399.

2481.   Woodward, Ralph Lee, Jr. "Economic Development and Dependency in Nineteenth-Century Guatemala." In *Crises in the Caribbean Basin,* edited by Richard Tardanico. Beverly Hills, CA: Sage, 1987. pp. 59-78.

GUYANA

Books and Monographs

2482. Braveboy-Wagner, Jacqueline Anne. *The Venezuela-Guyana Border Dispute: Britain's Colonial Legacy in Latin America.* Boulder, CO: Westview, 1984. 349p.

2483. Burrowes, Reynold A. *The Wild Coast: An Account of Politics in Guyana.* Cambridge, MA: Schenkman, 1984. 348p.

2484. Fauriol, Georges A. *Foreign Policy Behavior of Caribbean States: Guyana, Haiti and Jamaica.* Washington, DC: University Press of America, 1984. 338p.

2485. Hope, Kempe Ronald. *Guyana: Politics and Development in an Emergent Socialist State.* Oakville, Ontario; New York: Mosaic, 1985. 136p.

2486. James, Rudolph, and Harold A. Lutchman. *Law and the Political Environment in Guyana.* Georgetown, Guyana: Institute of Development Studies, University of Guyana, 1984. 215p.

2487. Jeffrey, Henry B., and Colin Baber. *Guyana Politics, Economics and Society: Beyond the Burnham Era.* London: Frances Pinter; Boulder, CO: Lynne Rienner, 1986. 203p.

2488. Lamur, Carlo. *The American Takeover: Industrial Emergence and Alcoa's Expansion in Guyana and Suriname, 1914-1921.* Dordrecht, Netherlands; Cinnaminson, NJ: Foris, 1985. 209p.

2489. Pierce, Paulette, *Noncapitalist Development: The Struggle to Nationalize the Guyanese Sugar Industry.* Totowa, NJ: Rowman & Allenheld, 1984. 200p.

2490. Quamina, Odida T. *Mineworkers of Guyana.* Atlantic Highlands, NJ: Humanities, 1987. 118p.

2491. Spinner, Thomas J., Jr. *A Political and Social History of Guyana, 1945-1983.* Boulder, CO: Westview, 1984. 244p.

2492.   Thomas, Clive Y. *Plantations, Peasants and State: A Study of the Mode of Sugar Production in Guyana.* Los Angeles: Center for Afro-American Studies, University of California, 1984. 214p.

Articles and Chapters

2493.   Butt Colson, Audrey. "El desarrollo nacional y los Akawaio y Pemón del Alto Mazaruni," *América Indígena* 43:3 (July-September 1983), 445-502.

2494.   Chandisingh, Rejendra. "The State, the Economy, and the Type of Rule in Guyana: An Assessment of Guyana's 'Socialist Revolution'," *Latin American Perspectives* 10:4 (Fall 1983), 59-74.

2495.   Danns, George K. "The Role of the Military in the National Security of Guyana." In *Militarization in the Non-Hispanic Caribbean,* edited by Alma H. Young and Dion E. Phillips. Boulder, CO: Lynne Rienner, 1986. pp. 112-138.

2496.   Hintzen, Percy C. "Bases of Elite Support for a Regime: Race, Ideology, and Clientelism as Bases for Leaders in Guyana and Trinidad," *Comparative Political Studies* 16:3 (October 1983), 363-391.

2497.   Hintzen, Percy. "Ethnicity, Class and Internal Capitalist Penetration in Guyana and Trinidad," *Social and Economic Studies* 34:3 (September 1985), 107-163.

2498.   Long, Frank, and Gillian Pollard. "An Examination of Patent Statistics in Guyana, 1903-1980," *Studies in Comparative International Development.* 19:3 (Fall 1984), 3-14.

2499.   Mitchell, Ivor. "Correlates of Consumer Shopping Behaviour in the Cooperative Socialist Republic of Guyana," *Social and Economic Studies* 34:2 (June 1985), 26-68.

2500.   Odie-Ali, Stella. "Women in Agriculture: The Case of Guyana," *Social and Economic Studies* 35:2 (June 1986), 241-289.

2501.   Sidell, Scott R. "Exploring the Effects of the Tied Development Loans on the Foreign Exchange and Liquidity Performance of Developing Countries: The Case of Guyana," *Inter-American Economic Affairs* 38:3 (Winter 1984), 3-48.

2502.   Strachan, Alan J. "Return Migration to Guyana," *Social and Economic Studies* 32:3 (September 1983), 121-142.

2503.   Thomas, Clive. "Guyana: The Rise and Fall of 'Co-operative Socialism'." In *Dependency under Challenge: The Political Economy of the Commonwealth Caribbean,* edited by Anthony Payne and Paul Sutton. Dover, NH: Manchester University Press, 1984. pp. 77-104.

2504.   Thompson, Alvin O. "The Guyana-Suriname Boundary Dispute: An Historical Appraisal, c. 1683-1816," *Boletín de Estudios Latinoamericanos y del Caribe* 39 (December 1985), 63-84.

HAITI

Books and Monographs

2505. Barros, Jacques. *Haiti de 1804 à nos jours.* Paris: L'Harmattan, 1984. 2 vols.

2506. Bellegard-Smith, Patrick. *In the Shadow of Powers: Dantes Bellegarde in Haitian Social Thought.* Atlantic Highlands, NJ: Humanities, 1985. 244p.

2507. Brinkerhoff, Derick W., and Jean-Claude Garcia-Zamor. *Politics, Projects and People: Institutional Development in Haiti.* New York: Praeger, 1986. 288p.

2508. Buckley, Roger Norman, ed. *The Haitian Journal of Lieutenant Howard, York Hussars, 1796-1798.* Knoxville: University of Tennessee Press, 1985. 194p.

2509. DeWind, Josh, and David H. Kinley, III. *Aiding Migration: The Impact of International Development Assistance on Haiti.* Boulder, CO: Westview, 1987. 170p.

2510. Di Tella, Torcuato S. *La rebelión de esclavos de Haití.* Buenos Aires: IDES, 1984. 118p.

2511. Fass, Simon M. *Political Economy in Haiti: The Drama of Survival.* New Brunswick, NJ: Transaction, 1987. 416p.

2512. Fauriol, Georges A. *Foreign Policy Behavior of Caribbean States: Guyana, Haiti and Jamaica.* Washington, DC: University Press of America, 1984. 338p.

2513. Foster, Charles R., and Albert Valdman, eds. *Haiti — Today and Tomorrow: An Inter-Disciplinary Study.* Lanham, MD: University Press of America, 1984. 389p.

2514.   Lundahl, Mats. *The Haitian Economy: Man, Lands and Markets.* New York: St. Martin's, 1983. 290p.

2515.   Miller, Jack C. *The Plight of Haitian Refugees.* New York: Praeger, 1984. 222p.

2516.   Moreau de Saint-Méry, M.L.E. *A Civilization That Perished: The Last Years of White Colonial Rule in Haiti.* Translated, abridged and edited by Ivor D. Spencer. Lanham, MD: University Press of America, 1985. 295p.

2517.   Nicholls, David. *Haiti in Caribbean Context: Ethnicity, Economy and Revolt.* New York: St. Martin's, 1985. 282p.

2518.   Paquin, Lyonel. *The Haitians: Class and Color Politics.* Brooklyn, NY: Multi-Type, 1983. 271p.

2519.   Plant, Roger. *Sugar and Modern Slavery: A Tale of Two Countries.* London: Zed, 1987. 177p.

2520.   Price-Mars, Jean. *So Spoke the Uncle.* Translated by Magdaline W. Shannon. Washington, DC: Three Continents, 1983. 252p.

2521.   Prince, Rod. *Haiti: Family Business.* London: Latin American Bureau, 1985. 86p.

2522.   Spector, Robert M. *W. Cameron Forbes and the Hoover Commissions to Haiti (1930).* Lanham, MD: University Press of America, 1985. 258p.

2523.   Stein, Robert Louis. *Léger Félicité Sonthonax: The Lost Sentinel of the Republic.* Rutherford, NJ: Fairleigh Dickinson University Press, 1985. 234p.

2524.   Weinstein, Brian, and Aaron Segal. *Haiti: Political Failures, Cultural Success.* New York: Praeger, 1984. 175p.

Articles and Chapters

2525.   Allman, James. "Conjugal Unions in Rural and Urban Haiti," *Social and Economic Studies* 34:1 (March 1985), 27-57.

2526.   Cástor, Susy. "Estructuras de dominación y de existencia campesina en Haití," *Boletín de Estudios Latinoamericanos y del Caribe* 35 (December 1983), 71-84.

2527.   Dupuy, Alex. "French Merchant Capital and Slavery in Saint-Dominique," *Latin American Perspectives* 12:3 (Summer 1985), 77-102.

2528.   Geggus, D.P. "Toussaint L'Ouverture and the Slaves of the Breda Plantations," *Journal of Caribbean History* 20:1 (1985-86), 30-48.

2529.   Grunwald, Joseph. "Restructuración de la industria maquiladora," *El Trimestre Económico* 50:200 (October-December 1983), 2123-2152.

2530.   Maingot, Anthony P. "Haiti: Problems of a Transition to Democracy in an Authoritarian Soft State," *Journal of Inter-American Studies and*

World Affairs 28:4 (Winter 1986-87), 75-102.

2531. Murray, Gerald F. "Bon-Dieu and the Rites of Passage in Rural Haiti: Structural Determinants of Postcolonial Theology and Ritual." In *The Catholic Church and Religions in Latin America,* edited by Thomas C. Bruneau, Chester E. Gabriel and Mary Mooney. Montreal, Canada: Centre for Developing Area Studies, McGill University, 1984. pp. 188-231.

2532. Plummer, Brenda Gayle. "The Metropolitan Connection: Foreign and Semiforeign Elites in Haiti, 1900-1915," *Latin American Research Review* 19:2 (1984), 119-142.

2533. Stein, Robert L. "From Saint Domingue to Haiti, 1804-1825," *Journal of Caribbean History* 19:2 (November 1984), 189-226.

2534. Stepick, Alex. "The Haitian Exodus: Flight from Terror and Poverty." In *The Caribbean Exodus,* edited by Barry B. Levine. New York: Praeger, 1987. pp. 131-151.

2535. Szlajfer, Henryk. "Against Dependent Capitalist Development in Nineteenth-Century Latin America: The Case of Haiti and Paraguay," *Latin American Perspectives* 13:1 (Winter 1986), 45-73.

HONDURAS

Books and Monographs

2536.   Arancibia, Juan. *Honduras: ¿Un Estado Nacional?* Tegucigalpa, Honduras: Guaymuras, 1985. 132p.

2537.   Carney, J. Guadalupe. *To Be a Revolutionary: An Autobiography.* San Francisco: Harper & Row, 1985. 473p.

2538.   Committee for the Defense of Human Rights in Honduras. *Human Rights in Honduras, 1984.* Washington, DC: Washington Office on Latin America and the World Council of Churches, 1985. 63p.

2539.   Delgado Fiallos, Aníbal. *Honduras, elecciones '85: más allá de la fiesta cívica.* Tegucigalpa: Guaymuras, 1986. 181p.

2540.   Fernández, Arturo. *Partidos políticos y elecciones en Honduras, 1980.* 2d ed. Tegucigalpa, Honduras: Guaymuras, 1983. 106p.

2541.   Funes de Torres, Lucila. *Los derechos humanos en Honduras.* Tegucigalpa: Centro de Documentación de Honduras, 1984. 194p.

2542.   Herrera Caceras, Héctor Roberto. *Diplomacia-política y desarrollo nacional de Honduras.* Tegucigalpa, Honduras: Universidad Nacional Autónoma de Honduras, Editorial Universitaria, 1983. 200p.

2543.   Lapper, Richard. *Honduras: State for Sale.* London: Latin American Bureau, 1985. 132p.

2544.   MacCameron, Robert. *Bananas, Labor, and Politics in Honduras: 1954-1963.* Syracuse, NY: Syracuse University, 1983. 166p.

2545.   Molina Chocano, Guillermo. *Estado liberal y desarrollo capitalista en Honduras.* 3d ed. Tegucigalpa, Honduras: Universidad Nacional Autónoma de Honduras, Editorial Universitaria, 1985. 136p.

2546.   Morris, James A. *Honduras: Caudillo Politics and Military Rulers.* Boulder, CO: Westview, 1984. 156p.

2547.   Newson, Linda A. *The Cost of Conquest: Indian Decline in Honduras under Spanish Rule.* Boulder, CO: Westview, 1986. 375p.

2548.   Paz Barnica, Edgardo. *La política exterior de Honduras, 1982-86.* Tegucigalpa: Ministerio de Relaciones Exteriores de Honduras; Madrid, Spain: Iberoamericana, 1986. 493p.

2549.   Peckenham, Nancy, and Annie Street, eds. *Honduras: Portrait of a Captive Nation.* New York: Praeger, 1985. 350p.

2550.   Rosenberg, Mark B., and Philip L. Shepherd, eds. *Honduras Confronts Its Future: Contending Perspectives on Critical Issues.* Boulder, CO: Lynne Rienner, 1986. 268p.

2551.   Swedberg, Richard. *The Honduran Trade Union Movement: 1920-1982.* Cambridge, MA: Central American Information Office, 1983. 44p.

Articles and Chapters

2552.   *América Indígena.* 45:3 (July-September 1984). Entire issue on the indigenous population of Honduras.

2553.   Brockett, Charles D. "The Commercialization of Agriculture and Rural Economic Insecurity: The Case of Honduras," *Studies in Comparative International Development* 22:1 (Spring 1987), 82-102.

2554.   Brockett, Charles D. "Public Policy, Peasants, and Rural Development in Honduras," *Journal of Latin American Studies* 19:1 (May 1987), 69-86.

2555.   Brown, Becky J., and Alexander Coles. "Café, cardamomo y agricultura de subsistencia: un estudio de sistemas agrícolas en la región de Quimistán, Honduras," *Estudios Sociales Centroamericanos* 42 (September-December 1986), 37-57.

2556.   Cid, Rafael del. "Los limites de la acción estatal bajo situaciones reformistas: los casos de Honduras, 1972-1975, y Panamá, 1968-1980," *Estudios Sociales Centroamericanos* 13:38 (May-August 1984), 13-39.

2557.   Cuevas, Carlos E., and Douglas H. Graham. "Agricultural Lending Costs in Honduras." In *Undermining Rural Development with Cheap Credit,* edited by Dale W. Adams, Douglas H. Graham, and J.D. Von Pischke. Boulder, CO: Westview, 1984. pp. 96-103.

2558.   Dennis, Philip A., and Michael D. Olien. "Kinship among the Miskito," *American Ethnologist* 11:4 (November 1984), 718-737.

2559.   Helms, Mary W. "Of Kings and Contexts: Ethnohistorical Interpretations of Miskito Political Structure and Function," *American Ethnologist* 13:3 (August 1986), 506-523.

2560.   Hernández Chávez, Alcides. "Política económica y pensamiento neoliberal: el caso de Honduras," *Estudios Sociales Centroamericanos* 13:37 (January-April 1984), 231-257.

2561. Kendall, Carl, Dennis Foote, and Reynaldo Martorell. "Anthropology, Communications, and Health: The Mass Media and Health Practices Program in Honduras," *Human Organization* 42:4 (Winter 1983), 353-360.

2562. Millett, Richard L. "The Honduras Dilemma," *Current History* 86:524 (December 1987), 409-416.

2563. Millett, Richard L. "Honduras: An Emerging Dilemma." In *From Gunboats to Diplomacy: New U.S. Policies for Latin America,* edited by Richard Newfarmer. Baltimore, MD: Johns Hopkins University Press, 1984. pp. 89-101.

2564. Morris, James A. "Honduras: The Burden of Survival in Central America." In *Central America: Crisis and Adaptation,* edited by Steve C. Ropp and James A. Morris. Albuquerque: University of New Mexico Press, 1984. pp. 189-225.

2565. Pastor, Rodolfo. "El ocaso de los cacicazgos: historia de la crisis del sistema político hondureño," *Foro Internacional* 26:1 (July-September 1985), 16-30.

2566. Rojas Aravena, Francisco. "Costa Rica y Honduras: a similares problemas soluciones distintas," *Estudios Sociales Centroamericanos* 43 (January-April 1987), 49-61.

2567. Rosenberg, Mark B. "Honduras: Bastion of Stability or Quagmire?" In *Revolution and Counterrevolution in Central America and the Caribbean,* edited by Donald E. Schulz and Douglas H. Graham. Boulder, CO: Westview, 1984. pp. 331-349.

2568. Rosenberg, Mark B. "Honduras: The Reluctant Democracy," *Current History* 85:515 (December 1986), 417-420.

2569. Rosenberg, Mark B. "Nicaragua and Honduras: Toward Garrison States," *Current History* 83:490 (February 1984), 59-62.

2570. Ruhl, J. Mark. "Agrarian Structure and Political Stability in Honduras," *Journal of Inter-American Studies and World Affairs* 26:1 (February 1984), 33-68.

2571. Ruhl, J. Mark. "The Honduran Agrarian Reform under Suazo Córdova, 1982-85: An Assessment," *Inter-American Economic Affairs* 39:2 (Autumn 1985), 63-80.

2572. Selser, Gregorio. "Honduras: de república bananera a enclave militar, 1980-1984," *Revista Mexicana de Sociología* 46:3 (July-September 1984), 241-269.

2573. Shepherd, Philip L. "Honduras." In *Confronting Revolution: Security through Diplomacy in Central America,* edited by Morris J. Bachman, William M. LeoGrande and Kenneth E. Sharpe. New York: Pantheon, 1986. pp. 125-155.

2574.   Volk, Steven. "Honduras: On the Border of War." In *Trouble in Our Backyard: Central America and the United States in the Eighties,* edited by Martin Diskin. New York: Pantheon, 1983. pp. 203-243.

2575.   Wonderly, Anthony. "Materials Symbolics in Pre-Columbian Households: The Painted Pottery of Naco, Honduras," *Journal of Anthropological Research* 42:4 (Winter 1986), 497-534.

JAMAICA

Books and Monographs

2576. Dance, Daryl C. *Folklore from Contemporary Jamaicans.* Knoxville: University of Tennessee Press, 1985. 229p.

2577. Edquist, Charles. *Capitalism, Socialism, and Technology: A Comparative Study of Cuba and Jamaica.* London: Zed (Totowa, NJ: Dist. by Biblio Distribution Center), 1985. 182p.

2578. Fauriol, Georges A. *Foreign Policy Behavior of Caribbean States: Guyana, Haiti and Jamaica.* Washington, DC: University Press of America, 1984. 338p.

2579. Feuer, Carl Henry. *Jamaica and the Sugar Worker Cooperatives: The Politics of Reform.* Boulder, CO: Westview, 1984. 219p.

2580. Forbes, John D. *Jamaica: Managing Political and Economic Change.* Washington, DC: American Enterprise Institute, 1985. 54p.

2581. Hector, Mario. *Death Row.* London: Zed, (Totowa, NJ: Dist. by Biblio Distribution Center.), 1984. 111p.

2582. Holzberg, Carol S. *Minorities and Power in a Black Society: The Jewish Community of Jamaica.* Lanham, MD: North-South, 1987. 259p.

2583. Kaufman, Michael. *Jamaica under Manley: Dilemmas of Socialism and Democracy.* London: Zed; Westport, CT: L. Hill, 1985. 282p.

2584. Looney, Robert. *The Jamaican Economy in the 1980s: Economic Decline and Structural Adjustment.* Boulder, CO: Westview, 1987. 257p.

2585. Manley, Michael. *Up the Down Escalator: Development and the International Economy. A Jamaican Case Study.* Washington, DC: Howard University Press, 1987. 332p.

2586.   Petras, Elizabeth McLean. *Jamaican Labor Migration: White Capital and Black Labor, 1850-1930.* Boulder, CO: Westview, 1987. 284p.

2587.   Stephens, Evelyne Huber, and John D. Stephens. *Democratic Socialism in Jamaica: The Political Movement and Social Transformation in Dependent Capitalism.* Princeton, NJ: Princeton University Press, 1986. 423p.

2588.   Stephens, Evelyne Huber, and John D. Stephens. *Jamaica's Democratic Socialist Path: An Evaluation.* Washington, DC: Latin American Program, Wilson Center. 1984. 50p.

2589.   Stone, Carl. *Class, State, and Democracy in Jamaica.* New York: Praeger, 1986. 198p.

2590.   Waters, Anita M. *Race, Class, and Political Symbols: Rastafari and Reggae in Jamaican Politics.* New Brunswick, NJ: Transaction, 1985. 343p.

Articles and Chapters

2591.   Anderson, Patricia Y. "Migration and Development in Jamaica." In *Migration and Development in the Caribbean,* edited by Robert A. Pastor. Boulder, CO: Westview, 1985. pp. 117-139.

2592.   August, Thomas. "Jewish Assimilation and Plural Society in Jamaica," *Social and Economic Studies* 36:2 (June 1987), 109-122.

2593.   Barbone, Luca, and Francisco Rivera-Batiz. "Foreign Capital and the Contractionary Impact of Currency Devaluation with an Application to Jamaica," *Journal of Development Economics* 26:1 (June 1987), 1-15.

2594.   Barrett, Ina. "The Ombudsman in Jamaica," *Social and Economic Studies* 34:1 (March 1985), 59-75.

2595.   Beckford, George L., ed. "Impact of Bauxite-Alumina on Rural Jamaica," *Social and Economic Studies* 36:1 (March 1987), entire issue.

2596.   Begashaw, Girma. "Evaluation of a Supervised Credit Project in Jamaica," *Social and Economic Studies* 32:1 (March 1983), 135-169.

2597.   Bélisle, François J. "Food Production and Tourism in Jamaica: Obstacles to Increasing Local Food Supplies to Hotels," *Journal of Developing Areas* 19:1 (October 1984), 1-20.

2598.   Bélisle, François J. "Tourism and Food Imports: The Case of Jamaica." *Economic Development and Cultural Change* 32:4 (July 1984), 819-842.

2599.   Bennett, Karl. "An Analysis of the Jamaican Foreign Exchange Auction," *Social and Economic Studies* 35:4 (December 1986), 93-110.

2600.   Bennett, Karl. "Exchange Rate Policy and External Imbalance: The Jamaican Experience 1973-1982," *Social and Economic Studies* 32:4 (December 1984), 51-72.

2601.   Berkaak, Odd Are. "Re-Settlement and Dislocation of Small Farmers in Alcoa's Mining Areas in the Mocho Mountains of Jamaica," *Journal of Peace Research* 20:3 (1983), 227-237.

2602.   Bernal, Richard L. "Crisis and Reform in Jamaica: Some Economic Lessons." In *Towards an Alternative for Central America and the Caribbean,* edited by George Irvin and Xabier Gorostiaga. London; Boston: Allen & Unwin, 1985. pp. 111-125.

2603.   Bernal, Richard L. "Foreign Investment and Development in Jamaica," *Inter-American Economic Affairs* 38:2 (Autumn 1984), 3-21.

2604.   Bernal, Richard L. "The IMF and Class Struggle in Jamaica, 1977-1980," *Latin American Perspectives* 11:3 (Summer 1984), 53-82.

2605.   Blustain, Harvey. "The Political Context of Soil Conservation Programs in Jamaica," *Human Organization* 44:2 (Summer 1985), 124-131.

2606.   Bolles, A. Lynn. "Economic Crisis and Female-Headed Households in Urban Jamaica." In *Women and Change in Latin America,* edited by June Nash and Helen Safa. South Hadley, MA: Bergin & Garvey, 1986. pp. 65-83.

2607.   Bourne, Compton. "Banking Boom and Bust Economies: Lessons from Trinidad and Tobago and Jamaica," *Social and Economic Studies* 34:4 (December 1985), 139-163.

2608.   Bourne, Compton. "Effects of Subsidized Credit on the Size Distribution of Farm Household Incomes," *Social and Economic Studies* 32:1 (March 1983), 81-101.

2609.   Bourne, Compton. "Structure and Performance of Jamaican Rural Financial Markets, *Social and Economic Studies* 32:1 (March 1983), 1-21.

2610.   Braveboy-Wagner, Jacqueline Anne. "The Politics of Developmentalism: U.S. Policy toward Jamaica." In *The Caribbean Challenge: U.S. Policy in a Volatile Region,* edited by H. Michael Erisman. Boulder, CO: Westview, 1984. pp. 160-179.

2611.   Bray, David. "Industrialization, Labor Migration and Employment Crises: A Comparison of Jamaica and the Dominican Republic." In *Crises in the Caribbean Basin,* edited by Richard Tardanico. Beverly Hills, CA: Sage, 1987. pp. 79-93.

2612.   Brodber, Erna. "Afro-Jamaican Women at the Turn of the Century," *Social and Economic Studies* 35:3 (September 1986), 23-54.

2613.   Bullock, Colin. "IMF Conditionality and Jamaica's Economic Policy in the 1980s," *Social and Economic Studies* 35:4 (December 1986), 129-176.

2614.   Daniel, S., A.A. Francis, D. Nelson, B. Nembhard, and D.H. Ramjeesingh. "A Structural Analysis of the Jamaican Economy: 1974," *Social and Economic Studies* 34:3 (September 1985), 1-69.

2615.   Davies, Omar. "An Analysis of the Management of the Jamaican Economy: 1972-1985," *Social and Economic Studies* 35:1 (March

1986), 73-109.

2616.   Davies, Omar. "Economic Transformation in Jamaica: Some Policy Issues," *Studies in Comparative International Development* 19:3 (Fall 1984), 40-58.

2617.   Dore, M.H.I. "Mineral Taxation in Jamaica: An Oligopoly Dictates Tax Policy," *American Journal of Economics and Sociology* 46:2 (April 1987), 179-203.

2618.   Duncan, W. Raymond. "Alternative Approaches." In *Politics, Policies, and Economic Development in Latin America,* edited by Robert G. Wesson. Stanford, CA: Hoover Institution Press, 1984. pp. 188-212.

2619.   Duncan, W. Raymond. "The Struggle in Jamaica." In *Crisis and Opportunity: U.S. Policy in Central America and the Caribbean,* edited by Mark Falcoff and Robert Royal. Washington, DC: Ethics and Public Policy Center, 1984. pp. 119-135.

2620.   Dunn, Richard S. "'Dreadful Idlers' in the Cane Fields: The Slave Labor Pattern on the Jamaican Sugar Estate, 1762-1831," *Journal of Interdisciplinary History* 17:4 (Spring 1987), 795-822.

2621.   Edie, Carlene J. "Domestic Politics and External Relations in Jamaica under Michael Manley, 1972-1980," *Studies in Comparative International Development* 21:1 (Spring 1986), 71-94.

2622.   Edie, Carlene J. "Jamaican Political Processes: A System in Search of a Paradigm," *Journal of Development Studies* 20:4 (July 1984), 248-270.

2623.   Eyre, L. Alan. "Political Violence and Urban Geography in Kingston, Jamaica," *Geographical Review* 74:1 (January 1984), 24-37.

2624.   Feuer, Carl. "Better Must Come: Sugar and Jamaica in the 20th Century," *Social and Economic Studies* 33:4 (December 1984), 1-49.

2625.   Figueroa, Mark. "An Assessment of Overvoting in Jamaican Elections," *Social and Economic Studies* 34:3 (September 1985), 71-106.

2626.   Goulbourne, Harold D. "Elementary School Teachers and Politics in Colonial Jamaica: The Formation of the Jamaica Union of Teachers, 1894," *Caribbean Quarterly* 31:3-4 (September-December 1985), 16-30.

2627.   Graham, Douglas H., and Stephen K. Pollard. "The Crop Lien Programme: Implications of a Credit Project Transformed into an Ad-Hoc Income Transfer Programme," *Social and Economic Studies* 32:1 (March 1983), 63-80.

2628.   Headley, Bernard D. "Behind a Manley Victory in Jamaica," *Monthly Review* 38:9 (February 1987), 17-30.

2629.   Headley, Bernard D. "Mr. Seaga's Jamaica: An Inside Look," *Monthly Review* 37:4 (September 1985), 35-42.

2630.   Hefferman, Peter J., and Stephen K. Pollard. "The Determinants of

Credit Use among Small Farmers in Jamaica," *Social and Economic Studies* 32:1 (March 1983), 23-41.

2631.   McBain, Helen. "Towards a Viable Water Utility in Jamaica," *Social and Economic Studies* 34:1 (March 1985), 77-96.

2632.   Meyers, Albert. "Household, Labor Relations, and Reproductive Strategies among Small Cane Farmers in Jamaica," *Review* 7:2 (Fall 1983), 255-283.

2633.   Mills, G.E., and M.L., Slyfield. "Public Service Reform in Jamaica: Human Resources Management," *International Review of Administrative Sciences* 53:3 (September 1987), 395-412.

2634.   Morrisey, Michael P. "A Rural-Urban Stratification of Jamaica for Sampling Procedures," *Social and Economic Studies* 33:4 (December 1984), 101-123.

2635.   Nyanin, Ohene Owusu. "Leading Costs, Institutional Viability and Agricultural Credit Strategies in Jamaica," *Social and Economic Studies* 32:1 (March 1983), 103-133.

2636.   Payne, Anthony. "Jamaica: The 'Democratic Socialist' Experiment of Michael Manley." In *Dependency under Challenge: The Political Economy of the Commonwealth Caribbean,* edited by Anthony Payne and Paul Sutton. Dover, NH: Manchester University Press, 1984. pp. 18-42.

2637.   Petras, James F., Miguel E. Correa, and Roberto P. Korzeniewicz. "The Crises in Market, Collectivist and Mixed Economies: Puerto Rico, Cuba, and Jamaica." In *Capitalist and Socialist Crises in the Late Twentieth Century,* by James F. Petras. Totowa, NJ: Rowman & Allanheld, 1984. pp. 296-318.

2638.   Pollard, Stephen K., and Douglas H. Graham. "The Performance of the Food-producing Sector in Jamaica, 1962-1979: A Policy Analysis," *Economic Development and Cultural Change* 33:4 (July 1985), 731-754.

2639.   Pollard, Stephen K., and Douglas H. Graham. "Price Policy and Agricultural Export Performance in Jamaica," *World Development* 13:9 (September 1985), 1067-1075.

2640.   Pollard, Stephen K., and Peter J. Hefferman. "Agricultural Productivity and Credit Use of Small Farmers in Jamaica," *Social and Economic Studies* 32:1 (March 1983), 42-62.

2641.   Rawlings, Glenville, "Measuring the Impact of IRDP II on the Technical Efficiency Level of Jamaican Peasant Farmers," *Social and Economic Studies* 34:2 (June 1985), 71-96.

2642.   Richardson, Mary. "Out of Many, One People; Aspiration or Reality?" *Social and Economic Studies* 32:3 (September 1983), 143-167.

2643.   Robotham, Don. "The Emergence of Sociology in Jamaica," *Social and Economic Studies* 33:1 (March 1984), 83-116.

2644.   Schuler, Monica. "Coloured Civil Servants in Post-Emancipation Jamaica: Two Case Studies," *Caribbean Quarterly* 30:3-4 (September-December 1984), 85-98.

2645.   Shepherd, Verene A. "The Dynamics of Afro-Jamaican-East Indian Relations in Jamaica, 1845-1945: A Preliminary Analysis," *Caribbean Quarterly* 32:3-4 (September-October 1986), 14-26.

2646.   Stephens, Evelyne Huber. "Minerals Strategies and Development: International Political Economy, State, Class and the Role of the Bauxite/Aluminum and Copper Industries in Jamaica and Peru," *Studies in Comparative International Development* 22:3 (Fall 1987), 60-102.

2647.   Stephens, Evelyne Huber, and John D. Stephens. "Democratic Socialism in Dependent Capitalism: An Analysis of the Manley Government in Jamaica," *Politics and Society* 12:3 (1983), 373-411.

2648.   Stephens, Evelyne Huber, and John D. Stephens. "Transition to Mass Parties and Ideological Politics: The Jamaican Experience since 1972," *Comparative Political Studies* 19:4 (January 1987), 443-483.

2649.   Stone, Carl. "Jamaica: From Manley to Seaga." In *Revolution and Counterrevolution in Central America and the Caribbean,* edited by Donald E. Schulz and Douglas H. Graham. Boulder, CO: Westview, 1984. pp. 385-419.

2650.   Stone, Carl. "Jamaican Public Opinion and the University of the West Indies," *Caribbean Quarterly* 31:3-4 (September-December 1985), 31-40.

2651.   Stone, Carl. "Reflections on Political Polling in Jamaica," *Social and Economic Studies* 33:1 (March 1984), 117-140.

2652.   Taylor, Frank F. "The Burial of the Past: The Promotion of the Early Jamaica Tourist Industry," *Boletín de Estudios Latinoamericanos y del Caribe* 40 (June 1986), 49-61.

2653.   Witter, Michael. "Exchange Rate Policy in Jamaica: A Critical Assessment," *Social and Economic Studies* 32:4 (December 1983), 1-50.

2654.   Witter, Michael, and Diaram Ramjeesingh. "An Analysis of the Internal Structure of the Jamaican Economy: 1969-1974," *Social and Economic Studies* 35:1 (March 1986), 1-72.

2655.   Woolcock, Joseph. "Class Conflict and Class Reproduction: An Historical Analysis of the Jamaican Educational Reforms of 1957 and 1962," *Social and Economic Studies* 33:4 (December 1984), 51-99.

2656.   Worrell, Keith. "Preliminary Estimates of the Demand for Money Function: Jamaica 1962-79," *Social and Economic Studies* 34:3 (September 1985), 265-281.

2657.   Zahedieh, Nuala. "Trade, Plunder, and Economic Development in Early English Jamaica, 1655-89," *Economic History Review* 39:2 (May 1986), 205-222.

LESSER ANTILLES

Books and Monographs

2658. Adelaide, Amedée, ed. *Guadeloupe, les quatre vérités.* Paris: Caribéennes, 1984. 89p.

2659. Bangou, Henri. *Le parti socialiste français face à la decolonisation, de Jules Guesde à François Mitterand: le cas de la Guadeloupe.* Paris: L'Harmattan, 1985. 287p.

2660. Blérald, Alain-Philippe. *Histoire économique de la Guadeloupe et de la Martinique, du XVIIe siecle a nos jours.* Paris: Karthala, 1986. 336p.

2661. Cabort-Masson, Guy. *Les puissances d'argent en Martinique.* 2d ed. Fort-de-France, Martinique: Laboratoire de Recherches de l'AMEP, 1985. 289p.

2662. Cox, Edward L. *Free Coloreds in the Slave Societies of St. Kitts and Grenada, 1763-1833.* Knoxville: University of Tennessee Press, 1984. 197p.

2663. Gaspar, David Barry. *Bondmen and Rebels: A Study of Master-Slave Relations in Antigua, with Implications for Colonial British America.* Baltimore, MD: Johns Hopkins University Press, 1985. 338p.

2664. Hartog, Johannes. *De Nederlandse Antillen en de Verenigde Staten van Amerika.* Zutphen, Netherlands: Walburg, 1983. 64p.

2665. Henry, Paget. *Peripheral Capitalism and Underdevelopment in Antigua.* New Brunswick, NJ: Transaction, 1985. 220p.

2666. Inniss, Probyn. *Whither Bound St. Kitts-Nevis?* St. Johns, Antigua: Antigua Printery, 1983. 99p.

2667.   Miles, William F.S. *Elections and Ethnicity in French Martinique: A Paradox in Paradise.* New York: Praeger, 1986. 284p.

2668.   Olwig, Karen Fog. *Cultural Adaptation and Resistance on St. John: Three Centuries of Afro-Caribbean Life.* Gainesville: University of Florida Press, 1985. 226p.

2669.   Pérotin-Dumon, Anne. *Être patriote sous les tropiques: La Guadeloupe, la colonisation et la révolution (1789-1994).* Basse-Terre, Guadeloupe: Sociéte D'Histoire de la Guadeloupe, 1985. 339p.

2670.   Petty, Colville, L. *Anguilla: Where There's a Will There's a Way.* East End: Anguilla: C.L. Petty, 1984. 127p.

2671.   Richardson, Bonham C. *Caribbean Migrants: Environment and Human Survival on St. Kitts and Nevis.* Knoxville: University of Tennessee Press, 1983. 209p.

2672.   Rubenstein, Hymie. *Coping with Poverty: Adaptive Strategies in a Caribbean Village.* Boulder, CO: Westview, 1987. 389p.

2673.   World Bank. *Dominica: Priorities and Prospects for Development.* Washington, DC: 1985. 120p.

Articles and Chapters

2674.   Gaspar, D. Barry. "'To Bring Their Offending Slaves to Justice': Compensation and Slave Resistance in Antigua 1669-1763," *Caribbean Quarterly* 30:3-4 (September-December 1984), 45-59.

2675.   Hendrickson, Embert. "Surinam and the Antilles: A New Perspective," *World Today* 40:6 (June 1984), 261-268.

2676.   Kelly, Deirdre. "St. Lucia's Female Electronics Factory Workers: Key Components in an Export-Oriented Industrialization Strategy," *World Development* 14:7 (July 1986), 823-838.

2677.   Midgett, Douglas K. "Distorted Development: The Resuscitation of the Antigua Sugar Industry," *Studies in Comparative International Development* 19:2 (Summer 1984), 33-58.

2678.   Miles, William F.S. "Mitterrand in the Caribbean: Socialism (?) Comes to Martinique," *Journal of Inter-American Studies and World Affairs* 27:3 (Fall 1985), 63-79.

2679.   Thomas, J. Paul. "The Caribs of St. Vincent: A Study in Imperial Maladministration, 1763-73," *Journal of Caribbean History* 18:2 (November 1983), 60-73.

2680.   Trouillot, Michel-Rolph. "Labour and Emancipation in Dominica: Contribution to a Debate," *Caribbean Quarterly* 30:3-4 (September-December 1984), 73-84.

MEXICO

Books and Monographs

2681.   Alvarado Mendoza, Arturo, ed. *Electoral Patterns and Perspectives in Mexico.* La Jolla: Center for U.S.-Mexican Studies, University of California, San Diego, 1987. 287p.

2682.   Anglade, Christian, and Carlos Fortín, eds. *The State and Capital Accumulation in Latin America.* Vol. 1: *Brazil, Chile, Mexico.* Pittsburgh, PA: University of Pittsburgh Press, 1985. 254p.

2683.   Ankerson, Dudley. *Agrarian Warlord: Saturnino Cedillo and the Mexican Revolution in San Luis Potosí.* DeKalb: Northern Illinois University Press, 1984. 303p.

2684.   Arrom, Silvia Marina. *The Women of Mexico City, 1790-1857.* Stanford, CA: Stanford University Press, 1985. 384p.

2685.   Aspe Armella, Pedro, and Paul E. Sigmund, eds. *The Political Economy of Income Distribution in Mexico.* New York: Holmes & Meier, 1984. 552p.

2686.   Austin, James E., and Gustavo Esteva, eds. *Food Policy in Mexico: The Search for Self-Sufficiency.* Ithaca, NY: Cornell University Press, 1987. 383p.

2687.   Azaola, Elena. *La clase obrera como sujeto de estudio en México, 1940-1980.* Mexico City: Centro de Investigaciones y Estudios Superiores en Antropología Social. 1984. 111p.

2688.   Bailey, Norman A., and Richard Cohen. *The Mexican Time Bomb.* New York: Priority, 1987. 61p.

2689.   Barrett, Elinore M. *The Mexican Colonial Copper Industry.* Albuquerque: University of New Mexico Press, 1987. 143p.

2690. Beezley, William H. *Judas at the Jockey Club and Other Episodes of Porfirian Mexico.* Lincoln: University of Nebraska Press, 1987. 181p.

2691. Benjamin, Thomas, and William McNellie, eds. *Other Mexicos: Essays on Regional Mexican History, 1876-1911.* Albuquerque: University of New Mexico Press, 1984. 319p.

2692. Bennett, Douglas C., and Kenneth E. Sharpe. *Transnational Corporations versus the State: The Political Economy of the Mexican Auto Industry.* Princeton, NJ: Princeton University Press, 1985. 299p.

2693. Bennett, Mark. *Public Policy and Industrial Development: The Case of the Mexican Auto Parts Industry.* Boulder, CO: Westview, 1986. 134p.

2694. Borah, Woodrow. *Justice by Insurance: The General Indian Court of Colonial Mexico and the Legal Aids of the Half-Real.* Berkeley: University of California Press, 1983. 482p.

2695. Borah, Woodrow, coord. *El gobierno provincial en la Nueva España, 1570-1787.* Mexico City: Universidad Nacional Autónoma de México, 1985. 249p.

2696. Brannon, Jeffery, and Eric N. Baklanoff. *Agrarian Reform and Public Enterprise in Mexico.* Tuscaloosa: University of Alabama Press, 1987. 237p.

2697. Bundage, Burr Cartwright. *The Jade Steps: A Ritual Life of the Aztecs.* Salt Lake City: University of Utah, 1985. 280p.

2698. Buve, R., ed. *Haciendas in Central Mexico from Late Colonial Times to the Revolution: Labour Conditions, Hacienda Management, and Its Relations to the State.* Amsterdam: Center for Latin American Research and Documentation, 1984. 307p.

2699. Camp, Roderic A. *Intellectuals and the State in Twentieth-Century Mexico.* Austin: University of Texas Press, 1985. 279p.

2700. Camp, Roderic A. *The Making of a Government: Political Leaders in Modern Mexico.* Tucson: University of Arizona Press, 1984. 237p.

2701. Camp, Roderic A., ed. *Mexico's Political Stability: The Next Five Years.* Boulder, CO: Westview, 1986. 279p.

2702. Cardoso, Gerald. *Negro Slavery in the Sugar Plantations of Veracruz and Pernabuco 1550-1680: A Comparative Study.* Lanham, MD: University Press of America, 1983. 211p.

2703. Carey, James C. *The Mexican Revolution in Yucatán, 1915-1924.* Boulder, CO: Westview, 1984. 251p.

2704. Carr, Barry, and Ricardo Anzaldúa Montoya, eds. *The Mexican Left, the Popular Movements, and the Politics of Austerity.* Translated by Sandra de Castillo. La Jolla: Center for U.S.-Mexican Studies, University of California, San Diego, 1986. 96p.

2705. Chase, Arlene F., and Prudence M. Rice, eds. *The Lowland Maya*

Postclassic. Austin: University of Texas Press, 1985. 352p.

2706.   Cleaves, Peter S. *Professions and the State: The Mexican Case.* Tucson: University of Arizona Press, 1987. 147p.

2707.   Clendinnen, Inga. *Ambivalent Conquests: Maya and Spaniard in Yucatán, 1517-1570.* Cambridge, England; New York: Cambridge University Press, 1987. 245p.

2708.   Cline, S.L. *Colonial Culhuacán, 1580-1600: A Social History of an Aztec Town.* Albuquerque: University of New Mexico Press, 1986. 258p.

2709.   Coerver, Don M., and Linda B. Hall. *Texas and the Mexican Revolution: A Study in State and National Border Policy, 1910-1920.* San Antonio, TX: Trinity University Press, 1984. 167p.

2710.   Conrad, Geoffrey W., and Arthur A. Demarest. *Religion and Empire: The Dynamics of Aztec and Inca Expansion.* Cambridge, England; New York: Cambridge University Press, 1984. 266p.

2711.   Cornelius, Wayne A. *The Political Economy of Mexico under de la Madrid: The Crisis Deepens, 1985-1986.* San Diego: Center for U.S.-Mexican Studies, University of California, San Diego, 1986. 50p.

2712.   Davis, Thomas B., and Amado Ricón, comps. *The Political Plans of Mexico.* Lanham, MD: University Press of America, 1987. 687p.

2713.   Dennis, Philip A. *Intervillage Conflict in Oaxaca.* New Brunswick, NJ: Rutgers University Press, 1987. 213p.

2714.   Durán, Esperanza. *Guerra y revolución: los grandes potencias y México, 1914-1918.* Mexico City: Colegio de México, Centro de Estudios Inernacionales, 1985. 277p.

2715.   Durand, Jorge. *La ciudad invade al ejido: proletarización, urbanización y lucha política en el Cerro del Judío, D.F.* Mexico City: Casa Chata, 1983. 145p.

2716.   El Guindi, Fadwa, with the collaboration of Abel Hernández Jiménez. *The Myth of Ritual: A Native's Ethnography of Zapotec Life-Crisis Rituals.* Tucson: University of Arizona Press, 1986. 147p.

2717.   Esteva, Gustavo, with the collaboration of David Barkin. *The Struggle for Rural Mexico.* South Hadley, MA: Bergin & Garvey, 1984. 309p.

2718.   Ewald, Ursala. *The Mexican Salt Industry, 1560-1980: A Study in Change.* New York: Gustav Fischer, 1985. 480p.

2719.   Fagan, Brian M. *The Aztecs.* New York: W.H. Freeman, 1984. 322p.

2720.   Falcón, Romana. *Revolución y caciquismo: San Luis Potosí, 1910-1938.* Mexico City: Colegio de México, 1984. 306p.

2721.   Falk, Pamela S., ed. *Petroleum and Mexico's Future.* Boulder, CO: Westview, 1987. 124p.

2722.   Farris, Nancy M. *Maya Society under Colonial Rule: The Collective*

Enterprise of Survival. Princeton, NJ: Princeton University Press, 1984. 585p.

2723.   Fernández-Kelly, María Patricia. *For We Are Sold, I and My People: Women and Industry in Mexico's Frontier.* Albany: State University of New York Press, 1983. 217p.

2724.   Freidel, David A., and Jeremy A. Sabloff. *Conzumel: Late Maya Settlement Patterns.* Orlando, FL: Academic, 1984. 208p.

2725.   Friedland, Joan, and Jesús Rodríguez y Rodríguez. *Seeking Safe Ground: The Legal Situation of Central American Refugees in Mexico.* San Diego, CA: Mexico-U.S. Law Institute, University of San Diego School of Law; Mexico City: Instituto de Investigaciones Jurídicas, Universidad Nacional Autónoma de México, 1987. 82p.

2726.   Friedrich, Paul. *The Princess of Naranja: An Essay in Anthrohistorical Method.* Austin: University of Texas Press, 1986. 305p.

2727.   Garza, Luis Alberto de la, et al. *Evolución del estado mexicano.* Mexico City: Caballito, 1986. 3 vols.

2728.   García de León, Antonio. *Resistencia y utopía: memorial de agravios y crónicas de revueltas y profecías acaecidas en la Provincia de Chiapas durante los últimos quinientos años de su historia.* Mexico City: Era, 1985. 2 vols.

2729.   Gentlemen, Judith. *Mexican Oil and Dependent Development.* New York: P. Lang, 1984. 260p.

2730.   Gentlemen, Judith, ed. *Mexican Politics in Transition.* Boulder, CO: Westview, 1987. 320p.

2731.   Gereffi, Gary. *The Pharmaceutical Industry and Dependency in the Third World.* Princeton, NJ: Princeton University Press, 1983. 291p.

2732.   Gibson, Lay James, and Alfonso Corona Renteria, eds. *The U.S. and Mexico: Borderland Development and the National Economies.* Boulder, CO: Westview, 1985. 262p.

2733.   Gilbert, Alan, and Peter M. Ward. *Housing, the State and the Poor: Policy and Practice in Three Latin American States.* Cambridge, England; New York: Cambridge University Press, 1985. 319p.

2734.   Gilly, Adolfo. *The Mexican Revolution.* Translated by Patrick Camiller. London: New Left Books, 1983. 407p.

2735.   Goldwert, Marvin. *Machismo and Conquest: The Case of Mexico.* Lanham, MD: University Press of America, 1983. 85p.

2736.   González Casanova, Pablo. *El estado y los partidos políticos en México.* Rev. ed. Mexico City: Era, 1986. 257p.

2737.   González Casanova, Pablo, coord. *Las elecciones en México: evolución y perspectivas.* Mexico City: Siglo Veintiuno, 1985. 385p.

2738.   González Casanova, Pablo, and Héctor Aguilar Camín, coords. *México*

ante la crisis. Mexico City: Siglo Veintiuno, 1985.
Vol. 1:   *El contexto internacional y la crisis económica,* 435p.
Vol. 2:   *El impacto social y cultural: las alternativas,* 425p.

2739.   González Navarro, Moisés. *La pobreza en México.* Mexico City: Colegio de México, 1985. 494p.

2740.   Goulet, Dennis. *Mexico: Development Strategies for the Future.* Notre Dame, IN: University of Notre Dame Press, 1983. 191p.

2741.   Grayson, George W. *The United States and Mexico: Patterns of Influence.* New York: Praeger, 1984. 215p.

2742.   Green, Stanley D. *The Mexican Republic: The First Decade, 1823-1833.* Pittsburgh, PA: University of Pittsburgh Press, 1987. 314p.

2743.   Gregory, Peter. *The Myth of Market Failure: Employment and the Labor Market in Mexico.* Baltimore, MD: Johns Hopkins University Press for the International Bank for Reconstruction and Development, 1986. 299p.

2744.   Guzmán, Oscar M., Antonio Yúnez-Naude, and Miguel S. Wionczek, eds. *Energy Efficiency and Conservation in Mexico.* Translated by Glenn Gardner and Rodnet Williamson. Boulder, CO: Westview, 1987. 354p.

2745.   Hamblin, Nancy L. *Animal Use by the Conzumel Maya.* Tucson: University of Arizona Press, 1984. 206p.

2746.   Hamilton, Nora, and Timothy F. Harding, eds. *Modern Mexico: State, Economy, and Social Conflict.* Beverly Hills, CA: Sage, 1986. 213p.

2747.   Hamnett, Brian R. *Roots of Insurgency: Mexican Regions, 1750-1824.* New York: Cambridge University Press, 1986. 276p.

2748.   Hanrahan, Gene Z. *The Bad Yankee: El peligro yankee: American Entrepreneurs and Financiers in Mexico.* Chapel Hill, NC: Documentary Publications, 1985. 2 vols.

2749.   Hart, John Mason. *Revolutionary Mexico: The Coming and Process of the Mexican Revolution.* Berkeley: University of California Press, 1987. 520p.

2750.   Harvey, H.R., and Hanns J. Prem, eds. *Explorations in Ethnohistory: Indians of Central Mexico in the Sixteenth Century.* Albuquerque: University of New Mexico Press, 1984. 312p.

2751.   Hassig, Ross. *Trade, Tribute, and Transportation: The Sixteenth Century Political Economy of the Valley of Mexico.* Norman: University of Oklahoma Press, 1985. 364p.

2752.   Hellman, Judith Adler. *Mexico in Crisis* 2d ed. New York: Holmes & Meier, 1983. 345p.

2753.   Hernández Laos, Enrique. *La productividad y el desarrollo industrial en México.* Mexico City: Fondo de Cultura Económica, 1985. 448p.

2754.   Hirth, Kenneth G., ed. *Trade and Exchange in Early Mesoamerica.*

Albuquerque: University of New Mexico Press, 1984. 338p.

2755. Hu-DeHart, Evelyn. *Yaqui Resistance and Survival: The Struggle for Land and Autonomy, 1821-1910.* Madison: University of Wisconsin Press, 1984. 293p.

2756. Ingham, John M. *Mary, Michael & Lucifer: Folk Catholicism in Central Mexico.* Austin: University of Texas Press, 1986. 216p.

2757. Jacobs, Ian. *Ranchero Revolt: The Mexican Revolution in Guerrero.* Austin: University of Texas Press, 1983. 234p.

2758. Johannsen, Robert W. *To the Halls of Montezuma: The Mexican War in the American Imagination.* New York: Oxford University Press, 1985. 363p.

2759. Johnson, Kenneth F. *Mexican Democracy: A Critical View.* 3d ed. New York: Praeger, 1984. 279p.

2760. Jones, Rodney W., and Steven A. Hildreth. *Modern Weapons and Third World Powers.* Boulder, CO: Westview, 1984. 125p.

2761. Joseph, Gilbert M. *Rediscovering the Past at Mexico's Periphery: Essays on the History of Modern Yucatán.* University: University of Alabama Press, 1986. 203p.

2762. Kendall, Carl, John Hawkins, and Laurel Bossen, eds. *Heritage of Conquest: Thirty Years Later.* Albuquerque: University of New Mexico Press, 1983. 368p.

2763. Kicza, John E. *Colonial Entrepreneurs: Families and Business in Colonial Mexico City.* Albuquerque: University of New Mexico Press, 1983. 313p.

2764. Kinsbruner, Jay. *Petty Capitalism in Spanish America: The Pulperos of Puebla, Mexico City, Caracas, and Buenos Aires.* Boulder, CO: Westview, 1987. 159p.

2765. Knight, Alan. *The Mexican Revolution.* New York: Cambridge University Press, 1986. 2 vols.
    Vol. 1:   *Porfirians, Liberals and Peasants,* 619p.
    Vol. 2:   *Counter Revolution and Reconstruction,* 679p.

2766. Kowalski, Jeff Karl. *The House of the Governor: A Maya Palace of Uxmal, Yucatán, Mexico.* Norman: University of Oklahoma Press, 1987. 298p.

2767. Kroeber, Clifton B. *Man, Land and Water: Mexico's Farmlands Irrigation Policies, 1885-1911.* Berkeley: University of California Press, 1983. 288p.

2768. Ladman, Jerry R., ed. *Mexico: A Country in Crisis.* El Paso: Texas Western Press, 1986. 169p.

2769. LaPointe, Marie. *Los Mayas rebeldes de Yucatán.* Zamora, Mexico: Colegio de Michoacán, 1983. 258p.

2770. Latell, Brian. *Mexico at the Crossroads: The Many Crises of the Political System.* Stanford, CA: Hoover Institution, 1986. 34p.

2771. Leahy, Margaret E. *Development Strategies and the Status of Women: A Comparative Study of the United States, Mexico, the Soviet Union and Cuba.* Boulder, CO: Lynne Rienner, 1986. 167p.

2772. Leiby, John S. *Colonial Bureaucrats and the Mexican Economy: Growth of a Patrimonial State, 1763-1821.* New York: P. Lang, 1986. 252p.

2773. Leiby, John S. *Report to the King: Colonel Juan Camargo y Cavallero's Historical Account of New Spain, 1815.* New York: P. Lang, 1984. 215p.

2774. León, Samuel, and Ignacio Marván. *En el cardenismo, 1934-1940.* Mexico City: Siglo Vientiuno, 1985. 313p. *(La clase obrera en la historia de México,* Vol. 10.)

2775. Levy, Daniel C., and Gabriel Székely. *Mexico: Paradoxes of Stability and Change.* 2d ed. Boulder, CO: Westview, 1987. 297p.

2776. Lindley, Richard B. *Haciendas and Economic Development: Guadalajara, Mexico, at Independence.* Austin: University of Texas Press. 1983. 156p.

2777. Lira, Andrés. *Comunidades indígenas frente a la Ciudad de México: Tenochtitlán y Tlateloco, sus pueblos y barrios, 1812-1919.* Michoacán: Colegio de México y Colegio de Michoacán, 1983. 426p.

2778. Litvak King, Jaime. *Ancient Mexico: An Overview* Albuquerque University of New Mexico Press, 1985. 134p.

2779. Logan, Kathleen. *Haciendo Pueblo: The Development of a Guadalajaran Suburb.* University: University of Alabama Press, 1984. 141p.

2780. Looney, Robert E. *Economic Policymaking in Mexico: Factors Underlying the 1982 Crisis.* Durham, NC: Duke University Press, 1985. 309p.

2781. López Monjardín, Adriana. *La lucha por los ayuntamientos: una utopía viable.* Mexico City: Siglo Vientiuno, 1986. 157p.

2782. López Villafañe, Víctor. *La formación del sistema político mexicano.* Mexico City: Siglo Veintiuno, 1986. 212p.

2783. Lucas de Rouffignac, Ann. *The Contemporary Peasantry in Mexico: A Class Analysis.* New York: Praeger, 1985. 203p.

2784. Luiselli Fernández, Cassio. *The Route to Food Self-Sufficiency in Mexico: Interactions with the U.S. Food System.* La Jolla: Center for U.S.-Mexican Studies, University of California, San Diego, 1985. 64p.

2785. McGuire, Thomas R. *Politics and Ethnicity on the Rio Yaqui: Potam Revisited.* Tucson: University of Arizona Press, 1986. 186p.

2786. Markman, Sidney David. *Architecture and Urbanization in Colonial Chiapas, Mexico.* Philadelphia, PA: American Philosophical Society,

1984. 443p.

2787.   Martin, Cheryl English. *Rural Society in Colonial Morelos.* Albuquerque: University of New Mexico Press, 1985. 255p.

2788.   Maxfield, Sylvia, and Ricardo Anzaldúa Montoya, eds. *Government and Private Sector in Contemporary Mexico.* La Jolla, CA: Center for U.S.-Mexican Studies, University of California, San Diego, 1987. 146p.

2789.   Meneses Morales, Ernesto. *Tendencias educativas oficiales en México, 1821-1911: la problemática de la educación mexicana en el siglo XIX y principios del siglo XX.* Mexico City: Porrúa, 1983. 787p.

2790.   Meyer, Michael C., and William L. Sherman. *The Course of Mexican History.* 3d ed. New York: Oxford University Press, 1987. 711p.

2791.   Middlebrook, Kevin J. *Political Liberalization in an Authoritarian Regime: The Case of Mexico.* La Jolla: Center for U.S.-Mexican Studies, University of California, San Diego, 1985. 36p.

2792.   Miller, Robert Ryal. *Mexico: A History.* Norman: University of Oklahoma Press, 1985. 414p.

2793.   Morley, Sylvanus G., and George W. Brainerd. *The Ancient Maya.* 4th ed. Revised by Robert J. Sharer. Stanford, CA: Stanford University Press, 1983. 708p.

2794.   Motolinía, Fray Toribio de. *Historia de los indios de la Nueva España.* Barcelona, Spain: Herederos de Juan Gili, 1914; reprint ed., Madrid, Spain: Clásicos Castalia, 1985. 404p.

2795.   Murphy, Michael E. *Irrigation in the Bajío Region of Colonial Mexico.* Boulder, CO: Westview, 1986. 226p.

2796.   Musgrave, Peggy B., ed. *Mexico and the U.S.: Studies in Economic Interaction.* Boulder, CO: Westview, 1985. 261p.

2797.   Newell G., Roberto, and Luis Rubio F. *Mexico's Dilemma: The Political Origins of Economic Crisis.* Boulder, CO: Westview, 1984. 319p.

2798.   Nutini, Hugh G. *Ritual Kinship: Ideological and Structural Integration of the Compadrazgo System in Rural Tlaxcala.* Vol. 2 Princeton, NJ: Princeton University Press, 1984. 505p.

2799.   Offner, Jerome A. *Law and Politics in Aztec Texcoco.* Cambridge, England: Cambridge University Press, 1983. 340p.

2800.   Paoli Bolio, Francisco José. *Estado y sociedad en México, 1917-1984.* Mexico City: Oceano, 1985. 137p.

2801.   Paoli Bolio, Francisco José. *Yucatán y los origenes del nuevo estado mexicano: gobierno de Salvador Alvarado, 1915-1918.* Mexico City: Era, 1984. 222p.

2802.   Pearce, Kenneth. *The View from the Top of the Temple: Ancient Maya Civilization and Modern Maya Culture.* Albuquerque: University of

New Mexico Press, 1984. 273p.

2803.   Peña, José F. de la. *Oligarquía y propiedad en la Nueva España, 1550-1624.* Mexico City: Fondo de Cultura Económica, 1983. 308p.

2804.   Philip, George, ed. *Politics in Mexico.* Dover, NH: Croom Helm, 1985. 223p.

2805.   Pichardo Pagaza, Ignacio. *Introducción a la administración pública de México.* Mexico City: Instituto Nacional de Administración Pública, 1984. 2 vols.

2806.   Pohl, Mary, ed. *Prehistoric Lowland Maya Environment and Subsistence Economy.* Cambridge, MA: Peabody Museum of Archaeology and Ethnology, Harvard University (dist. by Harvard University Press), 1985. 209p.

2807.   Raat, W. Dirk, and William H. Beezley, eds. *Twentieth-Century Mexico.* Lincoln: University of Nebraska Press, 1986. 318p.

2808.   Ramírez, Miguel D. *Development Banking in Mexico: The Case of Nacional Financiera S.A.* New York: Praeger, 1986. 228p.

2809.   Reina, Leticia, ed. *Las luchas populares en México en el siglo XIX.* Mexico City: Centro de Investigaciones y Estudios Superiores en Antropología Social, 1983. 522p.

2810.   Reynolds, Clark W., and Carlos Tello, eds. *U.S.-Mexico Relations: Economic and Social Aspects.* Stanford, CA: Stanford University Press, 1983. 375p.

2811.   Riding, Alan. *Distant Neighbors: A Portrait of the Mexicans.* New York: Knopf, 1985. 385p.

2812.   Riquelme, Marcial Antonio, and Yolanda Manzoni de Riquelme. *Migraciones internas y empleo: estudio de casos de un asentamiento irregular de la zona metropolitana de la ciudad de México.* Mexico City: Universidad Autónoma Metropolitana Iztapala, 1985. 269p.

2813.   Rivera Marín de Iturbe, Guadalupe. *La propiedad territorial en México, 1301-1810.* Mexico City: Siglo Veintiuno, 1983. 357p.

2814.   Ronfeldt, David, ed. *The Modern Mexican Military: A Reassessment.* La Jolla: Center for U.S.-Mexican Studies, University of California, San Diego, 1984. 218p.

2815.   Rosa, Martín de la, and Charles A. Reilly, coords. *Religion y política en México.* Mexico City: Siglo Veintiuno, 1985. 371p.

2816.   Rosenthal-Urey, Ina, ed. *Regional Impacts of U.S.-Mexican Relations.* San Diego: Center for U.S.-Mexican Studies, University of California, San Diego, 1986. 154p.

2817.   Roxborough, Ian. *Unions and Politics in Mexico: The Case of the Automobile Industry.* New York: Cambridge University Press, 1984. 209p.

2818.   Rubin-Kurtzman, Jane R. *The Socioeconomic Determinants of Fertility in Mexico: Changing Perspectives.* San Diego: Center for U.S.-Mexican Studies, University of California, San Diego, 1987. 66p.

2819.   Ruiz, Vicki L., and Susan Tiano, eds. *Women on the U.S.-Mexico Border: Responses to Change.* Boston, MA: Allen & Unwin, 1987. 247p.

2820.   Sabloff, Jeremy A., and E. Wyllys Andrews V., eds. *Late Lowland Maya Civilization: Classic to Postclassic.* Albuquerque: University of New Mexico Press, 1986. 526p.

2821.   Sanders, Sol W. *Mexico: Chaos on Our Doorstep.* Lanham, MD: Hamilton, 1986. 222p.

2822.   Sanderson, Steven E. *The Transformation of Mexican Agriculture: International Structure and the Politics of Rural Change.* Princeton, NJ: Princeton University Press, 1986. 324p.

2823.   Sanderson, Susan Walsh. *Land Reform in Mexico: 1910-1980.* Orlando, FL: Academic, 1984. 186p.

2824.   Schell, William, Jr. *Medieval Iberian Tradition and Development of the Mexican Hacienda.* Syracuse, NY: Maxwell School of Citizenship and Public Affairs, Syracuse University, 1986. 117p.

2825.   Schwaller, John Frederick. *Origins of Church Wealth in Mexico: Ecclesiastical Revenues and Church Finances, 1523-1600.* Albuquerque: University of New Mexico Press, 1985. 241p.

2826.   Silva Herzog, Jesús. *En defensa de México: Pensamiento económico político.* Mexico City: Nueva Imagen, 1984. 2 vols.

2827.   Simonelli, Jeanne M. *Two Boys, a Girl, and Enough! Reproductive and Economic Decisionmaking on the Mexican Periphery.* Boulder, CO: Westview, 1986. 231p.

2828.   Soustelle, Jacques. *The Olmec: The Oldest Civilization in Mexico.* Translated by Helen R. Land. Norman: University of Oklahoma Press, 1985. 214p.

2829.   Spalding, Rose J. *The Mexican Food Crisis: An Analysis of SAM.* La Jolla: Center for U.S.-Mexican Studies, University of California, San Diego, 1984. 44p.

2830.   Spores, Ronald. *The Mixtecs in Ancient and Colonial Times.* Norman: University of Oklahoma Press, 1985. 262p.

2831.   Spores, Ronald, and Ross Hassig, eds. *Five Centuries of Law and Politics in Central Mexico.* Nashville, TN: Vanderbilt University Press, 1984. 286p.

2832.   Stoddard, Ellwyn R. *Maquila: Assembly Plants in Northern Mexico.* El Paso: Texas Western Press, 1987. 91p.

2833.   Story, Dale. *Industry, the State, and the Public Policy in Mexico.* Austin: University of Texas Press, 1986. 275p.

2834.   Story, Dale. *The Mexican Ruling Party: Stability and Authority.* New York: Praeger, 1986. 160p.

2835.   Super, John C. *La vida en Querétaro durante la colonia, 1531-1810.* Mexico City: Fondo de Cultura Económica, 1983. 294p.

2836.   Taggart, James M. *Nahuat Myth and Social Structure.* Austin: University of Texas Press, 1983. 287p.

2837.   Tutino, John *From Insurrection to Revolution in Mexico: Social Bases of Agrarian Violence, 1750-1940.* Princeton, NJ: Princeton University Press, 1986. 425p.

2838.   van Zontwijk, Rudolph. *The Aztec Arrangement: The Social History of Pre-Spanish Mexico.* Norman: University of Oklahoma Press, 1985. 346p.

2839.   Vásquez, Carlos, and Manuel García y Griego, eds. *Mexican-U.S. Relations: Conflict and Convergence.* Los Angeles: UCLA Chicano Studies Research Center; UCLA Latin American Center, 1983. 490p.

2840.   Vásquez, Josefina Zoraida, and Lorenzo Meyer. *The United States and Mexico.* Chicago: University of Chicago Press, 1985. 220p.

2841.   Vélez-Ibañez, Carlos G. *Rituals of Marginality: Politics, Process, and Cultural Change in Central Urban Mexico, 1969-1974.* Berkeley; Los Angeles: University of California Press, 1983. 296p.

2842.   Villanueva Mukul, Eric. *Así tomamos las tierras: henequén haciendas en Yucatán durante el porfiriato.* Mérida, Yucatán: Maldonado, 1984. 136p.

2843.   Walker, David W. *Kinship, Business, and Politics: The Martínez del Río Family in Mexico, 1824-1867.* Austin: University of Texas Press, 1986. 278p.

2844.   Ward, Peter M. *Welfare Politics in Mexico: Papering over the Cracks.* London; Boston, MA: Allen & Unwin, 1986. 152p.

2845.   Warren, J. Benedict. *The Conquest of Michoacán: The Spanish Domination of the Tarascan Kingdom in Western Mexico.* Norman: University of Oklahoma Press, 1985. 352p.

2846.   Wasserman, Mark. *Capitalists, Caciques, and Revolution: The Native Elite and Foreign Enterprise in Chihuahua, Mexico, 1854-1911.* Chapel Hill: University of North Carolina Press, 1984. 232p.

2847.   Wasserstrom, Robert. *Class and Society in Central Chiapas.* Berkeley: University of California Press, 1983. 357p.

2848.   Weckmann, Luis. *La herencia medieval de México.* Mexico City: Colegio de México, 1984. 2 vols.

2849.   Weeks, Charles A. *The Juarez Myth in Mexico.* University: University of Alabama Press, 1987. 204p.

2850.   Weintraub, Sidney, ed. *Industrial Strategy and Planning in Mexico and the United States.* Boulder, CO: Westview, 1986. 279p.

2851.   Wells, Allen. *Yucatán's Gilded Age: Henequen, and International Harvester, 1860-1915.* Albuquerque: University of New Mexico Press, 1985. 239p.

2852.   Whiting, Van R., Jr. *Politics of Technology Transfer in Mexico.* La Jolla: Center for U.S.-Mexican Studies, University of California, San Diego, 1984. 57p.

2853.   Willey, Gordon Randolf. *Essays in Maya Archaeology.* Albuquerque: University of New Mexico Press, 1987. 245p.

2854.   Wionczek, Miguel S., and Regaei El Mallakh, eds. *Mexico's Energy Resources: Toward a Policy of Diversification.* Boulder, CO: Westview, 1985. 176p.

2855.   Wyman, Donald L., ed. *Mexico's Economic Crisis: Challenges and Opportunities.* La Jolla: Center for U.S.-Mexican Studies, University of California, San Diego, 1983. 126p.

2856.   Young, Gay, ed. *The Social Ecology and Economic Development of Ciudad Juárez.* Boulder, CO: Westview, 1986. 171p.

2857.   Zavala, Silvio. *El servicio personal de los indios en la Nueva España, 1521-1550.* Mexico City: Colegio de México, 1984-85. 2 vols.

Articles and Chapters

2858.   Aguayo Quezada, Sergio, and Laura O'Dogherty. "Los refugiados guatemaltecos en Campeche y Quintana Roo," *Foro Internacional* 27:2 (October-December 1986), 266-295.

2859.   Aguirre Beltrán, Gonzalo. "La polémica indigenista en México en los años setenta, *América Indígena* 44 (December 1984), 7-28.

2860.   Alarcón, Gustavo. "Los ingresos del trabajo y las determinantes de sus diferencias," *El Trimestre Económico* 52:206 (April-June 1985), 499-529.

2861.   Alberro-Semerena, José Luis, and María Dolores Nieto-Ituarte. "Empirical Estimates of Marxism Categories in Mexico: 1970-1975," *Review of Radical Political Economics* 18:4 (Winter 1986), 32-46.

2862.   Alejo, Francisco Javier. "Crecimiento, estabilidad y distribución: los tres grandes problemas del desarrollo. El caso de México," *El Trimestre Económico* 51:201 (January-March 1984), 33-72.

2863.   Alisky, Marvin. "Mexico." In *Arms Production in Developing Countries: An Analysis of Decision Making,* edited by James Everett Katz. Lexington, MA: Lexington, 1984. pp. 247-263.

2864.   Almaráz, Félix D., Jr. "San Antonio's Old Franciscan Missions: Material Decline and Secular Avarice in the Transition from Hispanic to Mexican Control," *The Americas* 44:1 (July 1987), 1-22.

2865.   Amieva-Huerta, Juan. "Aspectos teóricos de un modelo macro-econométrico para la economía mexicana," *El Trimestre Económico* 52:205 (January-March 1985), 139-173.

2866.   Anderson, Joan B., and Roger S. Frantz. "Production Efficiency among Mexican Apparel Assembly Plants," *Journal of Developing Areas* 19:3 (April 1985), 369-377.

2867.   Anderson, Joan B., and Roger S. Frantz. "The Response of Labour Effort to Falling Real Wages: The Mexican Peso Devaluation of February 1982," *World Development* 12:7 (July 1984), 759-766.

2868.   Andrews, Anthony P. "The Political Geography of the Sixteenth Century Yucatán Maya," *Journal of Anthropological Research* 40:4 (Winter 1984), 589-596.

2869.   Anna, Timothy E. "The Rule of Agustín de Iturbide: A Reappraisal," *Journal of Latin American Studies* 17:1 (May 1985), 79-110.

2870.   Arizpe, Lourdes. "The Rural Exodus in Mexico and Mexican Migration to the United States." In *The Border That Joins: Mexican Migrants and U.S. Responsibility,* edited by Peter G. Brown and Henry Shue. Totowa, NJ: Rowman & Allenheld, 1983. pp. 162-183.

2871.   Arizpe, Lourdes, and Josefina Aranda. "Women Workers in the Strawberry Agribusiness in Mexico." In *Women's Work: Development and the Division of Labor by Gender,* edited by Eleanor Burke Leacock and Helen I. Safa. South Hadley, MA: Bergin & Garvey, 1986. pp. 174-193.

2872.   Arrendondo Ramírez, Pablo, and María de Lourdes. "La política informativa de Televisa en los Estados Unidos: El caso de '24 Horas'." *Mexican Studies* 2:1 (Winter 1986), 83-105.

2873.   Arriola, Carlos, and Juan Gustavo Galindo. "Los empresarios y el Estado en México, 1976-1982," *Foro Internacional* 25:2 (October-December 1984), 118-137.

2874.   Arrom, Silvia M. "Changes in Mexican Family Law in the Nineteenth Century: The Civil Codes of 1870 and 1884," *Journal of Family History* 10:3 (Fall 1985), 305-317.

2875.   Ashby, Joe C. "The Dilemma of the Mexican Trade Union Movement," *Mexican Studies* 1:2 (Summer 1985), 277-301.

2876.   Aspe, Pedro, and Carlos M. Jarque. "Expectativas racionales: un modelo trimestral para la economía mexicana," *El Trimestre Económico* 52:207 (July-September 1985), 649-682.

2877.   Aubry, Andrés. "Indígenas y movimientos populares," *Boletín de Antropología Americana* 8 (December 1983), 59-62.

2878.   Ayala, José, and Clemente Ruiz Durán. "Development and Crisis in Mexico: A Structuralist Approach." In *Latin American Political Economy: Financial Crisis and Political Change,* edited by Jonathan Hartlyn and Samuel A. Morley. Boulder, CO: Westview, 1986. pp. 243-264.

2879. Báez-Jorge, Felix. "Articulaciones e intercambios desde la perspectiva del Compadrinazgo entre los Zoque-Popoluca," *América Indígena* 44:2 (April-June 1984), 283-302.

2880. Bagley, Bruce M. "Mexico in Central America: The Limits of Regional Power." In *Political Change in Central America: Internal and External Dimensions,* edited by Wolf Grabendorff, Heinrich-W. Krumwiede and Jörg Todt. Boulder, CO: Westview, 1984. pp. 261-284.

2881. Bagley, Bruce M. "The Politics of Asymmetrical Interdependence: U.S.-Mexican Relations in the 1980s." In *The Caribbean Challenge: U.S. Policy in a Volatile Region,* edited by H. Michael Erisman. Boulder, CO: Westview, 1984. pp. 141-159.

2882. Baklanoff, Eric N., and Jeffery T. Brannon. "Forward and Backward Linkages in a Plantation Economy: Immigrant Entrepreneurship and Industrial Development in Yucatán, Mexico," *Journal of Developing Areas* 19:1 (October 1984), 83-94.

2883. Balassa, Bela. "Trade Policy in Mexico," *World Development* 11:9 (September 1983), 795-811.

2884. Baldwin, Deborah. "Broken Traditions: Mexican Revolutionaries and Protestant Allegiances," *The Americas* 40:2 (October 1983), 229-258.

2885. Barkin, David. "The End to Food Self-Sufficiency in Mexico," *Latin American Perspectives* 14:3 (Summer 1987), 271-297.

2886. Barrientos, Gustavo. "La salud de las trabajadoras de la salud," *Revista Mexicana de Sociología* 45:3 (July-September 1983), 877-914.

2887. Bartra, Roger, and Gerardo Otero. "Agrarian Crisis and Social Differentiation in Mexico," *Journal of Peasant Studies* 14:3 (April 1987), 334-362.

2888. Basáñez, Miguel, and Roderic A. Camp. "La nacionalización de la banca y la opinión pública en México," *Foro Internacional* 25:2 (October-December 1984), 202-216.

2889. Bastian, Jean-Pierre. "Los propagandistas del constitucionalismo en México, 1910-1920," *Revista Mexicana de Sociología* 45:2 (April-June 1983), 321-351.

2890. Becker, Marjorie. "Black and White and Color: *Cardenismo* and the Search for a *Campesino* Ideology," *Comparative Studies in Society and History* 29:3 (July 1987), 453-465.

2891. Beelen, George D. "The Harding Administration and Mexico: Diplomacy by Economic Persuasion," *The Americas* 41:2 (October 1984), 177-189.

2892. Beezley, William H. "In Search of Everyday Mexicans in the Revolution," *Inter-American Review of Bibliography* 33:3 (1983), 366-382.

2893. Behar, Ruth. "Sex and Sin, Witchcraft and the Devil in Late-Colonial Mexico," *American Ethnologist* 14:1 (February 1987), 34-54.

2894. Behar, Ruth. "The Visions of a Guachichil Witch in 1599: A Window on the Subjugation of Mexico's Hunter-Gatherers," *Ethnohistory* 34:2 (Spring 1987), 115-138.

2895. Bejarano González, Fernando. "La irregularidad de la tenencia de la tierra en las colonias populares, 1976-1982," *Revista Mexicana de Sociología* 45:3 (July-September 1983), 797-827.

2896. Benjamin, Thomas, and Marcial Ocasio-Meléndez. "Organizing the Memory of Modern Mexico: Porfirian Historiography in Perspective, 1880s-1980s," *Hispanic American Historical Review* 64:2 (May 1984), 323-364.

2897. Berdan, Frances F. "Cotton in Aztec Mexico: Production, Distribution and Uses," *Mexican Studies* 3:2 (Summer 1987), 235-262.

2898. Berndt, Ernst R., and German Botero. "Energy Demand in the Transportation Sector of Mexico," *Journal of Development Economics* 17:3 (April 1985), 219-238.

2899. Berndt, Ernst R., and Ricardo Samaniego. "Residential Electricity Demand in Mexico: A Model Distinguishing Access from Consumption," *Land Economics* 60:3 (August 1984), 268-277.

2900. Binford, Leigh. "Political Conflict and Land Tenure in the Mexican Isthmus of Tehuantepec," *Journal of Latin American Studies* 17:1 (May 1985), 179-200.

2901. Bizberg, Ilán. "Las perspectivas de la oposición sindical en México," *Foro Internacional* 23:4 (April-June 1983), 331-358.

2902. Bizberg, Ilán. "Política laboral y acción sindical en México, 1976-1982," *Foro Internacional* 25:2 (October-December 1984), 166-189.

2903. Blair, Calvin P. "Buy, Beg, Borrow and Steal: The Forms and Fashions of Technology Transfer," *Mexican Studies* 2:2 (Summer 1986), 215-233.

2904. Blanco, Herminio, and Peter M. Garber. "Recurrent Devaluation and Speculative Attacks on the Mexican Peso," *Journal of Political Economy* 94:1 (February 1986), 148-166.

2905. Blitzer, Charles R., and Richard S. Eckaus. "Energy-Economy Interactions in Mexico: A Multiperiod General Equilibrium Models," *Journal of Development Economics* 21:2 (May 1986), 259-281.

2906. Blomström, Magnus. "El comportamiento de las empresas nacionales y extranjeras en México: una revisión del estudio de Fajnzylber y Martínez Tarragó," *El Trimestre Económico* 52:205 (January-March 1985), 175-194.

2907. Blomström, Magnus. "Multinationals and Market Structure in Mexico," *World Development* 14:4 (April 1986), 523-530.

2908. Boils M., Guillermo. "Los militares en México: 1965-1985," *Revista Mexicana de Sociología* 47:1 (January-March 1985), 169-185.

2909.   Booth, John A., and Mitchell A. Seligson. "The Political Culture of Authoritarianism in Mexico: A Reexamination," *Latin American Research Review* 19:1 (1984), 106-124.

2910.   Borah, Woodrow. "El status jurídico de los indios en Nueva España," *América Indígena* 45:2 (April-June 1985), 257-276.

2911.   Bortz, Jeffrey. "The Dilemma of Mexican Labor," *Current History* 86:518 (March 1987), 105-108.

2912.   Brading, D.A. "Facts and Figments in Bourbon Mexico," *Bulletin of Latin American Research* 4:1 (1985), 61-64.

2913.   Brandes, Stanley H. "Animal Metaphors and Social Control in Tzintzuntzan," *Ethnology* 23:3 (July 1984), 207-215.

2914.   Brannon, Jeffrey, and Eric N. Baklanoff. "The Political Economy of Agrarian Reform in Yucatán, Mexico," *World Development* 12:11-12 (November-December 1984), 1131-1141.

2915.   Browner, C.H. "Gender Roles and Social Change: A Mexican Case Study," *Ethnology* 25:2 (April 1986), 89-106.

2916.   Bueno, Gerardo. "Alternative Forms, Fashions and Politics for Technology Transfer: A Mexican Perspective," *Mexican Studies* 2:2 (Summer 1986), 235-252.

2917.   Bueno, Gerardo. "Endeudamiento externo y estrategias de desarrollo en México, 1976-1982," *Foro Internacional* 24:1 (July-September 1983), 78-89.

2918.   Bueno, Gerardo M. "La influencia de Estados Unidos sobre la economía mexicana," *Foro Internacional* 24:4 (April-June 1984), 484-498.

2919.   Byerlee, Derek, and Edith Hesse de Polanco. "Farmers' Stepwise Adoption of Technological Packages: Evidence from the Mexican Altiplano," *American Journal of Agricultural Economics* 68:3 (August 1986), 519-527.

2920.   Camp, Roderic A. "An Image of Mexican Intellectuals," *Mexican Studies* 1:1 (Winter 1985), 61-82.

2921.   Camp, Roderic A. "The Political Technocrat in Mexico and the Survival of the Political System," *Latin American Research Review* 20:1 (1985), 97-118.

2922.   Camp, Roderic A. "Relaciones familiares en la política mexicana," *Foro Internacional* 26:3 (January-March 1986), 349-372.

2923.   Camp, Roderic A. "El tecnócrata en México," *Revista Mexicana de Sociología* 45:2 (April-June 1983), 579-599.

2924.   Canabal Cristiani, Beatriz. "El campo y los campesinos, hacia 1985," *Revista Mexicana de Sociología* 47:1 (January-March 1985), 207-219.

2925.   Cancian, Frank. "Las listas de espera en el sistema de cargos de Zinacantán: cambios sociales, políticos y económicos, 1952-1980,"

América Indígena 46:3 (July-September 1986), 477-494.

2926. Carbó, Teresa. "¿Cómo habla el poder legislativo en México?" *Revista Mexicana de Sociología* 49:2 (April-June 1987), 165-180.

2927. Carmagnani, Marcello. "The Inertia of Clio: The Social History of Colonial Mexico," *Latin American Research Review* 20:1 (1985), 149-166.

2928. Carr, Barry. "Crisis in Mexican Communism: The Extraordinary Congress of the Mexican Communist Party," *Science and Society* 50:4 (Winter 1986-1987), 391-414.

2929. Carr, Barry. "Crisis in Mexican Communism: The Extraordinary Congress of the Mexican Communist Party - Part II," *Science and Society* 51:1 (Spring 1987), 43-67.

2930. Carr, Barry. "Mexican Communism, 1968-1981: Eurocommunism in the Americas?" *Journal of Latin American Studies* 17:1 (May 1985), 201-228.

2931. Carr, Barry. "The Mexican Communist Party and Agrarian Mobilization in the Laguna, 1920-1940: A Worker-Peasant Alliance?" *Hispanic American Historical Review* 67:3 (August 1987), 371-404.

2932. Caso-Raphael, Agustín, and Jorge Miranda. "Patrones de política monetaria y gasto público en México: el desarrollo estabilizador," *El Trimestre Económico* 51:203 (July-September 1984), 591-614.

2933. Castañeda, Jorge G. "Don't Corner Mexico!" *Foreign Policy* 60 (Fall 1985), 75-90.

2934. Castañeda, Jorge G. "Mexico at the Brink," *Foreign Affairs* 64:2 (Winter 1985-86), 287-303.

2935. Castañeda, Jorge G. "Mexico's Coming Challenges," *Foreign Policy* 64 (Fall 1986), 120-139.

2936. Castorena, Guadalupe. "Concentración vertical de productores campesinos por el Estado," *Revista Mexicana de Sociología* 45:3 (July-September 1983), 829-855.

2937. Cerutti, Mario. "Burguesía regional, mercados y capitalism. Apuntes metodológicos y referencias sobre un caso latinoamericano: Monterey, 1850-1910," *Revista Mexicana de Sociología* 45:1 (January-March 1983), 129-148.

2938. Cervantes González, Jesús A. "Inflación y distribución del ingreso y de la riqueza en México," *El Trimestre Económico* 50:200 (October-December 1983), 2017-2040.

2939. Chacón, Ramón D. "Rural Education Reform in Yucatán: From the Porfiriato to the Era of Salvador Alvarado, 1910-1918," *The Americas* 42:2 (October 1985), 207-228.

2940. Chacón, Ramón D. "Salvador Alvarado and the Roman Catholic Church: Church-State Relations in Revolutionary Yucatán, 1914-1918,"

Journal of Church and State 27:2 (Spring 1985), 245-266.

2941.   Chandler, D.S. "The Montepios and Regulation of Marriage in the Mexican Bureaucracy, 1770-1821," *The Americas* 43:1 (July 1986), 47-68.

2942.   Chant, Silvia. "Family Formation and Female Roles in Querétaro, Mexico," *Bulletin of Latin American Research* 4:1 (1985), 17-32.

2943.   Chant, Sylvia. "Household Labour and Self-Help Housing in Querétaro, Mexico," *Boletín de Estudios Latinoamericanos y de Caribe* 37 (December 1984), 45-68.

2944.   Chavez, Leo R. "Mexican Immigration and Health Care: A Political Economy Perspective," *Human Organization* 45:4 (Winter 1986), 344-352.

2945.   Cochrane, James. "Secretarios de Relaciones Exteriores y Secretarios de Estado, 1935-1985: sus carreras y experiencias profesionales," *Foro Internacional* 27:1 (July-September 1986), 60-74.

2946.   Collier, George A. "Peasant Politics and the Mexican State," *Mexican Studies* 3:1 (Winter 1987), 71-98.

2947.   Cook, Scott. "Peasant Economy, Rural Industry and Capitalist Development in the Oaxaca Valley, Mexico," *Journal of Peasant Studies* 12:1 (October 1984), 3-40.

2948.   Cook, Scott. "Rural Industry, Social Differentiation, and the Contradictions of Provincial Mexican Capitalism," *Latin American Perspectives* 11:4 (Fall 1984), 60-85.

2949.   Cook, Scott, and Leigh Binford. "Petty Commodity Production, Capital Accumulation, and Peasant Differentiation: Lenin vs. Chayanov in Rural Mexico," *Review of Radical Political Economics* 18:4 (Winter 1986), 1-31.

2950.   Corbett, Jack. "Mexico: The Policy Context of Social Impact Analysis." In *Social Impact Analysis and Development Planning in the Third World,* edited by William Derman and Scott Whiteford. Boulder, CO: Westview, 1985. pp. 50-66.

2951.   Cordera, Rolando. "Economía y dependencia," *Revista Mexicana de Sociología* 47:1 (January-March 1985), 15-24.

2952.   Cornelius, Wayne A. "The Political Economy of Mexico under De la Madrid: Austerity, Routinized Crisis, and Nascent Recovery," *Mexican Studies* 1:1 (Winter 1985), 83-123.

2953.   Cothran, Dan A. "Budgetary Secrecy and Policy Strategy: Mexico under Cárdenas," *Mexican Studies* 2:1 (Winter 1986), 35-58.

2954.   Cott, Kennett. "Mexican Diplomacy and the Chinese Issue, 1876-1910," *Hispanic American Historical Review* 67:1 (February 1987), 63-85.

2955.   Couturier, Edith. "Women and the Family in Eighteenth-Century Mexico: Law and Practice," *Journal of Family History* 10:3 (Fall 1985), 294-

304.

2956.   Cummins, Victoria Hennessey. "Imperial Policy and Church Income: The Sixteenth Century Mexican Church," *The Americas* 43:1 (July 1986), 87-103.

2957.   Dahlman, Carl J., and Mariluz Cortes. "Exports of Technology by Newly-Industrializing Countries: Mexico," *World Development* 12:5-6 (May-June 1984), 601-624.

2958.   Danks, Noblet Barry. "The Labor Revolt in 1766 in the Mining Community of Real Del Monte," *The Americas* 44:2 (October 1987), 143-165.

2959.   Dávila Aldas, Francisco. "La economía mexicana, sus problemas y repercusiones sociopolíticas, 1976-1982," *Revista Mexicana de Sociología* 45:3 (July-September 1983), 751-779.

2960.   Davis, Charles L. "Political Regimes and the Socioeconomic Resource Model of Political Mobilization: Some Venezuelan and Mexican Data," *Journal of Politics* 45:2 (May 1983), 422-448.

2961.   Deeds, Susan M. "Land Tenure Patterns in Northern New Spain," *The Americas* 41:4 (April 1985), 446-461.

2962.   De Olloqui, José Juan. "Un enfoque bancario sobre la crisis mexicana de pagos en 1982," *El Trimestre Económico* 51:203 (July-September 1984), 527-544.

2963.   DeVoss, David. "Mexico City's Limits." In *Bordering on Trouble: Resources and Politics in Latin America,"* edited by Andrew Maguire and Janet Welsh Brown. Bethesda, MD: Adler & Adler, 1986. pp. 13-54.

2964.   DeWalt, Billie R. "Mexico's Second Green Revolution," *Mexican Studies* 1:1 (Winter 1985), 29-60.

2965.   Dewey, Kathryn G. "Nutrition, Social Impact, and Development: A Mexican Case." In *Social Impact Analysis and Development Planning in the Third World,* edited by William Derman and Scott Whiteford. Boulder, CO: Westview, 1985. pp. 160-177.

2966.   Doolittle, William E. "Agriculture Expansion in a Marginal Area of Mexico," *Geographical Review* 73:3 (July 1983), 301-313.

2967.   Douglas, H. Eugene, and Victor Basiuk. "The Private Sector and Technology Transfer to Mexico," *Mexican Studies* 2:2 (Summer 1986), 253-273.

2968.   Dumond, Don E. "The Talking Crosses of Yucatán: A New Look at Their History," *Ethnohistory* 32:4 (December 1985), 291-308.

2969.   Durán, Esperanza. "Mexico and the South Atlantic Conflict: Solidarity or Ambiguity?" *International Affairs* 60:2 (Spring 1984), 221-232.

2970.   Durán, Esperanza. "Mexico: Economic Realism and Political Efficiency," *World Today* 41:5 (May 1985), 96-99.

2971.   Earl, Duncan M. "El simbolismo de la política y la política del simbolismo: el Carnaval Chamula y el mantenimiento de la comunidad," *América Indígena* 46:3 (July-September 1986), 545-567.

2972.   Epstein, Erwin E. "National Consciousness and Education in Mexico." In *Education in Latin America*, edited by Colin Brock and Hugh Lawlor. Dover, NH: Croom Helm, 1985. pp. 50-78.

2973.   Erb, Guy F., and Cathryn Thorup. "Las relaciones entre México y Estados Unidos: cuestiones futuras," *Foro Internacional* 26:4 (April-June 1986), 480-510.

2974.   Estrada I., Margarita. "Trabajo femenino y reproducción de la fuerza de trabajo industrial," *Boletín de Antropología Americana* 8 (December 1983), 133-140.

2975.   Fábregas, Andrés. "El análisis antropológico de la política: el caso de México," *Boletín de Antropología Americana* 8 (December 1983), 5-40.

2976.   Fairchild, Loretta G., and Kim Sosin. "Manufacturing Firms in Mexico's Financial Crisis: Determinants of Severity and Response," *Mexican Studies* 3:1 (Winter 1987), 127-150.

2977.   Felstehausen, Herman, and Heliodoro Díaz-Cisneros. "The Strategy of Rural Development: The Puebla Initiative," *Human Organization* 44:4 (Winter 1985), 285-292.

2978.   Ferris, Elizabeth, G. "Mexico's Foreign Policies: A Study in Contradictions." In *The Dynamics of Latin American Foreign Policies*, edited by Jennie K. Lincoln and Elizabeth G. Ferris. Boulder, CO: Westview, 1984. pp. 213-227.

2979.   Ferris, Elizabeth G. "The Politics of Asylum: Mexico and the Central American Refugees," *Journal of Inter-American Studies and World Affairs* 26:3 (August 1984), 357-384.

2980.   Flamm, Kenneth. "Transfer of Advanced Technology: Recent Trends and Implications for Mexico," *Mexican Studies* 2:2 (Summer 1986), 195-213.

2981.   Fournier, Patricia. "Arqueología histórica en la Ciudad de México," *Boletín de Antropología Americana* 11 (July 1985), 27-31.

2982.   Fox, Jonathan. "Agrarian Reform and Populist Politics: A Discussion of Stephen Sanderson's *Agrarian Populism and the Mexican State*," *Latin American Perspectives* 12:3 (Summer 1985), 29-41.

2983.   Franco Hijuelos, Claudia. "Las ventas de crudo mexicano para la reserva estratégica petrolera de Estados Unidos," *Foro Internacional* 27:4 (April-June 1987), 543-561.

2984.   Frieden, Jeff. "Third World Indebted Industrialization: International Finance and State Capitalism in Mexico, Brazil, Algeria, and South Korea." In *Postimperialism: International Capitalism and Development in the Late Twentieth Century*, edited by David G. Becker, Jeff Frieden, Sayre P. Schatz, and Richard L. Sklar.

Boulder, CO: Lynne Rienner, 1987. pp. 131-159.

2985.   Fukurai, Hiroshi, James B. Pick, Edgar W. Butler, and Swapan Nag. "An Analysis of Interstate Migration in Mexico: Impact of Origin and Destination States on Migration Patterns," *Mexican Studies* 3:2 (Summer 1987), 365-396.

2986.   Funes Rodríguez, Guillermo. "Public Policy and Technology Transfer: A Mexican Perspective," *Mexican Studies* 2:2 (Summer 1986), 275-298.

2987.   Gallardo, Julio López. "La distribución del ingreso en México: estructura y evolución," *El Trimestre Económico* 50:200 (October-December 1983), 2227-2256.

2988.   García, Brígida, and Orlandina de Oliveira. "Dinámica poblacional en México: tendencias recientes," *Revista Mexicana de Sociología* 47:1 (January-March 1985), 189-205.

2989.   García Argañarás, Fernando. "Historical Structures, Social Forces, and Mexican Independence," *Latin American Perspectives* 13:1 (Winter 1986), 19-43.

2990.   Garma Navarro, Carlos. "Liderazgo protestante en una lucha campesina en México," *América Indígena* 44:1 (January-March 1984), 127-141.

2991.   Garner, Paul. "Federalism and Caudillismo in the Mexican Revolution: The Genesis of the Oaxaca Sovereignty Movement, 1915-20," *Journal of Latin American Studies* 17:1 (May 1985), 111-133.

2992.   Garner, Richard L. "Further Consideration of 'Facts and Figments in Bourbon Mexico'," *Bulletin of Latin American Research* 6:1 (1987), 55-63.

2993.   Garner, Richard L. "Price Trends in Eighteenth-Century Mexico," *Hispanic American Historical Review* 65:2 (May 1985), 279-325.

2994.   Garza Elizondo, Humberto. "Desequilibrios y contradicciones en la política exterior de México," *Foro Internacional* 24:4 (April-June 1984), 443-457.

2995.   Garza Elizondo, Humberto. "Mexican-Soviet Relations." In *Soviet-Latin American Relations in the 1980s,* edited by Augusto Varas. Boulder, CO: Westview, 1987. pp. 197-210.

2996.   Garza Elizondo, Humberto. "México y Canadá en el decenio de los ochenta," *Foro Internacional* 27:1 (July-September 1986), 45-59.

2997.   Garza Elizondo, Humberto, "La Ostpolitik de México: 1977-1982," *Foro Internacional* 24:3 (January-March 1984), 341-357.

2998.   Hall, Linda B., and Don M. Coever. "Oil and the Mexican Revolution: The Southwestern Connection," *The Americas* 41:2 (October 1984), 229-244.

2999.   Hamel, Ranier Enrique. "Socio-Cultural Conflict and Bilingual Education: The Case of the Otomí Indians in Mexico," *International Social Science Journal* 36:1 (1984), 113-128.

3000.   Hamilton, Nora. "State-Class Alliances and Conflicts: Issues and Actors in the Mexican Economic Crisis," *Latin American Perspectives* 11:4 (Fall 1984), 6-32.

3001.   Hanks, William F. "Authenticity and Ambivalence in the Text: A Colonial Maya Case," *American Ethnologist* 13:4 (November 1986), 721-744.

3002.   Hanratty, Dennis M. "Mexican Policy toward Central American and the Caribbean." In *Revolution and Counterrevolution in Central America and the Caribbean,* edited by Donald E. Schulz and Douglas H. Graham. Boulder, CO: Westview, 1984. pp. 423-446.

3003.   Harris, Martha Caldwell. "Public Policy and Technology Transfer: A View from the United States," *Mexican Studies* 2:2 (Summer 1986), 299-316.

3004.   Hartland-Thunberg, Penelope, and Charles K. Ebinger. "Mexico's Economic Anguish." In *Banks, Petrodollars, and Sovereign Debtors,* edited by Penelope Hartland-Thunberg and Charles K. Ebinger. Boulder, CO: Westview, 1986. pp. 55-98.

3005.   Haskett, Robert S. "Indian Town Government in Colonial Cuernavaca: Persistence, Adaptation, and Change," *Hispanic American Historical Review* 67:2 (May 1987), 203-223.

3006.   Haviland, John B. "La creación del ritual: la Pascua de 1981 en Nabenchauk," *América Indígena* 46:3 (July-September 1986), 453-475.

3007.   Heath, John Richard. "Constraints on Peasant Maize Production: A Case Study from Michoacán," *Mexican Studies* 3:2 (Summer 1987), 263-286.

3008.   Hector, Cary. "La izquierda mexicana hoy," *Mexican Studies* 2:1 (Winter 1986), 1-33.

3009.   Helms, Brigit S. "Pluralismo limitado en México: estudio de un caso de consulta pública sobre la membresía del GATT," *Foro Internacional* 26:2 (October-December 1985), 172-189.

3010.   Henderson, Paul V.N. "Woodrow Wilson, Victoriano Huerta, and the Recognition Issue in Mexico," *The Americas* 41:2 (October 1984), 151-176.

3011.   Hernández Rodríguez, Rogelio. "Empresarios, estado y condiciones laborales durante la sustitución de importaciones," *Foro Internacional* 26:2 (October-December 1985), 157-171.

3012.   Hernández Rodríguez, Rogelio. "La política y los empresarios después de la nacionalización bancaria," *Foro Internacional* 27:2 (October-December 1986), 247-265.

3013.   Herrera, René, and Mario Ojeda. "La política de México en la región de Centroaméricana," *Foro Internacional* 23:4 (April-June 1983), 423-440.

3014.   Herrera-Lasso M., Luis. "México y la distensión internacional en el período 1976-1982: balance y perspectivas," *Foro Internacional* 24:3 (January-March 1984), 358-369.

3015.   Hererra Prats, Rocío B. de. "La política indigenista en la actualidad," *Boletín de Antropología Americana* 8 (December 1983), 41-58.

3016.   Herrera Zúñiga, René, and Manuel Chavarría. "México en Contadora: una búsqueda de límites a su compromiso en Centroamérica," *Foro Internacional* 24:4 (April-June 1984), 458-483.

3017.   Herwig, Holger H., and Christon I. Archer. "Global Gambit: A German General Staff Assessment of Mexican Affairs, November 1913," *Mexican Studies* 1:2 (Summer 1985), 303-321.

3018.   Herzog, Lawrence A. "The Cross Cultural Dimensions of Urban Land Use Policy on the U.S.-Mexican Border: A San Diego-Tiajuana Case Study," *Social Science Journal* 22:3 (July 1985), 29-46.

3019.   Giarraca, Norma. "Complejos agroindustriales y la subordinación del campesinado: algunas reflexiones y el caso de los tabacaleros mexicanos," *Estudios Rurales Latinoamericanos* 8:1 (January-April 1985), 21-39.

3020.   Gibson, Bill, Nora Lustig, and Lance Tayler. "Terms of Trade and Class Conflict in a Computable General Equilibrium Model for Mexico," *Journal of Development Studies* 33:1 (October 1986), 40-59.

3021.   Gilbert, M. Joseph, and Allen Wells. "Summer of Discontent: Economic Rivalry among Elite Factions during the Late Porfiriato in Yucatán," *Journal of Latin American Studies* 18:2 (November 1986), 255-282.

3022.   Giménez Montiel, Gilberto. "La controversia ideológica en torno al VI Informe de José López Portillo: ensayo de análisis argumentativo," *Revista Mexicana de Sociología* 45:2 (April-June 1983), 507-544.

3023.   Glade, William. "Party-Led Development." In *Politics, Policies, and Economic Development in Latin America,* edited by Robert G. Wesson. Stanford, CA: Hoover Institution Press, 1984. pp. 94-123.

3024.   Gómez Pompa, Arturo. "Maya Silviculture," *Mexican Studies* 3:1 (Winter 1987), 1-17.

3025.   González, María Luisa. "México ante el diálogo Norte-Sur," *Foro Internacional* 24:3 (January-March 1984), 327-340.

3026.   Grabowski, Richard, and Onesimo Sánchez. "Technological Change in Mexican Agriculture: 1950-1979," *Social and Economic Studies* 36:2 (June 1987), 187-205.

3027.   Grajales V., Carolina, and Felipe Lara Rosano. "Las decisiones políticas en transporte: el caso del aeropuerto de la ciudad de México," *Revista Mexicana de Sociología* 45:3 (July-September 1983), 915-932.

3028.   Greenleaf, Richard E. "The Inquisition Brotherhood: Cofradía de San Pedro Martír of Colonial Mexico," *The Americas* 40:2 (October 1983), 171-207.

3029.   Grindle, Merilee S. "Rhetoric, Reality, and Self-Sufficiency: Recent Initiatives in Mexican Rural Development," *Journal of Developing Areas* 19:2 (January 1985), 171-184.

3030.   Grunwald, Joseph. "Restructuración de la industria maquiladora," *El Trimestre Económico* 50:200 (October-December 1983), 2123-2152.

3031.   Gruzinski, Serge. "La red agujerada: identidades étnicas y occidentalización en el México colonial, siglos XVI-XIX, *América Indígena* 46:3 (July-September 1986), 411-434.

3032.   Guevara Niebla, Gilberto. "El tema de la educación," *Revista Mexicana de Sociología* 47:1 (January-March 1985), 233-241.

3033.   Gutiérrez, Ramón A. "Honor Ideology, Marriage Negotiation, and Class-Gender Domination in New Mexico, 1690-1846," *Latin American Perspectives* 12:1 (Winter 1985), 81-104.

3034.   Gutiérrez R., Roberto. "Precios del petróleo, deuda externa y crisis: la trascendencia del manejo de los instrumentos de política económica," *Foro Internacional* 27:4 (April-June 1987), 523-542.

3035.   Gutiérrez R., Roberto. "El trasfondo teórico de la política económica de México en los últimos años," *Foro Internacional* 26:4 (April-June 1986), 567-577.

3036.   Gwatkin, Davidson R. "The State of the World's Population Movement: Implications of the 1984 Mexico City Conference," *World Development* 13:4 (April 1985), 557-569.

3037.   Hirabayashi, Lane R. "Formación de Asociaciones de Pueblos migrantes a México: Mixtecos y Zapotecos," *América Indígena* 45:3 (July-September 1985), 579-598.

3038.   Hojman, David E. "From Mexican Plantations to Chilean Mines: The Theoretical and Empirical Relevance of Enclave Theories in Contemporary Latin America," *Inter-American Economic Affairs* 39:3 (Winter 1985), 27-53.

3039.   Holian, John. "The Fertility of Maya and Latino Women," *Latin American Research Review* 20:2 (1985), 87-103.

3040.   Holloway, Susan D., Kathleen S. Gorman, and Bruce Fuller. "Child-Rearing Attributions and Efficacy among Mexican Mothers and Teachers," *Journal of Social Psychology* 127:5 (October 1987), 499-510.

3041.   Horn, James J. "The Mexican Revolution and Health Care, or the Health of the Mexican Revolution," *Latin American Perspectives* 10:4 (Fall 1983), 24-39.

3042.   Horta, Raul Machado. "Constituição e direitos individuais," *Revista Brasileira de Estudos Políticos* 59 (July 1984), 41-68.

3043.   Huber, Brad R. "The Reinterpretation and Elaboration of Fiestas in the Sierra Norte de Puebla, Mexico," *Ethnology* 26:4 (October 1987), 281-296.

3044. Huerta Ríos, César. "El compadrazgo y sus relaciones con el caciquismo entre los Triquis de Oaxaca," *América Indígena* 44:2 (April-June 1984), 303-310.

3045. Ingham, John M. "Human Sacrifice at Tenochtitlan," *Comparative Studies in Society and History* 26:3 (July 1984), 378-400.

3046. Ireson, W. Randall. "Landholding, Agriculture Modernization and Income Concentration: A Mexican Example," *Economic Development and Cultural Change* 35:2 (January 1987), 351-366.

3047. Isaac, Barry L. "The Aztec 'Flowery War': A Geopolitical Explanation," *Journal of Anthropological Research* 39:4 (Winter 1983), 415-432.

3048. Ize, Alain. "Regideces fiscales e inestabilidad cambiaria: el caso de México," *El Trimestre Económico* 54:214 (April-June 1987), 311-332.

3049. Jackson, Robert H. "Demographic Change in Northwestern New Spain," *The Americas* 41:4 (April 1985), 462-479.

3050. John, Elizabeth A.H. "La situación y visión de los indios de la frontera norte de Nueva España, siglos XVI-XVIII," *América Indígena* 45:3 (July-September 1985), 465-483.

3051. Joseph, Gilbert M. "From Caste War to Class War: The Historiography of Modern Yucatán, c. 1750-1940," *Hispanic American Historical Review* 65:1 (February 1985), 111-134.

3052. Jrade, Ramón. "Inquiries into the Cristero Insurrection against the Mexican Revolution," *Latin American Research Review* 20:2 (1985), 53-69.

3053. Karim, M. Bazlul. "Rural Development Projects — Comilla, Puebla, and Chilalo: A Comparative Assessment," *Studies in Comparative International Development* 20:4 (Winter 1985-86), 3-42.

3054. Karl, Terry. "Mexico, Venezuela, and the Contadora Initiative." In *Confronting Revolution: Security through Diplomacy in Central America,* edited by Morris J. Blachman, William M. LeoGrande and Kenneth Sharpe. New York: Pantheon, 1986. pp. 271-292.

3055. Kaufman, Robert R. "Democratic and Authoritarian Response to the Debt Issue: Argentina, Brazil, Mexico," *International Organization* 39:2 (Summer 1985), 473-503.

3056. Kehoe, Timothy J., and Jaime Serra-Puche. "A General Equilibrium Analysis of Price Controls and Subsidies on Food in Mexico," *Journal of Development Economics* 21:1 (April 1986), 65-87.

3057. Kellog, Susan. "Aztec Inheritance in Sixteenth-Century Mexico City: Colonial Patterns, Prehispanic Influences," *Ethnohistory* 33:3 (Summer 1986), 313-330.

3058. Kemper, Robert V. "El compadrazgo en las ciudades mexicanas," *América Indígena* 44:2 (April-June 1984), 327-351.

3059. Keremitsis, Dawn. "Latin American Women Workers in Transition: Sexual

Division of the Labor Force in Mexico and Colombia in the Textile Industry," *The Americas* 40:4 (April 1984), 491-499.

3060.   Kim, Kwan S. "Industrial Development in Mexico: Problems, Policy Issues and Perspectives." In *Debt and Development in Latin America,* edited by Kwan S. Kim and David F. Ruccio. Notre Dame, IN: University of Notre Dame Press, 1985. pp. 205-226.

3061.   Kim, Kwan S., and Gerardo Turrubiate. "Structures of Foreign Trade and Income Distribution: The Case of Mexico," *Journal of Development Economics* 16:3 (December 1984), 263-278.

3062.   Kirk, Rodney C. "Parentesco en el compadrazgo yucateco: ¿Patrón de tradición o deadaptación?" *América Indígena* 44:2 (April-June 1984), 311-326.

3063.   Köhler, Ulrich. "Ciclos de poder en una comunidad indígena de México: política local y sus vínculos con la vida nacional," *América Indígena* 46:3 (July-September 1986), 435-451.

3064.   Knight, Alan. "Mexican Peonage: What Was It and Why Was It?" *Journal of Latin American Studies* 18:1 (May 1986), 41-74.

3065.   Knight, Alan. "The Mexican Revolution: Bourgeois? Nationalist? Or Just a 'Great Rebellion'?" *Bulletin of Latin American Research* 4:2 (1985), 1-37.

3066.   Knight, Alan. "The Political Economy of Revolutionary Mexico, 1900-1940." In *Latin America, Economic Imperialism and the State,* edited by Christopher Abel and Colin M. Lewis. London; Dover, NH: Athlone, 1985. pp. 288-317.

3067.   Knight, Alan. "The Working Class and the Mexican Revolution, c. 1900-1920," *Journal of Latin American Studies* 16:1 (May 1984), 51-79.

3068.   Kurtz, Donald V. "Strategies of Legitimation and the Aztec State," *Ethnology* 23:4 (October 1984), 301-314.

3069.   LaBarge, Richard A. "Questionable Records? Some Inconsistencies in the Gross Domestic Product of Mexico," *Inter-American Economic Affairs* 39:2 (Autumn 1985), 3-9.

3070.   LaFrance, David G. "Francisco I. Madero and the 1911 Interim Governorship in Puebla," *The Americas* 42:3 (January 1986), 311-331.

3071.   LaFrance, David G. "Germany, Revolutionary Nationalism and the Downfall of President Francisco I. Madero: The Covadonga Killings," *Mexican Studies* 2:1 (Winter 1986), 59-82.

3072.   LaFrance, David G. "Labour and the Mexican Revolution: President Francisco I. Madero and the Puebla Textile Workers," *Boletín de Estudios Latinoamericanos y del Caribe* 34 (June 1983), 59-74.

3073.   Lavrin, Asunción. "El capital eclesiástico y las elites sociales en Nueva España," *Mexican Studies* 1:1 (Winter 1985), 1-28.

3074.   León-Portilla, Miguel. "La imagen de sí mismo: testimonios indígenas del periodo colonial," *América Indígenas* 45:2 (April-June 1985), 277-307.

3075. Lerner de Sheinbaum, Bertha. "1983: la ruptura frente al populismo, el compromiso con la austeridad y la renovación moral," *Revista Mexicana de Sociología* 45:2 (April-June 1983), 545-577.

3076. LeVine, Sarah Ethel, Clara Sunderland Correa, and F. Medardo Tapia Uribe. "The Martial Morality of Mexican Women: An Urban Study," *Journal of Anthropological Research* 42:2 (Summer 1986), 183-202.

3077. Levy, Daniel C. "The Mexican Government's Loosening Grip?" *Current History* 86:518 (March 1987), 113-116.

3078. Levy, Daniel C., and Gabriel Székely. "Mexico: Challenges and Responses," *Current History* 85:507 (January 1986), 16-20.

3079. Levy, Santiago. "Cambio tecnológio y uso de la energía en México," *El Trimestre Económico* 52:208 (October-December 1985), 1141-1163.

3080. Lindau, Juan David. "Percepciones mexicanas de la política exterior de Estados Unidos: el caso Camarena Salazar," *Foro Internacional* 27:4 (April-June 1987), 562-675.

3081. Loaeza, Soledad. "La iglesia y la democracia en México," *Revista Mexicana de Sociología* 47:1 (January-March 1985), 161-168.

3082. Loaeza, Soledad. "La Iglesia Católica mexicana y el reformismo autoritario," *Foro Internacional* 25:2 (October-December 1984), 138-165.

3083. Loaeza, Soledad. "El papel político de las clases medias en el México contemporaneo," *Revista Mexicana de Sociología* 45:2 (April-June 1983), 407-439.

3084. Looney, Robert E. "Inflation in Pre-Crisis Mexico: A Monetarist Interpretation of the Relative Importance of Internal and External Factors," *Mexican Studies* 3:2 (Summer 1987), 319-346.

3085. Looney, Robert E. "Mechanism of Mexican Economic Growth: The Role of Deteriorating Sources of Growth in the Current Economic Crisis," *Journal of Social, Political and Economic Studies* 12:1 (Spring 1987), 77-94.

3086. Looney, Robert E. "Mexican Economic Performance during the Echeverría Administration: Bad Luck or Poor Planning?" *Bulletin of Latin American Research* 2:2 (May 1983), pp. 57-68.

3087. Looney, Robert E. "Structural Origins of Mexican Inflation: 1951-1980," *Social and Economic Studies* 34:3 (September 1985), 165-198.

3088. Lozoya, Jorge Alberto. "México y la diplomacia multilateral," *Foro Internacional* 24:4 (April-June 1984), 427-442.

3089. Luna, Matilde. "Transformaciones del corporativismo empresarial y tecnocratización de la política," *Revista Mexicana de Sociología* 47:1 (January-March 1985), 125-137.

3090.   Luna, Matilde. "Las transformaciones del régimen político mexicano en la década de 1970," *Revista Mexicana de Sociología* 45:2 (April-June 1983), 453-472.

3091.   McCaa, Robert. *"Calidad, Clase,* and Marriage in Colonial Mexico: The Case of Parral, 1788-90," *Hispanic American Historical Review* 64:3 (August 1984), 477-501.

3092.   Macune, Charles W., Jr. "The Impact of Federalism on Mexican Church-State Relations, 1824-1835: The Case of the State of Mexico," *The Americas* 40:4 (April 1984), 505-529.

3093.   McGoodwin, James R. "Mexico's Conflictual Inshore Pacific Fisheries: Problem Analysis and Policy Recommendations," *Human Organization* 46:3 (Fall 1987), 221-232.

3094.   Madrid H., Miguel de la. "Mexico: The New Challenge," *Foreign Affairs* 63:1 (Fall 1984), 72-76.

3095.   Mares, David R. "Explaining Choice of Development Strategies: Suggestions from Mexico, 1970-1982," *International Organization* (Autumn 1985), 667-697.

3096.   Mares, David R. "Mexico's Challenges: Sovereignty and National Autonomy under Interdependence," *Third World Quarterly* 9:3 (July 1987), 788-803.

3097.   Mares, David R. "La política comercial: regionalización, liberalización y vulnerabilidad," *Foro Internacional* 24:3 (January-March 1984), 294-310.

3098.   Márquez, Javier. "La banca en México: 1830-1983," *El Trimestre Económico* 50-200 (October-December 1983), 1873-1914.

3099.   Martínez Assad, Carlos. "Ayer y hoy: la problemática regional en México," *Revista Mexicana de Sociología* 45:1 (January-March 1983), 221-232.

3100.   Martínez Assad, Carlos, and Alicia Ziccardi. "El municipio entre la sociedad y el Estado," *Mexican Studies* 3:2 (Summer 1987), 287-318.

3101.   Masferrer Kan, Elio. "Las condiciones históricas de la etnicidad entre los Totonacos," *América Indígena* 46:4 (October-December 1986), 733-749.

3102.   Masferrer Kan, Elio. "Religión y política en la Sierra Norte de Puebla," *América Indígena* 46:3 (July-September 1986), 531-544.

3103.   Masferrer Kan, Elio, Carlos Bravo Marentes, Heber Morales Carranza, and Carlos Garma Navarro. "El compadrazgo entre los Totonacos de la Sierra," *América Indígena* 44:2 (April-June 1984), 375-402.

3104.   Massey, Douglas S. "Understanding Mexican Migration to the United States," *American Journal of Sociology* 92:6 (May 1987), 1372-1403.

3105.   Mathews, Holly F. "'We are Mayordomo': A Reinterpretation of Women's Roles in the Mexican Cargo System," *American Ethnologist* 12:2

(May 1985), 285-301.

3106.   Maviglia, Sandra F. "Mexico's Guidelines for Foreign Investment: The Selective Promotion of Necessary Industries," *American Journal of International Law* 80:2 (April 1986), 281-304.

3107.   Mayer Celis, Leticia. "El escenario y los actores: los líderes de una profesión," *Mexican Studies* 3:2 (Summer 1987), 347-364.

3108.   Mayo, John. "Consuls and Silver Contraband on Mexico's West Coast in the Era of Santa Ana," *Journal of Latin American Studies* 19:2 (November 1987), 389-411.

3109.   Meissner, Frank. "Mexican Border and Free Zone Areas: Implications for Development." In *U.S.-Latin American Trade Relations,* edited by Michael R. Czinkota. New York: Praeger, 1983. pp. 244-252.

3110.   Menéndez, Eduardo L. "Centralización o autonomía: la 'Nueva' política del sector salud en México," *Boletín de Antropología Americana* 10 (December 1984), 85-95.

3111.   Menéndez, Eduardo L. "Estructura social y mortalidad en Yucatán, México," *Boletín de Antropología Americana* 8 (December 1983), 111-131.

3112.   Mertens, L., and P.J. Richards. "Recession and Employment in Mexico," *International Labour Review* 126:2 (March-April 1987), 229-243.

3113.   Middlebrook, Kevin J. "Political Liberalization in an Authoritarian Regime: The Case of Mexico." In *Transition from Authoritarian Rule,* edited by Guillermo O'Donnell, Philippe C. Schmitter and Laurence Whitehead. Baltimore, MD: Johns Hopkins University Press, 1986. pp. 123-147.

3114.   Mier y Terán, Marta, and Cecilia Rabell. "Características demográficas de los grupos domésticos en México," *Revista Mexicana de Sociología* 45:1 (January-March 1983), 263-292.

3115.   Miller, Barbara. "The Role of Women in the Mexican Cristero Rebellion: *Las Señores y Las Religiosas,"* *The Americas* 40:3 (January 1984), 303-323.

3116.   Miller, Richard W. "Class, Politics, and Family Organization in San Cosme Xalostoc, Mexico," *Ethnology* 23:4 (October 1984), 289-300.

3117.   Miller, Simon. "The Mexican Hacienda between the Insurgency and the Revolution: Maize Production and Commercial Triumph on the *Temporal,"* *Journal of Latin American Studies* 16:2 (November 1984), 309-336.

3118.   Molinar, Juan, and Leonardo Valdés. "Las elecciones de 1985 en el Distrito Federal," *Revista Mexicana de Sociología* 49:2 (April-June 1987), 183-215.

3119.   Mora-Echeverría, Jesús Ignacio. "Prácticas y conceptos prehispánicos sobre espacio y tiempo: a propósito del origen del calendario ritual mesamericano," *Boletín de Antropología Americana* 9 (July 1984), 5-

46.

3120.   Morales, Isidro. "Las negociaciones del gas entre 1977 y 1979," *Foro Internacional* 26:4 (April-June 1986), 511-549.

3121.   Morales Troncoso, Carlos, Salvador Romero Orozco, Heinz Von Wobeser, and Héctor Orrico de la Vega. "Small- and Medium-Sized Companies in the Exportation of Manufactured Goods: The Situation in Mexico." In *U.S.-Latin American Trade Relations,* edited by Michael R. Czinkota. New York: Praeger, 1983. pp. 143-154.

3122.   Mumme, Steven P. "The Cananea Copper Controversy: Lessons for Environmental Diplomacy," *Inter-American Economic Affairs* 38:1 (Summer 1984), 3-22.

3123.   Mummert, Gail. "The Transformation of the Forms of Social Organization of Production in a Mexican Ejido, 1924-81," *International Social Science Journal* 39:4 (November 1987), 523-542.

3124.   Nalven, Joseph. "Environmental Cooperation in the U.S.-Mexican Border Region: Social and Cultural Aspects of Technical Relationships," *Mexican Studies* 2:1 (Winter 1986), 107-127.

3125.   Navarro, Bernardo. "El metro de la ciudad de México," *Revista Mexicana de Sociología* 46:4 (October-December 1984), 85-102.

3126.   Niblo, Stephen R. "British Propaganda in Mexico during the Second World War: The Development of Cultural Imperialism," *Latin American Perspectives* 10:4 (Fall 1983), 114-126.

3127.   Nichols, Deborah L. "Risk and Agricultural Intensification during the Formative Period in the Northern Basin of Mexico," *American Anthropologist* 89:3 (September 1987), 596-616.

3128.   Ojeda, Mario. "El lugar de México en el mundo contemporáneo," *Foro Internacional* 24:4 (April-June 1984), 415-426.

3129.   Olson, Wayne. "Crisis and Social Change in Mexico's Political Economy," *Latin American Perspectives* 12:3 (Summer 1985), 7-28.

3130.   Ortiz, Andrés. "Organización sociopolítica en los altos de Chiapas," *América Indígena* 46:3 (July-September 1986), 569-583.

3131.   Ortiz, Guillermo, and Jaime Serra-Puche. "A Note on the Burden of the Mexican Foreign Debt," *Journal of Development Economics* 21:1 (April 1986), 111-129.

3132.   Ortiz de Montellano, Bernard. *"Caida de Mollera:* Aztec Sources for a Mesoamerican Disease of Alleged Spanish Origin," *Ethnohistory* 34:4 (Fall 1987), 381-399.

3133.   Ouweneel, Arij. "Schedules in Hacienda Agriculture: The Cases of Santa Ana Aragón, 1765-1768, and San Nicolas de los Pilares, 1793-1795, Valley of Mexico," *Boletín de Estudios Latinoamericanos y del Caribe* 40 (June 1986), 63-97.

3134.   Paddock, John. "Tezcatlipoca in Oaxaca," *Ethnohistory* 32:4 (December

1985), 309-325.

3135.   Pansters, Wil. "Petty Commodity Production and Social Relations of Production: The Case of Ciudad Juárez, Mexico," *Boletín de Estudios Latinoamericanos y del Caribe* 39 (December 1983), 45-61.

3136.   Pardo, María del Carmen. "La ley federal de entidades paraestatales: un nuevo intento para regular el sector paraestatal," *Foro Internacional* 27:2 (October-December 1986), 234-246.

3137.   Pardo, María del Carmen. "La reforma administrativa para el desarrollo social en México," *Foro Internacional* 25:2 (October-December 1984), 101-117.

3138.   Parlee, Lorena M. "The Impact of United States Railroad Unions on Organized Labor and Government Policy in Mexico (1880-1911)," *Hispanic American Historical Review* 64:3 (August 1984), 443-475.

3139.   Partridge, William L., and Antoinette B. Brown. "Desarrollo agrícola entre los Mazatecos reacomodados," *América Indígena* 43:2 (April-June 1983), 343-362.

3140.   Patch, Robert W. "Agrarian Change in Eighteenth-Century Yucatán," *Hispanic American Historical Review* 65:1 (February 1985), 21-49.

3141.   Paz Salinas, María Emilia. "Crisis y expropiación, un análisis comparativo: 1938-1982," *Revista Mexicana de Sociología* 45:2 (April-June 1983), 441-451.

3142.   Paz Salinas, María Emilia. "La frontera sur," *Revista Mexicana de Sociología* 47:1 (January-March 1985), 25-37.

3143.   Peñaloza Webb, Tomás. "La productividad de la banca en México 1980-1983," *El Trimestre Económico* 52:206 (April-June 1985), 465-497.

3144.   Percy, Allison. "The Revolutionary Potential of Mexico in the 1980s," *Journal of International Affairs* 40:2 (Winter-Spring 1987), 373-385.

3145.   Perló, Manuel, and Martha Schteingart. "Movimientos sociales urbanos en México," *Revista Mexicana de Sociología* 46:4 (October-December 1984), 105-125.

3146.   Philip, George. "Mexican Politics and the Journals," *Bulletin of Latin American Research* 5:1 (1986), 121-132.

3147.   Pírez, Pedro. "Modalidades de desarrollo y política regional en México, 1960-1980," *Revista Mexicana de Sociología* 45:1 (January-March 1983), 149-168.

3148.   Platt, D.C.M. "British Finance in Mexico, 1821-1867," *Bulletin of Latin American Research* 3:1 (January 1984), 45-62.

3149.   Poston, Dudley L., Jr., Elizabeth Brody, Katherine Trent, and Harley L. Browing. "Modernization and Childlessness in the States of Mexico," *Economic Development and Cultural Change* 34:3 (April 1985), 503-519.

3150. Powell, Thomas G. "Spain and Mexico." In *The Iberian-Latin American Connection: Implications for U.S. Foreign Policy,* edited by Howard J. Wiarda. Boulder, CO: Westview, 1986. 253-292.

3151. Prock, Jerry. "Mexico's Monetary Changes and Border Banks: An Impact Study," *Inter-American Economic Affairs* 39:3 (Winter 1985), 71-78.

3152. Pucciarelli, Alfred R. "Contradicciones del desarrollo regional polarizado: el papel de la agricultura en la microregión Lázaro Cárdenas," *Revista Mexicana de Sociología* 45:1 (January-March 1983), 107-128.

3153. Pucciarelli, Alfredo J. "El dominio estatal de la agricultura campesina: estudio sobre los egidatarios minifundistas de la Comarca Lagunera en México," *Estudios Rurales Latinoamericanos* 9:3 (September-December 1986), 29-67.

3154. Raat, W. Dirk. "U.S. Intelligence Operations and Covert Action in Mexico, 1900-47," *Journal of Contemporary History* 22:4 (October 1987), 615-637.

3155. Rama, Ruth. "Do Transnational Agribusiness Firms Encourage the Agriculture of Developing Countries? The Mexican Experience," *International Social Science Journal* 37:3 (1985), 331-343.

3156. Rama, Ruth. "Las empresas transnacionales y la agricultura de los países en desarrollo: el caso de México," *Estudios Rurales Latinoamericanos* 9:2 (May-August 1986), 7-32.

3157. Rama, Ruth. "Some Effects of the Internationalization of Agriculture on the Mexican Agricultural Crisis." In *The Americas in the New International Division of Labor,* edited by Steven E. Sanderson. New York: Holmes & Meier, 1985. pp. 69-94.

3158. Ramírez, Miguel D. "Mexico's Development Experience, 1950-84: Lessons and Future Prospects," *Journal of Inter-American Studies and World Affairs* 28:2 (Summer 1986), 39-65.

3159. Ramírez Rancano, Mario. "Carranza ¿victima de una conjura industrial?" *Revista Mexicana de Sociología* 45:2 (April-June 1983), 353-374.

3160. Ramos-Escandón, Carmen. "La política obrera del Estado Mexicano de Díaz a Madero: el caso de los trabajadores textiles," *Mexican Studies* 3:1 (Winter 1987), 19-47.

3161. Randall, Robert W. "Mexico's Pre-Revolutionary Reckoning with Railroads," *The Americas* 42:1 (July 1985), 1-28.

3162. Rausch, Jane M. "Frontiers in Crisis: The Breakdown of the Missions in Far Northern Mexico and New Granada, 1821-1849," *Comparative Studies in Society and History* 29:2 (April 1987), 340-359.

3163. Redclift, Michael. "Peasant Movements and Urbanisation in Contemporary Morelos: To What Do We Owe Our Ignorance?" *Bulletin of Latin American Research* 5:1 (1986), 95-100.

3164. Restrepo, Iván. "La ecología," *Revista Mexicana de Sociología* 47:1

(January-March 1985), 221-231.

3165.   Reynolds, Clark W. "Alternative Forms, Fashions, and Policies for Technology Transfer: A Binational Perspective," *Mexican Studies* 2:2 (Summer 1986), 317-332.

3166.   Reynolds, Clark W. "El mercado de mano de obra de México y de los Estados Unidos en el futuro," *El Trimestre Económico* 50:200 (October-December 1983), 2321-2337.

3167.   Reynolds, Clark W., and Robert McCleery. "Modeling United States-Mexico Economic Linkages," *American Economic Review* 75:2 (May 1985), 217-222.

3168.   Richmond, Douglas W. "Confrontations and Reconciliation: Mexicans and Spaniards during the Mexican Revolution, 1910-1920," *The Americas* 41:2 (October 1984), 215-228.

3169.   Richmond, Douglas W. "Nationalism and Class Conflict in Mexico, 1910-1920," *The Americas* 43:3 (January 1987), 279-303.

3170.   Rico F., Carlos. "Mexico and Latin America: The Limits of Cooperation," *Current History* 86-518 (March 1987), 121-124.

3171.   Riley, James D. "Crown Law and Rural Labor in New Spain: The Status of *Gañanes* during the Eighteenth Century," *Hispanic American Historical Review* 64:2 (May 1984), 259-285.

3172.   Rivera, Juan M. "Desarrollo, crecimiento y estrategia gubernamental: los modelos de Formosa y Corea del Sur como posibles respuestas a la crisis económica de México," *El Trimestre Económico* 53:210 (April-June 1986), 393-409.

3173.   Rochin, Refugio I. "Mexico's Agriculture in Crisis: A Study of Its Northern States," *Mexican Studies* 1:2 (Summer 1985), 255-275.

3174.   Rodríguez, Federico, and Javier Salas. "Estructura y funcionamiento del mercado de crédito interbancario en México," *El Trimestre Económico* 52:206 (April-June 1985), 293-312.

3175.   Rodríguez Araujo, Octavio. "Partidos políticas y elecciones en México, 1964 a 1985," *Revista Mexicana de Sociología* 47:1 (January-March 1985), 41-104.

3176.   Ronfeldt, David. "The Modern Mexican Military." In *Armies and Politics in Latin America*, edited by Abraham F. Lowenthal and Samuel Fitch. Rev. ed. New York: Holmes & Meier, 1986. pp. 224-261.

3177.   Roniger, Luis. "Caciquismo and Coronelismo: Contextual Dimensions of Patron Brokerage in Mexico and Brazil," *Latin American Research Review* 22:2 (1987), 71-99.

3178.   Roniger, Luis. "Coronelismo, Caciquismo, and Oyabun-Kobun Bonds: Divergent Implications of Hierarchical Trust in Brazil, Mexico and Japan," *British Journal of Sociology* 38:3 (September 1987), 310-330.

3179.   Roxborough, Ian. "State, Multinationals and the Working Class in Brazil and Mexico." In *Latin America, Economic Imperialism and the State,* edited by Christopher Abel and Colin M. Lewis. London; Dover, NH: Athlone, 1985. pp. 430-450.

3180.   Salas, Javier, and José Julián Sidaoui. "Evolución y perspectivas de las exportaciones de manufacturas," *El Trimestre Económico* 50:200 (October-December 1983), 2339-2371.

3181.   Salehizadeh, Mehdi, and Jorge Garza-Adame. "Mexico's Protectionist Policies and Their Implications for the Computer Industry," *Inter-American Economic Affairs* 38:1 (Summer 1984), 85-101.

3182.   Salisbury, Richard V. "Mexico, the United States, and the 1926-27 Nicaraguan Crisis," *Hispanic American Historical Review* 66:2 (May 1986), 319-339.

3183.   Sanderson, Steven E. "Presidential Succession and Political Rationality in Mexico," *World Politics* 35:3 (April 1983), 315-334.

3184.   Sanderson, Susan Walsh. "Mexico's Agricultural Policy," *Current History* 86:518 (March 1987), 109-112.

3185.   Sandos, James A. "Northern Separatism during the Mexican Revolution: An Inquiry into the Role of Drug Trafficking, 1919-1920," *The Americas* 41:2 (October 1984), 191-214.

3186.   Santley, Robert S. "The Political Economy of the Aztec Empire," *Journal of Anthropological Research* 41:3 (Fall 1985), 327-337.

3187.   Sawyer, W. Charles, and Richard L. Sprinkle. "The Effects of Mexico's Devaluation and Tariff Changes on U.S. Exports," *Social Science Journal* 23:1 (Spring 1986), 55-62.

3188.   Schmidt, Henry C. "The Mexican Foreign Debt and the Sexennial Transition from López Portillo to De la Madrid," *Mexican Studies* 1:2 (Summer 1985), 227-254.

3189.   Schmitt, Karl. "Church and State in Mexico: A Corporatist Relationship," *The Americas* 40:3 (January 1984), 349-376.

3190.   Schryer, Frans J. "Class Conflict and the Corporate Peasant Community: Disputes over Land in Nahuatl Villages," *Journal of Anthropological Research* 43:2 (Summer 1987), 99-120.

3191.   Schryer, Frans J. "Ethnicity and Politics in Rural Mexico: Land Invasions in Huejutla," *Mexican Studies* 3:1 (Winter 1987), 99-126.

3192.   Schryer, Frans J. "From *rancheros* to *pequeños propietarios:* Agriculture, Class Structure and Politics in the Sierra de Jacala, Mexico," *Boletín de Estudios Latinoamericanos y del Caribe* 34 (June 1983), 41-58.

3193.   Schryer, Frans J. "Peasants and the Law: A History of Land Tenure and Conflict in the Huasteca," *Journal of Latin American Studies* 18:2 (November 1986), 285-311.

3194.   Schumacher, August. "Agricultural Development and Rural Employment:

A Mexican Dilemma." In *The Border That Joins: Mexican Migrants and U.S. Responsibility,* edited by Peter G.Brown and Henry Shue. Totowa, NJ: Rowman & Allenheld, 1983. pp. 141-161.

3195.   Schwaller, John Frederick. "The *Ordenanza del Patronazgo* in New Spain, 1574-1600," *The Americas* 42:3 (January 1986), 253-274.

3196.   Seed, Patricia. "The Church and the Patriarchal Family: Marriage Conflicts in Sixteenth- and Seventeenth-Century New Spain," *Journal of Family History* 10:3 (Fall 1985), 284-293.

3197.   Sefchovich, Sara. "Democracia y cultura," *Revista Mexicana de Sociología* 47:1 (January-March 1985), 243-250.

3198.   Segal, Aaron. "The Mexican Exodus: Setting the Patterns." In *The Caribbean Exodus,* edited by Barry B. Levine. New York: Praeger, 1987. pp. 67-92.

3199.   Segovia, Rafael. "La vida política de México dentro de 25 años," *Foro Internacional* 27:3 (January-March 1987), 375-389.

3200.   Sepúlveda Amor, Bernardo. "Reflexiones sobre la política exterior de México," *Foro Internacional* 24:4 (April-June 1984), 407-414.

3201.   Shadow, Robert D. "Lo indio está en la tierra: identidad social y lucha agraria entre los Tepecano en el norte de Jalisco," *América Indígena* 45:3 (July-September 1985), 521-578.

3202.   Sheldon, Sam. "Folk Economy and Impoverishment in Mexico's Zona Ixtlera," *Journal of Developing Areas* 17:4 (July 1983), 453-472.

3203.   Sloan, John W. "The Mexican Variant of Corporatism," *Inter-American Economic Affairs* 38:4 (Spring 1985), 3-18.

3204.   Smith, Michael E. "The Aztlan Migration of the Nahuatl Chronicles: Myth or History?" *Ethnohistory* (July-August-September 1984), 153-186.

3205.   Smith, Peter H. "Mexico: The Continuing Quest for a Policy." In *From Gunboats to Diplomacy: New U.S. Policies for Latin America,* edited by Richard Newfarmer. Baltimore, MD: Johns Hopkins University Press, 1984. pp. 37-53.

3206.   Smith, Peter H. "Uneasy Neighbors: Mexico and the United States," *Current History* 86:518 (March 1987), 97-100.

3207.   Smith, Peter H. "U.S.-Mexican Relations: The 1980s and Beyond," *Journal of Inter-American Studies and World Affairs* 27:1 (February 1985), 91-101.

3208.   Spalding, Rose J. "Structural Barriers to Food Programming: An Analysis of the 'Mexican Food System'," *World Development* 13:12 (December 1985), 1249-1262.

3209.   Stebbins, Kenyon Rainier. "Politics, Economics, and Health Services in Rural Oaxaca, Mexico," *Human Organization* 45:2 (Summer 1986), 112-119.

3210. Stevens, Donald F. "Economic Fluctuations and Political Instability in Early Republican Mexico," *Journal of Interdisciplinary History* 16:4 (Spring 1986), 635-665.

3211. Storey, Rebecca. "An Estimate of Mortality in a Pre-Columbian Urban Population," *American Anthropologist* 87:3 (September 1985), 519-535.

3212. Story, Dale. "Policy Cycles in Mexican Presidential Politics," *Latin American Research Review* 20:3 (1985), 139-161.

3213. Street, James H. "Can Mexico Break the Vicious Circle of 'Stop-Go' Policy? An Institutional Overview," *Journal of Economic Issues* 20:2 (June 1986), 601-612.

3214. Street, James H. "Development Planning and the Public Enterprise: The Case of PEMEX," *Journal of Inter-American Studies and World Affairs* 27:4 (Winter 1985-86), 141-154.

3215. Street, James H. "Mexico's Development Crisis," *Current History* 86:518 (March 1987), 101-104.

3216. Székely, Gabriel. "Notas sobre la política energética de Canadá y México en los años ochenta," *Foro Internacional* 24:4 (April-June 1984), 499-513.

3217. Tardanico, Richard. "México revolucionario, 1920-1928: capitalismo transnacional, luchas locales y formación del nuevo Estado," *Revista Mexicana de Sociología* 45:2 (April-June 1983), 375-405.

3218. Tardanico, Richard. "State Responses to the Great Depression, 1929-1934: Toward a Comparative Analysis of 'Revolutionary' Mexico and 'Non-revolutionary' Colombia." In *Crises in the Caribbean Basin,* edited by Richard Tardanico. Beverly Hills, CA: Sage, 1987. pp. 113-140.

3219. Taylor, J. Edward. "Undocumented Mexico-U.S. Migration and Returns to Households in Rural Mexico," *American Journal of Agricultural Economics* 69:3 (August 1987), 626-638.

3220. Taylor, Lance. "Mexico's Adjustment in the 1980s: Look Back before Leaping Ahead." In *Adjustment Crisis in the Third World,* edited by Richard E. Feinberg and Valeriana Kallab. Rutgers, NJ: Transaction, 1984. pp. 147-158.

3221. Taylor, Lawrence D. "The Great Adventure: Mercenaries in the Mexican Revolution, 1910-1915," *The Americas* 43:1 (July 1986), 25-45.

3222. Taylor, William B. "The Virgin of Guadalupe in New Spain: An Inquiry Into the Social History of Marian Devotion," *American Ethnologist* 14:1 (February 1987), 9-33.

3223. Thomas, John S., and Michael C. Robbins. "Social Status and Settlement Pattern Features: A Tojolabal Maya Example," *Human Organization* 44:2 (Summer 1985), 172-176.

3224. Thomson, Guy P.C. "Protectionism and Industrialization in Mexico, 1821-

1854: The Case of Puebla." In *Latin America, Economic Imperialism and the State,* edited by Christopher Abel and Colin M. Lewis. London; Dover, NH: Athlone, 1985. pp. 125-146.

3225.   Tirado, Ricardo. "Los empresarios y la derecha en México," *Revista Mexicana de Sociología* 47:1 (January-March 1985), 105-123.

3226.   Torchia Estrada, Juan Carlos. "Pedro Henríquez Ureña y el desplazamiento del positivismo en México," *Inter-American Review of Bibliography* 35:2 (1985), 143-165.

3227.   Tornell, Aaron. "¿Es el libre comercio la mejor opción? Comercio Heckscher-Ohlin vs. comercio intraindustrial," *El Trimestre Económico* 53:211 (July-September 1986), 529-560.

3228.   Trejo Delarbre, Raúl. "Disparidades y dilemas en el sindicalismo mexicano," *Revista Mexicana de Sociología* 47:1 (January-March 1985), 139-160.

3229.   Turrent, Isabel. "Las relaciones commerciales de México con América Latina, 1976-1982," *Foro Internacional* 24:3 (January-March 1984), 311-326.

3230.   Tutino, John. "Family Economies in Agrarian Mexico, 1750-1910," *Journal of Family History* 10:3 (Fall 1985), 258-271.

3231.   Urquidi, Víctor I. "Technology Transfer between Mexico and the United States," *Mexican Studies* 2:2 (Summer 1986), 179-193.

3232.   Urquidi, Víctor L. "Transferencia de tecnología entre México y Estados Unidos: experiencia y perspectivas," *Foro Internacional* 26:3 (January-March 1986), 317-330.

3233.   Valdés, Dennis N. "The Decline of Slavery in Mexico," *The Americas* 44:2 (October 1987), 167-194.

3234.   Vanderwood, Paul J. "Nineteenth-Century Mexico's Profiteering Bandits." In *Bandidos: The Varieties of Latin American Banditry,* edited by Richard W. Slatta. Westport, CT: Greenwood, 1987. pp. 11-31.

3235.   Van Young, Eric. "Conflict and Solidarity in Indian Village Life: The Guadalajara Region in Late Colonial Period," *Hispanic American Historical Review* 64:1 (February 1984), 55-79.

3236.   Van Young, Eric. "Mexican Rural History since Chevalier: The Historiography of the Colonial Hacienda," *Latin American Research Review,* 18:3 (1983), 5-61.

3237.   Van Young, Eric. "Millennium on the Northern Marches: The Mad Messiah of Durango and Popular Rebellion in Mexico, 1800-1815," *Comparative Studies in Society and History* 28:3 (July 1986), 385-413.

3238.   Van Young, Eric. "Recent Anglophone Scholarship on Mexico and Central America in the Age of Revolution, 1750-1850," *Hispanic American Historical Review* 65:4 (November 1985), 725-743.

3239.   Varley, Ann. "Urbanization and Agrarian Law: The Case of Mexico City," *Bulletin of Latin American Research* 4:1 (1985), 1-16.

3240.   Vaughan, Mary Kay. "Primary Schooling in the City of Puebla, 1821-60," *Hispanic American Historical Review* 67:1 (February 1987), 39-62.

3241.   Velasco Avila, Cuauhtémoc. "Labour Relations in Mining: Real del Monte and Pachuca, 1824-1874." In *Miners and Mining in the Americas,* edited by Thomas Greaves and William Culver. Manchester, England; Dover, NH: Manchester University Press, 1985. pp. 47-67.

3242.   Velázquez Guzman, María Guadalupe. "Política educativa y estructura agraria: una visión compesina," *Revista Mexicana de Sociología* 45:3 (July-September 1983), 781-795.

3243.   Vellinga, Menno. "The Small Margins of Autonomous Development: Cooptation and Control of Urban Social Movements in Monterrey, Mexico," *Boletín de Estudios Latinoamericanos y del Caribe* 41 (December 1986), 53-69.

3244.   Vignal, Adriana Novelo. "La política exterior de México en el sureste de Asia," *Foro Internacional* 24:3 (January-March 1984), 370-392.

3245.   Villabona Blanco, María Pilar. "La constitución mexicana de 1917 y la española de 1931," *Revista de Estudios Políticos* 31:32 (January-April 1983), 199-208.

3246.   Villanueva, Margaret A. "From Calpixaui to Corregidor: Appropriations of Women's Cotton Textile Production in Early Colonial Mexico," *Latin American Perspectives* 12:1 (Winter 1985), 17-40.

3247.   Villegas Montiel, Francisco Gil. "La crisis de legitimidad en la última etapa del sexenio de José López Portillo," *Foro Internacional* 25:2 (October-December 1984), 190-201.

3248.   Walker, David W. "Business as Usual: The Empress del Tabaco in Mexico, 1837-44," *Hispanic American Historical Review* 64:4 (November 1984), 675-705.

3249.   Warman, Arturo. "The Cauldron of the Revolution: Agrarian Capitalism and Sugar Industry in Morelos, Mexico, 1880-1910." In *Crisis and Change in the International Sugar Economy, 1860-1914,* edited by Bill Albert and Adrian Graves. Edinburgh, Scotland: ISC Press, 1984. pp. 165-180.

3250.   Warman, Arturo. "Desarrollo rural en areas indígenas: reflexiones a partir de la experiencia mexicana," *América Indígena* 44 (December 1984), 63-83.

3251.   Wasserman, Mark. "Strategies for Survival of the Porfirian Elite in Revolutionary Mexico: Chihuahua during the 1920s," *Hispanic American Historical Review* 67:1 (February 1987), 87-107.

3252.   Weiner, Mervyn L. "Improving Federal Management in Mexico: An Essay on Institutional Reform," *International Review of Administrative Sciences* 53:2 (June 1987), 183-195.

3253. Wiemers, Eugene L., Jr. "Agriculture and Credit in Nineteenth-Century Mexico: Orizaba and Cordoba, 1822-71," *Hispanic American Historical Review* 65:3 (August 1985), 519-546.

3254. Wells, Miriam J., and Jacob Climo. "Parallel Process in the World System: Intermediate Agencies and Local Factionalism in the United States and Mexico," *Journal of Development Studies* 20:2 (January 1984), 151-170.

3255. Wilk, Richard B. "The Ancient Maya and the Political Present," *Journal of Anthropological Research* 41:3 (Fall 1985), 307-326.

3256. Willey, Gordon R. "Changing Conceptions of Lowland Maya Culture History," *Journal of Anthropological Research* 40:1 (Spring 1984), 41-59.

3257. Williams, Edward J. "Mexico's Central American Policy: National Security Considerations." In *Rift and Revolution: The Central American Imbroglio,* edited by Howard J. Wiarda. Washington, DC: American Enterprise Institute, 1984. pp. 303-328.

3258. Wionczek, Miguel S. "Algunas reflexiones sobre la futura política petrolera de México," *Desarrollo Económico* 23:89 (April-June 1983), 59-78.

3259. Wionczek, Miguel S. "Industrialización, capital extranjero y transferencía de tecnológia: la experiencia mexicana, 1930-1985. *Foro Internacional* 26:4 (April-June 1986), 550-566.

3260. Weiss, John. "Alliance for Production: Mexico's Incentives for Private Sector Industrial Development," *World Development* 12:7 (July 1984), 723-742.

3261. Wright, Angus. "Rethinking the Circle of Poison: The Politics of Pesticide Poisoning among Mexican Farm Workers," *Latin American Perspectives* 13:4 (Fall 1986), 26-59.

3262. Wu, Celia. "The Population of the City of Querétaro in 1791," *Journal of Latin American Studies* 16:2 (November 1984), 277-307.

3263. Zedillo Ponce de León, Ernesto. "The Mexican External Debt: The Last Decade." In *Politics and Economics of External Debt Crisis: The Latin American Experience,* edited by Miguel S. Wionczek in collaboration with Luciano Tomassini. Boulder, CO: Westview, 1985. pp. 294-324.

3264. Zedillo Ponce de León, Ernesto. "Mexico's Recent Balance-of-Payments Experience and Prospects for Growth," *World Development* 14:8 (August 1986), 963-991.

3265. Zepeda P., Jorge. "Las elecciones federales de 1985 en Michoacán," *Revista Mexicana de Sociología* 49:2 (April-June 1987), 217-232.

3266. Zermeño, Sergio. "De Echeverría a De la Madrid: ¿hacia un régimen burocrático-autoritario?" *Revista Mexicana de Sociología* 45:2 (April-June 1983), 473-506.

3267.   Zermeño, Sergio. "Hacia una democracia como identidad restringida: sociedad y política en México," *Revista Mexicana de Sociología* 49:2 (April-June 1987), 57-87.

NICARAGUA

Books and Monographs

3268.   Alisky, Marvin. *"La Prensa" of Managua: Chronicler of Its Country.* Tempe, AZ: Bevin Company BC Monographs, 1986. 11p.

3269.   Belli, Humberto. *Breaking Faith: The Sandinista Revolution and Its Impact on Freedom and Christian Faith in Nicaragua.* Westchester, IL: Crossway, 1985. 271p.

3270.   Booth, John A. *The End and the Beginning: The Nicaraguan Revolution.* 2d ed. Boulder, CO: Westview, 1985. 363p.

3271.   Brody, Reed. *Contra Terror in Nicaragua: Report of a Fact-Finding Mission: September 1984-January 1985.* Boston, MA: South End, 1985. 206p.

3272.   Burns, E. Bradford. *At War in Nicaragua: The Reagan Doctrine and the Politics of Nostalgia.* New York: Harper & Row, 1987. 211p.

3273.   Cabestrero, Teófilo. *Blood of the Innocent: Victims of the Contras' War in Nicaragua.* Translated by Robert R. Barr. Maryknoll, NY: Orbis, 1985. 104p.

3274.   Cabestrero, Teófilo. *Revolutionaries for the Gospel: Testimonies of Fifteen Christians in the Nicaraguan Government.* Translated by Phillip Berryman. Maryknoll, NY: Orbis, 1986. 148p.

3275.   Cabezas, Omar. *Fire from the Mountain: The Making of a Sandinista.* Translated by Kathleen Weaver. New York: Crown, 1985. 233p.

3276.   Christian, Shirley. *Nicaragua: Revolution in the Family.* New York: Random House, 1985. 337p.

3277.   Colburn, Forrest D. *Post-Revolutionary Nicaragua: State, Class, and the Dilemmas of Agrarian Policy.* Berkeley; Los Angeles: University of California Press, 1986. 145p.

3278.   Collins, Joseph, with Frances Moore Lappé, Nick Allen, and Paul Rice. *Nicaragua: What Difference Could a Revolution Make?* 3d ed. New York: Grove, 1986. 311p.

3279.   Conroy, Michael E., ed., with the assistance of María Verónica Frenkel. *Nicaragua: Profiles of the Revolutionary Public Sector.* Boulder, CO: Westview, 1987. 247p.

3280.   Coraggio, José Luis. *Nicaragua: Revolution and Democracy.* Winchester, MA: Allen & Unwin, 1986. 109p.

3281.   Crawley, Eduardo. *Nicaragua in Perspective.* Rev. ed. New York: St. Martin's, 1984. 200p.

3282.   Davis, Peter. *Where is Nicaragua?* New York: Simon & Schuster, 1987. 349p.

3283.   Dickey, Christopher. *With the Contras: A Reporter in the Wilds of Nicaragua.* New York: Simon and Schuster, 1985. 327p.

3284.   Dixon, Marlene, ed. *On Trial: Reagan's War against Nicaragua: Testimony of the Permanent People's Tribunal.* San Francisco, CA: Synthesis, 1985. 269p.

3285.   Dixon, Marlene, and Susanne Jonas, eds. *Nicaragua under Siege.* San Francisco, CA: Synthesis, 1984. 234p.

3286.   Donahue, John M. *The Nicaraguan Revolution in Health: From Somoza to the Sandinistas.* South Hadley, MA: Bergin & Garvey, 1986. 156p.

3287.   Dozier, Craig L. *Nicaragua's Mosquito Shore: The Years of British and American Presence.* University: University of Alabama Press, 1985. 269p.

3288.   Eich, Dieter, and Carlos Rincón. *The Contras: Interviews with Anti-Sandinistas.* San Francisco: Synthesis, 1985. 193p.

3289.   Harris, Richard L., and Charlos M. Vilas, eds. *Nicaragua: A Revolution under Siege.* London: Zed (Totowa, NJ: Dist. by Biblio Distribution Center), 1985. 250p.

3290.   Hirshon, Sheryl L., and Judy Butler. *And Also Teach Them to Read.* Westport, CT: L. Hill, 1983. 224p.

3291.   Hodges, Donald C. *Intellectual Foundations of the Nicaraguan Revolution.* Austin: University of Texas Press, 1986. 378p.

3292.   Jones, Jeffrey, ed. *Brigadista: Harvest and War in Nicaragua.* Westport, CT: Praeger, 1986. 227p.

3293.   Kimmens, Andrew C., ed. *Nicaragua and the United States.* New York: H.W. Wilson, 1987. 267p.

3294.   McCuen, Gary E., ed. *The Nicaraguan Revolution: Ideas in Conflict.* Hudson, WI: Gary E. McCuen, 1986. 184p.

3295.   McGinnis, James. *Solidarity with the People of Nicaragua.* Maryknoll,

NY: Orbis, 1985. 162p.

3296. Marcus, Bruce, ed. *Nicaragua: The Sandinista People's Revolution.* New York: Pathfinder, 1985. 412p.

3297. Melrose, Dianna. *Nicaragua: The Threat of a Good Example.* Oxford, England: Oxfam (Boston, MA: Dist. by Oxfam America), 1985. 68p.

3298. Miller, Valerie. *Between Struggle and Hope: The Nicaraguan Literacy Crusade.* Boulder, CO: Westview, 1985. 258p.

3299. Newson, Linda A. *Indian Survival in Colonial Nicaragua.* Norman: University of Oklahoma Press, 1987. 466p.

3300. Nolan, David. *FSLN: The Ideology of the Sandinistas and the Nicaraguan Revolution.* Coral Gables, FL: Institute of Interamerican Studies, Graduate School of International Studies, University of Miami, 1984. 203p.

3301. Ohland, Klaudine, and Robin Schneider, eds. *National Revolution and the Indigenous Identity: The Conflict between Sandinists and Miskito Indians on Nicaragua's Atlantic Coast.* Copenhagen: International Work Group for Indigenous Affairs, 1983. 302p.

3302. O'Shaughnessy, Laura, and Luis H. Serra. *The Church and Revolution in Nicaragua.* Athens: Latin American Studies Program, Center for International Studies, Ohio University, 1986. 118p.

3303. Pastor, Robert A. *Condemned to Repetition: The United States and Nicaragua.* Princeton, NJ: Princeton University Press, 1987. 392p.

3304. Payne, Douglas W. *The Democratic Mask: The Consolidation of the Sandinista Revolution.* New York: Freedom House, 1985. 107p.

3305. Robinson, William I., and Ken Norsworthy. *David and Goliath: The U.S. War against Nicaragua.* New York: Monthly Review Press, 1987. 400p.

3306. Rosset, Peter, and John Vandermeer, eds. *The Nicaragua Reader: Documents of a Revolution under Fire.* New York: Grove, 1983. 359p.

3307. Rosset, Peter, and John Vandermeer, eds. *Nicaragua, Unfinished Revolution: The New Nicaraguan Reader.* New York: Grove, 1986. 505p.

3308. Selser, Gregorio. *Nicaragua: de Walker a Somoza.* Mexico City: Mex-Sur, 1984. 332p.

3309. Spalding, Rose J., ed. *The Political Economy of Revolutionary Nicaragua.* Boston, MA: Allen & Unwin, 1987. 256p.

3310. Stanislawski, Dan. *The Transformation of Nicaragua, 1519-1548.* Berkeley: University of California Press, 1983. 150p.

3311. Trobo, Claudio. *Lo que pasé en Nicaragua.* Mexico City: Siglo Veintiuno, 1984. 252p.

3312.   Valenta, Jiri, and Esperanza Durán, eds. *Conflict in Nicaragua: A Multidimensional Perspective.* Winchester, MA: Allen & Unwin, 1987. 441p.

3313.   Vanderlaan, Mary B. *Revolution and Foreign Policy in Nicaragua.* Boulder, CO: Westview, 1986. 404p.

3314.   Vilas, Carlos María. *The Sandinista Revolution: National Liberation and Social Transformation in Central America.* Translated by Judy Butler. New York: Monthly Review Press; Berkeley, CA: Center for the Studies of the Americas, 1986. 317p.

3315.   Walker, Thomas W. *Nicaragua: The Land of Sandino.* 2d ed. Boulder, CO: Westview, 1986. 170p.

3316.   Walker, Thomas W., ed. *Nicaragua: The First Five Years.* New York: Praeger, 1985. 561p.

3317.   Walker, Thomas W., ed. *Reagan versus the Sandinistas: The Undeclared War on Nicaragua.* Boulder, CO: Westview, 1987. 337p.

3318.   White, Steven F. *Culture and Politics in Nicaragua: Testimonies of Poets and Writers.* New York: Lumen, 1986. 134p.

3319.   Zwerling, Philip, and Connie Martin. *Nicaragua: A New Kind Revolution.* Westport, CT: L. Hill, 1985. 251p.

Articles and Chapters

3320.   Austin, James, Jonathan Fox, and Walter Kruger. "The Role of the Revolutionary State in the Nicaraguan Food System," *World Development* 13:1 (January 1985), 15-40.

3321.   Azicri, Max. "Nicaragua's Foreign Relations: The Struggle for Survival." In *The Dynamics of Latin American Foreign Policies,* edited by Jennie K. Lincoln and Elizabeth G. Ferris. Boulder, CO: Westview, 1984, 229-250.

3322.   Baktiari, Bahman. "Revolution and the Church in Nicaragua and El Salvador," *Journal of Church and State* 28:1 (Winter 1986), 14-42.

3323.   Baumeister, Eduardo. "Estructura y reforma agraria en el proceso sandinista," *Desarrollo Económico* 24:94 (July-September 1984), 187-202.

3324.   Baumeister, Eduardo. "Notas para la discusión del problema agrario en Nicaragua," *Estudios Rurales Latinoamericanos* 8:2 (May-August 1985), 199-220.

3325.   Baumeister, Eduardo, and Oscar Neira Cuadra. "The Making of a Mixed Economy: Class Struggle and State Policy in the Nicaragua Transition." In *Transition and Development: Problems of Third World Socialism,* edited by Richard R. Fagen, Carmen Diana Deere and José Luis Coraggio. New York: Monthly Review Press, 1986. 171-191.

3326.   Behrman, Jere R., Barbara L. Wolfe, and David M. Blau. "Human Capital and Earnings Distribution in a Developing Country: The Case of Prerevolutionary Nicaragua," *Economic Development and Cultural Change* 34:1 (October 1985), 1-29.

3327. Bendaña, Alejandro. "Nicaragua's Position in the Region." In *Conflict in Central America: Approaches to Peace and Security,* edited by Jack Child. London: C. Hurst, 1985. 48-53.

3328. Berríos, Rubén. "Economic Relations between Nicaragua and the Socialist Countries," *Journal of Inter-American Studies and World Affairs* 27:3 (Fall 1985), 111-139.

3329. Berríos, Rubén. "Relations between Nicaragua and the Socialist Countries." In *Soviet-Latin American Relations in the 1980's,* edited by Augusto Varas. Boulder, CO: Westview, 1987. 144-173.

3330. Blau, David M. "Fertility, Child Nutrition, and Child Mortality in Nicaragua: An Economic Analysis of Interrelationships," *Journal of Developing Areas* 20:2 (January 1986), 185-201.

3331. Booth, John A. "The Revolution in Nicaragua: Through a Frontier of History." In *Revolution and Counterrevolution in Central America and The Caribbean,* edited by Donald E. Schulz and Douglas H. Graham. Boulder, CO: Westview, 1984. 301-330.

3332. Booth, John A. "War and the Nicaraguan Revolution," *Current History* 85:515 (December 1986), 405-408.

3333. Bourgois, Philippe. "Las minorías étnicas en la revolución nicaragüense," *Estudios Sociales Centroamericanos* 13:39 (August-December 1984), 13-31.

3334. Bourgois, Philippe. "Nicaragua's Ethnic Minorities in the Revolution, *Monthly Review* 36:8 (January 1985), 22-44.

3335. Brumberg, Abraham. "Nicaragua: A Mixture of Shades," *Dissent* (Spring 1986), 173-178.

3336. Brumberg, Abraham. "Nicaragua, The Inner Struggle: Is There Still a Chance for Political Pluralism," *Dissent* (Summer 1986), 294-303.

3337. Cantarero, Rodrigo F., and Forrest D. Colburn. "The Structural Basis of Rural Employment in Postrevolutionary Nicaragua," *Journal of Developing Areas* 21:1 (October 1986), 49-61.

3338. Castillo Rivas, Donald. "Reasons for the Success of the Nicaraguan Revolution." In *Political Change in Central America: Internal and External Dimensions,* edited by Wolf Grabendorff, Heinrich-W. Krumwiede and Jörg Todt. Boulder, CO: Westview, 1984. 53-63.

3339. Center for Research and Studies of the Agrarian Reform, ed. "Agrarian Reform in Nicaragua: The First Three Years," *International Journal of Sociology* 13:2 (Summer 1983), 9-91.

3340. Chamorro, Jaime. "How 'La Prensa' Was Silenced," *Commentary* 83:1 (January 1987), 39-44.

3341.   Chavez, Roberto. "Urban Planning in Nicaragua: The First Five Years," *Latin American Perspectives* 14:2 (Spring 1987), 226-236.

3342.   Christian, Shirley. "Nicaragua and the United States," *World Affairs* 149:4 (Spring 1987), 177-182.

3343.   Clayton, Lawrence A. "The Nicaragua Canal in the Nineteenth Century: Prelude to American Empire in the Caribbean," *Journal of Latin American Studies* 19:2 (November 1987), 323-352.

3344.   Colburn, Forrest D. "Class, State, and Revolution in Rural Nicaragua: The Case of *Los Cafetaleros,*" *Journal of Developing Areas* 18:4 (July 1984), 501-517.

3345.   Colburn, Forrest D. "Embattled Nicaragua," *Current History* 86:524 (December 1987), 405-408.

3346.   Colburn, Forrest D. "Nicaragua under Siege," *Current History* 84:500 (March 1985), 105-108.

3347.   Colburn, Forrest D. "Rural Labor and the State in Postrevolutionary Nicaragua," *Latin American Research Review* 19:3 (1984), 103-117.

3348.   Colburn, Forrest D., and Silvio De Franco. "Privilege, Production, and Revolution: The Case of Nicaragua," *Comparative Politics* 17:3 (April 1985), 277-290.

3349.   Conroy, Michael E. "External Dependence, External Assistance, and Economic Aggression against Nicaragua," *Latin American Perspectives* 12:2 (Spring 1985), 39-67.

3350.   Coraggio, José Luis. "Economics and Politics in the Transition to Socialism: Reflections on the Nicaragua Experience." In *Transition and Development: Problems of Third World Socialism,* edited by Richard R. Fagen, Carmen Diana Deere, and José Luis Coraggio. New York: Monthly Review Press, 1986. 143-170.

3351.   Coraggio, José Luis. "Revolución y democracia en Nicaragua," *Estudios Sociales Centroamericanos* 13:38 (May-August 1984), 83-113.

3352.   Coraggio, José Luis, and George Irvin. "Revolution and Democracy in Nicaragua, *Latin American Perspectives* 12:2 (Spring 1985), 23-37.

3353.   Coraggio, José Luis, and George Irvin. "Revolution and Pluralism in Nicaragua." In *Towards an Alternative for Central America and the Caribbean,* edited by George Irvin and Xabier Gorostiaga. London; Boston: Allen & Unwin, 1985. 251-263.

3354.   Corradi, Juan E. "Nicaragua: Can It Find Its Own Way," *Dissent* (Summer 1984), 275-284.

3355.   Deere, Carmen Diana, Peter Marchetti, and Nola Reinhardt. "The Peasantry and the Development of Sandinista Agrarian Policy, 1979-1984," *Latin American Research Review* 20:3 (1985), 75-109.

3356.   Dennis, Philip A., and Michael D. Olien. "Kinship among the Miskito," *American Ethnologist* 11:4 (November 1984), 718-737.

3357. Dodson, Michael. "Nicaragua: The Struggle for the Church." In *Religion and Political Conflict in Latin America,* edited by Daniel H. Levine. Chapel Hill: University of North Carolina Press, 1986. 79-105.

3358. Donahue, John M. "The Politics of Health Care in Nicaragua before and after the Revolution of 1979," *Human Organization* 42:3 (Fall 1983), 264-272.

3359. Donahue, John M. "The Profession and the People: Primary Health Care in Nicaragua," *Human Organization* 45:2 (Summer 1986), 96-103.

3360. Dore, Elizabeth. "Nicaragua: The Experience of the Mixed Economy." In *Latin American Political Economy: Financial Crisis and Political Change,* edited by Jonathan Hartlyn and Samuel A. Morley. Boulder, CO: Westview, 1986. 319-350.

3361. Dosal, Paul J. "Accelerating Dependent Development and Revolution: Nicaragua and the Alliance for Progress," *Inter-American Economic Affairs* 38:4 (Spring 1985), 75-96.

3362. Fagen, Richard. "Revolution and Crisis in Nicaragua." In *Trouble in Our Backyard: Central America and the United States in the Eighties,* edited by Martin Diskin. New York: Pantheon, 1983. 125-154.

3363. Falcoff, Mark. "Nicaraguan Harvest," *Commentary* 80:1 (July 1985), 21-28.

3364. Fitzgerald, E.V.K. "Agrarian Reform as a Model of Accumulation: The Case of Nicaragua since 1979," *Journal of Development Studies* 22:1 (October 1985), 208-226.

3365. Fitzgerald, E.V.K. "Estado y política económica en la nueva Nicaragua," *Estudios Sociales Centroamericanos* 13:37 (January-April 1984), 259-268.

3366. Fitzgerald, E.V.K. "Stabilization and Economic Justice: The Case of Nicaragua." In *Debt and Development in Latin America,* edited by Kwan S. Kim and David F. Ruccio. Notre Dame, IN: University of Notre Dame Press, 1985. 191-204.

3367. Garfield, Richard M. "Health and the War against Nicaragua, 1981-84," *Journal of Public Health Policy* 6:1 (March 1985), 116-131.

3368. Gilbert, Dennis. "Nicaragua." In *Confronting Revolution: Security through Diplomacy in Central America,* edited by Morris J. Blachman, William M. LeoGrande and Kenneth E. Sharpe. New York: Pantheon, 1986. 88-124.

3369. Gismondi, Michael A. "Transformations in the Holy: Religious Resistance and Hegemonic Struggles in the Nicaraguan Revolution," *Latin American Perspectives* 13:3 (Summer 1986), 13-36.

3370. Gleijeses, Piero. "Nicaragua: Resist Romanticism," *Foreign Policy* 54 (Spring 1984), 122-138.

3371. Gorman, Stephen M. "Social Change and Political Revolution: The Case of Nicaragua." In *Central America: Crisis and Adaptation,* edited by

Steve C. Ropp and James A. Morris. Albuquerque: University of New Mexico Press, 1984. 33-66.

3372. Gorostiaga, Xabier. "Dilemmas of the Nicaraguan Revolution." In *The Future of Central America,* edited by Richard R. Fagen and Olga Pellicer. Stanford, CA: Stanford University Press, 1983. 47-66.

3373. Gould, Jeffrey L. "'For an Organized Nicaragua': Somoza and the Labour Movement, 1944-1948," *Journal of Latin American Studies* 19:2 (November 1987), 353-387.

3374. Gutman, Roy. "Nicaragua: America's Diplomatic Charade," *Foreign Policy* 56 (Fall 1984), 3-23.

3375. Harris, Richard L. "The Revolutionary Process in Nicaragua," *Latin American Perspectives* 12:2 (Spring 1985), 3-21.

3376. Harris, Richard L. "The Revolutionary Transformation of Nicaragua," *Latin American Perspectives* 14:1 (Winter 1987), 3-18.

3377. Helms, Mary W. "Of Kings and Contexts: Ethnohistorical Interpretations of Miskito Political Structure and Function," *American Ethnologist* 13:3 (August 1986), 506-523.

3378. Hertz, Michael K. "Misunderstandings: Nicaragua," *Monthly Review* 36:4 (September 1984), 35-48.

3379. Highet, Keith. "Evidence, the Court and the Nicaragua Case," *American Journal of International Law* 81:1 (January 1987), 1-56.

3380. Hintermeister, Alberto. "El empleo agrícola en una estructura en transformación: el caso de Nicaragua," *Estudios Rurales Latinoamericanos* 6:2-3 (May-December 1983), 201-218.

3381. Horowitz, David. "Nicaragua: A Speech to My Former Comrades on the Left," *Commentary* 81:6 (June 1986), 27-31.

3382. Jameson, Fredric. "Tomás Borge on the Nicaraguan Revolution," *New Left Review* 164 (July-August 1987), 53-64.

3383. Jentoft, Svein. "Organizing Fishery Cooperatives: The Case of Nicaragua," *Human Organization* 45:4 (Winter 1986), 353-358.

3384. Jonas, Susanne. "The New Cold War and the Nicaraguan Revolution: The Case of U.S. 'Aid' to Nicaragua." In *Revolution and Intervention in Central America,* edited by Marlene Dixon and Susanne Jonas. Rev. ed. San Francisco: Synthesis, 1983. 219-236.

3385. Judson, Fred. "Sandinista Revolutionary Morale," *Latin American Perspectives* 14:1 (Winter 1987), 19-42.

3386. Kaimowitz, David. "Nicaraguan Debates on Agrarian Structure and Their Implications for Agricultural Policy and the Rural Poor," *Journal of Peasant Studies* 14:1 (October 1986), 100-117.

3387. Kaimowitz, David, and David Stanfield. "The Organization of Production Units in the Nicaraguan Agrarian Reform. *Inter-*

American Economic Affairs 39:1 (Summer 1985), 51-77.

3388. Kemble, Penn, and Arturo J. Cruz, Jr. "How the Nicaraguan Resistance Can Win," *Commentary* 82:6 (December 1986), 19-29.

3389. Kirk, John. "John Paul II and the Exorcism of Liberation Theology: A Retrospective Look at the Pope in Nicaragua," *Bulletin of Latin American Research* 4:1 (1985), 33-47.

3390. Kleinbach, Russell. "Nicaraguan Literacy Campaign: Its Democratic Essence," *Monthly Review* 37:3 (July-August 1985), 75-84.

3391. Krumwiede, Heinrich-W. "Sandinist Democracy: Problems of Institutionalization." In *Political Change in Central America: Internal and External Dimensions,* edited by Wolf Grabendorff, Heinrich-W. Krumwiede and Jörg Todt. Boulder, CO: Westview, 1984. 64-81.

3392. Kusnetzoff, Fernando. "Democratización del Estado, gobiernos locales y cambio social: experiencias comparativas en Chile y Nicaragua," *Revista Mexicana de Sociologia* 45:1 (January-March 1983), 191-219.

3393. Landau, Saul. "Inside Nicaragua's Class War," *Socialist Review* 13:5 (September-October 1983), 9-28.

3394. Lobel, Jules. "The New Nicaraguan Constitution: Uniting Participatory and Representative Democracy," *Monthly Review* 39:7 (December 1987), 1-17.

3395. López y Rivas, Gilberto, and Eckart Boege. "Los Miskitos y la cuestión nacional en Nicaragua," *Boletín de Antropología Americana* 9 (July 1984), 99-107.

3396. Luciak, Ilja. "National Unity and Popular Hegemony; the Dialectics of *Sandinista* Agrarian Reform Policies, 1979-1986," *Journal of Latin American Studies* 19:1 (May 1987), 113-140.

3397. Luciak, Ilja. "Popular Democracy in the New Nicaragua: The Case of a Rural Mass," *Comparative Politics* 20:1 (October 1987), 35-55.

3398. McDougal, Myres. "Presentation before the International Court of Justice: *Nicaragua vs. United States,*" *World Affairs* 148:1 (Summer 1985), 35-46.

3399. Maier, Harold G., ed. "Appraisals of the ICJ's Decision: *Nicaragua v. United States* (Merits)," *American Journal of International Law* 81:1 (January 1987), 77-183.

3400. Marchetti, Peter E. "War, Popular Participation, and Transition to Socialism: The Case of Nicaragua." In *Transition and Development: Problems of Third World Socialism,* edited by Richard R. Fagen, Carmen Diana Deere and José Luis Coraggio. New York: Monthly Review Press, 1986. 303-330.

3401. Marini, Ruy Mauro. "The Nicaraguan Revolution and the Central American Revolutionary Process." In *Revolution and Intervention in Central America,* edited by Marlene Dixon and Susanne Jonas. Rev.

ed. San Francisco: Synthesis, 1983. 175-182.

3402.   Mattelard, Armand. "La communicación en Nicaragua entre la guerra y la democracia," *Estudios Sociales Centroamericanos* 41 (May-August 1986), 17-40.

3403.   Matthews, Robert P. "Sandinista Relations with the West: The Limits of Nonalignment." In *Crisis in the Caribbean Basin,* edited by Richard Tardanico. Beverly Hills, CA: Sage, 1987. 191-215.

3404.   Millett, Richard L. "From Somoza to the Sandinistas: The Roots of Revolution in Nicaragua." In *Political Change in Central America: Internal and External Dimensions,* edited by Wolf Grabendorff, Heinrich-W. Krumwiede and Jörg Todt. Boulder, CO: Westview, 1984. 37-52.

3405.   Millett, Richard L. "Nicaragua's Frustrated Revolution," *Current History* 85:507 (January 1986), 5-8.

3406.   Moore, John H. "The Miskitu National Question in Nicaragua," *Science and Society* 50:2 (Spring 1986), 132-147.

3407.   Muravchik, Joshua, Susan Alberts, and Antony Korenstein. "Sandinista Anti-Semitism and Its Apologists," *Commentary* 82:3 (September 1986), 25-29.

3408.   Obando y Bravo, Miguel. "Nicaragua: The Sandinistas Have 'Gagged and Bound' Us," *World Affairs* 148:4 (Spring 1986), 229-231.

3409.   Olien, Michael D. "E. G. Squier and the Miskito: Anthropological Scholarship and Political Propaganda," *Ethnohistory* 32:2 (May 1985), 111-133.

3410.   Olien, Michael D. "Micro/Macro-Level Linkages: Regional Political Structures on the Mosquito Coast, 1845-1864," *Ethnohistory* 34:3 (Summer 1987), 256-287.

3411.   Ortega, Marvin. "Workers' Participation in the Management of the Agro-Enterprises of the APP," *Latin American Perspectives* 12:2 (Spring 1985), 69-82.

3412.   Ortiz, Roxanne Dunbar. "Indigenous Rights and Regional Autonomy in Revolutionary Nicaragua," *Latin American Perspectives* 14:1 (Winter 1987), 43-66.

3413.   Philip, George. "The Nicaraguan Conflict: Politics and Propaganda," *World Today* 41:12 (December 1985), 222-224.

3414.   Radu, Michael. "The Origins and Evolution of the Nicaraguan Insurgencies, 1979-1985," *Orbis* 29:4 (Winter 1986), 821-840.

3415.   Reding, Andrew. "Nicaragua's New Constitution: A Close Reading," *World Policy Journal* 4:2 (Spring 1987), 257-294.

3416.   Reding, Andrew. "Seeds of a New and Renewed Church: The 'Ecclesiastical Insurrection' in Nicaragua," *Monthly Review* 39:3 (July-August 1987), 24-55.

3417. Reinhardt, Nola. "Agro-Exports and the Peasantry in the Agrarian Reforms of El Salvador and Nicaragua," *World Development* 15:7 (July 1987), 941-959.

3418. Robinson, William I, and Kent Norsworthy. "Elections and U.S. Intervention in Nicaragua," *Latin American Perspectives* 12:2 (Spring 1985), 83-110.

3419. Robinson, William I., and Kent Norsworthy. "Nicaragua: The Strategy of Counterrevolution," *Monthly Review* 37:7 (December 1985), 11-24.

3420. Rosenberg, Mark B. "Nicaragua and Honduras: Toward Garrison States," *Current History* 83:490 (February 1984), 59-62.

3421. Russell, George. "Can the Sandinistas Still Be Stopped," *Commentary* 84:1 (July 1987), 26-34.

3422. Salisbury, Richard V. "Mexico, the United States, and the 1926-1927 Nicaraguan Crisis," *Hispanic American Historical Review* 66:2 (May 1986), 319-339.

3423. Samandú, Luis E. "Los poderosos de la tierra se preocupan como en tiempos de Jesús: fe y compromiso político entre los campesinos de Julapa, Nicaragua," *Boletín de Estudios Latinoamericanos y del Caribe* 35 (December 1983), 85-99.

3424. Saul, John S. "Nicaragua under Fire," *Monthly Review* 36:10 (March 1985), 47-54.

3425. Schoultz, Lars. "Nicaragua: The United States Confronts a Revolution." In *From Gunboats to Diplomacy: New U.S. Policies for Latin America,* edited by Richard Newfarmer. Baltimore, MD: John Hopkins University Press, 1984. 116-134.

3426. Schwartz, Stephen. "Nicaraguan Journey," *Commentary* 82:5 (November 1986), 64-69.

3427. Sepúlveda, Cristián. "Capitalismo agroexportador, estado y rentabilidad: el circuito cafetalero y azucarero en Nicaragua," *Estudios Sociales Centroamericanos* 13:38 (May-August 1984), 55-81.

3428. Shapiro, Michael. "Bilingual-Bicultural Education in Nicaragua's Atlantic Coast Region," *Latin American Perspectives* 14:1 (Winter 1987), 67-86.

3429. Shaw, Royce Q. "U.S. Policy toward Revolutionary Nicaragua," *Journal of Third World Studies* 3:2 (Fall 1986), 102-109.

3430. Sholk, Richard. "The National Bourgeoisie in Post-Revolutionary Nicaragua," *Comparative Politics* 16:3 (April 1984), 253-276.

3431. Shugart, Matthew Soberg. "States, Revolutionary Conflict and Democracy: El Salvador and Nicaragua in Comparative Perspective," *Government and Opposition* 22:1 (Winter 1987), 13-32.

3432. Shugart, Matthew Soberg. "Thinking about the Next Revolution: Lessons from U.S. Policy in Nicaragua," *Journal of Inter-American Studies and World Affairs* 29:1 (Spring 1987), 73-92.

3433.   Slater, David. "Socialismo, democracia y el imperativo territorial: elementos para una comparación de las experiencias cubana y nicaragüense," *Estudios Sociales Centroamericanos* 44 (May-August 1987), 20-40.

3434.   Smith, Wayne S. "Lies about Nicaragua," *Foreign Policy* 67 (Summer 1987), 87-103.

3435.   Spalding, Rose J. "La expansión económica del Estado en Nicaragua después de la revolución," *Foro Internacional* 25:1 (July-September 1984), 14-32.

3436.   Spalding, Rose J. "Food Politics and Agricultural Change in Revolutionary Nicaragua, 1979-82." In *Food, Politics, and Society in Latin America,* edited by John C. Super and Thomas C. Wright. Lincoln: University of Nebrasks Press, 1985. 199-227.

3437.   Trindade, Antônio Augusto Cançado. "Nicarágua versus Estados Unidos," *Revista Brasileira de Estudos Políticos* 63-64 (July 1986-January 1987), 139-170.

3438.   Trupp, L. Ann. "Políticas gubernamentales sobre el uso de plaguicidas: los casos en Costa Rica y Nicaragua," *Estudios Sociales Centroamericanos* 42 (September-December 1986), 59-75.

3439.   Ullman, Richard H. "At War with Nicaragua," *Foreign Affairs* 62:1 (Fall 1983), 39-58.

3440.   Vaky, Viron P. "Positive Containment in Nicaragua," *Foreign Policy* 68 (Fall 1987), 42-58.

3441.   Valenta, Jiri. "Nicaragua: Soviet Pawn or Non-Aligned Country?" *Journal of Inter-American Studies and World Affairs* 27:3 (Fall 1985), 163-175.

3442.   Valenta, Jiri, and Virginia Valenta. "Sandinistas in Power," *Problems of Communism* 34:5 (September-October 1985), 1-28.

3443.   Vanden, Harry E., and Waltraud Queiser Morales. "Nicaraguan Relations with the Non-Aligned Movement," *Journal of Inter-American Studies and World Affairs* 27:3 (Fall 1985), 141-161.

3444.   Vanegas, Manuel, and Jerome Hammond. "Un modelo oferta-demanda de la industria lechera de Nicaragua," *El Trimestre Económico* 53:212 (October-December 1986), 813-833.

3445.   Van Tassell, G. Lane. "The Case for Political Pluralism in Sandinista Nicaragua," *Journal of Third World Studies* 4:1 (Spring 1987) 95-104.

3446.   Vilas, Carlos M. "Insurgencia popular y revoluciones sociales: centorno a la Revolución sandinista," *Revista Mexicana de Sociología* 46:3 (July-September 1986), 185-209.

3447.   Vilas, Carlos M. "The Mass Organizations in Nicaragua: The Current Problematic and Perspectives for the Future," *Monthly Review* 38:6

(November 1986), 20-31.

3448. Vilas, Carlos M. "Nicaragua: una transición diferente," *Revista Mexicana de Sociología* 45:3 (July-September 1983), 935-979.

3449. Vilas, Carlos M. "Sobre la estrategia económica de la Revolución sandinista," *Desarrollo Económico* 26:101 (April-June 1986), 121-142.

3450. Vilas, Carlos M. "El sujeto social de la insurrección popular: la Revolución Sandinista," *Latin American Research Review* 20:1 (1985), 119-147.

3451. Walker, Thomas W. "Nicaraguan-U.S. Friction: The First Four Years, 1979-1983." In *The Central American Crisis: Sources of Conflict and the Failure of U.S. Policy,* edited by Kenneth M. Coleman and George C. Herring. Wilmington, DE: Scholarly Resources, 1985. 157-189.

3452. Weeks, John. "Las elecciones nicaragüenses de 1984," *Foro Internacional* 26:1 (July-September 1985), 85-106.

3453. Wilde, Kathleen L. "The Cuban and Nicaraguan Revolutions: Viewpoints of a Peace and Social Justice Activist," *Journal of Third World Studies* 3:2 (Fall 1986), 111-116.

3454. Williams, Philip J. "The Catholic Hierarchy in the Nicaraguan Revolution," *Journal of Latin American Studies* 17:2 (November 1985), 341-369.

3455. Wilson, Patricia A. 'Regionalization and Decentralization in Nicaragua," *Latin American Perspectives* 14:2 (Spring 1987), 237-254.

3456. Yopo H., Boris. "Soviet Military Assistance to Cuba and Nicaragua, 1980-1984." In *Soviet-Latin American Relations in the 1980's,* edited by Augusto Varas. Boulder, CO: Westview, 1987. 105-126.

3457. Zalkin, Michael. "Food Policy and Class Transformation in Revolutionary Nicaragua, 1979-86," *World Development* 15:7 (July 1987), 961-984.

PANAMA

Books and Monographs

3458. Arias Calderón, Ricardo. *Panamá: desastre o democracia.* Panama City: República de Panamá, Programa de Desarrollo Democrático de la Fundación ECAM, 1985. 219p.

3459. Araúz, Virgilo. *Reflexiones sobre la crisis educativa panameña.* Panama: Siglo XXI, 1985. 108p.

3460. Bourgois, Phillippe. *Ethnic Diversity on a Corporate Plantation: Guaymí Labor on a United Brands Subsidiary in Costa Rica and Panama.* Cambridge, MA: Cultural Survival, 1985. 52p.

3461. Conniff, Michael L. *Black Labor on a White Canal: Panama, 1903-1981.* Pittsburgh, PA: University of Pittsburgh Press, 1985. 221p.

3462. Dodd, Thomas J. *La crisis de Panamá: Cartas de Tomás Herrán, 1900-1904.* Bogotá: Banco de la República, 1985. 454p.

3463. Evans, G. Russell. *The Panama Canal Treaties Swindle: Consent to Disaster.* Carrboro, NC: Signal, 1986. 286p.

3464. Farnsworth, David N., and James W. McKenney. *U.S.-Panama Relations, 1903-1978: A Study in Linkage Politics.* Boulder, CO: Westview, 1983. 313p.

3465. Figueroa Navarro, Alfredo. *El desarrollo de las ciencias sociales en Panamá: estudio introductorio, antología y bibliografía.* Panama City: Universidad de Panamá, 1983. 535p.

3466. Furlong, William L., and Margaret E. Scranton. *The Dynamics of Foreign Policymaking: The President, the Congress, and the Panama Canal Treaties.* Boulder, CO: Westview, 1984. 263p.

3467.   Jorden, William J. *Panama Odyssey: From Colonialism to Partnership.*
        Austin: University of Texas Press, 1984. 746p.

3468.   Howe, James. *The Kuna Gathering: Contemporary Village Politics in
        Panama.* Austin: University of Texas Press, 1986. 326p.

3469.   Knapp, Herbert, and Mary Knapp. *Red, White and Blue Paradise: The
        American Canal Zone in Panama.* San Diego: Harcourt Brace
        Jovanovich, 1985. 306p.

3470.   Mena García, María del Carmen. *La sociedad de Panamá en el siglo
        XVI.* Seville, Spain: Diputación Provincial de Seville, 1984. 448p.

3471.   Moffett, George D., III. *The Limits of Victory: The Ratification of the
        Panama Canal Treaties.* Ithaca, NY: Cornell University Press, 1985.
        263p.

3472.   Newton, Velma. *The Silver Men: West Indian Labour Migration to
        Panama, 1850-1914.* Mona, Jamaica: Institute of Social and Economic
        Research, University of West Indies, 1984. 218p.

3473.   Priestley, George. *Military Government and Popular Participation in
        Panama: The Torrijos Regime, 1968-1975.* Boulder, CO: Westview,
        1986. 166p.

3474.   Torrijos Herrera, Omar. *Papeles del general.* Madrid, Spain: Centro de
        Estudios Torrijistas, 1984. 207p.

3475.   Wali, Alaka. *Kilowatts and Crisis: A Study of Development and Social
        Change in Panama.* Boulder, CO: Westview, 1987. 250p.

Articles and Chapters

3476.   Aguilar, Pilar, and Gonzalo Retamal. "Educational Policy and Practice in
        Panama: A Focus on Adult Education." In *Education in Latin
        America,* edited by Colin Brock and Hugh Lawlor. Dover, NH: Croom
        Helm, 1985. 79-91.

3477.   Arias Calderón, Ricardo. "Panama: Disaster or Democracy," *Foreign
        Affairs,* 66:2 (Winter 1987/88), 328-347.

3478.   Bort, John R. "The Impact of Development on Panama's Small-Scale
        Fishermen," *Human Organization* 46:3 (Fall 1987), 233-242.

3479.   Bossert, Thomas John. "Panama." In *Confronting Revolution: Security
        through Diplomacy in Central America,* edited by Morris J.
        Blachman, William M. LeoGrande and Kenneth E. Sharpe. New York:
        Pantheon, 1986. 183-205.

3480.   Bourgois Irwin, Philippe. "Etnicidad y lucha clases en una subsidiaria de
        la United Fruit Company en Costa Rica y Panamá," *Boletín de
        Antropología Americana* 8 (December 1983), 63-74.

3481.   Castro, Nils, and Oydén Ortega. "Canal de Panamá: a cinco años del
        Tratado, nuevas causas de conflicto," *Foro Internacional* 26:1 (July-
        September 1985), 31-36.

3482. Cid, Rafael del. "Los limites de la acción estatal bajo situaciones reformistas: los casos de Honduras, 1972-1975, y Panamá, 1968-1980," *Estudios Sociales Centroamericanos* 13:38 (May-August 1984), 13-39.

3483. Harrell, Marielouise W., and Jerry B. Leonard. "Income Effects of Donated Commodities in Rural Panama," *American Journal of Agricultural Economics* 69:1 (February 1987), 115-122.

3484. Harris, Lewis D. "Rodrigo de Bastidas and the Discovery of Panama," *Geographical Review* 74:2 (April 1984), 170-182.

3485. Moore, Alexander. "From Council to Legislature: Democracy, Parliamentarianism, and the San Blas Cuna," *American Anthropologist* 86:1 (March 1984), 28-42.

3486. Moore, Alexander. "Lore and Life: Cuna Indian Pageants, Exorcism, and Diplomacy in the Twentieth Century," *Ethnohistory* 30:2 (Spring 1983), 93-106.

3487. Moreno Rojas, Cecilia Sadith. "Acerca de la problemática indígena en Panamá: el caso Guaymí," *Boletín de Antropología Americana* 8 (December 1983), 75-81.

3488. Ropp, Steve. "General Noriega's Panama," *Current History* 85:515 (December 1986), 421-424.

3489. Ropp, Steve C. "Leadership and Political Transformation in Panama: Two Levels of Regime Crisis." In *Central America: Crisis and Adaptation,* edited by Steve C. Ropp and James A. Morris. Albuquerque: University of New Mexico Press, 1984. 227-255.

3490. Ropp, Steve C. "Panama's Struggle for Democracy," *Current History* 86:524 (December 1987), 421-424.

3491. Smith W., David A. "La frontera Panamá-Costa Rica: relaciones económicas y sociales," *Estudios Sociales Centroamericanos* 40 (January-April 1986), 77-85.

3492. Thiesenhusen, William C. "Incomes on Some Agrarian Reform Asentamientos in Panama," *Economic Development and Cultural Change* 35:4 (July 1987), 809-831.

3493. Turner, Jorge. "Panamá: ahora y después," *Revista Mexicana de Sociología* 46:3 (July-September 1984), 271-299.

3494. Weeks, John. "Panama: The Roots of Current Political Instability," *Third World Quarterly* 9:3 (July 1987), 763-787.

PARAGUAY

Books and Monographs

3495. Benítez, Luis G. *Historia del Paraguay: época colonial.* Asunción, Paraguay: Comuneros, 1985. 263p.

3496. Cardiel, José. *Compendio de la historia del Paraguay, 1780.* Buenos Aires: Fundación para la Educación, la Ciencia y la Cultura, 1984. 212p.

3497. Enriquez Gamón, Efraín. *Economía paraguaya: planteamientos.* Asunción: Instituto Paraguayo de Estudios Geopolíticos e Internacionales, 1985. 317p.

3498. Fogel, Ramón B. *Movimientos campesinos en el Paraguay.* Asunción: Centro Paraguayo de Estudios Sociológicos, 1986. 230p.

3499. Garavaglia, Juan Carlos. *Mercado interno y economía colonial: tres siglos de historia de la yerba mate.* Mexico City: Grijalbo, 1983. 507p.

3500. Herken Krauer, Juan Carlos. *Ferrocarriles, conspiraciones, y negocios en el Paraguay, 1910-1914.* Asunción, Paraguay: Arte Nuevo, 1984. 191p.

3501. Herken Krauer, Juan Carlos. *El Paraguay rural entre 1869 y 1913.* Asunción: Centro Paraguayo de Estudios Sociológicos, 1984. 224p.

3502. Herken Kraus, Juan Carlos, and María Isabel Giménez de Herken. *Gran Bretaña y la Guerra de la Triple Alianza.* Asunción, Paraguay: Arte Nuevos, 1983. 167p.

3503. Plá, Josefina. *Los británicos en el Paraguay, 1850-1870.* Asunción, Paraguay: Arte Nuevo, 1984. 316p.

3504. Prieto Yegros, Leandro. *La infiltración comunista en los partidos políticos paraguayos.* Asunción, Paraguay: Cuadernos Republicanos, 1985. 521p.

3505.   Seiferheld, Alfredo M. *Nazismo y fascismo en el Paraguay*. Asunción, Paraguay: Histórica. 2 vols.
    Vol. 1:   *Vísperas de la II Guerra Mundial: gobiernos de Rafael Franco y Félix Paiva, 1936-1939*, 1985. 224p.
    Vol. 2:   *Los años de la guerra, 1939-1945*, 1986. 331p.

3506.   Warren, Harris G., with the assistance of Katherine F. Warren. *Rebirth of the Paraguayan Republic: The First Colorado Era, 1878-1904*. Pittsburgh, PA: University of Pittsburgh Press, 1985. 397p.

Articles and Chapters

3507.   Achilli, Elena Libia. "'Cultura Escolar': el olvido de la heterogeneidad en la escuela," *Revista Paraguaya de Sociología* 21:60 (May-August 1984), 93-102.

3508.   Baer, Werner, and Luis Breuer. "From Inward to Outward Oriented Growth: Paraguay in the 1980s," *Journal of Inter-American Studies and World Affairs* 28:3 (Fall 1986), 125-147.

3509.   Baer, Werner, and Melissa H. Birch. "Expansion of the Economic Frontier: Paraguayan Growth in the 1970s," *World Development* 12:8 (August 1984), 783-798.

3510.   Centro Latinoamericano de Demografía, Ministerio de Salud Pública y Bienestar Social, Paraguay. "Paraguay: la mortalidad infantil según variables socioeconomicas y geográficas, 1955-1980," *Revista Paraguaya de Sociología* 23:67 (September-December 1986), 73-117.

3511.   Corvalán, Grazziella. "El bilingüismo en la educación en el Paraguay: ¿Es creativo u opresivo?" *Latin American Research Review* 18:3 (1983), 109-126.

3512.   Fanger, Ulrich. "Administración educativa y reforma curricular en el Paraguay: un análisis de la enseñanza técnica y profesional de nivel medio," *Revista Paraguaya de Sociología* 21:60 (May-August 1984), 49-92.

3513.   Fogel, Ramón R. "Movimientos campesinos y transición democrática en el Paraguay," *Revista Paraguaya de Sociología* 23:67 (September-December 1986), 175-196.

3514.   Godoy Ziogas, Marilyn. "Condiciones de vida y estructura domésticas campesinas. Del grupo doméstico guaraní a la familia nuclear paraguaya," *Revista Paraguaya de Sociología* 20:56 (January-April 1983), 99-113.

3515.   Granda, Germán de. "Origen, función y estructura de un pueblo de negros y mulatos libres en el Paraguay del siglo XVIII: San Agustín de la Emboscada," *Revista Paraguaya de Sociología* 20:57 (May-August 1983), 7-36.

3516.   Ground, Richard Lynn. "'La evolución de la economía paraguaya en 1983'," *Revista Paraguaya de Sociología* 21:61 (September-December 1984), 243-298.

3517. Kaminsky, Mario. "Metodología de regionalización agropecuaria por tipificación: una aplicación al caso de Paraguay," *Revista Paraguaya de Sociología* 21:59 (January-April 1984), 125-150.

3518. Lago, Luiz Aranha Corrêa. "Fundación e inicial desarrollo de Curuguaty: notas sobre un 'censo' socioeconómico de una población paraguaya en 1716," *Revista Paraguaya de Sociología* 21:61 (September-December 1984), 225-242.

3519. Reber, Vera Blinn. "Commerce and Industry in Nineteenth Century Paraguay: The Example of *Yerba Mate,*" *The Americas* 42:1 (July 1985), 29-53.

3520. Roa Bastos, Augusto. "Fragments from a Paraguayan Autobiography," *Third World Quarterly* 9:1 (January 1987), 212-228.

3521. Rosa, J. Eliseo da. "Economics, Politics, and Hydroelectric Power: The Paraná River Basin," *Latin American Research Review* 18:3 (1983), 77-107.

3522. Shapiro, Judith. "From Tupã to the Land without Evil: The Christianization of Tupi-Guarani Cosmology," *American Ethnologist* 14:1 (February 1987), 126-139.

3523. Szlajfer, Henryk. "Against Dependent Capitalist Development in Nineteenth-Century Latin America: The Case of Haiti and Paraguay," *Latin American Perspectives* 13:1 (Winter 1986), 45-73.

3524. Williams, John Hoyt. "Paraguay's Stroessner: Losing Control?" *Current History* 86:516 (January 1987), 25-28.

PERU

Books and Monographs

3525. Adorno, Rolena. *Guaman Poma: Writing and Resistance in Colonial Peru.* Austin: University of Texas Press, 1986. 189p.

3526. Alberts, Tom. *Agrarian Reform and Rural Poverty: A Case Study of Peru.* Boulder, CO: Westview, 1983. 306p.

3527. Alvarez, Elena. *Política económica y agricultura en el Perú, 1969-1979.* Lima: Instituto de Estudios Peruanos, 1983. 343p.

3528. Anderle, Adam. *Los movimientos políticos en el Perú entre las dos guerras mundiales.* Havana, Cuba: Casa de las Américas, 1985. 455p.

3529. Andreas, Carol. *When Women Rebel: The Rise of Popular Feminism in Peru.* Westport, CT: L. Hill, 1985. 234p.

3530. Andrien, Kenneth J. *Crisis and Decline: The Viceroyalty of Peru in the Seventeenth Century.* Albuquerque: University of New Mexico Press, 1985. 287p.

3531. Becker, David, Jr. *The New Bourgeoisie and the Limits of Dependency: Mining, Class, and Power in "Revolutionary" Peru.* Princeton, NJ: Princeton University Press, 1983. 419p.

3532. Booth, David, and Bernardo Sorj. eds. *Military Reformism and Social Classes: The Peruvian Experience, 1986-1980.* New York: St. Martin's, 1983. 210p.

3533. Brown, Kendall W. *Bourbons and Brandy: Imperial Reform in Eighteenth Century Arequipa.* Albuquerque: University of New Mexico Press, 1986. 319p.

3534. Brundage, Burr Cartwright. *Lords of Cuzco: A History and Description of the Inca People in Their Final Days.* 2d ed. Norman: University of Oklahoma Press, 1985. 458p.

3535.   Bunster, Ximena, and Elsa M. Chaney. *Sellers and Servants: Working Women in Lima, Peru.* New York: Praeger, 1985. 258p.

3536.   Campodónico, Humberto. *La política petrolera 1970-1985: el estado, las contratistas y PetroPeru.* Lima, Peru: DESCO, 1986. 356p.

3537.   Chang-Rodríguez, Eugenio. *Opciones políticas peruanas 1985.* Lima, Peru: Centro de Documención Andina, 1985. 466p.

3538.   Conrad, Geoffrey W., and Arthur A. Demarest. *Religion and Empire: The Dynamics of Aztec and Inca Expansion.* Cambridge, England; New York: Cambridge University Press, 1984. 266p.

3539.   Daly, Jorge L. *The Political Economy of Devaluation: The Case of Peru, 1975-1978.* Boulder, CO: Westview, 1983. 127p.

3540.   Davies, Keith A. *Landowners in Colonial Peru.* Austin: University of Texas Press, 1984. 237p.

3541.   Deustua, José, and José Luis Rénique. *Intelectuales, indigenismo y descentralismo en el Perú, 1897-1931.* Cuzco, Peru: Centro de Estudios Rurales Andinos "Bartolomé de las Casas," 1984. 132p.

3542.   Fernández-Baca, Jorge, Carlos Parodi Zevallos, and Fabian Tumes Torres. *Agroindustria y transnacionales en el Peru.* Lima, Peru: DESCO, 1983. 260p.

3543.   Fernández Llerena, Raúl. *Los origenes del movimiento obrero en Arequipa.* Lima, Peru: Tarea, 1984. 271p.

3544.   Figueroa, Adolfo. *Capitalist Development and the Peasant Economy in Peru.* Cambridge, England; New York: Cambridge University, 1984. 140p.

3545.   Friedman, Douglas. *The State and Underdevelopment in Spanish America: The Political Roots of Dependency in Peru and Argentina.* Boulder, CO: Westview, 1984. 236p.

3546.   Glave, Luis Miguel, and María Isabel Remy. *Estructura agraria y vida rural en una región andina: Ollantaytambo entre los siglos XVI y XIX.* Cuzco, Peru: Centro de Estudios Rurales Andinos Bartolomé de Las Casas, 1983. 584p.

3547.   Gonzales, Michael J. *Plantation Agriculture and Social Control in Northern Peru, 1875-1933.* Austin: University of Texas Press, 1985. 235p.

3548.   Gonzales de Olarte, Efraín. *Economía de la communidad campesina: aproximación regional.* Lima: Instituto de Estudios Peruanos, 1984. 260p.

3549.   González Gómez, Andrés. *Economía política de la crisis: las contradicciones de la acumulación en el Perú, 1950-1975.* Lima, Peru: Facultad de Ciencias Económicas, Universidad Nacional Mayor de San Marcos, 1985. 314p.

3550.   Gray, Andrew. *And after the Gold Rush...? Human Rights and Self-*

Development among the Amarakaeri of Southeastern Peru.
Cambridge, MA: Cultural Survival, 1986. 125p.

3551. Guerra-García, Francisco. *Velasco: del estado oligarquico al capitalismo
de estado.* Lima, Peru: Centro de Estudios para el Desarrollo y la
Participación, 1983. 119p.

3552. Hecker, Gisela, and Wolfgang Hecker. *Pacatnamú y sus construcciones:
centro religioso prehispánico en la Costa Norte Peruana.* Frankfurt,
West Germany: Klaus Dieter Vervuert, 1985. 244p.

3553. Henríquez, Narda, and Javier Iguíñiz, eds. *El problema del empleo en el
Perú.* Lima: Pontificia Universidad Católica del Perú, 1983. 463p.

3554. Hyslop, John. *The Inka Road System.* Orlando, FL: Academic, 1984. 377p.

3555. Hyslop, John. *Inkawasi, the New Cuzco.* Oxford, England: British
Archaeological Reports; New York: Institute of Andean Research,
1985. 147p.

3556. Iguíñiz, Javier. *Política económica 1985-1986: deslindes mirando al
futuro.* Lima, Peru: DESCO, 1986. 153p.

3557. Lohmann Villena, Guillermo. *Los regidores perpetuos del cabildo de Lima
(1535-1821): crónica y estudio de un grupo de gestión.* Sevilla,
Spain: Diputación Provincial de Sevilla, 1983. 2 vols.

3558. Long, Norman, and Bryan Roberts. *Miners, Peasants, and Entrepreneurs:
Regional Development in the Central Highlands of Peru.* New York:
Cambridge University Press, 1984. 288p.

3559. Mallon, Florencia E. *The Defense of Community in Peru's Central
Highland: Peasant Struggle and Capitalist Transition.* Princeton, NJ:
Princeton University Press, 1983. 384p.

3560. Manrique, Nelson. *Colonialismo y pobreza campesina: Caylloma y el valle
del Colca siglos XVI-XX.* Lima, Peru: DESCO, 1985. 237p.

3561. Manrique, Nelson. *Mercado interno y región: la sierra central 1920-
1930.* Lima, Peru: DESCO, 1987. 281p.

3562. Martín, Luis. *Daughters of the Conquistadores: Women of the Viceroyalty of Peru.* Albuquerque: University of New Mexico Press,
1983. 354p.

3563. Matos Mar, José. *Desborde popular y crisis del estado: el nuevo rostro
del Perú en la década de 1980.* Lima: Instituto de Estudios
Peruanos, 1984. 107p.

3564. Molina Martínez, Miguel. *El Real Tribunal de Minería de Lima, 1785-
1821.* Seville, Spain: Diputación Provincial de Seville, 1986. 396p.

3565. Nörner, Magnus. *The Andean Past: Land, Societies and Conflict.* New
York: Columbia University Press, 1985. 300p.

3566. O'Phelan Godoy, Scarlett. *Rebellions and Revolts in Eighteenth Century
Peru and Upper Peru.* Cologne, West Germany: Böhlau, 1985. 345p.

3567. Pike, Frederick B. *The Politics of the Miraculous in Peru: Haya de la Torre and the Spiritualist Tradition.* Lincoln: University of Nebraska Press, 1986. 391p.

3568. Ramírez, Susan E. *Provincial Patriarchs: Land Tenure and the Economics of Power in Colonial Peru.* Albuquerque: University of New Mexico Press, 1986. 471p.

3569. Reid, Michael. *Peru: Paths to Poverty.* London: Latin American Bureau, 1985. 130p.

3570. Rodríguez Beruff, Jorge. *Los militares y el poder: un ensayo sobre la doctrina militar en el Perú, 1948-1968.* Lima, Peru: Mosca Azul, 1983. 264p.

3571. Rostworowski de Diez Canesco, María. *Estructuras andinas del poder: ideología religioso y política.* Lima: Instituto de Estudios Peruanos, 1983. 202p.

3572. Saba, Raúl P. *Political Development and Democracy in Peru: Continuity in Change and Crisis.* Boulder, CO: Westview, 1987. 180p.

3573. Salinas, Patricia W., with José Garzón, and Carol Wise. *Problematic regional y política central en el Perú.* Lima, Peru: Centro de Investigación de la Universidad del Pacífico, 1983. 75p.

3574. Sánchez Albavera, Fernando. *El capital extranjero en la economía peruana: políticas y negociaciones en la década de los setenta.* Santiago, Chile; New York: United Nations, 1984. 178p.

3575. Scheetz, Thomas E. *Peru: and the International Monetary Fund.* Pittsburgh, PA: University of Pittsburg Press, 1986. 257p.

3576. Spalding, Karen. *Huarochirí: An Andean Society under Inca and Spanish Rule.* Stanford, CA: Stanford University Press, 1984. 364p.

3577. Stein, William W., ed. *Peruvian Contexts of Change.* New Brunswick, NJ: Transaction, 1984. 400p.

3578. Taylor, Lewis. *Maoism in the Andes: Sendero Luminoso and the Contemporary Guerrilla Movement in Peru.* Liverpool, England: Centre for Latin American Studies, University of Liverpool, 1983. 40p.

3579. Vanden, Harry E. *National Marxism in Latin America: José Carlos Mariátegui's Thought and Politics.* Boulder, CO: Lynne Rienner, 1986. 215p.

3580. Verdera, Francisco. *El empleo en el Perú: un nuevo enfoque.* Lima, Peru: IEP, 1983. 158p.

3581. Weeks, John. *Limits to Capitalist Development: The Industrialization of Peru, 1950-1980.* Boulder, CO: Westview, 1985. 254p.

3582. Wise, Carol. *Economía política del Perú: rechazo a la receta ortodoxa.* Lima: Instituto de Estudios Peruanos, 1986. 57p.

Articles and Chapters

3583. Abugattas, Luis A. "Populism and After: The Peruvian Experience." In *Authoritarians and Democrats: Regime Transition in Latin America*, edited by James M. Malloy and Mitchell A. Seligson. Pittsburgh, PA: University of Pittsburgh Press, 1987. pp. 121-143.

3584. Albert, Bill. "External Forces and the Transformation of Peruvian Coastal Agriculture, 1880-1930." In *Latin America, Economic Imperialism and the State*, edited by Christopher Abel and Colin M. Lewis. London; Dover, NH: Athlone, 1985. pp. 231-249.

3585. Albert, Bill. "The Labour Force on Peru's Sugar Plantations 1820-1930: A Survey." In *Crisis and Change in the International Sugar Economy, 1860-1914*, edited by Bill Albert and Adrian Graves. Edinburgh, Scotland: ISC Press, 1984. pp. 199-216.

3586. Andrien, Kenneth J. "Corruption, Inefficiency, and Imperial Decline in the Seventeenth-Century Viceroyalty of Peru," *The Americas* 41:1 (July 1984), 1-20.

3587. Angell, Alan. "The Difficulties of Policy Making and Implementation In Peru," *Bulletin of Latin American Research* 3:1 (January 1984), 25-43.

3588. Angell, Alan. "El gobierno militar peruano de 1968 a 1980: el fracaso de la revolución desde arriba," *Foro Internacional* 25:1 (July-September 1984), 33-56.

3589. Angotti, Thomas. "The Contributions of José Carlos Mariátegui to Revolutionary Theory," *Latin American Perspectives* 13:2 (Spring 1986), 33-57.

3590. Assies, Willem. "The Agrarian Question in Peru," *Journal of Peasant Studies* 14:4 (July 1987), 500-532.

3591. Avery, William P. "Origins and Consequences of the Border Dispute between Ecuador and Peru," *Inter-American Economic Affairs* 38:1 (Summer 1984), 65-77.

3592. Babb, Florence E. "From the Field to the Cooking Pot: Economic Crisis and the Threat to Marketers in Peru," *Ethnology* 26:2 (April 1987), 137-149.

3593. Babb, Florence E. "Producers and Reproducers: Andean Marketwomen in the Economy." In *Women and Change in Latin America*, edited by June Nash and Helen Safa. South Hadley, MA: Bergin & Garvey, 1986. pp. 53-64.

3594. Babb, Florence E. "Women in the Marketplace: Petty Commerce in Peru," *Review of Radical Political Economics* 16:1 (Spring 1984), 45-59.

3595. Becker, David G. "'Bonanza Development' and the 'New Bourgeoisie': Peru Under Military Rule." In *Postimperialism: International Capitalism and Development in the Late Twentieth Century*, edited by David G. Becker, Jeff Frieden, Sayre P. Schatz, and Richard L.

Sklar. Boulder, CO: Lynne Rienner, 1987. pp. 63-105.

3596.   Becker, David G. "Peru after the 'Revolution' Class, Power, and Ideology," *Studies in Comparative International Development* 20:3 (Fall 1985), 3-30.

3597.   Becker, David G. "The Workers of the Modern Mines in Southern Peru: Socio-economic Change, and Trade Union Militancy in the Rise of a Labour Elite." In *Miners and Mining in the Americas,* edited by Thomas Greaves and William Culver. Manchester, England; Dover, NH: Manchester University Press, 1985. pp. 226-256.

3598.   Beckerman, Paul. "Inflation and Dollar Accounts in Peru's Banking System, 1978-84," *World Development* 15:8 (August 1987), 1087-1106.

3599.   Bedoya Garland, Eduardo. "Intensification and Degradation in the Agricultural Systems of the Peruvian Upper Jungle: The Upper Huallaga Case." In *Lands at Risk in the Third World: Local-Level Perspectives,* edited by Peter D. Little and Michael M. Horowitz. Boulder, CO: Westview, 1987. pp. 290-315.

3600.   Berg, Ronald H. *"Sendro Luminoso* and Peasants of Andahuaylas," *Journal of Inter-American Studies and World Affairs* 28:4 (Winter 1986-87), 165-196.

3601.   Berriós, Rubén. "Relations between Peru and the Socialist Countries." In *Soviet-Latin American Relations in the 1980s,* edited by Augusto Varas. Boulder, CO: Westview, 1987. pp. 211-229.

3602.   Bogdanowicz-Bindert, Christine A. "Portugal, Turkey and Peru: Three Successful Stabilization Programmes under the Auspices of the IMF," *World Development* 11:1 (January 1983), 65-70.

3603.   Bonner, Fred. "Peruvian Historians Today: Historical Setting," *The Americas* 43:3 (January 1987), 245-277.

3604.   Brading, D.A. "The Incas and the Renaissance: *The Royal Commentaries* of Inca Garcilaso de la Vega," *Journal of Latin American Studies* 18:1 (May 1986), 1-23.

3605.   Brass, Tom. *"Cargos* and Conflicts: The Fiesta System and Capitalist Development in Eastern Peru," *Journal of Peasant Studies* 13:3 (April 1986), 45-62.

3606.   Brass, Tom. "Unfree Labour and Capitalist Restructuring in the Agrarian Sector: Peru and India," *Journal of Peasant Studies* 14:1 (October 1986), 50-77.

3607.   Brown, Kendall W. "Jesuit Wealth and Economic Activity within the Peruvian Economy: The Case of Colonial Southern Peru," *The Americas* 44:1 (July 1987), 23-43.

3608.   Brush, Stephen B. "Diversity and Change in Andean Agriculture." In *Lands at Risk in the Third World: Local-Level Perspectives,* edited by Peter D. Little and Michael M. Horowitz. Boulder, CO: Westview, 1987. 271-289.

3609. Bunker, Stephen G. "Ritual, Respect and Refusal: Drinking Behavior in an Andean Village," *Human Organization* 46:4 (Winter 1987), 334-342.

3610. Caballero, José María. "Agriculture and the Peasantry under Industrialization Pressures: Lessons from the Peruvian Experience," *Latin American Research Review* 19:2 (1984), 3-41.

3611. Cahill, David. *"Curas* and Social Conflict in the *Doctrinas* of Cuzco, 1780-1814," *Journal of Latin American Studies* 16:2 (November 1984), 241-276.

3612. Campbell, Leon G. "Women and the Great Rebellion in Peru, 1780-1783," *The Americas* 42:2 (October 1985), 163-196.

3613. Carter, William E. "Religion in the Andes." In *The Catholic Church and Religions in Latin America,* edited by Thomas C. Bruneau, Chester E. Gabriel and Mary Mooney. Montreal, Canada: Centre for Developing Area Studies, McGill University, 1984. pp. 88-118.

3614. Celestino, Olinda. "Land and People in Peru: The Chancay Valley from the 16th to the 20th Century," *International Social Science Journal* 39:4 (November 1987), 505-522.

3615. Chang-Rodríguez, Eugenio. "Religión y evolución en Mariátegui," *Inter-American Review of Bibliography* 34:1 (1984), 72-88.

3616. Ciudad Reynaud, Adolfo. "Labour Relations in Peru," *International Labour Review* 126:4 (July-August 1987), 457-466.

3617. Clayton, Lawrence A. "Private Matters: The Origins and Nature of United States-Peruvian Relations, 1820-1850," *The Americas* 42:4 (April 1986), 377-417.

3618. Cleaves, Peter S. "Implementation of the Agrarian and Educational Reforms in Peru." In *The Public Sector in Latin America,* edited by Alfred H. Saulniers. Austin: Institute of Latin American Studies, University of Texas, 1984. pp. 141-161.

3619. Cleaves, Peter S., and Henry Pease García. "State Autonomy and Military Policy Making." In *Armies and Politics in Latin America,* edited by Abraham F. Lowenthal and Samuel Fitch. Rev. ed. New York: Holmes & Meier, 1986. pp. 335-366.

3620. Cole, Jeffrey A. "Viceregal Persistence versus Indian Mobility: The Impact of the Duque de la Palata's Reform Program on Alto Perú, 1681-1692," *Latin American Research Review* 19:1 (1984), 37-56.

3621. Collins, Jane. "The Maintenance of Peasant Coffee Production in a Peruvian Valley," *American Ethnologist* 11:3 (August 1984), 413-438.

3622. Contreras, Jesús. "El compadrazgo y los cambios en la estructura de poder local en Chinchero," Perú," *América Indígena* 44:2 (April-June 1984), 353-374.

3623. Cotler, Julio. "Military Interventions and 'Transfer of Power to

Civilians' in Peru," In *Transition from Authoritarian Rule*, edited by Guillermo O'Donnell, Philippe C. Schmitter and Laurence Whitehead. Baltimore, MD: Johns Hopkins University Press, 1986. pp. 148-172.

3624.   Cotler, Julio. "The Political Radicalization of Working Class Youth in Peru," *CEPAL Review* 29 (August 1986), 107-118.

3625.   Crabtree, John. "The Consolidation of Alan García's Government in Peru," *Third World Quarterly* 9:3 (July 1987), 804-824.

3626.   Crabtree, John. "Peru: From Belaúnde to Alan García," *Bulletin of Latin American Research* 4:2 (1985), 75-83.

3627.   D'Altroy, Terence N. "Transitions in Power: Centralization of Wanka Political Organization under Inka Rule," *Ethnohistory* 34:1 (Winter 1987), 78-102.

3628.   Deere, Carmen Diana. "Rural Women and Agrarian Reform in Peru, Chile, and Cuba." In *Women and Change in Latin America*, edited by June Nash and Helen Safa. South Hadley, MA: Bergin & Garvey, 1986. pp. 189-207.

3629.   De la Piedra, Enrique. "Peru and Its Private Bankers: Scenes from an Unhappy Marriage." In *Politics and Economics of External Debt Crisis: The Latin American Experience*, edited by Miguel S. Wionczek in collaboration with Luciano Tomassini. Boulder, CO: Westview, 1985. pp. 383-426.

3630.   Dietz, Henry, "Aspects of Peruvian Politics: Electoral Politics in Peru, 1978-86," *Journal of Inter-American Studies and World Affairs* 28:4 (Winter 1986-87), 139-163.

3631.   Eguren López, Fernando. "La Tierra y el desarrollo rural: el caso del Perú," *Estudios Rurales Latinoamericanos* 6:1 (January-April 1983), 77-94.

3632.   Ennew, Judith. *Mujercita y Mamacita:* Girls Growing up in Lima," *Bulletin of Latin American Research* 5:2 (1986), 49-66.

3633.   Ferrero Costa, Eduardo. "Peruvian Foreign Policy: Current Trends, Constraints and Opportunities," *Journal of Inter-American Studies and World Affairs* 29:2 (Summer 1987), 55-78.

3634.   Fins, Stephanie. "Los Machiguenga y las empresas misioneras," *América Indígena* 44:1 (January-March 1984), 101-110.

3635.   Flores, Luis G., and Ralph F. Catalanello. "Personal Value Systems and Organizational Roles in Peru," *Journal of Social Psychology* 127:6 (December 1987), 629-638.

3636.   Fonseca, César. "Estudios antropológicos de las comunidades andinas," *Boletín de Antropología Americana* 7 (July 1983), 49-56.

3637.   Garrett, Roger M. "Disparities and Constraints in Peruvian Education." In *Education in Latin America*, edited by Colin Brock and Hugh Lawlor. Dover, NH: Croom Helm, 1985. pp. 109-129.

3638. Gonzales, Michael J. "Economic Crisis, Chinese Workers and the Peruvian Sugar Planters 1875-1900: A Case Study of Labour and the National Elite." In *Crisis and Change in the International Sugar Economy, 1860-1914,* edited by Bill Albert and Adrian Graves. Edinburgh, Scotland, ISC Press, 1984. pp. 181-198.

3639. Gonzales, Michael J. "Neo-colonialism and Indian Unrest in Southern Peru, 1867-1898," *Bulletin of Latin American Research* 6:1 (1987), 1-26.

3640. González Martínez, José Luis. "El huanca y la cruz: migración y transformación de la mitología andina en las barridas de Lima," *América Indígena* 45:4 (October-December 1985), 747-785.

3641. Gros, Christian. "Luchas indígenas y prácticas autogestionarias: algunas reflexiones a partir de tres estudios de caso," *Estudios Rurales Latinoamericanos* 10:1 (January-April 1987), 55-69.

3642. Guillet, David. "Paleotecnologías hidraúlicas en el altiplano peruano y su potencial económico," *América Indígena* 46:2 (April-June 1986), 331-348.

3643. Hampe Martínez, Teodoro. "Continuidad en el mundo andino: los indígenas del Perú frente a la legislación colonial (Siglo XVI)," *América Indígena* 45:2 (April-June 1985), 357-390.

3644. Herzog, Lawrence A. "The Integrated Spatial Development Model and Regional Planning in the Peruvian Andes: A Critique," *International Review of Administrative Sciences* 52:3 (September 1986), 301-324.

3645. Hopkins, Diane E. "The Peruvian Agrarian Reform: Dissent from Below," *Human Organization* 44:1 (Spring 1985), 18-32.

3646. Huizer, Gerrit. "Social Polarisation as a Disruptive Force in Cooperatives: The Case of the Te Huyro Central Cooperative in La Convención, Peru," *Boletín de Estudios Latinoamericanos y del Caribe* 35 (December 1983), 21-38.

3647. Hunt, Shane J. "Growth and Guano in Nineteenth-Century Peru." In *The Latin American Economies: Growth and the Export Sector, 1880-1930,* edited by Roberto Cortés and Shane J. Hunt. New York: Holmes & Meier, 1985. 255-318.

3648. Jacobsen, Nils. "Cycles and Booms in Latin American Export Agriculture: The Example of Southern Peru's Livestock Economy, 1855-1920," *Review* 7:3 (Winter 1984), 443-507.

3649. Jaworski C., Helan. "Peru: The Military Government's Foreign Policy in Its Two Phases, 1968-1980." In *Latin American Nations in World Politics,* edited by Heraldo Muñoz and Joseph S. Tulchin. Boulder, CO: Westview, 1984. pp. 200-215.

3650. Jongkind, C. Fred. "Ethnic Solidarity and Social Stratification: Migrants' Organizations in Argentina and Peru," *Boletín de Estudios Latino-americanos y del Caribe* 40 (June 1986), 37-48.

3651. Klaiber, Jeffrey L. "The Battle over Private Education in Peru, 1968-

1980: An Aspect of the Internal Struggle in the Catholic Church," *The Americas* 43:2 (October 1986), 137-158.

3652. Klaiber, Jeffrey L. "The Catholic Lay Movement in Peru: 1867-1959," *The Americas* 40:2 (October 1983), 149-170.

3653. Laite, Julian, and Norman Long. "Fiestas and Uneven Capitalist Development in Central Peru," *Bulletin of Latin American Research* 6:1 (1987), 27-53.

3654. LaLone, Mary B., and Darrell E. LaLone. "The Inka State in the Southern Highlands: State Administrative and Production Enclaves," *Ethnohistory* 34:1 (Winter 1987), 47-62.

3655. LeVine, Terry Yarov. "Inka Labor Service at the Regional Level: The Functional Reality," *Ethnohistory* 34:1 (Winter 1987), 14-46.

3656. Lincoln, Jennie K. "Peruvian Foreign Policy since the Return to Democratic Rule." In *The Dynamics of Latin American Foreign Policies,* edited by Jennie K. Lincoln and Elizabeth G. Ferris. Boulder, CO: Westview, 1984. pp. 137-149.

3657. McClintock, Cynthia. "After Agrarian Reform and Democratic Government: Has Peruvian Agriculture Developed?" In *Food, the State and International Political Economy,* edited by F. LaMond Tullis and W. Ladd Hollist. Lincoln: University of Nebraska Press, 1986. pp. 74-98.

3658. McClintock, Cynthia. "Sendero Luminoso: Peru's Maoist Guerrillas," *Problems of Communism* 32:5 (September-October 1983), 19-34.

3659. McClintock, Cynthia. "Why Peasants Rebel: The Case of Peru's Sendero Luminoso," *World Politics* 37:1 (October 1984), 48-84.

3660. MacCormack, Sabine. "'The Heart Has Its Reasons': Predicaments of Missionary Christianity in Early Colonial Peru," *Hispanic American Historical Review* 65:3 (August 1985), 443-466.

3661. Mallon, Florencia E. "Gender and Class in the Transition to Capitalism: Household and Mode of Production in Central Peru," *Latin American Perspectives* 13:1 (Winter 1986), 147-174.

3662. Masterson, Daniel M. "Caudillismo and Institutional Change: Manuel Odría and the Peruvian Armed Forces, 1948-1956," *The Americas* 40:4 (April 1984), 479-489.

3663. Monguió, Luis. "La ilustración peruana y el indio," *América Indígena* 45:2 (April-June 1985), 343-355.

3664. Monnier, Alain. "Evangelización estructural: el ejemplo de los Mashco el sureste peruano," *América Indígena* 44:1 (January-March 1984), 191-200.

3665. Mooney, Mary. "Cautious Change in a Reformist Context: The Church in Peru." In *The Catholic Church and Religions in Latin America,* edited by Thomas C. Bruneau, Chester E. Gabriel and Mary Mooney. Montreal, Canada: Centre for Developing Area Studies, McGill

University, 1984. pp. 41-66.

3666. Moore, Thomas R. "El ILV y una 'Tribu Recién Encontrada': la experiencia Amarakaeri," *América Indígena* 44:1 (January-March 1984), 25-48.

3667. Mora Bernasconi, Carlos. "Reflexiones acerca del problema territorial de las communidades indígenas de la Amazonía," *América Indígena* 43:3 (July-September 1983), 569-584.

3668. Morales, Edmundo. "Coca and Cocaine Economy and Social Change in the Andes of Peru," *Economic Development and Cultural Change* 35:1 (October 1986), 143-161.

3669. North, Liisa L. "Problems of Democratization in Peru and Ecuador." In *Latin American Prospects for the 1980s,* edited by Archibald R.M. Ritter and David H. Pollock. New York: Praeger, 1983. pp. 214-239.

3670. Norton, George W., Victor G. Ganoza, and Carlos Pomareda. "Potential Benefits of Agricultural Research and Extension in Peru," *American Journal of Agricultural Economics* 69:2 (May 1987), 247-257.

3671. Oviedo, José Miguel. "Peru: Can This Nation Save Itself?" *Dissent* (Spring 1987), 171-178.

3672. Painter, Michael. "The Political Economy of Food Production in Peru," *Studies in Comparative International Development* 18:4 (Winter 1983), 34-52.

3673. Palmer, David Scott. "The Changing Political Economy of Peru under Military and Civilian Rule," *Inter-American Economic Affairs* 37:4 (Spring 1984), 37-62.

3674. Palmer, David Scott. "Military and Civilian Political Economy." In *Politics, Policies, and Economic Development in Latin America,* edited by Robert G. Wesson. Stanford, CA: Hoover Institution Press, 1984. pp. 74-93.

3675. Palmer, David Scott. "Rebellion in Rural Peru: The Origins and Evolution of Sendero Luminoso," *Comparative Politics* 18:2 (January 1986), 127-146.

3676. Peloso, Vincent C. "Cotton Planters, The State, and Rural Labor Policy: Ideological Origins of the Peruvian *República Aristocrática,* 1895-1908," *The Americas* 40:2 (October 1983), 209-228.

3677. Peloso, Vincent C. "Succulence and Sustenance: Region, Class, and Diet in Nineteenth-Century Peru." In *Food, Politics, and Society in Latin America,* edited by John C. Super and Thomas C. Wright. Lincoln: University of Nebraska Press, 1985. pp. 46-64.

3678. Petras, James, Morris Morley, and A. Eugene Havens. "Peru: Capitalist Democracy in Transition," *New Left Review* 142 (November-December 1983), 30-53.

3679. Pozorski, Thomas, Sheila Pozorski, Carol J. Mackey, and Alexandra M. Ulana Klymyshyn. "Pre-Hispanic Ridged Fields of the Casma Valley,

Peru," *Geographical Review* 73:4 (October 1983), 407-416.

3680.   Quilter, Jeffrey, and Terry Stocker. "Subsistence Economies and the Origins of Andean Complex Societies," *American Anthropologist* 85:3 (September 1983), 545-562.

3681.   Radcliffe, Sarah A. "Gender Relations, Peasant Livelihood Strategies and Migration: A Case Study from Cuzco, Peru," *Bulletin of Latin American Research* 5:2 (1986), 29-47.

3682.   Ramírez, Susan E. "The *'Dueño de Indios'*: Thoughts on the Consequences of the Shifting Bases of Power of the *'Curaca de los Viejos Antiguos'* under the Spanish in Sixteenth-Century Peru," *Hispanic American Historical Review* 67:4 (November 1987), 575-610.

3683.   Revesz, Bruno. "La reforma de la reforma en el agro costeño del Perú," *Estudios Rurales Latinoamericanos* 9:1 (January-April 1986), 43-62.

3684.   Roca, Santiago, and Rodrigo Prialé. "La devaluación y los programas de estabilización en el Perú," *El Trimestre Económico* 53:212 (October-December 1986), 835-881.

3685.   Roett, Riordan. "Peru: The Message from García," *Foreign Affairs* 64:2 (Winter 1985/86), 274-286.

3686.   Ronzelen de González, Teresa van. "Víctor Apaza, la emergencia de un Santo: descripción y análisis del proceso de formación de un nuevo culto popular," *América Indígena* 45:4 (October-December 1985), 647-668.

3687.   Rubio Correa, Marcial. "Militares y Sendero Luminoso frente al sistema democrático peruano," *Revista de Estudios Políticos* 53 (September-October 1986), 161-174.

3688.   St John, Ronald Bruce. "Peru: Democracy under Siege," *World Today* 40:7 (July 1984), 299-306.

3689.   Sallnow, Michael J. "Manorial Labour and Religious Ideology in the Central Andes: A Working Hypothesis," *Bulletin of Latin American Research* 2:2 (May 1983), 39-56.

3690.   Samaniego, Carlos. "Estado, acumulación y agricultura en el Perú," *Estudios Rurales Latinoamericanos* 7:3 (September-December 1984), 199-262.

3691.   Schaedel, Richard P. "Paleohidrologías y política agraria en el Perú," *América Indígena* 46:2 (April-June 1986), 319-329.

3692.   Scheetz, Thomas. "Gastos militares en Chile, Perú y la Argentina," *Desarrollo Económico* 25:99 (October-December 1985), 315-328.

3693.   Schuldt, Jurgen. "Desinflación selectiva y reactivación generalizada en el Perú, 1985-1986," *El Trimestre Económico* 54:Special (September 1987), 313-350.

3694.   Schydlowsky, Daniel M. "The Macroeconomic Effect of Nontraditional Exports in Peru," *Economic Development and Cultural Change* 34:3

(April 1986), 491-509.

3695. Schydlowsky, Daniel M. "The Tragedy of Lost Opportunity in Peru." In *Latin American Political Economy: Financial Crisis and Political Change,* edited by Jonathan Hartlyn and Samuel A. Morley. Boulder, CO: Westview, 1986. pp. 217-242.

3696. Scott, C.D. "The Decline of an Export Industry, or the Growth of Peruvian Sugar Consumption in the Long Run," *Journal of Development Studies* 21:2 (January 1985), 253-281.

3697. Scott, C.D. "Strategies of Technical Choice in the Peruvian Sugar Industry," *Journal of Peasant Studies* 12:4 (July 1985), 26-56.

3698. Seligmann, Linda J. "The Chicken in Andean History and Myth: The Quechua Concept of Wallpa," *Ethnohistory* 34:2 (Spring 1987), 139-170.

3699. Smith, Richard C. "La ideología liberal y las comunidades indígenas en el Perú republicano," *América Indígena* 43:3 (July-September 1983), 585-600.

3700. Stallings, Barbara. "International Lending and the Relative Autonomy of the State: A Case Study of Twentieth-Century Peru," *Politics and Society* 14:3 (1985), 257-288.

3701. Stephens, Evelyne Huber. "Minerals Strategies and Development: International Political Economy, State, Class and the Role of the Bauxite/Aluminum and Copper Industries in Jamaica and Peru," *Studies in Comparative International Development* 22:3 (Fall 1987), 60-102.

3702. Stocks, Anthony. "Native Enclaves in the Upper Amazon: A Case of Regional Non-integration," *Ethnohistory* 30:2 (Spring 1983), 77-92.

3703. Taylor, Lewis. "Agrarian Unrest and Political Conflict in Puno, 1985-1987," *Bulletin of Latin American Research* 6:2 (1987), 135-162.

3704. Taylor, Lewis. "Cambios capitalistas en las Haciendas Cajamarquinas del Perú, 1900-1935," *Estudios Rurales Latinoamericanos* 7:1 (April 1984), 93-129.

3705. Thorp, Rosemary. "The APRA Alternative in Peru: Preliminary Evaluation of Garcia's Economic Policies," *Bulletin of Latin American Research* 6:2 (1987), 162-182.

3706. Thorp, Rosemary. "La opción del APRA en el Perú," *El Trimestre Económico* 54:Special (September 1987), 351-368.

3707. Vanden, Harry E. "The Making of a Latin Marxist: José Carlos Mariátegui's Intellectual Formation," *Inter-American Review of Bibliography* 36:1 (1986), 5-28.

3708. Varón Gabai, Rafael, and Auke Pieter Jacobs. "Peruvian Wealth and Spanish Investments: The Pizarro Family during the Sixteenth Century," *Hispanic American Historical Review* 67:4 (November 1987), 657-695.

3709. Vellinga, M., and D. Kruijt. "The State, Regional Development, and Regional Bourgeoisie in Latin America: Case Studies of Peru and Colombia," *Inter-American Economic Affairs* 37:3 (Winter 1983), 3-31.

3710. Vreeland, James M., Jr. "Una perspectiva antropología de la paleotecnología en el desarrollo agrario del norte de Perú," *América Indígena* 46:2 (April-June 1986), 275-318.

3711. Wallace, James M. "Urban Anthropology in Lima: An Overview," *Latin American Research Review* 19:3 (1984), 57-85.

3712. Webb, Richard. "La gestación del plan antinflacionario del Perú," *El Trimestre Económico* 54:Special (September 1987), 295-311.

3713. Wehkamp, Andy. "Luchas colectivas de las obreras peruanas: los motivos de participación y alejamiento," *Boletín de Estudios Latino-americanos y del Caribe* 37 (December 1984), 69-83.

3714. Werlich, David P. "Debt, Democracy and Terrorism in Peru," *Current History* 86:516 (January 1987), 29-32.

3715. Werlich, David P. "Peru: The Shadow of the Shining Path," *Current History* 83:490 (February 1984), 78-82.

3716. Wilson, Fiona. "Conflict on a Peruvian Hacienda," *Bulletin of Latin American Research* 5:1 (1986), 65-94.

3717. Wilson, Patricia A., and Carol Wise. "The Regional Implications of Public Investment in Peru, 1968-1983," *Latin American Research Review* 21:2 (1986), 93-116.

3718. Works, Martha Adrienne. "Aguaruna Agriculture in Eastern Peru," *Geographical Review* 77:3 (July 1987), 343-358.

3719. Young, Grace Ester. "The Myth of Being 'Like a Daughter'," *Latin American Perspectives* 14:3 (Summer 1987), 365-380.

3720. Zuidema, R.T. "Hierarchy and Space in Incaic Social Organization," *Ethnohistory* 30:2 (Spring 1983), 49-75.

3721. Zulawski, Ann. "Wages, Ore Sharing, and Peasant Agriculture: Labor in Oruro's Silver Mines, 1607-1720," *Hispanic American Historical Review* 67:3 (August 1987), 405-430.

PUERTO RICO

Books and Monographs

3722. Acosta-Belem, Edna, ed. *The Puerto Rican Woman: Perspectives on Culture, History, and Society.* 2d ed. New York: Praeger, 1986. 212p.

3723. Bergad, Laird W. *Coffee and the Growth of Agrarian Capitalism in Nineteenth-Century Puerto Rico.* Princeton, NJ: Princeton University Press, 1983. 242p.

3724. Bloomfield, Richard J., ed. *Puerto Rico: The Search for a National Policy.* Boulder, CO: Westview, 1985, 192p.

3725. Carr, Raymond. *Puerto Rico: A Colonial Experiment.* New York: New York University Press, 1984. 477p.

3726. Delgado Pasapera, Germán. *Puerto Rico: sus luchas emancipadoras, 1850-1898.* Río Piedras, Puerto Rico: Cultural, 1984. 609p.

3727. Duncan, Ronald J., et al. *Social Research in Puerto Rico: Science, Humanism, and Society.* San Juan, Puerto Rico: Inter American University Press, 1983. 218p.

3728. Falk, Pamela S., ed. *The Political Status of Puerto Rico.* Lexington, MA: Lexington, 1986. 125p.

3729. García-Passalacqua, Juan M. *Puerto Rico: Equality and Freedom at Issue.* New York: Praeger, 1984. 175p.

3730. Heine, Jorge, ed. *Time for Decision: The United States and Puerto Rico.* Lanham, MD: North-South, 1983. 302p.

3731. Jiménez de Wagenheim, Olga. *Puerto Rico's Revolt for Independence: El Grito de Lares.* Boulder, CO: Westview, 1985. 127p.

3732. Morales, Julio. *Puerto Rican Poverty and Migration: We Just Had to Try Elsewhere.* New York: Praeger, 1986. 253p.

3733.   Morales Carrión, Arturo, et al. *Puerto Rico: A Political and Cultural History.* New York: W.W. Norton, 1983. 384p.

3734.   Nelson, Anne. *Murder under Two Flags: The U.S., Puerto Rico, and the Cerro Maravilla Cover-up.* New York: Ticknow and Fields, 1986. 269p.

3735.   Nistal-Moret, Benjamín, ed. *Esclavos prófugos y cimarrones: Puerto Rico, 1770-1870.* Río Piedras: Editorial de la Universidad de Puerto Rico, 1984. 287p.

3736.   Ortiz, Altagracia. *Eighteenth-Century Reforms in the Caribbean: Miguel de Muesas, Governor of Puerto Rico, 1769-76.* East Brunswick, NJ: Farleigh Dickinson University Press, 1983. 258p.

3737.   Picó, Fernando. *Los gallos peleados.* Río Piedras, Puerto Rico: Huracán, 1983. 179p.

3738.   Ramírez de Arellano, Annette B., and Conrad Seipp. *Colonialism, Catholicism, and Contraception: A History of Birth Control in Puerto Rico.* Chapel Hill: University of North Carolina Press, 1983. 219p.

3739.   Scarano, Francisco A. *Sugar and Slavery in Puerto Rico: The Plantation Economy of Ponce, 1800-1850.* Madison: University of Wisconsin Press, 1984. 242p.

3740.   Weisskoff, Richard. *Factories and Food Stamps: The Puerto Rico Model of Development.* Baltimore, MD: Johns Hopkins University Press, 1985. 190p.

Articles and Chapters

3741.   Alameda, José I., and Wilfredo Ruiz Oliveras. "La fuga de capital humano en la economía de Puerto Rico: reto para la actual década," *Revista de Ciencias Sociales* 24:1-2 (January-June 1985), 3-34.

3742.   Bonilla, Frank, and Ricardo Compos. "Evolving Patterns of Puerto Rican Migration." In *The Americas in the New International Division of Labor,* edited by Steven E. Sanderson. New York: Holmes & Meier, 1985. pp. 177-205.

3743.   Brass, Tom. "Coffee and Rural Proletarianization," *Journal of Latin American Studies* 16:1 (May 1984), 143-152.

3744.   Cabán, Pedro A. "Industrialization, the Colonial State, and Working Class Organizations in Puerto Rico," *Latin American Perspectives* 11:3 (Summer 1984), 149-172.

3745.   Collo, Martin J. "Capital Imports and Endogenous Productive Capacity: The Puerto Rican Experience," *Journal of Third World Studies* 4:2 (Fall 1987), 132-142.

3746.   Cruz Báez, Angel David. "El geógrafo, el ambiente y Puerto Rico," *Revista de Ciencias Sociales* 24:3-4 (July-December 1985), 455-469.

3747. Flores, Juan. "The Puerto Rico That José Luis González Built: Comments on Cultural History," *Latin American Perspectives* 11:3 (Summer 1984), 173-184.

3748. García Muñiz, Humberto. "Puerto Rico en las Naciones Unidas: la etapa de transición, 1960-1967," *Revista de Ciencias Sociales* 24:1-2 (January-June 1985), 113-152.

3749. González Díaz, Emilio, and Nemesio Vargas Acevedo. "Hacia una sociología de la vida cotidiana en Puerto Rico," *Revista de Ciencias Sociales* 25:1-2 (January-June 1986), 3-15.

3750. Gottfried, Robert R. "The Potential Impact of High-Test Molasses from Energy Cane on the Rum Industry of Puerto Rico," *World Development* 14:10-11 (October-November 1986), 1347-1356.

3751. Hernández Cruz, Juan E. "¿Migración de retorno o circulación de obreros boricuas?" *Revista de Ciencias Sociales* 24:1-2 (January-June 1985), 81-110.

3752. Levine, Barry B. "The Puerto Rican Exodus: Development of the Puerto Rican Circuit: In *The Caribbean Exodus,* edited by Barry B. Levine. New York: Praeger, 1987. pp. 93-105.

3753. López Cantos, Angel. "El comercio legal de Puerto Rico con las colonias extranjeras de América: 1700-1783," *Revista de Ciencias Sociales* 24:1-2 (January-June 1985), 201-228.

3754. Mann, Arthur J. "Economic Development, Income Distribution, and Real Income Levels: Puerto Rico, 1953-1977," *Economic Development and Cultural Change* 34:3 (April 1985), 485-502.

3755. Mann, Arthur J., and Robert Smith. "Public Transfers, Family Socioeconomic Traits, and the Job Search Behavior of the Unemployed: Evidence from Puerto Rico," *World Development* 15:6 (June 1987), 831-840.

3756. Negrón Porillo, Mariano, and Raúl Mayo Santana. "Trabajo, producción y conflictos en el siglo XIX: una revisión crítica de las nuevas investigaciones históricas en Puerto Rico," *Revista de Ciencias Sociales* 24:3-4 (July-December 1985), 469-496.

3757. Pantojas García, Emilio. "La crisis del modelo desarrollista y la reestructuración capitalista en Puerto Rico: hacia una redefinición del rol de Puerto Rico en la economía hemisférica," *Estudios Sociales Centroamericanos* 13:39 (August-December 1984), 33-61.

3758. Pantojas-García, Emilio. "Desarrollismo y lucha de clases: los límites del proyecto populista en Puerto Rico durante la década del cuarenta," *Revista de Ciencias Sociales* 24:3-4 (July-December 1985), 355-391.

3759. Pantojas-García, Emilio. "The U.S. Caribbean Basin Initiative and the Puerto Rican Experience: Some Parallels and Lesson," *Latin American Perspectives* 12:4 (Fall 1985), 105-128.

3760. Pastor, Robert. "The International Debate on Puerto Rico: The Costs of Being an Agenda-Taker," *International Organization* 38:3 (Summer

Being an Agenda-Taker," *International Organization* 38:3 (Summer 1984), 575-595.

3761.   Petras, James F., Miguel E.Correa, and Roberto P. Korzeniewicz. "The Crises in Market, Collectivist and Mixed Economies: Puerto Rico, Cuba, and Jamaica." In *Capitalist and Socialist Crises in the Late Twentieth Century.* By James F. Petras. Totowa, NJ: Rowman & Allanheld, 1984. 296-318.

3762.   Picó, Isabel. "Los estudiantes universitarios de la década del treinta: del nacionalismo cultural al nacionalismo político," *Revista de Ciencias Sociales* 24:3-4 (July-December 1985), 515-552.

3763.   Picó de Hernández, Isabel. "Los orígenes del movimiento estudiantil universitario: 1903-1930," *Revista de Ciencias Sociales* 24:1-2 (January-June 1985), 35-77.

3764.   Quintero Rivera, Angel G. "Economía y política en Puerto Rico, 1900-1934: algunos elementos regional-estructurales del crecimiento azucarero y el análisis de la política obrera," *Revista de Ciencias Sociales* 24:3-4 (July-December 1985), 393-454.

3765.   Ramos Mattei, Andres A. "The Growth of the Puerto Rican Sugar Industry Under North American Domination: 1899-1910." In *Crisis and Change in the International Sugar Economy, 1860-1914,* edited by Bill Albert and Adrian Graves. Edinburgh, Scotland: ISC Press, 1984. pp. 121-132.

3766.   Safa, Helen I. "Female Employment in the Puerto Rican Working Class." In *Women and Change in Latin America,* edited by June Nash and Helen Safa. South Hadley, MA: Bergin & Garvey, 1986. pp. 84-105.

3767.   Santiago, Carlos E. "Closing the Gap: The Employment and Unemployment Effects of Minimum Wage Policy in Puerto Rico," *Journal of Development Economics* 23:2 (October 1986), 293-311.

3768.   Santiago, Carlos E., and Erik Thorbecke. "Regional and Technological Dualism: A Dual-Dual Development Framework Applied to Puerto Rico," *Journal of Development Studies* 20:4 (July 1984), 271-289.

3769.   Stevens, Robert William. "Los arrabales de San Juan: una perspectiva histórica," *Revista de Ciencias Sociales* 24:1-2 (January-June 1985), 155-197.

3770.   Wessman, James W. "Sugar and Demography: Population Dynamics in the Spanish Antilles during the Nineteenth and Twentieth Centuries." In *Crisis and Change in the International Sugar Economy, 1860-1914,* edited by Bill Albert and Adrian Graves. Edinburgh, Scotland: ISC Press, 1984. pp. 95-110.

SURINAM

Books and Monographs

3771. Chin, Henk E., and Hans Buddingh. *Surinam: Politics, Economics and Society,* London; New York: Pinter, 1987. 192p.

3772. Hoogbergen, Wilhelmus S.M. *De Boni-oorlogen, 1757-1860: Marronage en Guerilla in Oost-Suriname.* Utrecht, Netherlands: Centrum voor Caraibishe Studies, 1985. 523p.

3773. Inter-American Commission on Human Rights. *Second Report on the Human Rights Situation in Suriname.* Washington, DC: Organization of American States, 1985. 69p.

3774. Lamur, Carlo. *The American Takeover: Industrial Emergence and Alcoa's Expansion in Guyana and Suriname, 1914-1921.* Dordrecht, Netherlands; Cinnaminson, NJ: Foris, 1985. 209p.

3775. Scholtens, Ben. *Suriname Tijdens de Tweede Wereldoorlog.* Paramaribo: Anton de Kom Universiteit van Suriname, 1985. 88p.

3776. Stephen, Henri J.M. *Winti: Afro-Surinaamse religie en magische rituelen in Suriname en Nederland.* Amsterdam: Karnak, 1985. 131p.

Articles and Chapters

3777. Brana-Shute, Gary. "Back to the Barracks? Five Years 'Revo' in Suriname," *Journal of Inter-American Studies and World Affairs* 28:1 (Spring 1986), 93-121.

3778. Hendrickson, Embert. "Surinam and the Antilles: A New Perspective," *World Today* 40:6 (June 1984), 261-268.

3779. Moreno, Jan. "Agricultural Cooperatives in Surinam: Complex Problems and Policy Responses," *Boletín de Estudios Latinoamericanos y del Caribe* 35 (December 1983), 51-70.

3780.   Sedoc-Dahlberg, Betty. "Interest Groups and the Military Regime in Suriname." In *Militarization in the Non-Hispanic Caribbean,* edited by Alma H. Young and Dion E. Phillips. Boulder, CO: Lynne Rienner, 1986. pp. 90-111.

3781.   Thompson, Alvin O. "The Guyana-Suriname Boundary Dispute: An Historical Appraisal, c. 1683-1816," *Boletín de Estudios Latino-americanos y del Caribe* 39 (December 1985), 63-84.

TRINIDAD AND TOBAGO

Books and Monographs

3782. Basdeo, Sahadeo. *Labour Organization and Labour Reform in Trinidad, 1919-1939.* St. Augustine, Trinidad: Institute for Social and Economic Research, University of the West Indies, 1983. 285p.

3783. Boodhoo, Ken I., ed. *Eric Williams: The Man and the Leader.* Lanham, MD: University Press of America, 1986. 143p.

3784. Clarke, Colin G. *East Indians in a West Indian Town: San Fernando, Trinidad, 1930-1970.* Boston, MA: Allen & Unwin, 1986. 193p.

3785. MacDonald, Scott B. *Trinidad and Tobago: Democracy and Development in the Caribbean.* New York: Praeger, 1986. 231p.

3786. Millette, James. *Society and Politics in Colonial Trinidad.* 2d ed. London: Zed (Totowa, NJ: Dist. by Biblio Distribution Center), 1985. 295p.

3787. Trotman, David Vincent. *Crime in Trinidad: Conflict and Control in a Plantation Society, 1838-1900.* Knoxville: University of Tennessee Press, 1986. 345p.

Articles and Chapters

3788. Auty, Richard, and Alan Gelb. "Oil Windfalls in a Small Parliamentary Democracy: Their Impact on Trinidad and Tobago," *World Development* 14:9 (September 1986), 1161-1175.

3789. Baksh, Ishmael J. "Factors Influencing Occupational Expectations of Secondary School Children in Trinidad and Tobago," *Social and Economic Studies* 33:3 (September 1984), 1-29.

3790. Basdeo, Sahadeo. "Indian Participation in Labour Politics in Trinidad, 1919-1939," *Caribbean Quarterly* 32:3-4 (September-October 1986), 50-65.

3791.   Boomert, Arie. "The Arawak Indians of Trinidad and Coastal Guiana, ca 1500-1650," *Journal of Caribbean History* 19:2 (November 1984), 123-188.

3792.   Bourne, Compton. "Banking Boom and Bust Economies: Lessons from Trinidad and Tobago and Jamaica," *Social and Economic Studies* 34:4 (December 1985), 139-163.

3793.   Brereton, Bridget. "Post-Emancipation Protest in the Caribbean: The 'Belmanna Riots' in Tobago, 1976," *Caribbean Quarterly* 30:3-4 (September-December 1984), 110-123.

3794.   Debysingh, Molly. "Cultural Change and Adaptation as Reflected in the Meat-Eating Habits of the Trinidad Indian Population," *Caribbean Quarterly* 32:3-4 (September-October 1986), 66-77.

3795.   Driver, Edwin D., and Aloo E. Driver. "Gender, Society and Self-Conceptions: India, Iran, Trinidad-Tobago, and the United States," *International Journal of Comparative Sociology* 24:3-4 (1983), 200-217.

3796.   Farrell, Terrence, Annette Najjar, and Hazel Marcelle. "Corporate Financing and Use of Bank Credit in Trinidad and Tobago," *Social and Economic Studies* 35:4 (December 1986), 1-65.

3797.   Haraksingh, Kusha. "Labour, Technology and the Sugar Estates in Trinidad, 1879-1914." In *Crisis and Change in the International Sugar Economy, 1860-1914,* edited by Bill Albert and Adrian Graves Edinburgh, Scotland: ISC Press, 1984. pp. 133-146.

3798.   Hintzen, Percy C. "Bases of Elite Support for a Regime: Race, Ideology, and Clientelism as Bases for Leaders in Guyana and Trinidad," *Comparative Political Studies* 16:3 (October 1983), 363-391.

3799.   Hintzen, Percy C. "Ethnicity, Class and Internal Capitalist Penetration in Guyana and Trinidad," *Social and Economic Studies* 34:3 (September 1985), 107-163.

3800.   Ince, Basil A. "Coping with Oil Wealth: The Case of Trinidad/Tobago and the Commonwealth Caribbean." In *Latin American Prospects for the 1980s,* edited by Archibald R.M. Ritter and David H. Pollock. New York: Praeger, 1983. pp. 111-134.

3801.   Kula, Erhun. "The Analysis of Social Interest Rate in Trinidad and Tobago," *Journal of Development Studies* 22:4 (July 1986), 731-739.

3802.   López, Consuelo. "C.L.R. James: 'Cleaning up the Mess' in the 1966 Trinidad-Tobago Election," *Caribbean Quarterly* 30:2 (June 1984), 18-32.

3803.   Najjar, Annette, and Hazel Marcelle. "Estimating a National Savings Series for Trinidad and Tobago," *Social and Economic Studies* 34:4 (December 1985), 165-197.

3804.   Nevadomsky, Joseph. "Developmental Sequences of Domestic Groups in an East Indian Community in Rural Trinidad," *Ethnology* 24:1 (January 1985), 1-11.

3805. Nevadomsky, Joseph. "Economic Organisation, Social Mobility and Changing Social Status in Rural Trinidad," *Social and Economic Studies* 33:3 (September 1984), 31-62.

3806. Parris, Carl. "Power and Privilege in Trinidad and Tobago," *Social and Economic Studies* 34:2 (June 1985), 97-109.

3807. Pollard, H.J. "The Erosion of Agriculture in an Oil Economy: The Case of Export Crop Production in Trinidad," *World Development* 13:7 (July 1985), 819-835.

3808. Ramsaran, Ramesh. "The Retail Price Index of Trinidad and Tobago and Its Relevance as a Measure of Changes in the Cost of Living," *Social and Economic Studies* 32:4 (December 1983), 73-106.

3809. Reddock, Rhoda. "Indian Women and Indentureship in Trinidad and Tobago, 1845-1917: Freedom Denied," *Caribbean Quarterly* 32:3-4 (September-October 1986), 27-49.

3810. Sudama, Trevor. "Class, Race, and the State in Trinidad and Tobago," *Latin American Perspectives* 10:4 (Fall 1983), 75-96.

3811. Sutton, Paul. "Trinidad and Tobago: Oil, Capitalism and the 'Presidential Power' of Eric Williams." In *Dependency under Challenge: The Political Economy of the Commonwealth Caribbean,* edited by Anthony Payne and Paul Sutton. Dover, NH: Manchester University Press, 1984. pp. 43-76.

3812. Trotman, David V. "Women and Crime in Late Nineteenth Century Trinidad," *Caribbean Quarterly* 30:3-4 (September-December 1984), 60-72.

URUGUAY

Books and Monographs

3813. Amnesty International. *Report on Human Rights Violations in Uruguay.* London, 1983. 34p.

3814. Ardito Barletta, Nicolas, Mario I. Blejer, and Luis Landau, eds. *Economic Liberalization and Stabilization Policies in Argentina, Chile and Uruguay: Applications of the Monetary Approach to the Balance of Payments.* Washington, DC: World Bank, 1984. 163p.

3815. Barrán, José P., and Benjamín Nahum. *Batlle, los estancieros y el imperio británico.* Montevideo: Banda Oriental. 7 vols.
    Vol. 4: *Las primeras reformas, 1911-1913,* 1983. 196p.
    Vol. 5: Barrán, José P. *La reacción imperial-conservadora, 1911-1913,* 1984. 210p.
    Vol. 6: *Crisis y radicalización, 1913-1916,* 1985, 257p.
    Vol. 7: Barrán, José P. *Lucha política y enfrentamiento social, 1913-1916,* 1986. 268p.

3816. Blinder, Samuel. *Uruguay, las visperas de la democracia.* Montevideo, Uruguay: Agencia Latinoamericana, 1984. 57p.

3817. D'Elia, Germán, and Armando Miraldi. *Historia del movimiento obrero en el Uruguay: desde sus origines hasta 1930.* Montevideo, Uruguay: Banda Oriental, 1984. 184p.

3818. Gillespie, Charles. *The Breakdown of Democracy in Uruguay: Alternative Political Models.* Washington, DC: Latin American Program, Wilson Center, 1984. 43p.

3819. Gillespie, Charles. *From Suspended Animation to Animated Suspension: Political Parties and the Difficult Birth of Uruguay's Transition, 1973-1983.* Montevideo: Centro de Informaciones y Estudios del Uruguay, 1985. 90p.

3820.   Gillespie, Charles, comp. *Uruguay y la democracia.* Papers from a seminar held at the Woodrow Wilson International Center for Scholars, Washington, D.C. Montevideo, Uruguay: Banda Oriental, 1984-85. 2 vols.

3821.   González, Luis E. *Political Parties and Redemocratization in Uruguay.* Montevideo: Centro de Informaciones y Estudios del Uruguay, 1984. 55p.

3822.   Kneit, Julio. *Uruguay 1985: la luz tras las tinieblas.*   Montevideo, Uruguay: J. Kneit, 1985. 202p.

3823.   Lawyers Committee for International Human Rights Staff. *The Generals Give Back Uruguay: A Report on Human Rights.* New York, 1985. 62p.

3824.   Ramos, Joseph. *Neoconservative Economics in the Southern Cone of Latin America, 1973-1983.* Baltimore, MD: Johns Hopkins University Press, 1986. 200p.

3825.   Rocha Imaz, Ricardo. *Nacionalism, socialismo y el Uruguay moderno.* Montevideo, Uruguay: Blancas (dist. by Banda Oriental), 1984. 92p.

3826.   Rocha Imaz, Ricardo, Roberto Varesi, and Dante Pizzirusso Lefiego. *Compendio de historia uruguay, 1800-1985.* Montevideo, Uruguay: Blancas, 1985. 92p.

3827.   Rodríguez Villamil, Silva, and Graciela Sapriza. *Mujer, Estado y política en el Uruguay del siglo XX.* Montevideo, Uruguay: Banda Oriental, 1984. 134p.

3828.   Rial Roade, Juan. *Población y desarrollo de un pequeño país, Uruguay 1830-1930.* Montevideo, Uruguay: Acali, 1983. 187p.

3829.   Sierra, Geronimo de. *Dependencia, democracia representativa y dictadura en el Uruguay.* Montevideo: Centro Interdisciplinario de Estudios sobre el Desarrollo, Uruguay, 1984. 102p.

3830.   Terra, Juan Pablo. *Distribución social del ingreso en el Uruguay: estratos de ingresos, categorías socio-profesionales y clases sociales alrededor de 1960.* Montevideo, Uruguay: Centro Latinoamericano de Economía Humana, 1983. 203p.

3831.   Terra, Juan Pablo. *El proceso de la vivienda de 1963 a 1980.* Montevideo, Uruguay: Centro Latinoamericano de Economía Humana, 1983. 179p.

Articles and Chapters

3832.   Aguiar, César Alberto. "Clivajes sociales, tiempos políticos y redemocratización," *Revista Mexicana de Sociología* 47:2 (April-June 1985), 21-43.

3833.   Aguiar, César Alberto. "Uruguay: escenas políticas y subsistemas electorales," *Desarrollo Económico* 24:96 (January-March 1985), 517-542.

3834. Alonso, José María, and Carlos Paolino. "Modernización y concentración en el agro uruguayo," *Revista Paraguaya de Sociología* 20:58 (September-December 1983), 83-98.

3835. Astori, Danilo. "Neoliberalismo authoritario en el Uruguay: peculiaridades internas e impulsos externos," *Revista Mexicana de Sociología* 47:2 (April-June 1985), 123-153.

3836. Barbato de Silva, Celia, and Luis Macadar. "Uruguay: una visión de su posible redinamización económica," *Revista Mexicana de Sociología* 47:2 (April-June 1985), 155-172.

3837. Barrán, José Pedro, and Benjamín Nahum. "Uraguayan Rural History," *Hispanic American Historical Review* 64:4 (November 1984), 655-673.

3838. Benton, Lauren A. "Reshaping the Urban Core: The Politics of Housing in Authoritarian Uruguay," *Latin American Research Review* 21:2 (1986), 33-52.

3839. Blejer, Mario I. "Liberalization and Stabilization Policies in the Southern Cone Countries," *Journal of Inter-American Studies and World Affairs* 25:4 (November 1983), 431-444.

3840. Blejer, Mario I., and José Gil Díaz. "Domestic and External Factors in the Determination of the Real Interest Rate: The Case of Uruguay," *Economic Development and Cultural Change* 34:3 (April 1986), 589-606.

3841. Corbo, Vittorio, Jaime de Melo, and James Tybout. "What Went Wrong with the Recent Reforms in the Southern Cone," *Economic Development and Cultural Change* 34:3 (April 1986), 607-640.

3842. Falcoff, Mark. "Spain and the Southern Cone." In *The Iberian-Latin American Connection: Implications for U.S. Foreign Policy,* edited by Howard J. Wiarda. Boulder, CO: Westview, 1986. pp. 337-359.

3843. Filgueira, Carlos H. "Mediación política y apertura democrática en el Uruguay," *Revista Mexicana de Sociología* 47:2 (April-June 1985), 45-65.

3844. Finch, Henry. "Democratisation in Uruguay," *Third World Quarterly* 7:3 (July 1985), 594-609.

3845. Finch, Henry. "The Military Regime and Dominant Class Interests in Uruguay, 1973-1983.: In *Generals in Retreat: The Crisis of Military Rule in Latin America,* edited by Philip J. O'Brien and Paul Cammack. Dover, NH: Manchester University Press, 1985. pp. 89-114.

3846. Finch, M.H.J. "British Imperialism in Uruguay: The Public Utility Companies and the Batllista State, 1900-1930." In *Latin America, Economic Imperialism and the State,* edited by Christopher Abel and Colin M. Lewis. London; Dover, NH: Athlone, 1985. pp. 250-266.

3847. Fortuna, Juan Carlos. "Los cambios en el escenario estructural de los movimientos laborales," *Revista Mexicana de Sociología* 47:2 (April-

June 1985), 233-248.

3848.   Gillespie, Charles G. "Uruguay's Return to Democracy," *Bulletin of Latin American Research* 4:2 (1985), 99-107.

3849.   Gillespie, Charles G. "Uruguay's Transition form Collegial Military-Technocratic Rule." In *Transition from Authoritarian Rule,* edited by Guillermo O'Donnell, Phillippe C. Schmitter and Laurence Whitehead. Baltimore, MD: Johns Hopkins University Press, 1986. pp. 173-195.

3850.   González, Luis E. "El sistema de partidos y las perspectivas de la democracia uruguaya," *Revista Mexicana de Sociología* 47:2 (April-June 1985), 67-84.

3851.   González, Luis E. "Uruguay, 1980-1981: An Unexpected Opening," *Latin American Research Review* 18:3 (1983), 63-76.

3852.   Hanson, James, and Jaime de Melo. "External Shocks, Financial Reforms, and Stabilization Attempts in Uruguay during 1974-83," *World Development* 13:8 (August 1985), 917-939.

3853.   Hanson, James, and Jaime de Melo. "The Uruguayan Experience with Liberalization and Stabilization, 1974-1981," *Journal of Inter-American Studies and World Affairs* 25:4 (November 1983), 477-508.

3854.   Kaztman, Rubén. "Youth and Unemployment in Montevideo," *CEPAL Review* 29 (August 1986), 119-131.

3855.   Lanzaro, Jorge Luis. "Movimiento obrero y reconstitución democrática," *Revista Mexicana de Sociología* 47:2 (April-June 1985), 173-209.

3856.   McDonald, Ronald H. "Confrontation and Transition in Uruguay," *Current History* 84:499 (February 1985), 57-60.

3857.   Mann, Arthur J., and Carlos E. Sánchez. "Labor Market Responses to Southern Cone Stabilization Policies: The Cases of Argentina, Chile, Uruguay," *Inter-American Economic Affairs* 38:4 (Spring 1985), 19-39.

3858.   Melgar, Alicia, and Walter Cancela. "Concentración del ingreso y desarticulación productiva: un desafío al proceso de democratización," *Revista Mexicana de Sociología* 47:2 (April-June 1985), 211-231.

3859.   Melo, Jaime de, and James Tybout. "The Effects of Financial Liberalization on Savings and Investment in Uruguay," *Economic Development and Cultural Change* 34:3 (April 1986), 561-587.

3860.   Melo, Jaime de, Ricardo Pascale, and James Tybout. "Microecomonic Adjustments in Uruguay during 1973-81: The Interplay of Real and Financial Shocks," *World Development* 13:8 (August 1985), 995-1015.

3861.   Paoline, Carlos. "Diferenciación y cambio técnico: el caso de los productores lecheros de la Cuenca de Montevideo," *Estudios Rurales Latinoamericanos* 8:1 (January-April 1985), 81-100.

3862.   Ransom, David. "Uruguay after the Dictatorship," *New Left Review* 163 (May-June 1987), 114-120.

3863. Rial, Juan. "Political Parties and Elections in the Process of Transition in Uruguay." In *Comparing New Democracies: Transition and Consolidation in Mediterranean Europe and the Southern Cone,* edited by Enrique A. Baloyra. Boulder, CO: Westview, 1987. pp. 241-265.

3864. Rial, Juan. "Las reglas del jeugo electoral en el Uruguay y sus implicaciones," *Revista Mexicana de Sociología* 47:2 (April-June 1985), 85-110.

3865. Riz, Liliana de. "Uruguay: la transición desde una perspectiva comparada," *Revista Mexicana de Sociología* 47:2 (April-June 1985), 5-20.

3866. Sierra, Gerónimo de. "La izquierda en la transición," *Revista Mexicana de Sociología* 47:2 (April-June 1985), 111-121.

3867. Weinstein, Martin. "Military Rule and Economic Failure." In *Politics, Policies, and Economic Development in Latin America,* edited by Robert G. Wesson. Stanford, CA: Hoover Institution Press, 1984. 38-52.

3868. Williams, John Hoyt. "Observations on Blacks and Bondage in Uruguay, 1800-1836," *The Americas* 43:4 (April 1987), 411-427.

VENEZUELA

Books and Monographs

3869. Bitar, Sergio, and Eduardo Troncoso. *El desafío industrial de Venezuela.* Buenos Aires: Pomaire, 1983. 285p.

3870. Blank, David E. *Venezuela: Politics in a Petroleum Republic.* New York: Praeger, 1984. 225p.

3871. Braveboy-Wagner, Jacqueline Anne. *Venezuela-Guyana Border Dispute: Britain's Colonial Legacy in Latin America.* Boulder, CO: Westview, 1984. 349p.

3872. Carrera Damas, Germán. *La crisis de la sociedad colonial venezolana.* Caracas: Monte Avila, 1983. 103p.

3873. Carrera Damas, Germán. *Una nación llamada Venezuela: proceso socio-histórico de Venezuela, 1810-1974.* Caracas: Monte Avila, 1984. 219p.

3874. Chalbaud Zerpa, Carlos. *Historia de Mérida.* Mérida, Venezuela: Universidad de los Andes, 1983. 407p.

3875. Colchester, Marcus, ed. *The Health and Survival of the Venezuelan Yanomami,* Cambridge, MA: Cultural Survival, 1985. 105p.

3876. Coronel, Gustavo. *The Nationalization of the Venezuelan Oil Industry: From Technocratic Success to Political Failure.* Lexington, MA: D.C. Health, 1983. 292p.

3877. Ewell, Judith. *Venezuela: A Century of Change.* Stanford, CA: Stanford University Press, 1984. 258p.

3878. Gilbert, Alan, and Patsy Healey. *The Political Economy of Land: Urban Development in an Oil Economy.* Brookfield, VT: Gower, 1985. 163p.

3879.   Gilbert, Alan, and Peter M. Ward. *Housing, the State and the Poor: Policy and Practice in Three Latin American Cities.* Cambridge, England; New York: Cambridge University Press, 1985. 319p.

3880.   Godio, Julio. *El movimiento obrero venezolano, 1850-1980.* Caracas: Ateneo, 1980-83. 3 vols.

3881.   Hanson, E. Mark. *Educational Reform and Administrative Development: The Cases of Colombia and Venezuela.* Stanford, CA: Hoover Institution Press, 1986. 246p.

3882.   Herwig, Holger H. *Germany's Vision of Empire in Venezuela, 1871-1914.* Princeton, NJ: Princeton University press, 1986. 285p.

3883.   Kinsbruner, Jay. *Petty Capitalism in Spanish America: The Pulperos of Puebla, Mexico City, Caracas, and Buenos Aires.* Boulder, CO: Westview, 1987. 159p.

3884.   Lizot, Jacques. *Tales of the Yanomami: Daily Life in the Venezuelan Forest.* Translated by Ernest Simon. Cambridge, England: Cambridge, University Press, 1985. 201p.

3885.   Looney, Robert E. *The Political Economy of Latin American Defense Expenditures: Case Studies of Venezuela and Argentina.* Lexington, MA: Lexington, 1986. 325p.

3886.   McBeth, Brian S. *Juan Vicente Gómez and the Oil Companies in Venezuela, 1908-1935.* Cambridge, England; New York: Cambridge University Press, 1983. 275p.

3887.   McKinley, P. Michael. *Pre-Revolutionary Caracas: Politics, Economy and Society 1777-1811.* Cambridge, England; New York: Cambridge University Press, 1986. 245p.

3888.   Martz, John D., ed. *Venezuela: The Democratic Experience.* Rev. ed. New York: Praeger, 1986. 489p.

3889.   Oropeza, Luis J. *Tutelary Pluralism: A Critical Approach to Venezuelan Democracy.* Cambridge, MA: Center for International Affairs, Harvard University, 1983. 127p.

3890.   Peeler, John A. *Latin American Democracies: Colombia, Costa Rica, Venezuela.* Chapel Hill: University of North Carolina, 1985. 193p.

3891.   Roseberry, William. *Coffee and Capitalism in the Venezuelan Andes.* Austin: University of Texas Press, 1983. 256p.

3892.   Serbin, Andres, ed. *Geopolítica de las relaciones de Venezuela con El Caribe.* Caracas, Venezuela: Fundación Fondo Editorial Acta Científica, 1983. 317p.

3893.   Vásquez Carrizosa, Alfredo. *Las relaciones de Colombia y Venezuela: la historia atormentada de dos naciones.* Bogotá: Tercer Mundo, 1983. 451p.

Articles and Chapters

3894. Allor, David J. "Venezuela: From Doctrine to Dialogue to Participation in the Processes of Regional Development," *Studies in Comparative International Development* 19:1 (Spring 1984), 86-97.

3895. Arvelo-Jiménez, Nelly, and Abel Perozo. "Programas de desarrollo entre poblaciones indígenas de Venezuela: antecedentes, consecuencias y una crítica," *América Indígena* 43:3 (July-September 1983), 503-536.

3896. Balderrama, Rafael. "Papel de la investigación agronómica en la modernización de la agricultura venezolana, 1937-1960," *Estudios Rurales Latinoamericanos* 10:1 (January-April 1987), 95-121.

3897. Barrera, Cristina. "La migración femenina internacional: el caso Colombia-Venezuela," *Estudios Rurales Latinoamericanos* 9:3 (September-December 1986), 69-80.

3898. Berglund, Susan. "Mercantile Credit and Financing in Venezuela, 1830-1870," *Journal of Latin American Studies* 17:2 (November 1985), 371-396.

3899. Berlin, Margalit. "Migrant Female Labor in the Venezuelan Garment Industry." In *Women and Change in Latin America,* edited by June Nash and Helen Safa. South Hadley, MA: Bergin & Garvey, 1986. pp. 260-272.

3900. Bigler, Gene, and Franklin Tugwell. "Banking on Oil in Venezuela." In *Bordering On Trouble: Resources and Politics in Latin America,* edited by Andrew Maguire and Janet Welsh Brown. Bethesda, MD: Adler & Adler, 1986. pp. 152-189.

3901. Boersner, Demetrio. "Venezuelan Policies toward Central America." In *Political Change in Central America: Internal and External Dimensions,* edited by Wolf Grabendorff, Heinrich-W. Krumwiede and Jörg Todt. Boulder, CO: Westview, 1984. pp. 245-260.

3902. Carrillo, Jorge, and María Matilde Suárez. "La organización económica de la pesca en la península de Paraguaná," *Estudios Rurales Latino-americanos* 9:1 (January-April 1986), 99-125.

3903. Crist, Raymond E. "Development and Agrarian Reform in Venezuela's Pioneer Zone," *American Journal of Economics and Sociology* 43:2 (April 1984), 149-158.

3904. Crist, Raymond E. "Westward Thrusts the Pioneer Zone in Venezuela," *American Journal of Economic and Sociology* 42:4 (October 1983), 451-462.

3905. Davis, Charles L. "Political Regimes and the Socioeconomic Resource Model of Political Mobilization: Some Venezuelan and Mexican Data," *Journal of Politics* 45:2 (May 1983), 422-448.

3906. Eastwood, David A. "Reality or Delusion: Migrant Perception of Levels of Living and Opportunity in Venezuela, 1961-1971," *Journal of Developing Areas* 17:4 (July 1983), 491-497.

3907.   Ellner, Steven B. "Inter-Party Agreement and Rivalry in Venezuela: A Comparative Perspective," *Studies in Comparative International Development* 19:4 (Winter 1984-85), 38-66.

3908.   Ellner, Steven B. "The MAS Party in Venezuela," *Latin American Perspectives* 13:2 (Spring 1986), 81-107.

3909.   Ewell, Judith. "Venezuela: Interim Report on a Social Pact," *Current History* 85:507 (January 1986), 25-28.

3910.   Gómez J., Alcides, and Luz Marina Díaz M. "La migración colombiana a Venezuela: los trabajadores azucareros y condiciones de trabajo," *Estudios Rurales Latinoamericanos* 7:1 (April 1984), 59-77.

3911.   Grayson, George W. "Venezuela and the Puerto Ordaz Agreement," *Inter-American Economic Affairs* 38:3 (Winter 1984), 49-73.

3912.   Hazleton, William A. "The Foreign Policies of Venezuela and Colombia: Collaboration, Competition, and Conflict." In *The Dynamics of Latin American Foreign Policies,* edited by Jennie K. Lincoln and Elizabeth G. Ferris. Boulder, CO: Westview, 1984. pp. 151-170.

3913.   Hellinger, Daniel. "Populism and Nationalism in Venezuela: New Perspectives on Acción Democrática," *Latin American Perspectives* 11:4 (Fall 1984), 33-59.

3914.   Hernández Alvarez, Oscar, and Héctor Lucena. "Political and Economic Determinants of Collective Bargaining in Venezuela," *International Labour Review* 124:3 (May-June 1985), 363-376.

3915.   Hill, Jonathan D. "Los misioneros y las fronteras," *América Indígena* 44:1 (January-March 1984), 183-190.

3916.   Hill, Jonathan D. "Social Equality and Ritual Hierarchy: The Arawkan Wakuénai of Venezuela," *American Ethnologist* 11:3 (August 1984), 528-544.

3917.   Hurtado, Samuel. "Las políticas agrarias del Estado y la cuestión campesina en Venezuela, 1936-1958," *Estudios Rurales Latinoamericanos* 6:1 (January-April 1983), 51-64.

3918.   Izard, Miguel, and Richard W. Slatta. "Banditry and Social Conflict on the Venezuelan Llanos." In *Bandidos: The Variation of Latin American Banditry,* edited by Richard W. Slatta. Westport, CT: Greenwood, 1987. pp. 33-47.

3919.   Karl, Terry Lynn. "Mexico, Venezuela, and the Contadora Initiative." In *Confronting Revolution: Security through Diplomacy in Central America.* New York: Pantheon, 1986. pp. 271-292.

3920.   Karl, Terry Lynn. "Petroleum and Political Pacts: The Transition to Democracy in Venezuela," *Latin American Research Review* 22:1 (1987), 63-94.

3921.   Levine, Daniel H. "The Transition to Democracy: Are There Lessons from Venezuela?" *Bulletin of Latin American Research* 4:2 (1985), 47-61.

3922. Looney, Robert E. "Venezuela's Economic Crisis: Origins and Successes in Stabilization," *Journal of Social, Political and Economic Studies* 11:3 (Fall 1986), 327-337.

3923. McCoy, Jennifer L. "The Politics of Adjustment: Labor and the Venezuelan Debt Crisis," *Journal of Inter-American Studies and World Affairs* 28:4 (Winter 1986-87), 103-138.

3924. Maingot, Anthony P. "Perceptions as Realities: The United States, Venezuela and Cuba in the Caribbean." In *Latin American Nations in World Politics,* edited by Heraldo Muñoz and Joseph S. Tulchin. Boulder, CO: Westview, 1984. pp. 63-82.

3925. Martz, John D. "The Crisis in Venezuelan Democracy," *Current History* 83:490 (February 1984), 73-78.

3926. Martz, John D. "Democratic Politics of Petroleum." In *Politics, Policies, and Economic Development in Latin America,* edited by Robert G. Wesson. Stanford, CA: Hoover Institution Press, 1984. pp. 161-187.

3927. Martz, John D. "Venezuelan Foreign Policy and the Role of Political Parties." In *Latin American Nations in World Politics,* edited by Heraldo Muñoz and Joseph S. Tulchin. Boulder, CO: Westview, 1984. pp. 133-149.

3928. Mayobre, Eduardo. "The Renegotiation of Venezuela's Foreign Debt during 1982 and 1983." In *Politics and Economics of External Debt Crisis: The Latin American Experience,* edited by Miguel S. Wionczek in collaboration with Luciano Tomassini. Boulder, CO: Westview, 1985. pp. 325-347.

3929. Melo, Oscar, and Michael G. Vogt. "Determinants of the Demand for Imports of Venezuela," *Journal of Development Economics* 14:3 (April 1984), 351-358.

3930. Miller, Gary M. "Status and Loyalty of Regular Army Officers in Late Colonial Venezuela," *Hispanic American Historical Review* 66:4 (November 1986), 667-696.

3931. Petras, James F., and Morris H. Morley. "Petro-dollars and the State: The Failure of State Capitalist Development in Venezuela," *Third World Quarterly* 5:1 (January 1983), 7-27.

3932. Rodríguez, Mario. "The First Venezuelan Republic and the North American Model," *Inter-American Review of Bibliography* 37:1 (1987), 3-17.

3933. Salgado, Rene. "Economic Pressure Groups and Policy-Making in Venezuela: The Case of FEDECAMARAS Reconsidered," *Latin American Research Review* 22:3 (1987), 91-105.

3934. Serbin, Andrés. "Estado, indigenismo e indianidad en Venezuela 1946-1979," *Boletín de Estudios Latinoamericanos y del Caribe* 34 (June 1983), 17-40.

3935. Slatta, Richard W. "'Llaneros' and gauchos: A Comparative View," *Inter-American Review of Bibliography* 35:4 (1985), 409-421.

3936.   Sonntag, Heinz R., and Rafael de la Cruz. "The State and Industrialization in Venezuela," *Latin American Perspectives* 12:4 (Fall 1985), 75-104.

3937.   Villabona Blanco, María Pilar. "Política y elecciones en Venezuela," *Revista de Estudios Políticos* 53 (September-October 1986), 215-237.

3938.   Werlhof, Claudia von. "El desarrollo agroindustrial y el nuevo movimiento campesino en Venezuela," *Boletín de Estudios Latinoamericanos y del Caribe* 39 (December 1985), 3-43.

3939.   Werlhof, Claudia von. "New Agricultural Cooperatives on the Basis of Sexual Polarisation Induced by the State: The 'Model' Collective Cooperative 'Cumparipa', Venezuela," *Boletín de Estudios Latinoamericanos y del Caribe* 35 (December 1983), 39-50.

3940.   Wright, Eleanor Witte. "Food Dependency and Malnutrition in Venezuela, 1958-74." In *Food, Politics, and Society in Latin America,* edited by John C. Super and Thomas C. Wright. Lincoln: University of Nebraska Press, 1985. pp. 150-173.

3941.   Wright, Robin M., and Jonathan D. Hill. "History, Ritual, and Myth: Nineteenth Century Millenarian Movements in Northwest Amazon," *Ethnohistory* 33:1 (January 1986), 31-54.

3942.   Yánez Betancourt, Leopoldo. "La economía venezolana: problemas y perspectivas," *El Trimestre Económico* 54:216 (October-December 1987), 727-768.

AUTHOR INDEX

Note: *The author index is arranged alphabetically, word by word. All characters or groups of characters separated by dashes, hyphens, diagonal slashes, spaces or periods are treated as separate words. Acronyms not separated by spaces or punctuation are alphabetized as though they are single words, while initials separated by spaces or punctuation are treated as if each letter is a complete word. Personal names beginning with capital Mc, M' and Mac are all listed under Mac as though the full form were used, and St. is alphabetized as if spelled out.*

Duncan, Tim, 1029, 1123
Duncan, W. Raymond, 717, 2089, 2157, 2618-2619
Duncan Baretta, Silvio R., 1500, 1594
Dunkerley, James, 326, 1319, 1339, 2374
Dunn, Marvin G., 718
Dunn, Peter M., 1078, 2381
Dunn, Richard S., 2620
Dunnett, Denzil, 1124
Dupuy, Alex, 2527
Durán, Esperanza, 327, 466-467, 719, 2714, 2969-2970, 3312
Durán Pérez, Teresa, 1804
Durand, Jorge, 2715

Eakin, Marshall C., 1501-1503
Earl, Duncan M., 2971
Early, John D., 2451
Eastwood, David A., 1340, 3906
Ebinger, Charles K., 1504, 3004
Eckaus, Richard S., 2905
Eckstein, Susan, 1341, 2158-2159, 2233
Economic Commission for Latin America, 247, 468-472, 1030, 1320, 1390, 2262
Economic Commission for Latin America and the Caribbean, 97, 473-475, 1391, 1901
ECLA Economic Projections Centre, 720
ECLA Mexican Office, 328
ECLAC Mexico Subregional Headquarters, 329
Eddins, John, 1642
Edelstein, Joel C., 452
Edie, Carlene J., 2621-2622
Edquist, Charles, 2090, 2160, 2577
Edwards, Alejandra Cox, 1745
Edwards, Keith L., 29
Edwards, Sebastian, 721, 1745, 1805-1806, 1953
Eguizábal, Cristina, 2343
Eguren López, Fernando, 3631
Eich, Dieter, 3288
El Guindi, Fadwa, 2716
Elkin, Judith Laikin, 77
Ellison, Herbert J., 2395
Ellner, Steven B., 3907-3908
El Mallakh, Regaei, 2854
Eltis, David, 722
Engbarth, Dennis, 564
Engerman, Stanley L., 121
England, Nora C., 24
English, Andrian J., 476
Engstrand, Iris H.W., 723
Ennew, Judith, 3632

Enriquez Gamón, Efraín, 3497
Epstein, Edward C., 724, 1125
Epstein, Erwin E., 2972
Equipo de trabajo del Departamento de Letras de la UCA, 2344
Erb, Guy F., 2973
Erber, Fabio Stefano, 1505
Erisman, H. Michael, 98, 2091
Escobar, Cristina, 1954
Escorcia, José, 1902
Escudé, Carlos, 1031-1032
Esquivel, Francisco, 2011
Esser, Klaus, 725
Esteva, Gustavo, 2686, 2717
Estrada I., Margarita, 2974
Etchepareborda, Roberto, 78-79, 1033
Etheredge, Lloyd S., 248
Evans, G. Russell, 3463
Evans, Hugh, 1366
Evans, Peter B., 1506-1508
Evanson, Robert K., 726-727
Everitt, John C., 1303
Evers, Tilman, 1509
Ewald, Ursula, 2718
Ewell, Judith, 3877, 3909
Executive Secretariat, ECLAC, 158, 728
Eyre, L. Alan, 2623

Fábregas, Andrés, 2975
Fagan, Brian M., 2719
Fagen, Patricia Weiss, 729
Fagen, Richard, 249-250, 3362
Fairchild, Loretta G., 730, 2976
Falcoff, Mark, 99-100, 251-252, 330-331, 477, 1126-1127, 1807-1809, 3363, 3842
Falcón, Ricardo, 1034, 1057
Falcón, Romana, 2720
Faletto, Enzo, 731, 900
Falk, Pamela S., 2092, 2161, 2721, 3728
Fallas Monge, Carlos Luis, 2012
Fals Borda, Orlando, 1903
Fanelli, José María, 1135-1136
Fanger, Ulrich, 3512
Farer, Tom J., 332-334, 732
Farnsworth, David N., 3464
Farrell, Joseph P., 1746
Farrell, Terrence, 3796
Farris, Nancy M., 2722
Fasano-Filho, Ugo, 1035
Fass, Simon M., 2511
Fauriol, Georges A., 120, 478, 2129, 2512, 2484, 2578
Fausto, Boris, 1392
Fearnside, Philip M., 1510

Wadsted, Otto G., 1718
Waggoner, Barbara Ashton, 71
Waggoner, George R., 71
Wagner Neto, José A., 1679
Waisman, Carlos H., 1059, 1252
Wali, Alaka, 3475
Walker, David W., 2848, 3248
Walker, Thomas W., 3315-3317, 3451
Wallace, Brian F., 1935
Wallace, James M., 3711
Wallich, Henry C., 405
Walter, Richard J., 1077, 1253
Ward, Christopher, 88
Ward, Peter M., 1904, 2733, 2844, 3879
Warman, Arturo, 3249-3250
Warren, Harris G., 3506
Warren, J. Benedict, 2845
Warren, Katherine F., 3506
Wasserman, Mark, 2846, 3251
Wasserstrom, Robert, 135, 606, 2847
Waters, Anita M., 2590
Waters, Maurice, 2413
Watkins, Alfred J., 607
Watson, Bruce W., 1078, 2381
Watson, Cynthia Ann, 1254
Watson, Hillbourne, 222
Webb, Michael A., 406
Webb, Richard, 1636, 3712
Webster, David, 2480
Weckmann, Luis, 2848
Weeks, Charles A., 2849
Weeks, John, 286, 407, 3581, 3452, 3494
Weeks, John M., 72
Wehkamp, Andy, 3713
Wehner, Peter, 563
Weinberg, Gregorio, 608, 986
Weiner, Mervyn L., 3252
Weinstein, Barbara, 1428
Weinstein, Brian, 2524
Weinstein, Martin, 3867
Weintraub, Sidney, 2850
Weis, W. Michael, 1719
Weiss, John, 3260
Weiss, Juan Carlos, 1633, 2129
Weiss, Wendy A., 2306
Weisskoff, Richard, 3740
Weitz, Richard, 987
Welch, Claude E., Jr., 609
Welch, David A., 2146
Welch, John H., 1720
Welch, Richard E., Jr., 2133
Wells, Allen, 2851, 3021
Wells, John, 1497
Wells, Miriam J., 3254
Werlhof, Claudia von, 3938-3939

Werlich, David P., 3714-3715
Werneck, Rogério L. Furquim, 1721-1722
Werner, Dennis, 1723
Wessman, James W., 2228, 3770
Wesson, Robert G., 610-611, 988, 2071
Westman, John, 1724
White, Averille, 223
White, Gordon, 2229
White, Richard Alan, 287
White, Steven F., 3318
Whiteford, Michael B., 2048, 2072
Whiteford, Scott, 505
Whitehall, Peter, 1287
Whitehead, Laurence, 408-409, 554, 1371
Whiting, Van R., Jr., 2852
Whitten, Norman E., Jr., 2271
Wiarda, Howard J., 288, 612-615, 989-991
Wiemers, Eugene L., Jr., 3253
Wiesner, Eduardo, 992
Wight, Jonathan, 1725
Wilde, Kathleen L., 2230, 3453
Wilhelmy, Manfred, 1888
Wilk, Richard R., 1314, 3255
Wilkie, Richard W., 73
Willey, Gordon Randolf, 289, 2853, 3256
Williams, Edward J., 3257
Williams, Gary W., 1726
Williams, John Hoyt, 3524, 3868
Williams, Marion, 224
Williams, Philip J., 3454
Williams, Robert G., 290
Willis, Eliza, 1863
Willmore, Larry N., 1727
Wilson, Fiona, 993, 3716
Wilson, Lofton, 74
Wilson, Patricia A., 3455, 3717
Winn, Peter, 1771
Wionczek, Miguel S., 616, 2744, 2854, 3258-3259
Wirth, John D., 617, 1429
Wise, Carol, 3573, 3582, 3717
Wise, Timothy, 994
Witter, Michael, 148, 2653-2654
Wogart, Jan Peter, 1255
Wolfe, Barbara L., 3326
Wolfe, Marshall, 995
Wonderly, Anthony, 2575
Wong, David C., 225
Wood, Beth, 5, 95
Wood, Bryce, 618
Wood, Charles H., 580, 1668
Wood, Richard E., 996
Wood, Robert D., 619

SUBJECT INDEX

Note: *The subject index is arranged alphabetically, word by word. All characters or groups of characters separated by dashes, hyphens, diagonal slashes, spaces or periods are treated as separate words. Acronyms not separated by spaces or punctuation are alphabetized as though they are single words, while initials separated by spaces or punctuation are treated as if each letter is a complete word. Asterisks (*) are used to identify references to foreign-language books and articles.*

About the Compiler

ROBERT L. DELORME received his Ph.D. from the University of Minnesota in 1968. He currently serves as a faculty member of California State University, teaching courses in Latin American Politics, U.S.-Latin American Relations, Latin American Political Systems, American Political Institutions, and State Government. In addition to the first and second volumes of *Latin America* (1981 and 1984), Professor Delorme authored *The Role of Foreign Investments in the Developmental Process: The Case of Mexico, 1884-1911* (1975), and coedited *The State of American Society* (1975).